BEYOND MARY OR MARTHA

EMORY STUDIES IN EARLY CHRISTIANITY

Vernon K. Robbins, General Editor
David B. Gowler, General Editor
Bart B. Bruehler, Associate Editor
Robert H. von Thaden Jr., Associate Editor
Richard S. Ascough
Juan Hernández Jr.
Susan E. Hylen
Brigitte Kahl
Mikeal C. Parsons
Russell B. Sisson
Shively T. J. Smith
Elaine M. Wainwright

Number 21

BEYOND MARY OR MARTHA
Reclaiming Ancient Models of Discipleship

Jennifer S. Wyant

SBL PRESS

Atlanta

Copyright © 2019 by Jennifer S. Wyant

Publication of this volume was made possible by the generous support of the Pierce Program in Religion of Oxford College of Emory University.

The editors of this series express their sincere gratitude to David E. Orton and Deo Publishing for publication of this series 2009–2013.

All rights reserved. No part of this work may be reproduced or transmitted in any form or by any means, electronic or mechanical, including photocopying and recording, or by means of any information storage or retrieval system, except as may be expressly permitted by the 1976 Copyright Act or in writing from the publisher. Requests for permission should be addressed in writing to the Rights and Permissions Office, SBL Press, 825 Houston Mill Road, Atlanta, GA 30329 USA.

Library of Congress Cataloging-in-Publication Data

Names: Wyant, Jennifer S., author.
Title: Beyond Mary or Martha : reclaiming ancient models of discipleship / Jennifer S. Wyant.
Description: Atlanta : SBL Press, 2019. | Includes bibliographical references and index.
Identifiers: LCCN 2019032586 (print) | LCCN 2019032587 (ebook) | ISBN 9781628372595 (paperback) | ISBN 9780884144137 (hardback) | ISBN 9780884144144 (ebook)
Subjects: LCSH: LCSH: Service (Theology)—Biblical teaching. | Bible. Luke, X, 38–42—Criticism, interpretation, etc. | Mary, of Bethany, Saint. | Martha, Saint. | Spiritual formation
Classification: LCC BS2595.6.S35 W93 2019 (print) | LCC BS2595.6.S35 (ebook) | DDC 226.4/06—dc23
LC record available at https://lccn.loc.gov/2019032586
LC ebook record available at https://lccn.loc.gov/2019032587

Cover design is an adaptation by Bernard Madden of Rick A. Robbins, Mixed Media (19" x 24" pen and ink on paper, 1981). Cover design used by permission of Deo Publishing.

Printed on acid-free paper.

To Elden

"The path is worn, but, for us, it's new."

Contents

Abbreviations ix

1. A New Problem, an Old Answer 1
2. A Literary Approach to Luke 10:38–42 33
3. Origen and Early Monastic Interpreters 71
4. Patristic Preachers 125
5. Medieval Readers 173
6. The Reformation and a Shift 223

Epilogue 265

Bibliography 277

Ancient Sources Index 293
Modern Authors Index 302
Subject Index 305

Abbreviations

AASD	Arte e Archeologia, Studi e documenti
AB	Anchor Bible
ACW	Ancient Christian Writers
Ag. Ap.	Josephus, *Against Apion*
Anna	Chrysostom, *De Anna*
APalph	Apophthegmata patrum alphabetica
APsys	Apophthegmata patrum systematica
ASNU	Acta Seminarii Neotestamentici Upsaliensis
ATA	Fitzgerald, Allen, ed. *Augustine through the Ages: An Encyclopedia*. Grand Rapids: Eerdmans, 1999.
ATLASP	*American Theological Library Association Summary of Proceedings*
BBB	Bonner biblische Beiträge
BDAG	Danker, Frederick W., Walter Bauer, William F. Arndt, and F. Wilbur Gingrich. *Greek-English Lexicon of the New Testament and Other Early Christian Literature*. 3rd ed. Chicago: University of Chicago Press, 2000.
BibTemps	Bible de tous les Temps
BJS	Brown Judaic Studies
BMW	The Bible in the Modern World
BTB	*Biblical Theology Bulletin*
BZNW	Beihefte zur Zeitschrift für die neutestamentliche Wissenschaft
Cant.	Richard of St. Victor, *Explicatio in Cantica Canticorum*
Catech.	Augustine, *De catechizandis rudibus*
CBQ	*Catholic Biblical Quarterly*
CBRA	*Collectanae Biblica et Religiosa Antiqua*
Claustr.	Hugh of Fouilloy, *De claustro animae*
CO	Calvin, John. *Ioannis Calvini opera quae supersunt omnia*. Edited by G. Baum, E. Cunitz, and E. Reuss.

	59 vols. Corpus Reformatorum 29–87. Brunswick: Schwetschke, 1863–1900.
Comm. Cant.	Origen, *Commentarius in Canticum*
Comm. Jo.	Origen, *Commentarii in evangelium Joannis*
Comm. Luc.	*Commentaria in Lucam*
Comm. Rom.	Origen, *Commentarii in Romanos*
Conc.	Joachim of Fiore, *Concordia novi ac veteris testamenti*
Conf.	Augustine, *Confessionum libri XIII*; John Cassian, *Conferences*
Const. App.	Apostolic Constitutions
CS	*Cistercian Studies*
CSS	Cistercian Studies Series
Dial.	Idungus of Regensburg, *Dialogs duorum monachorum*
Dial. Ott. Bamb.	Herbord of Michelsburg, *Dialogue de Ottone ep Bamberbensi*
Diat.	Ephrem, *Commentary on the Diatessaron*
Diatr.	Epictetus, *Diatribi* (*Dissertationes*)
Disp.	Simon of Tournae, *Disputationes*
Dist. mon.	Distinctiones monastiche
Doctr. chr.	Augustine, *De doctrina christiana*
EJL	Early Judaism and Its Literature
Enarrat. Ps.	Augustine, *Enarrationes in Psalmos*
Ep.	*Epistula(e)*
Evang. Luc.	Bede, *In Evangelium Lucae libros VI*; Bonaventura, *In Evangelium Lucae*
Faust.	Augustine, *Contra Faustum Manichaeum*
FB	Forschung zur Bibel
FC	Fathers of the Church
FCNTECW	Feminist Companion to the New Testament and Early Christian Writings
fol.	folio
Fr. 1 Reg.	Origen, *Fragmenta in librum primum Regnorum*
Fr. Jo.	Origen, *Fragmenta in evangelium Joannis*
Fr. Luc.	Origen, *Fragmenta in Lucam*
Fr. Matt.	Origen, *Fragmenta ex commentariis in evangelium Matthaei*
FS	*Franciscan Studies*
GCS	Die grieschischen christlichen Schriftsteller der ersten [drei]

Hist. eccl.	*Historia ecclesiastica*
HNT	Handbuch zum Neuen Testament
Hom.	*Homilia(e)*
Hom. 1 Thess.	John Chrysostom, *Homiliae in epistulam i ad Thessalonicenses*
Hom. Exod.	Origen, *Homiliae in Exodum*
Hom. Ezech.	Gregory the Great, *Homiliae in Ezechielem*
Hom. Gal.	John Chrysostom, *Homiliae in epistulam ad Galatas commentarius*
Hom. Gen.	Origen, *Homiliae in Genesim*
Hom. Jo.	John Chrysostom, *Homiliae in Joannem*
Hom. Judic.	Origen, *Homiliae in Judices*
Hom. Luc.	Origen, *Homiliae in Lucam*
Hom. Matt.	John Chrysostom, *Homiliae in Matthaeum*
Hom. Num.	Origen, *Homiliae in Numeros*
Hom. Phil.	John Chrysostom, *Homiliae in epistulam ad Philippenses*
Hom. Ps.	Origen, *Homiliae in Psalmos*
IAC	Iconographie de l'Art Chrétien
Ign. Smyrn.	Ignatius, *To the Smyrnaeans*
Impugn.	Aquinas, *Contra impugnantes Dei cultum et religionem*
Int. Castl.	Teresa of Ávila, *The Interior Castle*
JBL	*Journal of Biblical Literature*
JBRec	*Journal of the Bible and Its Reception*
JECS	*Journal of Early Christian Studies*
JFSR	*Journal of Feminist Studies in Religion*
JSSSup	Journal of Semitic Studies Supplement Series
LCC	Library of Christian Classics
LCL	Loeb Classical Library
Lib. Grad.	*Liber Graduum*
Lib. var. quest.	Isidore, *Liber de variis quaestionibus*
Liet.	Rudolf, *Vita Lietberti ep Camaeracensis*
Life	Possidius, *Life of St. Augustine*
LMW	Library of Medieval Women
LQ	*Lutheran Quarterly*
LSJ	Liddell, Henry George, Robert Scott, and Henry Stuart Jones. *A Greek-English Lexicon*. 9th ed. with revised supplement. Oxford: Clarendon, 1996.

LW	Luther, Martin. *Luther's Works*. 75 vols. Edited by Jaroslav Pelikan. St. Louis: Concordia, 1956–2011.
LXX	Septuagint
Mainz.	Siegfried of Mainz, *Mainzer Urkundenbuch*
Med.	Teresa of Ávila, *Meditations*
Med. or.	William of St. Thierry, *Meditative orationes*
MFC	Messages of the Fathers of the Church
MLST	Museum Lessianum section theologique
Moral.	Gregory the Great, *Moralia*
MS Bodl. 270B	MS Bodleian 270B. Oxford, Bodleian Library
NA28	Aland, Barbara, Kurt Aland, Johannes Karavidopoulos, Carlo M. Martini, and Bruce M. Metzger, eds. *Nestle-Aland Novum Testamentum Graece*. 28th rev. ed. Stuttgart: Deutsche Bibelgesellschaft, 2012.
NBf	*New Blackfriars*
NICNT	New International Commentary on the New Testament
NIGTC	New International Greek Testament Commentary
NovTSup	Supplements to Novum Testamentum
NPNF	Schaff, Philip, and Henry Wace, eds. *A Select Library of Nicene and Post-Nicene Fathers of the Christian Church*. 28 vols. in 2 series. 1886–1889. Reprint, Peabody, MA: Hendrickson, 1994.
NT	New Testament
NTS	*New Testament Studies*
NTTS	New Testament Tools and Studies
NTTSD	New Testament Tools, Studies, and Documents
OCP	*Orientalia Christiana Periodica*
OECS	Oxford Early Christian Studies
OT	Old Testament
ÖTK	Ökumenischer Taschenbuch-Kommentar
PatrSyr	Patrologia Syriaca
Perf.	Teresa of Ávila, *Way of Perfection*
PerspRelSt	*Perspectives in Religious Studies*
PETSE	*Papers of the Estonian Theological Society in Exile*
PG	Patrologia Graeca [= Patrologiae Cursus Completus: Series Graeca]. Edited by Jacques-Paul Migne. 162 vols. Paris, 1857–1886.
Philoc.	Origen, *Philocalia*

PL	Patrologia Latina [= Patrologia Cursus Completus: Series Latina]. Edited by Jacques-Paul Migne. 217 vols. Paris, 1844–1864.
PNTC	Pelican New Testament Commentaries
pref.	preface
Princ.	Origen, *De principiis*
prol.	prologue
PTS	Patristische Texte Und Studien
Quaest. ev.	Augustine, *Quaestionum evangelicarum*
Quis div.	Clement of Alexandria, *Quis dives salvetur*
RelLit	*Religion and Literature*
Renunc.	Innocent III, *On Renunciation*
Rer. mon. rat.	Evagrius, *Rerum monachalium rationes*
Rev.	Birgitta of Sweden, *Revelations*
RIL	*Religion and Intellectual Life*
Sac.	John Chrysostom, *De sacerdotio*
SBLDS	Society of Biblical Literature Dissertation Series
SCHT	Studies in Christian History and Thought
SCJ	*The Sixteenth Century Journal*
Sent.	*Sententiae*
Serm.	*Sermo(nes)*
Serm. 2	Bernard, *Sermon 2 in Assumptione*
Serm. 3	Bernard, *Sermon 3 de Diversis*
Serm. 51	Bernard, *Sermon 51 Song of Songs*
SJT	*Scottish Journal of Theology*
Smyrn.	Ignatius, *To the Smyrnaeans*
SNTSMS	Society for New Testament Studies Monograph Series
Solil.	Teresa of Ávila, *Soliloquies*
SP	Sacra Pagina
ST	Aquinas, *Summa Theologica*
ST	*Studia Theologica*
Stat.	John Chrysostom, *Ad populum Antiochenum de statuis*
StPatr	Studia Patristica
Str-B	Strack, Hermann Leberecht, and Paul Billerbeck. *Kommentar zum Neuen Testament aus Talmud und Midrasch*. 6 vols. Munich: Beck, 1922–1961.
StudMon	*Studia Monastica*
SVTG	*Septuaginta*. Vetus Testamentum Graecum auctoritate Academiae Scientiarum (first volumes: Societatis

	Literarum) Gottingensis editum, Göttingen: Vandenhoeck & Ruprecht, 1931–.
SWR	Series in Women and Religion
TC	*TC: A Journal of Textual Criticism*
Terr. mot.	John Chrysostom, *De terrae motu*
THKNT	Theologischer Handkommentar zum Neuen Testament
Tract. Ev. Jo.	Augustine, *In Evangelium Johannis tractatus*
TS	*Theological Studies*
TUGAL	Texte und Unteruschungen zur Geschichte der altchristlichen Literature
VCSup	Supplements to Vigiliae Christianae
Virginit.	*De virginitate*
VTT	Victorine Texts in Translation
Wolbod.	Reiner of St. Lawrence, *Vita Wolbodonis*

1
A New Problem, an Old Answer

> Every generation almost since the beginning of Christianity has tried to fit the story of Mary and Martha to its needs and to find in it a meaning suited to the Christian life of its time.
> — Giles Constable, *Three Studies in Religious and Social Thought*

> But in the history of oppression, simplistic views do as much damage as sophisticated ones, perhaps more.
> — Loveday C. Alexander, "Sisters in Adversity: Retelling Martha's Story"

The Passage: Luke 10:38–42

Mary and Martha's famous encounter with Jesus is only briefly described in the Third Gospel. Unlike the story of the two sisters in John 11:1–44, the entire Lukan account is only five short verses, nestled between the parable of the good Samaritan and the Lord's Prayer. Despite its brevity and familiarity, this story contains a paradox, which speaks to the difficulty of grasping the nature of being a disciple in Luke. This particular pericope appears only in Luke's Gospel and can be divided into three sections: Jesus's welcome into Martha's house (v. 38), a description of Mary and Martha's actions (vv. 39–40a), and Martha's complaint and Jesus's response that Mary has chosen the better part (vv. 40b–42).[1]

Ἐν δὲ τῷ πορεύεσθαι αὐτοὺς αὐτὸς εἰσῆλθεν εἰς κώμην τινά· γυνὴ δέ τις ὀνόματι Μάρθα ὑπεδέξατο αὐτόν.[2] καὶ τῇδε ἦν ἀδελφὴ καλουμένη Μαριάμ,

---

1. Of course, as already mentioned, John's Gospel also features Mary and Martha of Bethany, in John 11:1–44, but that story is focused on the resurrection of Lazarus and the sisters' reaction to Jesus and his delay. This will be discussed in later chapters.

2. Textual variant: several manuscripts (A, D, K, P, lat, sy, bo) include εἰς τὸν οἶκον αὐτῆς at the end of v. 38. François Bovon argues against Bruce Metzger that this

[ἣ] καὶ παρακαθεσθεῖσα πρὸς τοὺς πόδας τοῦ κυρίου ἤκουεν τὸν λόγον αὐτοῦ. ἡ δὲ Μάρθα περιεσπᾶτο περὶ πολλὴν διακονίαν·ἐπιστᾶσα δὲ εἶπεν· κύριε, οὐ μέλει σοι ὅτι ἡ ἀδελφή μου μόνην με κατέλιπεν διακονεῖν; εἰπὲ οὖν αὐτῇ ἵνα μοι συναντιλάβηται. ἀποκριθεὶς δὲ εἶπεν αὐτῇ ὁ κύριος· Μάρθα Μάρθα, μεριμνᾷς καὶ θορυβάζῃ[3] περὶ πολλά, ἑνὸς δέ ἐστιν χρεία[4] Μαριὰμ γὰρ τὴν ἀγαθὴν μερίδα ἐξελέξατο ἥτις οὐκ ἀφαιρεθήσεται αὐτῆς.

And as they were traveling, he went into a certain village, where a woman named Martha welcomed him. And she had a sister named Mary, who sat at the feet of the Lord and listened to his words. But Martha was worried about her many tasks. And she came and said, "Lord, does it not concern you that my sister has left me alone to serve? Tell her then to help me." And Jesus, answering her, said, "Martha, Martha, you are anxious and concerned about many things, but there is need of only one. For Mary has chosen the better part, which will not be taken away from her."[5]

This passage and the numerous ways it has been interpreted throughout history is the subject of this book. Specifically, I seek to engage the sharply divided contemporary hermeneutics surrounding Luke 10:38–42 by examining premodern approaches in order to open up new, liberative ways of reading the story of the two sisters and their strange encounter with Jesus.

The Question: Are You a Mary or a Martha?

At one time or another, most Christian women in the United States will be asked to ponder this question when reading about the two sisters from Bethany. It is a weighted question, one that often carries with it many

---

phrase was original, only to be dropped later because it seemed redundant, as the verb ὑποδέχομαι (to welcome) implies that Jesus is being welcomed into her house. This variant will be discussed in great detail in ch. 2. See Bovon, *Luke 2: A Commentary on the Gospel of Luke 9:51–19:27*, Hermeneia (Minneapolis: Fortress, 2013), 70 n. 20.

3. This is a *hapax legomenon*. Several manuscripts (A, K, P, f[13], etc.) appear to have changed it to τυρβάζειν, the more common verb.

4. There is a complicated textual critical problem here. In NA[28]'s critical apparatus, there are three variant readings: (1) an omission of the entire phrase μεριμνᾷς καὶ θορυβάζῃ περὶ πολλά, ἑνὸς δέ ἐστιν χρεία (attested by D and Ambrose), (2) ὀλίγον δέ ἐστιν χρεία (normally attested in Origen), and (3) ὀλίγον δέ ἐστιν χρεία ἢ ἑνός (attested in Basil, Jerome, and Cassian). See my discussion in ch. 2.

5. Unless otherwise indicated, all biblical translations are mine.

assumptions about the correct way to live as a female Christian. Women who are Marthas are seen as busy perfectionists; they work too hard and complain too much. Marys, on the other hand, are quiet and laid-back; they make sure to have personal quiet time with Jesus every day. They might still complete their daily tasks, but they would never let that get in the way of their faith. Marys are the very best of Christian women, while Marthas, despite their productivity, are often treated as though they have come up short. Thus, in the life of many Christian women, the question of which sister you are (or perhaps which one you are trying to be) is a serious one.

The popularity of this question has even led to the creation of personality quizzes one can easily find online or in the pages of Mary/Martha-themed devotionals. Mimicking the style of magazine quizzes designed to tell you your face shape or your dream vacation, these quizzes aim at helping women discover which sister they favor. One particular quiz asks a series of questions directed at helping uncover one's basic nature:[6]

- When life gets busy, does your time with God tend to get pushed aside?
- Overall, would you say that you tend to be a worrier?
- Do you find at times that you are easily angered by others?
- Would you say that it's easy for you to see others' faults?
- Do you like to create art or make to-do lists?

If a woman answers yes to any of the above questions, then the quiz reveals that she is a Martha, and by extension she likely enjoys going to choir practice and making to-do lists over prayer and devotions.[7] Such labeling implies this woman's faith is somehow inferior to the Marys of the group, because she struggles with anger, worry, and an overly critical spirit. She has let her daily tasks overwhelm her deeper purpose, which is to spend time with God. The subtext of this quiz and the question more broadly is a warning not to be too much like Martha. However, most women are assumed to be Marthas, as they are expected to be in charge of the house,

---

6. Jane Martin, "Are You a Mary or a Martha?," June 6, 2014, http://aproverbs-31wife.com/mary-martha/. This blog post was a guest post by Jane Martin, who at the time of writing this post was affiliated with MaryandMartha.com, a direct sales website that sells Christian home decor.

7. Martin, "Are You a Mary or a Martha?"

the entertaining, and the never-ending list of chores. This leads to an inevitable tension and a double burden placed on women: *you are a Martha, but you should want to be a Mary*. As Joanna Weaver writes in her devotional *Having a Mary Heart in a Martha World*: "Perhaps no passage of Scripture better describes the conflict we feel as women than the one we find in gospel of Luke. Just mention the names Mary and Martha around a group of Christian women and you'll get knowing looks and nervous giggles. We've all felt the struggle. We want to worship like Mary, but the Martha inside keeps bossing us around."[8]

This struggle between being Martha but wanting to be Mary is a central discussion point surrounding Luke 10:38–42 in many modern evangelical circles. Women are expected to do all the things that Marthas do but to do them with a Mary spirit. Women are called to live in this tension as they struggle to overcome their more Martha-like natures.

A particularly notable example of this interpretation can be found in the writing of popular women's writer and speaker Beth Moore, who has returned to this story numerous times. In her devotional *Jesus, the One and Only*, she acknowledges the vast time difference between the world of Mary and Martha and her modern audience, but she still argues that from this story we can see that while "our culture might be completely different, women have had the same challenges from the beginning of time."[9] She then offers a gentle critique to the Marys, who might be too busy praying to keep a clean and hospitable home, and then turns to criticize the Marthas, who allow themselves to be overly preoccupied with domestic and even ministerial tasks. She argues that if Martha had completed her preparations before Jesus arrived, then she too could have sat at his feet like her sister. God is doubly honored by the person who is able to prepare in such a way that she is distraction-free when the correct moment arrives to worship God. According to Moore, a woman should organize her life in a such way that she can be prepared to be a wonderful hostess at all times and not be distracted by all that might require. Moore makes clear that Martha's work is good and honorable. Her mistake, and the mistake of all Marthas out there, is to place more emphasis on the work than on a

---

8. Joanna Weaver, *Having a Mary Heart in a Martha World: Finding Intimacy with God in the Busyness of Life* (Colorado Springs: Waterbrook, 2000), 3.

9. Beth Moore, *Jesus, the One and Only* (Nashville: Broadman & Holman, 2013), 200. We will return to Moore's interpretation in ch. 6.

heart-to-heart relationship with Jesus Christ.[10] Moore's conclusion is that all Christian women should strive to be both a Martha and a Mary so that they can honor and love Christ to the fullest. While many of Moore's more nuanced points about finding ways to sit with Christ even in the midst of work could be easily be directed toward Christian men as well, she repeatedly directs her arguments to women in today's busy world.

Moore concisely presents the most frequent approach toward interpreting these verses within evangelical culture, and even within the mainstream Protestant denominations of Methodism, Presbyterianism, and Lutheranism, this reading is popular. The sentiment that this story can be directly applied to the lives of Christian women in the twenty-first century has led it to be firmly and almost exclusively located in the sphere of women's ministry. This story is for women. It represents a paradigm in which women readers are asked to place themselves in the position of Mary and Martha and live their lives accordingly.

The Rejoinder: The Feminists Respond

Feminist biblical scholars have responded to this line of interpretation, criticizing the double burden it places on women. Elisabeth Schüssler Fiorenza has noted that for some women this interpretation has led to an undercurrent of resentment toward the Marys, who seemingly do less for the Lord and yet are given more praise. More commonly, however, this has led to deep feelings of inadequacy for many women as they struggle to be both sisters at once, an evangelical version of trying to "have it all."[11] She argues: "Protestant interpreters ... insist that women must fulfill their duties as housekeepers. Nevertheless, they must not overdo it. In other words, they should be accomplished hostesses of the dinner parties and church suppers but they should take some time out to 'listen, pray and learn.'"[12]

---

10. Moore, *Jesus, the One and Only*, 201.
11. Elisabeth Schüssler Fiorenza, *But She Said: Feminist Practices of Biblical Interpretation* (Boston: Beacon, 1992), 55.
12. Schüssler Fiorenza, *But She Said*, 58. For similar statements of unease with typical interpretations of this passage see Robert M. Price, *The Widow Traditions in Luke-Acts: A Feminist-Critical Survey*, SBLDS 155 (Atlanta: Scholars Press, 1997), 178; Veronica Koperski, "Women and Discipleship in Luke 10:38–42 and Acts 6:1–7: The Literary Context of Luke-Acts," in *A Feminist Companion to Luke*, ed. Amy-Jill Levine

Most feminist scholars agree that this reading is harmful because it places an unnecessary and unrealistic burden on women, exemplifying a larger hermeneutic of the Bible that has privileged men and attempted to marginalize women. It follows that this reading should be corrected. Thus, over the past forty years, many feminist scholars have attempted to offer a more liberative reading of Luke 10:38–42, one that recognizes the vital but often ignored role women have played in the church.

However, while most agree that there is a problem with the conventional interpretation, there has been little agreement as to how to redeem or properly read this text. Two brief examples of feminist argumentation must suffice for now. One approach blames the problems in the text on the author of Luke and his misogynistic tendencies: Luke directly contributed to the oppression of women. The most prominent voice for this view is Schüssler Fiorenza herself. She argues that Luke intentionally sets the two sisters against one another in order to create conflict between women leaders in the early church. She concludes that Luke essentially "pits the apostolic women of the Jesus movement against each other.... Its rhetorical interests are to silence women leaders like Martha and at the same time to extol the silent and subordinate behavior of Mary."[13] For Schüssler Fiorenza, this text has always carried within it the intent to silence women. It reinforces the societal norms of the time and intentionally ignores the large roles Mary and Martha played in the early church. There is no redeeming the text itself. In order to redeem the story it tells, Schüssler Fiorenza argues that women must reimagine a completely new version. Thus, in her interpretation, she stresses the emphasis on Martha's service, διακονία, and argues that this reveals the ministry of word and table in which Martha historically participated. Once one recognizes this idea and erases the patriarchal structure in which this story is placed, one can retell the story in a way that honors the important and vibrant ministries of both sisters. Here is an excerpt of her retelling:

> I am Martha, the founder of the church in Bethany and the sister of Mary, the evangelist. All kinds of men are writing down the stories about Jesus but they don't get it right. Some use even our very own name to

---

(Cleveland: Pilgrim, 2004), 162; Elisabeth Moltmann-Wendel, *The Women around Jesus* (London: SCM, 1982), 52.

13. Elisabeth Schüssler Fiorenza, "A Feminist Critical Interpretation for Liberation: Martha and Mary, Lk 10:38–42," *RIL* 3 (1986): 32.

argue against women's leadership in the movement.... They had been travelling for a long time when they finally came to our village. I invited them to join my sister Mary and me. Jesus and the disciples with him sat down and began talking. Mary sat at the teacher's feet and I joined her in asking him about his latest journeys.... By the time the teacher finished this story evening had approached and it was time for sharing the meal. I asked Jesus if he would stay to eat with us. He said yes, and added: "Martha, don't go to a lot of trouble. Whatever you were going to have will be fine. Let me help you."[14]

As one can see, this is a dramatic departure from the original text of Luke 10:38–42 but a legitimate reading, if one believes that the text itself is corrupt.

On the other side of the spectrum, one discovers an apologetic reading in which the Third Gospel is seen as being entirely favorable to women. Many scholars hold this more apologetic view and have argued that it is the interpretations that are flawed, not the author, and that Luke actually creates a world in which women are able to move above typical gender roles by engaging in scholastic study and not typical domestic duties.[15] Luke is more of a liberator of women than an oppressor.

For instance, Irene Brennan argues that this story and others in the gospels offer an important corrective to a modern patriarchal culture that actively diminishes women's voices: "When Jesus quietly chides Martha for her insistence that Mary take the traditional woman's role, he makes it clear that he himself admits Mary into full discipleship. In so doing, Christ admits a woman to an equal place with men in that preparation which will enable her to be actively engaged in the establishment of the Kingdom."[16] In Brennan's reading, the story reflects an alternate historical reality in which women were admitted into the inner circles of Jesus's ministry. She argues that later glosses on this text are to blame for the current misinterpretations. At its core, the story of Mary and Martha at Bethany contains a liberative message for women.

---

14. Schüssler Fiorenza, "Feminist Critical Interpretation," 35.

15. It should be noted that this reflects a larger debate about Luke's treatment of women in his gospel. Scholarship is still divided on whether Luke is affirming of the ministries of his women characters or attempting to erase them. For a summary of this debate, see Jane Schaberg, "Luke," in *The Women's Bible Commentary*, ed. Carol A. Newsom and Sharon H. Ringe (Louisville: Westminster John Knox, 1992), 275–92.

16. Irene Brennan, "Women in the Gospels," *NBf* 52 (1971): 293.

Between these two poles, one can find almost every variation of these views as feminist scholars debate how Luke 10:38–42 can be read in relation to the role of women then and now.[17] However, what is most interesting about this debate is not the multitude of potential readings of Luke 10:38–42 but rather how each is focused, in one way or another, on answering a specific set of questions, namely, what Luke 10:38–42 can reveal to us about women in the early church. In fact, most modern biblical scholarship on Luke 10:38–42 intersects with the issue of women in the New Testament.[18] In one sense, this is logical, as this story does feature two named women. But such a tight focus leads to ignoring much of the richness of Luke 10:38–42. In many ways this story appears to linger in the niche market of texts about women's issues, allowing the majority of Lukan studies to ignore the text. Thus, one can see that even in feminist studies, Luke 10:38–42 primarily operates as a story about women for women, though the focus has shifted from paradigms for contemporary behavior to historical claims about women's roles.

While feminist readings are not oppressive or limiting of women in the same way as their Protestant evangelical counterparts, they reveal the same central issue: that Luke 10:38–42 has been limited to its contribution to gendered issues. The passage's potential contribution to the question of discipleship in Luke, and the nature of Christian discipleship more broadly, has been mostly ignored both in modern Protestant teaching and preaching and in significant parts of biblical scholarship.

---

17. See Barbara Reid, *Choosing the Better Part? Women in Gospel of Luke* (Collegeville, MN: Liturgical Press, 1996); Price, *Widow Tradition in Luke-Acts*, 175–90; Turid Karlsen Seim, *The Double Message: Patterns of Gender in Luke-Acts* (Nashville: Abingdon, 1994); Warren Carter, "Getting Martha Out of the Kitchen: Luke 10:38–42 Again," in Levine, *Feminist Companion to Luke*, 214–31. In particular, see Koperski, "Women and Discipleship," 161–96, for an overview on some of the more recent contributions. These views and several others will be discussed in greater detail in the final chapter.

18. There are, of course, other discussions about this passage, most notably within Lukan commentaries. The commentary tradition on this passage has focused on the following interpretative issues: form and source criticism, redaction criticism, and its relationship to other New Testament passages. These will be discussed in greater depth in ch. 2.

A New (Old) Approach: Finding a New Way to Discuss Luke 10:38–42

In order to enable a new way of reading this story, I undertake studying some very old ways of reading it. To that end, I present and analyze different premodern interpretations of the story of Mary and Martha. In the substantial reception history of this story, the passage has been placed in a number of different contexts and produced a range of interpretations, primarily on issues related to Christian discipleship. Consider, for example, Origen's interpretation from the third century:

> You might reasonably take Martha to stand for action and Mary for contemplation. For the mystery of love is lost to the active life unless one directs his teaching, and his exhortation to action, toward contemplation. For, there is no action without contemplation or contemplation without action. But we should say that Martha received the word more somatically, in her house, that is, in her soul, whereas Mary heard it spiritually, even if she sat at his feet. This means, she had already passed beyond what was handed down by way of introduction according to the plan of salvation, since she had put aside the things of a child but had not yet received what was perfect. (*Fr. Luc.* 171)[19]

Origen presents the paradigmatic nature of Mary and Martha as one of action and contemplation, spirituality and physicality, rather than two different types of female service. The women represent basic forms of Christianity. He does not mention the kitchen. Neither does he make allowances for their gender. He does not minimize or apologize for their respective roles. Gender is, at most, a secondary point in the larger argument. Or consider this later comment from Meister Eckhart in the thirteenth century:

> Martha was afraid her sister would remain clinging to consolation and sweetness, and she wished her to become as she herself was. This is why Christ said, "She has chosen the best part," as if to say, "Cheer up, Martha; this will leave her. The most sublime thing that can happen to a creature shall happen to her: She shall become as happy as you.... Mary sat at the feet of the Lord and listened to his words," and learned.... But after-

---

19. Translation from *Homilies on Luke*, trans. Joseph T. Lienhard. FC 94 (Washington, DC: Catholic University of America Press, 1996). Origen and the influence of his interpretation will be a core part of ch. 3.

> ward, when she had learned,…then she really for the first time began to serve…. Thus do the saints become saints; not until then do they really begin to practice virtue. (*Serm.* 86)[20]

In this sermon, we find an almost opposite reading of Luke 10:38–42 with respect to which sister represents greater progress in their Christian faith. Martha is elevated here as being further along in her Christian journey, while Mary is still needing space to learn. However, like in Origen, their gender is neither an advantage nor a hindrance within the larger argument. Not their gender but their understanding of the Christian faith is the central idea. Moreover, these are both sermons that appear to be directed to all Christians, and women are never explicitly called out as being the target audience.

These authors and others will be discussed in greater detail in the coming chapters, but I mention them here to illustrate that most, if not all, pre-Reformation readings of Luke 10:38–42 present Mary and Martha as models of discipleship. To be sure, patristic and medieval interpretations vary. Some interpreters elevate Mary, while others focus on Martha. Some take a more literal approach to highlight the importance of hospitality in discipleship, while others present a more spiritualized reading. Indeed, there is no standard premodern reading of this passage. What remains consistent, however, is a focus on the nature of discipleship for all Christians and a lack of specifically gendered interpretation.

I propose in this book that premodern readings of Luke 10:38–42 offer a way forward in reclaiming this story as one that is important for questions of discipleship, both ancient and modern. Within the history of interpretation, one finds this text being used to debate questions of eschatology, practical theology, and the nature of salvation, among others. Premodern readers were by no means flawless; many of them were deeply sexist, and I do not suggest that we should attempt to reclaim premodern modes of reading Scripture. Instead, my project seeks to bring those earlier interpretations back into the conversation about Luke 10:38–42. They offer an important corrective to modern Protestant readings, and they offer feminist readers a way to talk about Mary and Martha in a way that still elevates them but also highlights their influence on the shape of Christian understandings of discipleship. Premodern interpretations help

---

20. Translation from *The Complete Mystical Works*, trans. Maurice O'C Walshe (New York: Crossroads, 2009).

us see that while this text is gendered (women are the central figures), the primary meaning of the text is not gendered. Using female characters, the passage speaks to both men and women about the nature of Christian discipleship. By engaging with these old ways of reading, we are offered new insight into our postmodern readings of this story. They present us with alternate ways to explore this text, so that we might better "hold it up to light"[21] and explore its nuances.

In order to accomplish this, I first conduct a careful exegesis of Luke 10:38–42 in its Lukan context, emphasizing literary questions as opposed to historical-critical ones. In particular, I will focus on its relationship with the parable of the good Samaritan in Luke 10:25–37 and its location within Lukan travel narrative. Furthermore, I explore how this text, when read alongside other pericopes in Luke-Acts on discipleship, particularly Acts 6, can inform one's understanding of discipleship in Luke. As part of this literary approach, I also analyze the textual variants in this passage in order to unpack the potential diversity of interpretations during its transmission. Despite the brevity of the narrative, there is a significant variant in 10:41–42, which complicates interpretations of this passage.

I then conduct a literary and historical analysis of selected patristic, medieval, and Reformation texts, as well medieval and Reformation artwork, in order to examine how this story functioned in different exegetical cultures. I reject the claim that the history of interpretation must be studied as one might study evolution, examining how certain incorrect readings evolved into correct ones over time, as if the interpretation of the Bible can be viewed as progressing positively over time. Rather, I argue that, in different periods of time, different goals and priorities dictated how exegesis was conducted, leading to different outcomes for different purposes. The concerns of Origen when he read Luke 10:38–42 are different from the concerns of Schüssler Fiorenza. Old readings are not inherently better or worse due to their age or their origin in the precritical era; rather, their authors interpret through a different lens, one that is often ignored in the critical age of exegesis. The goal of this project is to examine what insights can be discovered when one places readings from different exegetical cultures in conversation with the modern era. In this, I agree with Peter Martens, who argues: "[Different] cultures *can*

---

21. Billy Collins, "Introduction to Poetry," in *The Apple That Astonished Paris* (Little Rock: University of Arkansas Press, 2006), 58.

communicate with one another and learn from one another even if they are oriented around different goals."²² This approach is the methodological basis for the history-of-interpretation sections of this project. Modern biblical scholars can and should engage with different exegetical cultures when studying a particular text. These exegetical cultures can be from the past (as this project engages), but they can also be from coexisting exegetical cultures as well. By engaging in this practice, scholars allow themselves to be exposed to ideas within the text that might have been obscured, leading to new ideas and, perhaps, better interpretations.

This project is attempt to practice that approach, using Luke 10:38–42 as a test case. When one studies patristic and medieval readings, one finds that the women of the story are considered as models of discipleship, whereas in contemporary piety/feminist readings, this element has been lost or ignored. The earlier ways of readings Luke 10:38–42 can be brought back to the conversation in order to offer a corrective. In many ways, earlier readings attest to a concern that appears to reflect Luke's own concerns about the nature of discipleship. The goal is to bring this passage out of subset of a texts labeled women's issues and back into broader conversations about discipleship in both Luke-Acts and Christianity more broadly.

A Question and a Concern

Therefore, the question underlying this project is a simple one: Are there meaningful interpretations of Luke 10:38–42 that have been hidden by the current discussions about the role of women in the first century and in the modern era? This work seeks to examine what happens when this text is read not against the backdrop of gender but against the backdrop of discipleship.

In many ways, I echo the concerns of many feminist-critical readings of Luke 10:38–42. Feminist-critical readings have been important for elevating the roles for women that previously were ignored, and they have been essential in identifying the patriarchal premises that have dominated modern evangelical readings. But I argue that this text has in fact been pigeonholed, leading to it being relevant only for the discussion of gender and little else. Mostly, the potential of this passage

---

22. Peter Martens, "Metaphors for Narrating the History of Biblical Interpretation," paper presented at Annual Meeting of the Society of Biblical Literature, San Antonio, Texas, November 20, 2016.

for understanding discipleship in Luke has been slighted. It is, indeed, a form of sexism to allow a passage that predominantly features women disciples to be written off as a niche text, only interesting to those who are concerned about women's ministry in the early church.

Similarly, evangelical Protestantism has removed this text from larger discussions about the question of discipleship. It is a woman's text for women. Mary and Martha retain their paradigmatic stature, but only for women in the household. This passage is a popular one for women's devotions and retreats, but, significantly, not for sermons. After all, the paradigm only applies to women, not to their male counterparts.

What Has Been Done: History of Research

While a more detailed analysis of the immense history of research conducted on this passage is found throughout this project, this section seeks to provide a wide overview of the predominant streams of research on Luke 10:38–42. These streams are loosely defined here as historical-critical approaches, literary approaches, textual criticism, and reception history. In this section, I will present a brief overview of the major figures in these streams in order to show where my own research both intersects and diverges from these previous projects.

Historical-Critical Approaches

In recent years, the predominant focus of most studies of Luke 10:38–42 has been historical in nature, as researchers have attempted to uncover the historical ministries of Christian women during the first century. In particular, these studies have focused on Martha's role in διακονία and Mary's role as a student of Jesus in order to uncover what ministries women participated in and how these ministries were received by their male counterparts. Thus, a large number of scholarly historical treatments of Luke 10:38–42 center on discovering Luke's position on the assumed disagreement in the early church on how women were allowed to serve. As Warren Carter notes, the primary question has become: "Is Luke an oppressor or a liberator?"[23]

---

23. Carter, "Getting Martha Out," 214.

As already briefly discussed, Schüssler Fiorenza analyzes this question from a historical perspective in a number of different books and articles.[24] In each, she famously argues that Martha's serving reflected an active role in word and table ministries for both the historical Martha and for other women in the early church and that Luke's own patriarchal impulses led him to attempt to erase those ministries.[25] She grounds her argument in the assertion that by the time Luke constructed his gospel, the term διακονία had come to refer to eucharistic ministry in house churches and included already a proclamation of the word alongside the table.[26] She argues that Luke is deeply uncomfortable with this role for women and thus attempts to marginalize Martha in his depiction of her in 10:38–42. In her view, Luke constructs his narrative in a such way as to silence her, and through her he attempts to erase all the voices of women ministers in the first century.[27] This conclusion leads to her claim that the text needs to be reconstructed to better reflect the historical reality of both Martha and Mary, but also to honor the roles women held in the first century.

Other scholars have found a more complicated role for Luke in his depiction of Mary and Martha and have pushed back against Schüssler Fiorenza's claims about διακονία. In particular, Barbara Reid and Turid Seim in their respective works argue that it is unclear whether διακονία refers in this instance to table ministry and a subsequent leadership role.[28] However, they both agree that this text reveals the complexities of women's ministries in the first century. Reid argues that what is at stake in this passage is not the question of whether women were regarded as Jesus's disciples but what ministries women were allowed to participate in as a result

---

24. Schüssler Fiorenza, *But She Said*, 54–76; Schüssler Fiorenza, "Feminist Critical Interpretation," 21–36; Schüssler Fiorenza, *In Memory of Her: A Feminist Theological Construction of Christian Origins* (New York: Crossroads, 1984); Schüssler Fiorenza, "The Practice of Biblical Interpretation: Luke 10:38–42," in *The Bible and Liberation: Political and Social Hermeneutics*, ed. Norman K. Gottwald and Richard A. Horsley (Maryknoll, NY: Orbis Books, 1992), 172–97.

25. Schüssler Fiorenza, *But She Said*, 58–60.

26. This argument is rooted in readings of Acts 6:1–7 and the service to the widows. She heavily draws on John Collins's work *Diakonia: Re-interpreting the Ancient Sources* (New York: Oxford University Press, 1990), 77–95. *Diakonia* as a concept within Luke-Acts will be discussed at greater length in ch. 2.

27. Schüssler Fiorenza, *But She Said*, 63.

28. Reid, *Choosing the Better Part?*, 147–48; Seim, *Double Message*, 100–101.

of that discipleship.²⁹ She holds that the early church was not clearly unified in its views on this issue and that the author of Luke, like the author of the Pastorals, sought to limit women's ministries.³⁰ Luke's depiction of the story reflects Martha's distress that Mary is being forced into a silent role, but Jesus ultimately affirms this as the better role. Reid emphasizes that this depiction of women in ministry only represents one side of the argument and that by engaging with other depictions of women in the New Testament, one can find a more realistic picture of women engaged in numerous ministries across the early church.³¹

Seim also argues that the role of women in the first-century church was a complex issue with numerous competing values at play. She ultimately concludes that Luke was a neutral figure, not attempting to either oppress or liberate women. She writes: "It is a preposterous simplification to ask whether Luke's writings were friendly or hostile to women.... The tension in Luke's narrative has indeed shown itself to be ambivalent evidence of both strong traditions about women on one hand and of the social and ideological controls that brought women to silence."³² Thus, Seim argues that Luke's depiction of Mary and Martha in Luke 10:38–42 is not intentionally constructed to limit the leadership roles for women. Rather, for Seim, Martha is indicative of a historical group of Christian women engaged with service and care of others, while Mary is indicative of women who were students and recipients (but not preachers) of the gospel message.³³ According to her, this explains the tension between Martha, who is engaged in ministry, and Mary, who is a silent observer, as the tension reflects the community that produced Luke. These roles were complex and based on societal norms on when women could speak or not, as revealed further in the New Testament in the letters of Paul. Seim's work reconstructing the roles of Christian women in the first century is particularly careful and detailed, and her claims about Luke being a more neutral figure are particularly compelling.

Seim has often been criticized for constructing a false dichotomy between Christian women and Jewish women.³⁴ She argues that Jewish

---

29. Reid, *Choosing the Better Part?*, 154–55.
30. Reid, *Choosing the Better Part?*, 154.
31. Reid, *Choosing the Better Part?*, 159–60.
32. Seim, *Double Message*, 249.
33. Seim, *Double Message*, 101–18.
34. Seim is in no way unique in this regard; several prominent readers of this text have argued that this passage points to the liberation of Christian women from the

women, as discussed in rabbinic literature, were prohibited from learning and participating in any forms of leadership. Thus, Christian women's ability to learn and participate in service marks a significant difference between Christianity and Judaism in the first century. This move has been severely questioned and critiqued, since it unnecessarily elevates Christianity over Judaism. It is historically inaccurate to suppose that by allowing Mary to listen to his teaching, Jesus was participating in an extraordinary liberative act that was always denied Jewish women.[35] As Stephen Davies notes, in order to make this claim, "One must overlook the fact that listening to men is far from an unusual or liberated role for a woman.... Unless it can be shown that such charismatic individuals normally refused to instruct women, then the portrait simply reflects reality as Luke knew it."[36] However, not all scholars agree that this dichotomy is inherently anti-Semitic; both Joel Green and John Donahue argue that it can be a neutral claim. They both argue, contra Schüssler Fiorenza, Davies, and others, that since women within Jewish culture were normally cast in the domestic role, the fact that Mary is allowed to do otherwise is revolutionary. They do not find such a statement to be anti-Jewish, and they draw heavily on Seim's work for their arguments.[37]

---

oppressive conditions endured by Jewish women, usually derived from readings of rabbinic texts that excluded women from learning. For other examples, see Brennan, "Women in the Gospels," 293; Richard J. Cassidy, *Jesus, Politics and Society: A Study of Luke's Gospel* (Maryknoll, NY: Orbis Books, 1978) 36; Frederick W. Danker, *Jesus and the New Age: A Commentary on St. Luke's Gospel* (Philadelphia: Fortress, 1988), 224–26.

35. For another brief example of this interpretation in modern scholarship, see Joseph Fitzmyer: "Moreover, Jesus in this scene does not hesitate to depict a woman as a disciple sitting at Jesus's feet.... Jesus rather encourages a woman to learn from him, contrast the attitude of the sages of Jewish rabbinic tradition" (*The Gospel according to Luke*, 2 vols., AB 28–28A [Garden City, NY: Doubleday, 1981–1985], 2:892). For a deeper look at this view in scholarship, see Koperski, "Women and Discipleship," 164–67.

36. Stephen Davies, "Third Gospel and New Testament Apocrypha," in *"Women Like This": New Perspectives on Jewish Women in the Greco-Roman World*, ed. Amy-Jill Levine, EJL 1 (Atlanta: Scholars Press, 1991), 186. Schüssler Fiorenza similarly argues: "A feminist critical hermeneutics of liberation must, however, reject such an anti-Jewish interpretation since it seeks to eliminate the oppression and marginality of Christian women by historically perpetuating that of Jewish women" ("Feminist Critical Interpretation," 28).

37. See Joel Green, *The Gospel of Luke*, NICNT (Grand Rapids: Eerdmans, 1997),

At its core, though, this argument is based on differing historical reconstructions of the roles of Jewish and Christian women and not on the text of Luke itself. From a literary perspective, there is no evidence in Luke's narrative to imply that Mary's act of listening is somehow revolutionary for Jewish women. Furthermore, the rabbinic evidence used to construct this dichotomy is much later and often used uncritically, as Seim herself admits.[38] This is an unnecessary exegetical decision that moves beyond the scope of the text and serves only to elevate Christian women and their ministries at the expense of Jewish women.

A second approach of historical-critical analysis, which should be briefly mentioned, rejects reconstructing the historical ministries of women in favor of reconstructing the form of this story. The most popular argument, originally found in Erling Laland's "Die Marte-Maria Perikope, Lukas 10, 38–42" and then reconstructed and expanded in Robert Price's *The Widow Tradition in Luke-Acts: A Feminist Critical Scrutiny*, states that the story went through multiple stages of development before ending up in its final form in Luke 10.[39] The earliest stage reflected advice on the correct treatment of itinerant missionaries, with Jesus himself being depicted as the paradigmatic preacher.[40] Thus, in its original form, the story was presented in such a way as to help Christians properly show hospitality to missionaries and looked similar to this: "He entered a village, and a woman named Martha received him into her home. But Martha was distracted with much serving. But the Lord said to her, 'Martha, Martha, you are anxious and troubled about many things; few things are needful, or only one.' "[41] Over time, additional elements were added to the story; the Mary subplot, an emphasis on asceticism, and an attempt to silence women created the story as it is found in Luke 10:38–42. Price argues that Luke co-opts the traditions around this story in its various layers to construct a narrative that is more suited to his negative view of women in ministry.[42]

---

435 n. 142; John R. Donahue, *The Gospel in Parable: Metaphor, Narrative and Theology in the Synoptic Gospels* (Philadelphia: Fortress, 1988), 138–39.

38. Seim, *Double Message*, 102 n. 15: "It is, however, important to make the reservation that an intensive investigation of Jewish sources from a feminist perspective may alter the picture of [the role of Jewish women] and add significant nuances to it."

39. Erling Laland, "Die Marte-Maria Perikope, Lukas 10, 38–42," *ST* 13 (1959): 70–85; Price, *Widow Tradition in Luke-Acts*, 175–201.

40. Laland, "Die Marte-Maria Perikope," 82.

41. Price, *Widow Tradition in Luke-Acts*, 177.

42. Price, *Widow Tradition in Luke-Acts*, 183. Here Price follows Schüssler Fio-

If one examines each layer in turn, one can see the different functions the story held. The original one can be traced to a historical event with an unknown hostess and an unknown "considerate and insightful itinerant."[43]

From both Price's reconstruction and Schüssler Fiorenza's, mentioned earlier, one can see an impulse to re-create the narrative in order to reflect a more historically accurate account of this (purported) event, because the text as it stands has been corrupted by Luke's editorializing and is need of historical correction.[44] While this approach raises important questions about the *Sitz im Leben* out of which this narrative arose and directs the conversation to necessary questions such as authorial intent, my project does not involve historical reconstructions. Unfortunately, the historical Mary and Martha are forever lost to modern scholars.

Literary Approaches

However, despite the historical limits of uncovering the real Mary and Martha, the text and the characters themselves remain. François Bovon correctly argues, "What counts in this story is not so much the label [or reconstruction] it is given, as is the narrative character."[45] Thus, some scholarly treatments have instead focused on literary readings of the passage in its Lukan context. In the following section, I highlight a few of those literary readings that are particularly informative for this project.

First, Loveday Alexander, in "Sisters in Adversity: Retelling Martha's Story," agrees with the assumption that the simple interpretation often preached in Protestant churches that Martha should stop nagging and become a more "quiet, tranquil soul" like her sister is harmful and inadequate to capture the complexities of the text.[46] She also recognizes, with Schüssler Fiorenza, that Martha often gets mistreated and demonized in many mainstream interpretations. She argues that instead of attempting to turn Martha and Mary into paradigms by which all Christian women's

---

renza's claims about the authorial intent of Luke, though he obviously disagrees with her claim that entire text is of Lukan composition.

43. Price, *Widow Tradition in Luke-Acts*, 178.

44. There are numerous other studies also engaged in a historical reconstruction of Mary and Martha and the women they represent.

45. Bovon, *Luke 2*, 69.

46. Loveday C. Alexander, "Sisters in Adversity: Retelling Martha's Story," in Levine, *Feminist Companion to Luke*, 198.

behavior should be mirrored, the text should be read as attempting to present a paradox.[47] Using literary analysis, she argues that Mary's behavior is bad by all accounts, but she is still vindicated. Martha, on the other hand, has impeccably good manners and yet she is rebuked. The intent, according to Alexander, is to overthrow expectations about what is good and bad in order to show Jesus in a new light. This, however, does not mean one should be a bad hostess or ignore work that needs to be done. She argues that to make this story about women's work or the historical nature of women's ministry in the early church is to "risk confining it to the ghetto: women's stories, notoriously are felt to have nothing to teach men."[48] This story, she argues, stresses that the business of discipleship, according to Luke, includes both men and women.

Ultimately, I find Alexander's emphasis persuasive and one that, I would argue, is reflected in how the reception history interacts with this passage. Her arguments about the intentionally paradoxical nature of Luke 10:38–42 are particularly important for my interpretation. I would argue that it is the paradox that leads to the creative and often conflicting interpretations found throughout the reception history. I disagree with Alexander's reading on one major point. She argues that one should push back against paradigmatic readings (particularly the contemplative-active paradigm) as being forced onto the text and not inherently embedded within it. However, I argue in coming chapters that the paradoxical and parabolic nature of this text naturally lends itself to such paradigmatic readings.

A second important literary analysis is Donahue's *Gospel in Parable*. He argues for a strong thematic connection between Luke 10:38–42 and the parable of the good Samaritan, which immediately precedes it in 10:25–37.[49] He argues that the story of Mary and Martha should also be viewed parabolically, even though it is not introduced as such, because the two stories represent personifications of the greatest commandment:

---

47. Alexander, "Sisters in Adversity," 212.
48. Alexander, "Sisters in Adversity," 213.
49. Donahue, *Gospel in Parable*, 136. In this, Donahue is not unique; many scholars hold the view these two texts should be read together. In particular, see Green, *Gospel of Luke*, 434; Luke Timothy Johnson, *The Gospel of Luke*, SP 3 (Collegeville, MN: Liturgical Press, 1991), 175. For the minority view that holds these passages are not connected, see Gerhard Schneider, *Evangelium nach Lukas*, ÖTK 3 (Gütersloh: Gütersloher Verlagshaus, 1977), 252; Fitzmyer, *Gospel according to Luke*, 2:891.

"The parable of the Good Samaritan with its exhortation to do mercy to the neighbor and the story of Mary and Martha with its praise of the one who sits and listens to the Lord form a two-fold parabolic illustration of the single command.... To love God with the whole heart and mind and the neighbor as the self demands both compassionate and effective entry into the world of the neighbor as well as undistracted attentiveness to the word of the Lord."[50] This reading informs his conclusion that Luke 10:38–42 should be classified as a parabolic narrative.[51] While I find Donahue's classification of this narrative compelling, I do not accept his exegetical argument that this pericope represents the "loving God" part of the greatest commandment. It is a disservice to Martha's role in the narrative to argue that she has failed to properly love God. Rather, I argue in the following chapter that the parabolic nature of the story is revealed in the way it challenges and reverses the reader's assumptions about the correct way to serve God and to participate in the act of hospitality.[52]

Another important piece of scholarship on this passage is Jutta Brutscheck's *Die Maria-Marta-Erzählung: Eine redaktionskritische Untersuchung zu Lk 10, 38–42*.[53] Brutscheck engages in both philology and literary analysis of the individual passage and its location in the travel narrative of Luke to conclude that correct treatment of others (i.e., hospitality) is rooted in attention to Jesus's words. A follower of Jesus is only able to properly exhibit hospitality (a major thematic element in this story) when she has heard the words of Jesus. In this way, Brutscheck argues that the narrative with Jesus and his hostesses was constructed to inform members of the early church as they sought a model for correctly hosting itinerant missionaries.[54] This connection between the relationship of the original audience with the world of the text is a particularly strong argument, as she finds a way to link the hospitality to itinerant missionaries without relying solely on stages of textual development. Furthermore, she emphasizes the importance of this story within the travel narrative

---

50. Donahue, *Gospel in Parable*, 136–37.
51. Donahue, *Gospel in Parable*, 134.
52. On this issue, I agree with Johnson that this text is deeply concerned with the question of hospitality (*Gospel of Luke*, 175–76).
53. Jutta Brutscheck, *Die Maria-Marta-Erzählung: Eine redaktionskritische Untersuchung zu Lk 10, 38–42*, BBB 64 (Frankfurt am Main: Hanstein, 1986).
54. For a brief summary of this work in English, see Frederick Danker, review of *Die Maria-Marta-Erzählung*, *CBQ* 50 (1988): 130–31.

as a whole.⁵⁵ However, she also rejects the claim of the early church that this story functions paradigmatically to represent contemplation and action, considering hospitality and the correct understanding of God's word to be the central themes. Her emphasis on the importance of this story's location in the travel narrative is shared by Warren Carter, whose work also should be briefly mentioned before transitioning to scholarly treatments of the reception history.⁵⁶ Carter argues that the narrative location of this story should shape one's reading of it and that the two sisters should not be read as opposing figures but rather as ministry partners, similar to the Seventy.⁵⁷ He finds other comparisons in Acts with the ministries of Stephen and the Seven and Barnabas and Paul. He views Luke as presenting a positive view of women's leadership, as the story uses female characters "to instruct the gospel readers and hearers about important aspects of the task of leadership and ministry."⁵⁸ Luke, therefore, is not attempting to silence women in his depiction of Mary and Martha but rather to elevate them as leaders within the early church. While Carter's continued focus on using this text to evaluate Luke's presentation of women is in line with most feminist scholarship, his point that this text speaks more broadly to questions of leadership, while using women as the primary characters, is important.

There are many other treatments of this passage in commentaries and articles that I have not dealt with, due to space limitations.⁵⁹ But this brief overview has presented the main interpretive methods used when

---

55. Brutscheck, *Die Maria-Marta-Erzählung*, 50–64.
56. Carter, "Getting Martha Out," 214–31.
57. Carter, "Getting Martha Out," 230.
58. Carter, "Getting Martha Out," 215. It should be noted that Carter here is expanding on the idea of women missionary partners first presented by Mary Rose D'Angelo in "Women Partners in the New Testament," *JFSR* 6 (1990): 65–86.
59. For instance, see Rudolf Bultmann, *The History of the Synoptic Tradition*, trans. John Marsh (Peabody, MA: Hendrickson, 1994), 33–34; Fitzmyer, *Gospel according to Luke*, 2:890–92; Bovon, *Luke 2*, 68–76; Koperski, "Women and Discipleship," 161–96; Luise Schottroff,. *Lydia's Impatient Sisters: A Feminist Social History of Early Christianity*, trans B. M. Rumscheidt (Louisville: Westminster John Knox, 1995); Adele Reinhartz, "From Narrative to History: The Resurrection of Mary and Martha," in Levine, "Women Like This," 161–64; Ben Witherington III, *Women in the Ministry of Jesus: A Study of Jesus' Attitudes in Women and Their Roles Reflected in this Earthly Life*, SNTSMS 51 (New York: Cambridge University Press, 1984), 99–105.

discussing Luke 10:38–42 as well as highlighted some of the primary scholars with whom I will be engaging in this project.

Secondary Scholarship on the Reception History

While a significant amount of work has been done to exegete this passage, the reception history has only been minimally discussed by New Testament scholars. One area of New Testament research where early Christian sources have come into play is the study of the textual variants in the passage, particularly in verses 41–42. At stake is Jesus's reply to Martha in verse 41. Does he say only one thing is needed, or are there a few things needed? Due to this notably complex textual variant in those verses, many scholars have examined the patristic evidence in an attempt to uncover the more original reading, since the popularity of the passage in the patristic period provides an abundance of evidence. Most significantly, Gordon D. Fee, in "'One Thing Needful'? (Luke 10:42)," conducts an in-depth analysis of the textual evidence for the different variants, drawing heavily on patristic sources.[60] He places the church fathers alongside each variant reading:

Table 1.1 Summary of Patristic Attestations[61]

Majority reading "there is only one thing needed"	Variant 1: omission "Martha, Mary has chosen ..."	Variant 2 "Few things are needed"	Variant 3 "Few things are needed, indeed only one"
Chrysostom	Ambrose	Origen (?)	Origen
Evagrius	Clement (?)		Basil
Pseudo-Macarius			Jerome
Augustine			Cassian
Gregory the Great			Cyril of Alexandria

The point of contention, according to Fee, is whether Origen actually attests to the second variant in his commentary on John. In his Lukan

---

60. Gordon D. Fee, "One Thing Needful? (Luke 10:42)," in *To What End Exegesis?* (Grand Rapids: Eerdmans, 2001), 3–16.
61. Fee, "One Thing Needful?," 4–5.

fragments, he clearly attests to the longer version. Aelred Baker, in "One Thing Necessary," argues that Origen himself must be the original source of the conflated variant, that he must have known multiple versions and combined them.[62] Fee, however, argues that Origen in his commentary on John is not quoting Luke 10:42 but rather paraphrasing it as he discusses John 11:2.[63] He holds that this removes an attestation of the second variant, leaving very few other references of it: a thirteenth-century codex, a fifth-century Syriac text, and two Bohairic texts (ninth and thirteenth centuries). He concludes that the third variant is most likely the original version of Luke 10:41–42 for two reasons: (1) it has significant early textual support among the patristics, and (2) it is the most difficult reading.[64] He concludes, alongside R. M. Grant, with the observation that the problem of textual critics using patristic sources is that often no one examines them closely enough to see what they actually support. Too often only the exact words are used and not the surrounding context, leading to a misuse of certain sources, as in the Origen example. He claims this is often the problem with critical analysis of Luke 10:41–42, and he attempts to correct it in his own thorough analysis.[65]

Such scholars attempt to use patristic evidence as a way to uncover the original form of the text and thus to uncover the original meaning of the text.[66] But the patristic sources themselves were less concerned with the original meaning of Luke and more concerned with the theological message encapsulated by Luke's words. Most patristic interpreters were not concerned with whether Jesus was referring to one dish or a few dishes in a literal sense. They are, rather, focused on what the few things or one thing mean for their understanding of discipleship. For instance, Cyril of Alexandria attests to variant three, whereas Augustine attests to the major-

---

62. Aelred Baker, "One Thing Necessary," *CBQ* 27 (1965): 136.
63. Fee, "One Thing Needful?," 11.
64. He renders the passage in the following way: "Martha, Martha, you are worried and troubled about many things. However, few things are needed, or if you will, only one. For that is what Mary has chosen …" (Fee, "One Thing Needful?," 14). His argument has been expanded on recently by Tommy Wasserman in "Bringing Sisters Back Together: Another Look at Luke 10:41–42," *JBL* 137 (2018): 439–61. He strongly agrees with Fee's support of the third variant.
65. Fee, "One Thing Needful?," 10. See also Robert M. Grant, "The Citation of Patristic Evidence in an Apparatus Criticus," in *New Testament Manuscript Studies*, ed. M. M. Parvis and A. Wikgren (Chicago: University of Chicago Press, 1977), 124.
66. Bovon, *Luke 2*, 74.

ity reading. However, Cyril interprets the passage as being primarily about the proper way to host a holy man who comes to your home; hence, only a few things are needed to serve, and the one most important thing is to learn from the holy man. Augustine, on the other hand, argues for an eschatological reading that focuses on the primary and eternal task of a Christian. The version of the text they had access to shifts the nature of their interpretation in a significant way.[67] This line of research is particularly important for this project because it highlights the complexity of the textual variants, and it reveals the seemingly paradoxical nature of Jesus's response to Martha and the various ways the patristic authors attempted to resolve that paradox.

Scholarly Treatments of the Reception History

There are a number of historical studies that have analyzed specific authors or time periods and their use of Luke 10:38–42. Most of these studies have been conducted by medieval historians, as Mary and Martha became important figures during that time period. For instance, Blake Heffner examines the view of Meister Eckhart and his interpretation of Martha as the better sister.[68] His work is useful in that he traces different developments of interpretation that he finds in Eckhart, who created a new interpretation out of different patristic pieces. Another example is found in the *Cambridge Companion to Mysticism*, which contains an article comparing the interpretations of Augustine, Eckhart, and Ignatius of Loyola in terms of their understanding of action and contemplation.[69] One study of the patristic period specifically focuses on the writings of Augustine on Mary and Martha. In "Les deux vies. Marthe et Marie (Luc 10:38–42)," Anne-Marie La Bonnardiere explores Augustine's numerous references to this story and the two different lives these two sisters

---

67. This is not to say that different early church fathers were intentionally changing the text but that in many instances these citations are being pulled from homilies, where they were not actually attempting to directly to quote the text but rather are summarizing, as Fee notes.

68. Blake Heffner, "Meister Eckhart and a Millennium with Mary and Martha," *LQ* 5 (1991): 171–85.

69. Charlotte Radler, "Actio et Contemplatio/Action and Contemplation," in *The Cambridge Companion to Mysticism*, ed. Amy Hollywood and Patricia Beckman (Cambridge: Cambridge University Press, 2012), 211–22.

represent: the present church and the future church.[70] These studies are short, appearing in journals or in collections of essays, and are not able to explore the significance of this passage in a detailed way.

However, there are four studies worth mentioning that focus on the reception history more broadly, moving beyond individual authors. The most important work on the reception history of Luke 10:38–42 is Daniel Csanyi's seventy-three-page article "Optima Pars: Die Auslegungsgeschichte von Lk 10,38–42 bei den Kirchen-vatern der ersten vier Jahrhunderte."[71] In this thorough and carefully researched article, Csanyi works through all the major occurrences of the passage in the first four hundred years of Christian history. Beginning with Clement of Alexandria and Origen and continuing until Augustine, he presents several key interpretations against the backdrop of each author's context. He is primarily focused on walking through the various relevant passages for his readers, making it a wonderful reference work for any seeking to understand how this passage operated in the early church. That said, several of his own interpretations have been questioned by others. For instance, he places Chrysostom's reading in conversation with the larger Messalian issues and argues that in order to properly understand Chrysostom's motivation, one must first understand the Messalian debate.[72] Since the almost-seventy years since his article was published, however, scholarly understanding of the Messalians has changed significantly, making his arguments about Chrysostom's reading fall flat. Overall, however, Csanyi is an important resource and one of the only scholars yet to engage in an in-depth study of the reception history of Luke 10:38–42.

Allie M. Ernst recently explored, in her monograph *Martha from the Margin*, all the references to Martha in early Christian liturgy, church orders, gnostic literature, the apocryphal acts, and artwork to depict Martha as an early church leader, respected by many in the early church.[73] She also examines early lectionaries, many of which do not include the previous story in Luke 10 (the good Samaritan) alongside Luke 10:38–42.

---

70. Anne-Marie La Bonnardiere, "Les deux vies: Marthe et Marie (Luc 10:38–42)," in *St. Augustin et la Bible*, BibTemps 3 (Paris: Beauchesne, 1986), 400–411.

71. Daniel Csanyi, "Optima Pars: Die Auslegungsgeschichte von Lk 10,38–42 bei den Kirchenvatern der ersten vier Jahrhunderte," *StudMon* 2 (1960): 5–78.

72. Csanyi, "Optima Pars," 84.

73. Allie M. Ernst, *Martha from the Margins: The Authority of Martha in Early Christian Tradition*, VCSup 98 (Leiden: Brill, 2009).

She argues, "Whereas modern exegetes are strongly predisposed to read and interpret the text in its current literary location, this context is by no means the only and probably not even the most common context in which early Christian readers and hearers would have encountered it."[74] Her work raises interesting questions about how the character of Martha was received by early Christians, since she concludes that Martha was a positive figure in the church. While her book primarily focuses on Martha in John 11, making her work mostly tangential to this study, her conclusion about the significance of Luke 10 is relevant: "That the story was put to such a broad range of purposes and was told and retold with a range of endings attest to the significance of the narrative in the early Christian tradition."[75] She recognizes that among these early Christian writers, this story and character of Martha more broadly served a host of rhetorical purposes as different Christian authors formed this story to examine their own theological convictions. Ernst's strength as a feminist reader is that, while recognizing the patriarchal impulses of many interpreters, she does not discount them and thus creates a space for exploring the variety of meaning this story holds, reclaiming Martha in a way that does not minimize Mary.

A third work, "Sibling Rivalry: Martha and Mary of Bethany" by Ena Giurescu Heller, examines depictions of Mary and Martha in Christian art through the centuries. Heller shows how different interpretations of Luke 10:38–42 can be seen through various artistic endeavors. While she shows that Mary often gets mistaken for another famous Mary, Mary Magdalene, Martha is consistently depicted as the personification of the active life.[76] She argues that in the late patristic and medieval periods, depictions of Martha were almost always positive and that it was not until after the Reformation that she was cast in a more negative light. She concludes that the painting "*Christ in the House of Martha and Mary*'s fortunes parallel the evolutions in both Christian writing and history.... In this respect, the scene becomes an exemplar of biblical art in its widest definition: art inspired by a biblical story, enriched by later writings, religious and secular

---

74. Ernst, *Martha from the Margins*, 213.
75. Ernst, *Martha from the Margins*, 220.
76. Ena Gierescu Heller, "Sibling Rivalry: Martha and Mary of Bethany," in *Women from the Margins: Women of the New Testament and Their Afterlives*, ed. Christine E. Joynes and Christopher C. Rowland, BMW 27 (Sheffield: Sheffield Phoenix, 2009), 2:245.

alike and by a lived history and tradition."⁷⁷ While Heller's view of early interpretations of Mary and Martha can sometimes border on the simplistic, her overall point about art reflecting the larger theological debate about Mary and Martha is an important one.⁷⁸ It is also important to note that most of the depictions of Martha before the Reformation were in fact positive ones, despite claims from feminist-critical scholars that Martha was often cast as the bad sister throughout history.

A final work is Giles Constable's *Three Studies in Medieval Religious and Social Thought*.⁷⁹ One of his case studies in this book is the reception of Mary and Martha in medieval history. While his primary focus is medieval authors, he brings in earlier sources to explain the general trends of interpretation his authors inherited. This is the most thorough English work on the reception history of Mary and Martha in Luke 10:38–42 written to date. He concludes:

> Every generation almost since the beginning of Christianity has tried to fit the story of Mary and Martha to its needs and to find in it a meaning suited to the Christian life of its time. Over the years its significance for the lives both of withdrawal and worldly activity and for this life and the next have changed, and the parts of Mary and Martha and the significance of Christ's words to Martha have been interpreted in different ways. The variety and ambiguity of these interpretations is evidence for the richness of the text and the ingenuity of the interpreters.⁸⁰

This concluding statement brilliantly presents one of the driving ideas behind my own thesis that the reception history is diverse and creative and that it offers to modern interpreters a way forward, whether to a feminist-critical scholar seeking to vindicate Martha or a preacher trying to free the story from being simply a women's story.

---

77. Heller, "Sibling Rivalry," 259.

78. For instance, not all early Christian writings drew on Origen's depiction of Mary as a contemplative and Martha as an active, as she claims (Heller, "Sibling Rivalry," 246). Augustine, in particular, creates a different image by drawing a comparison between Martha as the present church and Mary as the future church.

79. Giles Constable, "The Interpretation of Mary and Martha," in *Three Studies in Religious and Social Thought* (Cambridge: Cambridge University Press, 1995), 3–143.

80. Constable, "Interpretation of Mary and Martha," 141.

A Note about John 11

It is important to note that Luke 10 is not the only place in the gospels where Mary and Martha of Bethany make an appearance. John 11:17–44 contains a second story about the two sisters and their relationship with Jesus. However, due to the complexity of the Johannine text and the (already ambitious) scope of this study, I have decided to treat the Johannine text secondarily, focusing on it only in terms of its relationship to the Lukan narrative when it is brought into the discussion by the ancient interpreters themselves. Very early on, I noticed that interpretations of Luke 10 and John 11 were used to contribute to two different types of discussions, despite the fact the two passages feature the same characters. When most interpreters want to discuss and debate Mary and Martha and the constructions of discipleship they represent, they discuss Luke 10 and questions surrounding a correct interpretation of the "better part" Mary has chosen. In contrast, discussions of John 11 tend to highlight questions of resurrection, Jesus's interaction with two women, why Jesus was delayed, and so on, but not the characters of Mary and Martha more broadly. These two passages appear to operate mostly in distinct interpretive spheres.[81]

The same is also true for modern treatments of these passages. The story of Mary and Martha in evangelical circles primarily focuses on the Luke 10 passage and brings in the John 11 story as supplemental, primarily to flesh out the characteristics of the two sisters. Similarly, in modern biblical studies, one rarely finds overlap in discussions about the two stories other than to note that both Luke and John have an account of the two sisters and to raise questions about their historicity. Thus, while I do not ignore John 11:17–44, I treat in a supplemental fashion.

---

81. This is not to say that there is no overlap between the two texts. For instance, when Augustine is discussing Martha, he frequently supplements his argument about Martha's character with information provided in John 11 (*Serm.* 103–4). Thus, in my section about Augustine's readings of Mary and Martha, I will, of course, discuss how John 11 helps shape his reading of Luke 10. Another example of this overlap can be found in Chrysostom, who in one instance, during a homily about John 11 (*Hom. Jo.* 62.3), makes a turn to discuss Luke 10:38–42 instead. In order to get a full picture of Chrysostom's view of Luke 10:38–42, this homily must be included. Thus, interpretations about John 11 are not ignored in this work, but rather they are treated individually as they relate to the conversation at hand. In a similar way, other biblical passages will be treated as they intersect with these interpretations.

Chapter Outlines

Chapter 2: A Literary Approach to Luke 10:38–42

In this chapter I particularly draw on the work of Alexander and Donahue to argue that Luke 10:38–42 is best read as a parabolic narrative that challenges expectations about the call to follow Jesus. Furthermore, I argue that the story of Mary and Martha should be read alongside the story of the good Samaritan in order to better recognize the paradox that sometimes serving one's neighbor is what is needed to be a disciple, but at other times sitting and listening should be considered the better part. To do this, I examine Luke 10:38–42 in its Lukan context, particularly in the immediate context of Luke 10–11. I also address the primary exegetical and text-critical issues found in the text: the use of διαχονία to describe Martha's actions and its connection to Acts 6, the nature of Martha's complaint, the textual variant in verse 41/42, and the proper way to interpret Jesus's response. I show that the paradoxical nature of discipleship is already embedded in the passage itself; thus, the move to a theological reading regarding paradigms of discipleship is a natural interpretive decision, not a result of poor biblical scholarship.

Chapter 3: Origen and Early Monastic Interpreters

In this chapter I examine the beginning of interpretive tradition about Mary and Martha. I begin with Origen, since his interpretations have significant influence on the following centuries of interpretation. Contrary to common opinion, I show that Origen actually offers five interpretative options, and those who focus simply on the active-and-contemplative paradigm he introduces miss the depth of his reading. I then discuss how Origen's interpretations are adopted in the monastic tradition, with various authors adapting and expanding Origen's ideas about Mary and Martha as ascetic and nonascetic. This section draws on writers from the fourth and fifth centuries who are focused in particular on the developing nature of monasticism. In particular, I focus on the following authors/texts: the Liber Graduum, Pseudo-Macarius, the desert fathers, and Cassian. In this chapter I also briefly include those monastic texts that seem to be operating outside the majority position, specifically Basil's writings and Ephrem's *Commentary on the Diatessaron*. I show that, despite claims that all monastics adopted Origen's view whole cloth, there is actually significant evidence that his original readings were expanded and adapted, and even sometimes contradicted, in order to more fully flesh out competing understandings of the ultimate purpose of discipleship within early monasticism.

Chapter 4: Patristic Preachers

Here I study three important preachers and theologians from different parts of the Roman Empire. They each discuss Luke 10:38–42 at length but take distinct approaches. Chrysostom argues for Mary and Martha representing different seasons of life: there is a time to be a Martha and serve, and a time to be a Mary and listen. Augustine engages in a number of different approaches, as he focuses on this story in no fewer than six different homilies. In some homilies he presents the active/contemplative paradigm, whereas in other sermons he presents an eschatological paradigm. The third figure, Cyril of Alexandria, interprets the passage as a picture of hospitality, taking a more practical approach, but also revealing a reading that seems more directly connected the immediate context of Luke 10 in Luke-Acts. The concerns of these sermons are slightly different from ones preached to monastic communities, since they are directed to lay Christians, not monks.

Chapter 5: Medieval Readers

In this chapter I review a selection of medieval authors who discuss Luke 10:38–42. The story gained popularity during this period, leading to an abundance of creative interpretations that particularly seek to balance the relationship of service and spirituality. I analyze the ways in which the common threads of interpretation were picked up by medieval authors and adapted to fit their cultural context. While some have argued that writers in the medieval period merely copied early patristic writers, I show that they also expanded many interpretations. Furthermore, during this period, there were new developments. For instance, Martha in particular is painted in a more positive light during this period, and she is often portrayed more broadly as someone to emulate despite Jesus's seemingly critical response to her. Mary, on the other hand, became more linked with one of the other famous Marys of the New Testament: Mary Magdalene. Mary and Martha began to appear in artwork during this period, and the appearance of female interpreters enriches the discussion. While interpretation modulated during the medieval period, Mary and Martha remain for discipleship.

Chapter 6: The Reformation and a Shift

I here focus on Reformation readings of this story, particularly those of Martin Luther and John Calvin, to show how the Reformation introduced new ways of reading this passage. With the rejection of the action/contemplation paradigm, monasticism, and most of the patristic authors, so-called literal readings arose that focus on gender. The story began to place a double burden on women to work hard like Martha but to also make time for spiritual practices in their households. Holy women were those who were able to run their households and pray with a pleasant attitude. They were Marthas with a Mary-like heart. By using eulogies and practical texts written for women, I show how this gendered reading came into effect.

This focus on gender and Luke 10:38–42 continued into modern Christianity. To show this, I return to Moore and Schüssler Fiorenza and place them in conversation with each other to show how concerns about discipleship, which were central in early interpretations, have been replaced by a concern about the gender of Mary and Martha in both ecclesial and scholarly circles. Drawing on the work of Mary Beard, I argue that this overemphasis on gender leads to the text being mostly ignored.

Epilogue

The epilogue turns to three questions: (1) What has this study shown? (2) What questions have been raised? and (3) What areas of research remain to be studied in the future? I summarize my findings in order to offer a more helpful exegetical framework for interpreting Luke 10:38–42 for both ecclesial and academic settings.

Conclusion

Throughout this project, I argue that Luke 10:38–42 is a vibrant and living text with a rich interpretive past. This past, though often overlooked in the modern era, offers readers of the twenty-first century a new way to read this story outside the current paradigm, which dictates that the conversation must center on Mary and Martha as women rather than Mary and

Martha as disciples. This is not to say that modern readers should adopt a precritical lens when reading Luke 10, but rather that these premodern readers help reveal other interpretive options for approaching the story of Mary and Martha. When read in its Lukan context, this passage offers its readers insight into the nature and complexity of following Jesus. By reclaiming this focus, one can see a new way of preaching and teaching this text as more than a woman's story. It becomes again a story for all readers of the New Testament, and Mary and Martha become exemplars for all who seek to be disciples of Jesus Christ.

2
A Literary Approach to Luke 10:38–42

> Unfortunately, in the short story we are about to examine, Luke's manner of telling the story is allusive and the text often remains ambiguous. The "journey" of Jesus, Martha's "welcome," "service," and her "worries," Mary's "sitting at the Lord's feet" and her "listening to the word"—all these bring to mind certain existential questions of church life. Nevertheless, these elements of the text do not give direct answers to the questions we are asking.
>
> — François Bovon, *Luke 2*

Introduction

Luke's depiction of Mary and Martha and their encounter with Jesus raises several important questions about Christian discipleship. However, the text itself does not provide clear-cut answers to these questions. It is sparse on details, includes a host of unusual vocabulary, and has a number of textual variants. Throughout the centuries, interpreters have attempted to navigate these exegetical challenges. Before we can adequately adjudicate their readings, we must first become acquainted with the issues driving their discussions. Thus, in this chapter, I examine Luke 10:38–42 within its gospel context. I emphasize the questions raised by the text itself rather than historical-critical questions that may be at play behind the text.

The goal of this chapter is twofold. First, I intend to locate this passage within the literary world of Luke-Acts in order to show how the themes of Luke 10:38–42 connect to larger concerns of the Third Gospel. Second, I want to show how the passage's own internal ambiguity and multivalence allow for the diversity that we will see in the coming chapters. I hope to prove that the patristic and medieval readers who interpreted this passage, for all their flaws, were not careless readers of Scripture and that their readings are largely based in the questions that the story raises without clear resolution.

To accomplish these goals, I first examine the implications of this story being located in Luke's travel narrative (9:51–19:27), a connection that has often been overlooked in modern discussions of the text. I then turn to an examination of the characterizations of Martha and Mary in order to show how both sisters are primarily depicted positively and how they embody actions that elsewhere in Luke-Acts are presented as the legitimate actions of Christ followers. Finally, I turn to an in-depth analysis of Martha's request to Jesus and his response in 10:41–42. It is in this response that one finds the most complexity and textual instability, with different scribal traditions attempting to make sense of Jesus's confusing critique of Martha. Ultimately, my examination will prove that the story functions within the narrative to instruct Martha as a disciple and as a hostess, but also on a deeper level, to address Lukan concerns about the disorientation of service and the priority of listening to the word of God.

"And as They Were Traveling, He Came into a Certain Village": Setting in Luke's Gospel

Luke 10:38–42 is often analyzed outside its immediate literary context, which has led to the story operating as a stand-alone narrative. Joseph Fitzmyer goes so far as to claim that this passage is utterly unrelated to the passages that precede and follow it.[1] Such isolation makes it more challenging to observe the ways in which it echoes certain vocabulary and themes already being developed by Luke. Thus, before we can begin to properly analyze the characterization and textual issues of the passage, we must first analyze the narrative setting of Luke 10:38–42. The story of Martha and her sister is found in Luke's middle section, usually referred to as the travel narrative. This section, demarcated here as being located between Luke 9:51b and 19:28, recounts Jesus's final journey into Jerusalem before his trial, crucifixion, and resurrection.[2] It begins with an introductory summary statement in 9:51b: "When the days of his ascension were drawing

---

1. Fitzmyer, *Gospel according to Luke*, 2:891.
2. There is continued debate over the proper ending of the travel narrative. Suggested endings also include 18:30, 18:34, 19:10, 19:44, 19:46, 19:48, and 21:38. For a discussion of the different scholarly opinions on the question, see Filip Noël, *The Travel Narrative in the Gospel of Luke: Interpretation of Luke 9:51–10:28*, CBRA 5 (Brussels:

near, he set his face to go to Jerusalem." From there, Jesus begins a meandering journey into Jerusalem, though the chronology and the geography of that journey are not always clearly delineated. The primary purposes of this journey appear to be theological and dramatic, often making the geographical and historical features secondary within the narrative structure.³ Thematically, different sections are marked with repeated references to Jesus's and his disciples' journey, as Luke tells us that they are on the way (9:52, 53, 56, 57; 10:1, 38; 13:22, 31, 33; 14:25; 17:11; 18:31; 19:1, 11, 28), bringing the reader's attention back to this travel motif. In fact, the story of Mary and Martha is introduced in 10:38a with one of these markers, "And while they were traveling" (Εν δὲ τῷ πορεύεσθαι αὐτούς), immediately connecting this story to the larger journey Jesus is making.⁴

Within the larger structure of Luke, this section marks a departure from Luke's use of his Markan material as well as a significant departure from Mark's chronology.⁵ Indeed, much of the material in the travel narrative has no Markan parallel and appears to be from either Q or Luke's unique source. Throughout this section, one continually finds Jesus doing the work of a prophet and a teacher. In particular, Luke has constructed the travel narrative so that Jesus's own words are at the forefront as he engages with his disciples, the crowds, and his opponents. While most scholars acknowledge that Jesus's speech is clearly emphasized throughout this section, there is still significant disagreement about both its form and its function.⁶ Interpretations surrounding these questions are wide

---

Voor Wetenschappen en Kunsten, 2004), 249–328. Noël concludes in favor of 19:28 because he marks 19:29–46 as the introductory section of the entry to Jerusalem.

3. Luke Timothy Johnson, *The Literary Function of Possessions in Luke-Acts*, SBLDS 39 (Missoula, MT: Scholars Press, 1977), 105.

4. It also shares other vocabulary (εἰσῆλθεν and κώμη), which signals its connection within the overall travel narrative. For another discussion on the connections between the travel narrative and Luke 10:38–42, see Brutscheck, *Die Maria-Marta-Erzählung*, 50–64, .

5. While acknowledging the complexity surrounding the Synoptic problem, in this chapter I adopt the two-source hypothesis.

6. While most scholars hold this delineation to be helpful for interpreting Luke, in recent years a subset of Luke scholars have pushed back against the designation of the travel narrative, arguing that it is an artificial and unhelpful category that is not as clearly demarcated as most scholars argue. For instance, Reinhard von Bendemann argues that the travel narrative should be rebranded as the merely the central section of Luke, both rejecting the introductory statement in 9:51 as being indicative of any-

reaching and diverse.⁷ Some scholars, most notably David Moessner, have argued that this section is based on the Old Testament and is created to be a retelling of the biblical story, particularly Deuteronomy, as Jesus is depicted as the "prophet like Moses."⁸ Others have favored a more historical approach, arguing that this section reveals another Lukan source, specifically a travel narrative source that depicts Jesus's historical journey to Jerusalem and contains many of his teachings. This section of Luke is then primarily intended to be biographical and reflect Luke's concerns as a historian.⁹

However, the most dominant trend of interpretation is to highlight the christological themes of the section, following the work of Hans Conzelmann, who argues that the travel narrative functions not as a historical account of a literal journey but rather as a dramatic account pointing toward the identity of Christ and his upcoming suffering.¹⁰ Jesus does

---

thing and pointing out that there is still continued argument about the proper ending of the travel narrative. He argues that a new evaluation of the center section of Luke should be undertaken in order to see what new insights might be uncovered without the trappings of a travel narrative motif. See von Bendemann, *Zwischen ΔΟΞΑ und ΣΤΑΥΡΟΣ: Eine exegetische Untersuchung der Texte des sogenannten Reiseberichts im Lukasevangelium*, BNZW 101 (Berlin: de Gruyter , 2001), 101.

7. In a recent monograph, Filip Noël dissects the major interpretive theories surround the travel narrative that have developed over the last fifty years. In particular, he names four different categories of analysis of the travel narrative: redaction-critical, structural, Old Testament models, and historical. He helpfully presents the major figures in each category, highlighting the strengths and weaknesses of the various approaches. See Noël, *Travel Narrative*.

8. David Paul Moessner, *Lord of the Banquet: The Literary and Theological Significance of the Lucan Travel Narrative* (Minneapolis: Fortress, 1989). For other scholars who develop this idea in various forms, see Craig F. Evans, "The Central Section of St. Luke's Gospel," in *Studies in the Gospels: Essays in Memory of R. H. Lightfoot*, ed. D. N. Nineham (Oxford: Basil Blackwell, 1957), 37–53. This work was the first substantial analysis of the Septuagintalisms of this section. See also J. M. Dawsey, "Jesus's Pilgrimage to Jerusalem," *PerspRelSt* 14 (1987): 217–32; Ulrich Busse, *Die Wunder des Propheten Jesus: Die Rezeption, Komposition und Interpretation der Wundertradition im Evangelium des Lukas*, FB 24 (Stuttgart: Verlag Katholisches Bibelwerk, 1997); Willard Swartley, *Israel's Scripture Traditions and the Synoptic Gospels: Story Shaping Story* (Grand Rapids: Baker Academic, 1994).

9. In particular, see Armin Daniel Baum, *Lukas als Historiker der letzten Jesusreise* (Zurich: Braukhas, 1993).

10. Hans Conzelmann, *The Theology of St. Luke*, trans. Geoffrey Buswell (Minneapolis: Fortress, 1961).

2. A Literary Approach to Luke 10:38–42

refer to the inevitability of his coming suffering immediately before beginning his journey to Jerusalem in 9:43–45, and again in 13:33:

πλὴν δεῖ με σήμερον καὶ αὔριον καὶ τῇ ἐχομένῃ πορεύεσθαι, ὅτι οὐκ ἐνδέχεται προφήτην ἀπολέσθαι ἔξω Ἰερουσαλήμ.
Yet today, tomorrow, and the next day, it is necessary for me to be on my way, because it is impossible for a prophet to be killed outside Jerusalem.

Thus, Conzelmann's point that Christ's impending suffering is an important theme driving the narrative seems accurate. But, Filip Noël notes, while "Conzelmann's christological explanation remains an important point of reference, almost everyone points out that the travel section has richer thematic lines" beyond Christ's suffering.[11] In particular, Jürgen Schneider has noted the didactic and paraenetical nature of this section, which highlights the ethical and, perhaps more importantly, the ecclesiological implications of this passage.[12] This reading emphasizes the sheer volume of teaching Jesus does in this section. The didactic nature of the section for the life of the early church is rooted in the Jesus's identity as one who proclaims the word of God. Jesus is the Christ who instructs, calls to conversion, and condemns. As Jesus moves toward his death, his words provide a rich resource for the church that the Holy Spirit will subsequently gather in his name.

Here is where the form of the travel narrative comes into play. While at a glance the section appears rather helter-skelter, with Jesus traveling here and there in no discernible geographical or chronological order, many have attempted to find a coherent formal structure within these ten chapters.[13] However, many of these quickly become overly complex as they attempt to create a variety of chiastic structures to account for all the

---

11. Noël, *Travel Narrative*, 15.
12. Jürgen Schneider, "Zur Analyse des lukanischen Reiseberichtes," in *Synoptische Studien*, ed. Josef Schmid and A. Vögtle (Munich: Zink, 1953), 207–29. See also Bo Reicke, "Instruction and Discussion in the Travel Narrative," *Studia Evangelica* 73 (1959): 206–16.
13. The best-known proponent of this model is Michael Goulder. He sees seven topics that are repeated in reverse order: (1) the question of how to inherit eternal life, (2) faithful prayer, (3) healing story, (4) Pharisaic hypocrisy, (5) love of money, (6) repentance, and (7) rejection of Israel and the invitation to the outcasts. See Michael Goulder, "The Chiastic Structure of the Lucan Journey," in *Studia Evangelica* 2, ed. F. L. Cross (Berlin: Akademie, 1964), 195–202.

various pieces in the narrative. As Luke Timothy Johnson notes, "There are such points of balance to be discovered, obviously, otherwise such theories would be impossible. But the points of resemblance often result as much from the definitions given by scholars as the stories themselves."[14] Johnson himself offers a more straightforward structure that more simply accounts for the moves in the narrative. This structure is dictated by the most common event found in the travel narrative: Jesus speaking. Jesus interacts and speaks to three different groups of people throughout his journey: disciples, the crowds, and his opponents (usually the lawyers and Pharisees). As Johnson observes:

> We find that Luke has arranged Jesus's sayings and deeds in an alternating, contrasting pattern which might be described broadly as an alternation between the inside and the outside. Jesus address the crowd, for example, then turns from the crowd to address his disciples then turns from them to attack the Pharisees, etc. At times this pattern is more sharply indicated than at others, but as a formal pattern, it is present throughout these chapters.[15]

Throughout the journey, the type of speech Jesus uses to interact with these three groups is different. To his followers, he teaches, using parables and sermons to instruct them on how to follow him. To the crowds that surround him, he offers calls to turn and repent, warning them about the consequences of ignoring his message. To his opponents who attack him, he harshly criticizes, offering parables of rejection and condemnation. As one can see below, the pattern, while not absolute, shows a clear tendency of the author to alternate between outsiders and insiders, followers and opponents, as Jesus walks toward Jerusalem.

---

14. Johnson, *Gospel of Luke*, 163.
15. Johnson, *Literary Function of Possessions*, 108.

2. A Literary Approach to Luke 10:38–42

Table 2.1. Recipients of Jesus's Speech in the Travel Narrative[16]

9:51–56 (disciples)	15:1–32 (Pharisees)
9:57–62 (potential disciples)	16:1–13 (disciples)
10:1–12 (disciples)	16:14–31 (Pharisees)
10:13–15 (unrepentant cities)	17:1–10 (disciples)
10:16–23 (disciples)	17:11–19 (Samaritans)
10:24–37 (lawyer)	17:20–21 (Pharisees)
10:38–42 (Martha)	17:22–18:8 (disciples)
11:1–13 (disciples)	18:9–14 (pharisees)
11:14–36 (crowd)	18:26–34 (disciples)
11:37–53 (Pharisees and lawyer)	18:35–43 (crowds)
12:1–12 (Disciples)	18:15–17 (disciples)[17]
12:13–21 (crowd)	18:18–25 (rich ruler)
12:22–53 (disciples)	18:26–34 (disciples)
12:54–13:30 (crowd)	18:35–43 (crowds)
13:31–14:24 (pharisees)	19:1–27 (Zacchaeus/crowds)
14:25–35 (crowd)	

In particular, it is important to note speech directed toward the followers of Jesus. Jesus spends more time instructing them than on anything else in this section. He teaches them to pray, how to properly engage in missions, how to persevere in the midst of persecution, and so on. It is this repeated theme that causes Schneider and others to observe that the journey is not simply about depicting the nature of Jesus as the Messiah who will suffer, but also it is intended to instruct the disciples within the world of the narrative and the disciples in Luke's own community about the proper ways to serve Christ. As Johnson states, "In a word, the core of the faithful people

---

16. Table adapted from Johnson, *Literary Function of Possessions*, 108 n. 1. He concludes: "As with most formal patterns applied to the Gospels, the breakdown is not absolute, not are the classifications inarguable. The following listing of the passages together with a rough designation of the audience or participants at least shows that there is a definite alternation … between the insiders and the outsiders around Jesus."

17. In 18:15, Luke picks up the Markan chronology again.

is being prepared on the road to Jerusalem."[18] It is against this backdrop that one must approach the story of Martha and her sister in 10:38–42, as Jesus and his disciples come into their village on their journey.

Jesus's arrival into Martha's village in 10:38a, then, should not be read as a simple aside in the narrative, as if Luke merely inserted it in its current location for no other reason than that he needed to find a space for it. Rather, Luke intentionally reminds his reader of Jesus's journey as he introduces the story. If we take the claim seriously that Jesus is preparing his faithful people along the road, then we should assume that this story will likely point us toward a claim about how to properly participate in the kingdom of God. Of course, there is always the possibility that Jesus is not about to engage with a follower but rather with an opponent, a claim that is supported by a negative view of Martha. However, the story immediately follows the parable of the good Samaritan,[19] which clearly highlights the importance of radical hospitality and love of neighbor, and here we see Jesus entering into a village to himself receive hospitality. This arrangement of the section prepares the reader to expect that Jesus's host is likely a follower who will be receiving instruction. It is to this host and her positive characterization within the story that we will now turn in order to show that Jesus's interaction with her is not adversarial but rather pedagogical in nature.

"And a Certain Woman Named Martha Welcomed Him into Her Home": Martha's Characterization

Modern discussions about Luke 10:38–42 are quick to condemn Martha, emphasizing her stress and her seeming grumpiness in order to depict her as the story's villain, one who nags Jesus about her sister's inappropriate behavior. As Alexander observes, this seems unfair, as Martha is repeatedly depicted as the bad sister when set against the quiet and pious nature of Mary.[20] A close analysis of the characterization of Martha in these verses

---

18. Johnson, *Literary Function of Possessions*, 112.

19. The importance of the parable of the good Samaritan will be discussed at greater depth in the conclusion of this chapter.

20. Alexander, "Sisters in Adversity," 201. François Bovon remarks in his commentary that he easily fell into that trap that as well, depicting her as a very negative figure in his interpretation of Mary and Martha until several of his female PhD stu-

2. A Literary Approach to Luke 10:38–42

reveals that the passage itself presents her as a positive figure, a disciple who serves and welcomes.

She is, in fact, the central character in this vignette. As Seim argues, "Martha plays the active role that drives the narrative forward; she is the protagonist of the story."[21] The disciples fade away after "while they were traveling" in 10:38a, and the story shifts to focus on Martha's welcome of the Lord. This is our first introduction to Martha, that she welcomes (ὑπεδέξατο) Jesus into the house. The practice of welcoming guests into one's home is a recurring theme in Luke-Acts, appearing multiple times throughout both narratives (Luke 7:36–50; 9:51–10:24; 10:38–42; 19:1–10; 24:13–35; Acts 10:1–48; 11:1–18; 28:1–10). Hospitality more broadly is an important theme throughout Luke-Acts, with Luke drawing on ancient Mediterranean symbols and grammar to present his antagonists as violating cultural mores of hospitality and his protagonists as being proper hosts and hostesses.[22] The specific verb, ὑποδέχομαι, is a technical term indicating an act of hospitality.[23] The two other uses of ὑποδέχομαι in Luke-Acts are found in Luke 19:1–10, when Zacchaeus welcomes Jesus, and in Acts 17:7, when Jason is said to have welcomed Paul and Silas. In both of these stories, the hosts are presented as engaging in proper hospitality and true service. Thus, when Luke introduces Martha as welcoming Jesus, it is not a neutral statement of fact but rather one that conveys her as a sincere and

---

dents pushed back on his treatment of her, causing him to reevaluate his reading. See Bovon, *Luke 2*, 67 n. 1.

21. Seim, *Double Message*, 103.

22. Joshua W. Jipp, *Divine Visitations and Hospitality to Strangers: An Interpretation of the Malta Episode in Acts 28:1–10*, NovTSup 53 (Leiden: Brill, 2013), 171. Jipp offers an in-depth analysis of hospitality in the ancient Mediterranean world and Luke's use of that imagery and vocabulary. For an overview of Luke's depictions of hospitality, see chs. 5–6.

23. A few brief examples of this technical function can be found in elsewhere in first-century Jewish writings and early Christian literature. In James 2:25, Rahab is said to have received her justification through welcoming (ὑποδεξαμένη) and protecting the spies before the battle of Jericho. Ignatius, in his letter to Smyrnaeans, commends the community for receiving Philo and Rheus Agathopus ὑποδεξάμενοι ὡς διακόνους Θεοῦ (Ign. *Smyrn.* 10.1). Josephus also uses the word to express true expressions of hospitality throughout his writings. For instance, see *Ag. Ap.* 1.247: [ὁ τῶν Αἰθιόπων βασιλεύς] ὃς ὑποδεξάμενος καὶ τοὺς ὄχλους πάντας ὑπολαβὼν οἷς ἔσχεν ἡ χώρα. See Karl H. Rengstorf, ed., *The Complete Concordance of Flavius Josephus* (Leiden: Brill, 1973–1983), 4:253.

good hostess. Joshua Jipp even describes this story and Martha's behavior as encapsulating "the nature of hospitality that Jesus desires."[24]

Such hospitality is the expected response for a follower of Christ, following the criteria set out by Jesus earlier in the travel narrative. When Jesus sends out the Seventy in 10:1–12, he discusses the peace that will be with those towns and homes that receive (δέχομαι) the missionaries as opposed to those places that do not welcome them. Furthermore, in contrast to Martha's act of welcoming Jesus into her home after he enters her village (κώμη), the Samaritans are presented negatively in 9:52–53, when they do not receive him into their village (κώμη).[25] Furthermore, when read alongside the story that immediately precedes it, the parable of the good Samaritan in 10:25–37, one can see that Martha's hospitality reflects the actions of a true neighbor. As Warren Carter argues: "Martha appears in 10:38 as an embodiment of the positive responses named through chapter 10. In receiving Jesus, Martha is a child of peace (10:6) who has encountered God's reign (10:9). She is not subject to the curses and eschatological warnings of 10:12–15.... She appears as the model disciple in contrast to those in the previous verses who do not receive Jesus's messenger (9:52–53; 10:10)."[26] Thus, our introduction to Martha is entirely positive. She is doing what Luke has prepared his audience to expect from followers. She physically receives Christ into her home.

Before moving on to discuss the other aspects of her characterization, we must briefly address the question of whether the text originally included the phrase εἰς τὸν οἶκον αὐτῆς or some variation thereof. The current text of NA28 does not include it, suggesting that the inclusion of "in her house" was a later variant with wide attestation. Similarly, Bruce Metzger argues that "no motive is apparent for the deletion of the phrase 'into her house' if it were present in the text originally," arguing that it is more likely to be addition as ὑπεδέξατο seems to call for a concluding phrase.[27]

---

24. Jipp, *Divine Visitations and Hospitality to Strangers*, 226.

25. It is worth noting here κώμη is a common Lukan expression, showing up thirteen times in Luke-Acts, many of them in the travel narrative. Also, while the village mentioned in 10:38 is usually thought to be Bethany, the text does not supply that piece of information, leaving an unnamed village. Bethany is usually supplied because of John 11, which locates Mary, Martha, and their brother Lazarus as living in Bethany.

26. Carter, "Getting Martha Out," 219.

27. Bruce Metzger, *A Textual Commentary on the Greek New Testament* (Stuttgart: United Bible Societies, 1975), 153.

This claim, however, is not supported by the three other New Testament appearances of this phrase (Luke 19:6, Acts 17:7; James 2:25). A brief exploration of these three other appearances supports this point. In Luke 19:6, we find Zacchaeus climbing down the tree in order to host Jesus after Jesus as declared he will eat at Zacchaeus's house:

καὶ σπεύσας κατέβη καὶ ὑπεδέξατο αὐτὸν χαίρων
And quickly, he came down and *welcomed him* joyfully.

Similarly, in Acts 17:7a, when the Jews in Thessaloniki are accusing Paul and his companions before the rulers of that city, they turn to highlight Jason as well because he welcomed them:

Οἱ τὴν οἰκουμένην ἀναστατώσαντες οὗτοι καὶ ἐνθάδε πάρεισιν οὓς ὑποδέδεκται Ἰάσων
These people who have been turning the world upside down have come here also and *whom Jason welcomed*. (17:6b–7a)

Thus, one can see that within Luke-Acts the verb ὑποδέχομαι does not call for some sort of additional prepositional phrase. Furthermore, when studying the critical apparatus of both of those passages, one does not find any manuscripts that supply the additional phrase either. Those references did not seem incomplete without the added phrase to supply where they received their guests. That they received their guests into their homes is implied by the verb.

The fourth and final New Testament reference is James 2:25, wherein James offers Rahab as example of the relationship between faith and works:

ὁμοίως δὲ καὶ Ῥαὰβ ἡ πόρνη οὐκ ἐξ ἔργων ἐδικαιώθη ὑποδεξαμένη τοὺς ἀγγέλους καὶ ἑτέρᾳ ὁδῷ ἐκβαλοῦσα
Likewise, was not Rahab the prostitute also justified by works *when she welcomed the messengers* and sent them out by another road?

Thus, we can see that in every other occurrence of this verb within the New Testament, it never actually includes an additional prepositional phrase.[28]

---

28. Moreover, it is notable that one does not find any scribal correction to add a prepositional phrase within any of the critical apparatuses for these verses. It seems unlikely that it was grammatical concerns that led the majority of scribes to add a prepositional phrase.

This makes it unlikely that a scribe would introduce a prepositional phrase onto a verb that typically stands alone. The longer reading is a more difficult one, but it allows 10:38 to better align with Luke 10:5-7, which, as mentioned, discusses proper protocol for welcoming disciples into someone's οἰκία.[29]

Moreover, despite Metzger's claim that there are no reasons for omission, Bovon argues that there is a potential motive in that Martha's role as the apparent head of the household would have seemed improper to some early copyists.[30] He thinks that referring to the house as hers would imply ownership, a thought that would have been improper in some corners of the ancient Mediterranean world. Luke himself does not seem to have that particular concern, as we see another female homeowner in Acts when Lydia receives Paul and the others into her house.[31] Another potential reason for discomfort is that in John's account, in 12:1, it is Lazarus and not Martha who is explicitly called the homeowner. This discrepancy could have led to scribal harmonizing, which led to the phrase simply being omitted, eliminating both the contradiction and any potential impropriety.

Furthermore, a significant number of early manuscripts support the reading "into her house," including several early ones, such as Sinaiticus and Alexandrinus. In fact, there are only three Greek sources that omit the phrase: two papyri ($\mathfrak{P}^{45}$ and $\mathfrak{P}^{75}$) and Vaticanus. On its face, these are three highly reliable sources, but given the scribal tendency in papyri to omit small phrases, neither $\mathfrak{P}^{45}$ nor $\mathfrak{P}^{75}$ seems sufficient to justify the argument that the primitive text ended with αὐτόν.[32] This leaves Vaticanus against several other early majuscules, leading me to conclude that εἰς τὸν

---

29. Brutscheck, *Maria-Marta Erzählung*, 18.

30. Bovon, *Luke 2*, 70. This appears particularly evident in those manuscripts that omit "her," leaving Jesus to simply be welcomed into the house.

31. Similar language is used there. See Acts 16:15: ὡς δὲ ἐβαπτίσθη καὶ ὁ οἶκος αὐτῆς, παρεκάλεσεν λέγουσα· εἰ κεκρίκατέ με πιστὴν τῷ κυρίῳ εἶναι, εἰσελθόντες εἰς τὸν οἶκόν μου μένετε· καὶ παρεβιάσατο ἡμᾶς.

32. On $\mathfrak{P}^{45}$, see James Royse, *Scribal Habits in Early Greek New Testament Papyri*, NTTSD 36 (Leiden: Brill, 2007), 103–97, particularly, 131–41, 197. He concludes, "The scribe has a marked tendency to omit portions of the text, often as it seems accidentally, but perhaps also by deliberate pruning" (197). Colwell similarly argues for a tendency to omit phrases in $\mathfrak{P}^{45}$. See also Ernest C. Colwell, "Method in Evaluating Scribal Habits: A Study of $\mathfrak{P}^{45}$, $\mathfrak{P}^{66}$, and $\mathfrak{P}^{75}$," in *Studies in Methodology in Textual Criticism of the New Testament*, NTTS 9 (Leiden: Brill, 1969), 118–19. On

οἶκον αὐτῆς is to be preferred, following the argument of James Royse: "In particular, as long as the competing readings are all early, the preference must lie with the longer reading."[33] In this case, I think it is clear that when one examines the evidence, the shorter reading seems unlikely to have been the earlier version. However, regardless of whether we can definitely decide which version was the earliest, the text points to Martha being the primary figure and caretaker of this home. There is no mention of a husband or a brother. She and Jesus are the main characters in this narrative. She is the one who shows Jesus hospitality. Like the women mentioned in 8:1–3, she appears to be providing for Jesus out of her own resources. Dropping the phrase "into her home" obscures this important point.[34]

Martha is also depicted in the narrative as the one who serves (διακονέω) and as one engaged in service (διακονία). Διακονία is a complex word with a number of meanings in the ancient world, and it shows up repeatedly in different contexts throughout Luke-Acts. John Collins dedicates an entire monograph to analyzing these different meanings.[35] He concludes from an analysis of a wide range of Greco-Roman sources, including the New Testament, that διακονία had a broader sense in the ancient world than simple table serving. Rather, he argues that it often represented any kind of service that took place between two points. For instance, it can refer to the activity of relating a message, performing errands, participating in priestly roles, relating divine revelations, waiting tables, doing civil servant jobs, and many others.[36] Much has been written about implications of this language appearing in Luke 10:38–42 and what its usage might mean for women in ministry during the first century.[37] However, much of this work has been historical in nature, as scholars have attempted to reconstruct the types of ministry this word might have referred to in the early church and the debates regarding women's participation in them.[38]

𝔓75, see Royse, *Scribal Habits*, 615–704, particularly 662–65, 704: "The scribe has a low frequency of addition and omits more than three times as often as he adds" (704).

33. Royse, *Scribal Habits*, 734.

34. For more detailed work on this textual variant and its implications, see Jennifer S. Wyant, "Giving Martha Back Her House: Analyzing the Textual Variant in Luke 10:38b," *TC* 24 (forthcoming).

35. Collins, *Diakonia*.

36. Collins, *Diakonia*, 173–91.

37. For instance, see Reid, *Choosing the Better Part?*, 47–48; Schüssler Fiorenza, *But She Said*, 63; Seim, *Double Message*, 100–101.

38. It should be noted that John Collins has been critical of this debate and how it

Setting aside historical-critical questions, a literary approach can help us understand how διακον- language functions within Luke-Acts, which will in turn allow us to better understand how its usage in Luke 10:40 further defines Martha's character. First, one frequently finds διακονέω used in passages relating to women who serve Jesus. In Luke 4:39, Peter's mother-in-law is said to serve them immediately after her healing: παραχρῆμα δὲ ἀναστᾶσα διηκόνει αὐτοῖς. Similarly, in Luke 8:1–3, Luke describes a number of women who were traveling with Jesus and the Twelve, serving them out of their own resources, αἵτινες διηκόνουν αὐτοῖς ἐκ τῶν ὑπαρχόντων αὐταῖς. Thus, when Martha is described as serving she fits into a set of women who minister to Jesus during his life, supporting his ministry.

However, beyond references to women, Jesus uses διακον- language in his own teaching about the kingdom of God. In Luke 12:37, Jesus says that the slaves found waiting for their master (ὁ κύριος) will be blessed and that their master will have them sit and eat while he serves them (καὶ παρελθὼν διακονήσει αὐτοῖς). Here it is the κύριος who serves his slaves. This is their eschatological reward. It also represents the reversal that occurs in the kingdom of God. The greatest serve the least. This is further emphasized in during the Last Supper in Luke 22:26–27. Here Jesus settles a dispute between his disciples over who is the greatest among them, which is worth quoting in full:

> ὑμεῖς δὲ οὐχ οὕτως, ἀλλ' ὁ μείζων ἐν ὑμῖν γινέσθω ὡς ὁ νεώτερος καὶ ὁ ἡγούμενος ὡς ὁ διακονῶν. τίς γὰρ μείζων, ὁ ἀνακείμενος ἢ ὁ διακονῶν; οὐχὶ ὁ ἀνακείμενος; ἐγὼ δὲ ἐν μέσῳ ὑμῶν εἰμι ὡς ὁ διακονῶν.
> But not so with you; rather the greatest among you must become like the youngest, and the leader like one who *serves*. For who is greater, the one who is at the table or the one who *serves*? Is it not the one at the table? But I am among you as one who *serves*.

---

has appropriated his own research. He argues that διακονία is not referring to a specific ministry but rather can operate with a different meaning depending on the context: "The reason the words apply to women in three instances in the Gospel is simply that the narrative requires appropriate words for attendance upon guests or master; on the other hand, they apply to men in the public roles of mission and proclamation in Acts (and in Paul) because the words properly designate such activities, especially as these are of a religious character. The two applications owe nothing to Luke's estimations of women vis-a-vis men, provide no evidence of bias against women, and arise simply because of Luke's competence in the Greek language." See Collins, "Did Luke Intend a Disservice to Women in the Martha and Mary Story?," *BTB* 28 (1998): 110.

Jesus already embodied this service immediately prior in the narrative as he served his disciples during the meal. In the kingdom of God, there is an ethic of service, with Jesus himself providing the example. As I. Howard Marshall observes, the parable is set up to reinforce the contrast between Jesus and the secular world since Jesus is present to the disciples as a servant despite the fact that he is greater than the ones seated at the table with him.[39] Thus, when Martha serves Jesus in 10:40, she is participating in kingdom behavior. To engage in physical service is not a demeaning activity in Luke, but rather it is the action of Jesus himself, and those who also participate in that form of service imitate him.[40]

This positive view of service continues throughout Acts. In Acts 1:17 and 25, the apostles are searching for a replacement for Judas to join them in their διακονία. Here the word represents the ministry that the disciples are engaged in as they begin the work of the church. Similarly, in Acts 6:1-4, two different types of διακονία are displayed:

> Ἐν δὲ ταῖς ἡμέραις ταύταις πληθυνόντων τῶν μαθητῶν ἐγένετο γογγυσμὸς τῶν Ἑλληνιστῶν πρὸς τοὺς Ἑβραίους, ὅτι παρεθεωροῦντο ἐν τῇ διακονίᾳ τῇ καθημερινῇ αἱ χῆραι αὐτῶν. προσκαλεσάμενοι δὲ οἱ δώδεκα τὸ πλῆθος τῶν μαθητῶν εἶπαν· οὐκ ἀρεστόν ἐστιν ἡμᾶς καταλείψαντας τὸν λόγον τοῦ θεοῦ διακονεῖν τραπέζαις. ἐπισκέψασθε δέ, ἀδελφοί, ἄνδρας ἐξ ὑμῶν μαρτυρουμένους ἑπτά, πλήρεις πνεύματος καὶ σοφίας, οὓς καταστήσομεν ἐπὶ τῆς χρείας ταύτης, ἡμεῖς δὲ τῇ προσευχῇ καὶ τῇ διακονίᾳ τοῦ λόγου προσκαρτερήσομεν.
>
> Now during those days, when the disciples were increasing in number, the Hellenists complained against the Hebrews because their widows were being neglected in the daily distribution of food. And the twelve called together the whole community of the disciples and said, "It is not right that we should neglect the word of God in order *to wait on tables*. Therefore, friends, select from among yourselves seven men of good standing, full of the Spirit and of wisdom, whom we may appoint to this task, while we, for our part, will devote ourselves to prayer and to the *ministry* of the word."

---

39. I. Howard Marshall, *The Gospel of Luke*, NIGTC (Grand Rapids: Eerdmans, 1978), 814.

40. Another usage of διακονία in Luke is found in 17:7-10. There Jesus instructs his disciples that like slaves who serve without being thanked, they should also do all that is expected of them. In this, service appears to be part of the basic expectations for all who follow Christ.

Usually this passage is invoked to argue that Martha's form of service is comparable to the form of service done by the Seven who are appointed by the Twelve. The Seven, as one discovers in Acts, are engaged in a full and vibrant ministry that includes preaching the word and table fellowship. However, this seems to ignore the fact that words can operate with different meanings in different context. Simply because the word refers to a more technical form of ministry in Acts 6 does not necessarily mean we need to assume that technical form in Luke 10.

A better approach to the relationship between Acts 6 and Luke 10 is to examine the shared tension in both passages between a physical form of service on one hand and being concerned with the word of God on the other. After all, beyond the shared vocabulary, one can also see what appears to be a parallel structure. The Twelve are going to pray and serve the word, like Mary sitting at the feet of Jesus, while the Seven are going to serve tables, like Martha. Both of these are positive roles but reveal a tension between physical service and devotion, which, as Veronica Koperski argues, "manifests a tension that has been mirrored through the centuries in the variety of interpretations of the Lukan texts that express some sort of polarity."[41] Thus, when we return to the use of διακονία in Luke 10:40, we see that Luke is characterizing Martha as one engaged in physical service in order to take care of Jesus. Like the women in Luke 8:1–3, like Jesus himself in Luke 22:24–27, and like the Seven in Acts 6:1–4, Martha is participating in the kingdom of God through her service.

Thus, we can conclude that Martha's initial characterization is positive. She welcomes Jesus, and she serves him. Both of these acts confirm Martha's status as a true disciple. The first qualifying note comes in 10:40, where Luke describes Martha as being περιεσπᾶτο by much service. Περισπάω is a New Testament *hapax legomena*, meaning "to have one's attention directed from one thing to another, to be distracted, quite busy or overburdened."[42] Since there is no parallel usage in the New Testament, it will be useful to briefly examine some of the other contexts in which this verb appears. It is found six times in the LXX, mostly in the wisdom literature of Ecclesiastes and Sirach. In Ecclesiastes in particular, the verb holds the connotation of being distracted by the inevitable trials and worries of life, given to humanity by God:

---

41. Koperski, "Women and Discipleship," 194.
42. BDAG, s.v. "περισπάω," 804.

2. A Literary Approach to Luke 10:38–42

καὶ ἔδωκα τὴν καρδίαν μου τοῦ ἐκζητῆσαι καὶ τοῦ κατασκέψασθαι ἐν τῇ σοφίᾳ περὶ πάντων τῶν γινομένων ὑπὸ τὸν οὐρανόν· ὅτι περισπασμὸν πονηρὸν ἔδωκεν ὁ Θεὸς τοῖς υἱοῖς τῶν ἀνθρώπων τοῦ περισπᾶσθαι ἐν αὐτῷ.
And I applied my heart to seek out and examine by wisdom concerning all things that are done under heaven, for God has given to the sons of men an evil distraction to be distracted with.[43] (1:13)

εἶδον σὺν πάντα τὸν περισπασμόν, ὃν ἔδωκεν ὁ Θεὸς τοῖς υἱοῖς τῶν ἀνθρώπων τοῦ περισπᾶσθαι ἐν αὐτῷ.
I have seen all the distractions, which God has given to the sons of men to be distracted with. (3:10)

ὅτι οὐ πολλὰ μνησθήσεται τὰς ἡμέρας τῆς ζωῆς αὐτοῦ· ὅτι ὁ Θεὸς περισπᾷ αὐτὸν ἐν εὐφροσύνῃ καρδίας αὐτοῦ.
For he shall not much remember the days of his life; for God distracted him in the mirth of his heart. (5:19)

In these passages, the distractions are an inevitable part of the human condition, and they involve the everyday experiences of life, such as property and family. In this respect, it seems unavoidable that all humankind will be weighed down by these distractions. In other contexts, particularly in Stoic discourse, one finds these distractions can be avoided by proper orientation to the self. This usage is clearest in Epictetus, who uses περιεσπᾶτο when discussing how a philosopher is able to withstand the distractions of life:[44]

εὐσχολῶ γάρ· οὐ περισπᾶταί μου ἡ διάνοια. τί ποιήσω μὴ περισπώμενος;
For, I have plenty of leisure; my mind is not being dragged this way and that. What shall I do, seeing there is nothing that disturbs me? (*Diatr.* 3.9.19)

Ἡ πρώτη διαφορὰ ἰδιώτου καὶ φιλοσόφου· ὁ μὲν λέγει οὐαί μοι διὰ τὸ παιδάριον, διὰ τὸν ἀδελφόν, οὐαὶ διὰ τὸν πατέρα, ὁ δ', ἄν ποτ' εἰπεῖν ἀναγκασθῇ, οὐαί μοι ἐπιστήσας λέγει δι' ἐμέ.
The first difference between a layman and a philosopher: The one says, "Woe is me because of my child, my brother, woe because of my father";

---

43. Unless otherwise noted, all Septuagint translations are mine.
44. Translations of Epictetus come from *The Discourses, as Reported by Arrian, the Manual, and Fragments*, trans. W. A. Oldfather, 2 vols, LCL (Cambridge: Harvard University Press, 1926–1928).

and the other, if he can ever be compelled to say, "Woe is me," adds, after a pause, "because of myself." (*Diatr.* 3.19.1)

Epictetus argues that outside sources such as family and possessions are unfortunate distractions that are able to lead the nonphilosopher away from truly being able to focus on what matters, namely, controlling his or her own will.

He further develops this point in his discussion on the calling of a Cynic and whether they should marry in 3.22:

> τοιαύτης δ' οὔσης καταστάσεως, οἵα νῦν ἔστιν, ὡς ἐν παρατάξει, μή ποτ' ἀπερίσπαστον εἶναι δεῖ τὸν Κυνικόν, ὅλον πρὸς τῇ διακονίᾳ τοῦ θεοῦ, ἐπιφοιτᾶν ἀνθρώποις δυνάμενον, οὐ προσδεδεμένον καθήκουσιν ἰδιωτικοῖς οὐδ' ἐμπεπλεγμένον σχέσεσιν, ἃς παραβαίνων οὐκέτι σώσει τὸ τοῦ καλοῦ καὶ ἀγαθοῦ πρόσωπον,
> But in such an order of things as the present, which is like that of a battlefield, it is a question, perhaps, if the Cynic ought not to be free from distraction, wholly devoted to the service of God, free to go about among men, not tied down by the private duties of men, nor involved in relationships which he cannot violate and still maintain his role as a good and excellent man,

Here Epictetus argues that cares and concerns of running the household will inevitably distract the Cynic from his service (διακονία) to God. He will have to fetch water for his children's baths, take care of his wife, and have other daily distractions. These distractions keep one from that which is of greater importance, the pursuit of philosophical lifestyle. Freedom from distractions allow one to serve God.

Turning back to our passage, Martha has allowed herself to be distracted by her service to the Lord. She is distracted by all the physical service demanded by hosting and also, in some sense, by her sister's lack of service. According to Ecclesiastes, this περισπασμός is the inevitable distraction of life.[45] However, it seems as though Martha's problem here is not that these things are occurring, but rather that she has allowed herself to be troubled by them. Bovon argues, correctly, that often this word is assumed to reflect Martha's poor attitude, but that if we take into account her position as the head of the household hosting an important visitor,

---

45. The Greek translator of Ecclesiastes here chose περισπασμός to represent עִנְיָן, an unusual Hebrew word, meaning "to be busy," that only appears in Ecclesiastes.

"it is to be seen that this surfeit of activities understandable but disproportionate kept Martha from experiencing what was most important at that moment."[46] However, if we take into consideration the range of usage supplied by Epictetus's understanding of the word, we can see that it can also carry the sense of incorrect orientation, letting outside factors negatively affect one's own soul.[47] As I have already argued, Martha's service and hospitality are markers of her discipleship, but it appears that Luke is setting the reader up to understand that her good behavior may have the effect of her being improperly oriented toward Jesus. It is the first sign that this story will lead to a reversal of expectations over what is good and what is better.

In summary, Martha is introduced in Luke 10 as a positive character, who welcomes Jesus into her household and offers him hospitality. She takes care of Jesus out of her own resources like the women in 8:1–3, and she hosts him like Zacchaeus in 17:1–9. She fits into a line of men and women followers of Jesus who support his ministry and offer him hospitality. Furthermore, she is engaged in much service, another commendable act throughout Luke-Acts, one that reflects the behavior of the followers of Christ, whether they are engaged in the more menial tasks of waiting on tables or on the more ecclesial tasks of ministry. Both are equally presented as the actions of disciples. Martha is distracted by these actions, but this description does not suggest that we should read her character negatively, but rather suggests that the story is about to reveal the things on which Martha should properly focus. It is the beginning of the tension found in this story between two different types of good behavior. It should also be noted that none of her characterization is particularly rooted in her identity as a woman. As Alexander argues, "Her gender is simply part of the minimal background information which the narrator has to supply in order to explain the situation presupposed in the narrative."[48] Even her distraction is not something unique to her because of her gender, as it seems that all human beings are at risk of being distracted by the everyday tasks of living. Overall, we find that Martha is primarily depicted in the narrative as a disciple who hosts and serves.

---

46. Bovon, *Luke 2*, 71.

47. This is not to argue any sort of dependency between Epictetus and Luke or even Ecclesiastes and Luke necessarily, but rather to show that within the discourse of the first century, περισπάω held this range of meaning.

48. Alexander, "Sisters in Adversity," 208.

"And She Had a Sister Named Mary, Who Was Sitting at the Feet of the Lord": Mary's Characterization

Mary is introduced only through her familial relationship with Martha, and her overall characterization is also positive. While she never speaks in this story, a point that will be discussed later, she is described as sitting at the feet of the Lord and as listening to the word of the Lord, both of which are clear markers of her status as a disciple of Jesus. In this section I analyze these descriptions in the larger context of Luke-Acts to show that Luke is clearly depicting Mary in a positive light, as he did with her sister Martha, before turning to an analysis of her silence.

First, we find Mary sitting at the feet of Lord. This introduction sets the scene for Mary to also be seen as a disciple. The exact verb Luke uses, παρακαθίζω, is another New Testament *hapax legomenon*, meaning "to sit down beside."[49] However, what is more important is where she is sitting: at the feet of the Lord. This position denotes a recognition and respect of authority. For instance, this can be seen in Jesus's encounter with the sinful woman in Luke 7:36–50. In this story, the woman stands before the feet of Jesus (στᾶσα ὀπίσω παρὰ τοὺς πόδας αὐτοῦ) and then she bathes his feet (βρέχειν τοὺς πόδας αὐτοῦ) and kisses them (κατεφίλει τοὺς πόδας αὐτοῦ). This anointing and washing of Jesus's feet conveys a powerful moment in the gospel in which the woman shows her enormous respect and affection for Jesus. This is criticized by the host, Simon the Pharisee, as improper behavior, leading Jesus to defend her actions as appropriate and rooted. In this story the woman is vindicated and presented as the model disciple. Similarly, in Luke 17:11–19, Jesus heals ten lepers, but only one, a Samaritan, returns after realizing that he has been healed and falls before Jesus's feet (ἔπεσεν ἐπὶ πρόσωπον παρὰ τοὺς πόδας αὐτοῦ) to give thanks. Like the sinful woman in Luke 7, Luke also presents these actions positively as Jesus praises the Samaritan for his faith. In the narrative, both of these characters reveal their respect for Jesus by placing themselves before Jesus's feet. It illustrates that they recognize Jesus as an authority and that they are willing to show their gratitude by humbling themselves before him.[50]

---

49. BDAG, s.v. "παρακαθίζω," 765.

50. In Acts 4:32–37, the disciples are depicted as having authority as the members of the first church sell their possessions and place them at the feet of the apostles (παρὰ τοὺς πόδας τῶν ἀποστόλων). Similarly, in Acts 10:25, Cornelius falls at Peter's feet.

2. A Literary Approach to Luke 10:38–42

Furthermore, the specific construction used in 10:39, sitting at someone's feet, occurs two other times in Luke-Acts.[51] First, in Luke 8:35, the healed demoniac is found clothed, sane, and sitting at the feet of Jesus: εὗρον καθήμενον τὸν ἄνθρωπον ἀφ' οὗ τὰ δαιμόνια ἐξῆλθεν ἱματισμένον καὶ σωφρονοῦντα παρὰ τοὺς πόδας τοῦ Ἰησοῦ. Here the demoniac is depicted as a new convert of Christ who then seeks to go with Jesus. Similarly, in Acts 22:3, during Paul's speech after his arrest in Jerusalem, he identifies himself as a Jew brought up in the city at the feet of Gamaliel, ἀνατεθραμμένος δὲ ἐν τῇ πόλει ταύτῃ, παρὰ τοὺς πόδας Γαμαλιήλ. This phrasing clearly depicts Paul as a student and follower of Gamaliel. Thus, by placing Mary at Jesus's feet, Luke further emphasizes her role as a disciple, as she is learning from one with greater authority.

Despite claims that Luke's depiction of Mary reveals the countercultural nature of Jesus, who allowed women to learn from him, the text itself gives no indication that this is meant to be read as an abnormal occurrence. In fact, throughout Luke-Acts, Jesus and the leaders of the early church are depicted talking to and educating women. For instance, in Acts 16, Paul speaks to Lydia and goes to her household, with no mention of this being inappropriate. Reid argues that while social mores about interactions between men and women existed, they were not uniformly observed, particularly in the shifting world of the first century.[52] Rather, within the Greco-Roman and the Jewish world, there are examples of women being educated in philosophy and religion.[53] Thus, if the text itself does not present Mary's position as unique, then neither should modern readers. Instead of focusing on the degree of radicality of Jesus's acceptance of a woman, we should instead ask how Mary's depiction as a disciple affects

---

51. For a more in-depth discussion, see Brutscheck, *Die Maria-Marta Erzählung*, 124–26.

52. Reid, *Choosing the Better Part?*, 150.

53. For instance, see Musonius Rufus, *Fragment 3* (*That Women Too Should Study Philosophy*): "But above all a woman must be chaste and self-controlled.... I would add yet these: to control her temper, not to be overcome by grief, to be superior to uncontrolled emotion of every kind. Now these are the things which the teaching of philosophy transmit and the person who has learned them and practices them would seem to me to have become a well-ordered and seemly character, whether man or woman." See Abraham Malherbe, ed., *Moral Exhortation: A Greco-Roman Sourcebook* (Philadelphia: Westminster, 1986), 133.

the interpretation of the passage.⁵⁴ While Martha welcomes Jesus, Mary sits at his feet and listens to his words.

That Mary is said to be "hearing the word" (ἤκουεν τὸν λόγον αὐτοῦ) is particularly important for correctly reading this story. The theme of listening to the word of the Lord is a recurring one in Luke-Acts (Luke 5:1; 6:47; 7:29; 8:14, 21; 10:16; 11:28; 14:35; Acts 2:22; 4:4; 10:22; 13:7, 44; 15:7; 19:10) and appears as a core element of authentic discipleship. For Luke, the true disciple listens to the word of God and then obeys it. Jesus addresses this point directly later in the travel narrative, in 11:28, when a woman calls out from the crowd: "Blessed is the womb that bore and the breasts that nursed you" (μακαρία ἡ κοιλία ἡ βαστάσασά σε καὶ μαστοὶ οὓς ἐθήλασας). Jesus responds to the woman's blessing by responding that one who is actually blessed is the one who hears the word of God and obeys it (μακάριοι οἱ ἀκούοντες τὸν λόγον τοῦ θεοῦ καὶ φυλάσσοντες). Jesus's mother actually qualifies under both blessings, as she is the first example of listening and obeying in the gospel. In Luke 1:38, she responds with a spirit of obedience to the angel's message from God about her upcoming pregnancy. As Johnson observes, "For Luke, Mary does hear the word and keep it."⁵⁵

Similarly, in Luke 8:21, Jesus responds that his true family are the ones who listen to the word of God and do it (ὁ μήτηρ μου καὶ ἀδελφοί μου οὗτοί εἰσιν οἱ τὸν λόγον τοῦ θεοῦ ἀκούοντες καὶ ποιοῦντες). And in the parable of the sower and the seeds in Luke 8:4–15, Jesus tells the disciples that the good soil is the one who hears the word and holds onto it. All of these passages emphasize the underlying claim that listening to the word of God is central to correctly participating in discipleship. In Luke's Gospel, listening is not simply a passive act but one that leads to action. It is against this backdrop that one should read Luke's description of Mary as she sits listening to Jesus's words. By depicting her in this manner, Luke also conveys the

---

54. For a fuller discussion of the complex and at times contradictory nature of women's roles in the Greco-Roman world and the early church, see Susan Hylen, *The Modest Apostle: Thecla and the History of Women in the Early Church* (Oxford: Oxford University Press, 2015). For a deeper look at the roles of women in the Jewish context, see Bernadette J. Brooten, *Women Leaders in the Ancient Synagogue*, BJS 36 (Chico, CA: Scholars Press, 1982). Brooten analyzes inscriptional evidence to show that women served at times in leadership roles in synagogues throughout the ancient Mediterranean world.

55. Johnson, *Commentary on the Gospel of Luke*, 133.

2. A Literary Approach to Luke 10:38–42

expectation that Mary, like the mother of God, is among those who are the good soil, who listen and act accordingly.

This raises the question of Mary's silence in the text. All of the dialogue in this narrative is between Martha and Jesus; Mary is a silent character who is discussed but does not enter the conversation herself. Feminist scholars have argued that it is Mary's silence and passivity that has made her the favorite sister of interpreters throughout history.[56] We cannot ignore the patriarchal impulse to favor silent women over women who speak, but the question is whether Luke is intentionally favoring Mary because she is silent within the passage itself. In some ways, her silence is expected, given the inner logic of the text itself. As Seim points out, "Mary's silent listening is not exceptional: at the outset, this is true of everyone. In relation to the word of the Jesus, they find themselves in the position of the listener. First, one must listen and be taught."[57] In Seim's reading, there is no intentional silencing of her character.

Alexander also argues that Mary's silence is anticipated by the story itself, but for a different reason. According to her interpretation, Mary does not speak because Mary is not a main character.[58] She is a background character meant to spur the conversation between Martha and Jesus. Martha acts and speaks, whereas Mary's actions are described in a subclause relating to her familial relationship to Martha. She holds that this story is not Mary and Martha's story but rather Martha's story: "What we have then is not a three-cornered scene but, as so often in the gospels a dialogue between two characters, Jesus and Martha; Mary's actions provoke the dialogue, but she does not herself speak or appear on stage."[59] This is why Mary does not speak: because her speech is unnecessary to the story itself.[60] If we treat Mary as background character around whom the

---

56. Elisabeth Moltmann-Wendel discusses the male exegete's privileging of Mary because of her silence and the problems that stem from that reading. See Moltmann-Wendel, *The Women around Jesus* (London: SCM, 1982), 51–54. See also Alexander, "Sisters in Adversity," 198–200; Schussler Fiorenza, *But She Said*, 60–62. This exegetical tendency could reflect the influence of 1 Tim 2:15, in which the author argues that women should be silent in church.

57. Seim, *Double Message*, 112.

58. Alexander, "Sisters in Adversity," 198–206.

59. Alexander, "Sisters in Adversity," 206.

60. This follows a common trend in short, contained narratives in Luke: they are self-contained, stripped to the essential details, usually between two characters or two groups of characters. See Donahue, *The Gospel in Parable*, 21–22.

action revolves but who herself is not a part of the conversation, then her lack of speech is not actually notable.

The view that Mary is a background character, however, is not universally held. Bovon actually argues the opposite; he claims that Mary is the main character of this story, around which the entire story centers despite her lack of recorded speech.[61] Most readings treat the two sisters as equal characters, emphasizing a three-pronged narrative.[62] This dispute over how to fit Mary into the narrative begins to reveal the tension inherent in the construction of the story itself. While Martha is clearly the dominant sister in the narrative, given most of the action and the speech, Mary's characterization moves beyond that of a secondary character. She is clearly depicted by Luke as a disciple, albeit one who takes a different form from her sister. She is also characterized positively. Thus, unlike readings that try to place the two sisters in opposition to each other, one can see that the comparison seems to be between two different goods. As Alexander argues, "In terms of gospel discourse, however, the story offers a choice between two good types of behavior, listening to Jesus and serving him, and this is the heart of the paradox."[63] The paradox is seen in stronger terms when we turn to examine Martha's request and Jesus's response 10:40–42.

"Lord, Do You Not Care?": Martha's Accusation and Request

As previously discussed, Martha is said to be distracted by her serving and hospitality. This distraction, Luke tells us, leads her to turn to Jesus, her guest of honor, with an accusation and a request. It is at this point in the narrative that many popular interpretations have argued that complaining Martha descends into nagging the Lord about her saintly sister. However, a nuanced look at verse 40 reveals several complex interpretative decisions that must be made about the nature of Martha's statement. First, what is the impact of ἐφίστημι in this verse? Second, what is at the root of Martha's rhetorical question to Jesus and her accusation of her sister? Third and finally, how should one understand the nature of her command to Jesus?

---

61. Bovon, *Luke 2*, 68.
62. Brutscheck, *Die Marie-Marta-Erzählung*, 30–49.
63. Alexander, "Sisters in Adversity," 211. Bovon similarly argues the characterization of the two sisters represents "a harmonious and symmetrical presentation of Martha's welcome and Mary's listening" (*Luke 2*, 71).

My discussion will show how Martha's question begins to reveal the root of her misorientation and how her question itself forces Jesus to adjudicate between the two forms of discipleship that Martha and her sister embody.

Luke includes an interesting detail at the beginning of Martha's speech to Jesus. He describes her as coming up to him to speak (ἐπιστᾶσα δὲ εἶπεν). The specific verb, ἐφίστημι, is a Lukan favorite, meaning in this instance to "stand at or near a specific place or living entities often with the connation of suddenness."[64] Sometimes it is divine visitors who appear in this sudden manner. For instance, the angel of the Lord appears suddenly to the shepherds in Luke 2:9, and the men at the tomb appear in the same manner in 24:4. Other times, it is opponents or enemies who come up in this way, as in Luke 20:1, when the scribes and chief priests approach Jesus to trap him, or in Acts 6:12, when the scribes come on Stephen to arrest him. Sometimes, it carries a more neutral tone, reflecting the basic suddenness of an act, as in Luke 2:38 when Anna, the faithful widow, comes on the holy family in the temple. The question, then, is, In what sense should we read Martha's appearance next to Jesus? Should we read ἐφίστημι as a negative descriptor of Martha? Is she rushing up to Jesus, accusatory, angry, and out of sorts? Or is it a more neutral description, a literary flourish included to show her urgency and to build the narrative tension around their encounter?

I think it is likely the latter. Martha is not an opponent of Jesus. She is not trying to trick him like the religious leaders often try to do. Luke has already established Martha as acting like a disciple. One could argue that Martha is instead being cast as an opponent of Mary, whose actions she views as unacceptable, and Luke uses ἐφίστημι here to emphasize this displeasure. However, it is unlikely that this detail is intended to indicate some overtly negative or manipulative behavior on Martha's part. This is an encounter with Jesus over what Martha perceives to be a legitimate wrong.

Martha begins her address with a seemingly rhetorical question: "Lord, do you not care that my sister has left me alone to serve?" (κύριε, οὐ μέλει σοι ὅτι ἡ ἀδελφή μου μόνην με κατέλιπεν διακονεῖν;). The verb, μέλω, only appears here in Luke and only once in Acts, but it evokes a similar sense as the disciples' plea to Jesus in Mark 4:38, "Lord, do you not care

---

64. BDAG, s.v. "ἐφίστημι," 418; see also LSJ, s.v. "ἐφίστημι," which differentiates between hostile and nonhostile uses of the word. Of the twenty-one uses of ἐφίστημι in the New Testament, eighteen of those appear in Luke-Acts.

that we are perishing?"[65] Both seem to be an accusation focusing on Jesus's seeming indifference to a problem immediately at hand. Here Martha is concerned that her sister has left her alone to serve. Interestingly, she does not refer to Mary by her name but rather by her familial connection. Martha's distraction at serving appears to be further heightened by her sister's lack of service. This further reveals Martha's disorientation. Martha clearly feels abandoned by her sister in her time of need. Instead of directing her attention to the Lord and to her own actions, she instead is focused on her sister and her sister's actions. By allowing her sister's behavior to upset her, she is participating in the type of distraction Epictetus warns against by allowing familial issues to cause internal grief.

This disorientation leads her to accuse her sister, and she demands that Jesus resolve their domestic dispute.[66] She commands him to speak to her: εἰπὲ οὖν αὐτῇ ἵνα μοι συναντιλάβηται. On one hand, her request is not unreasonable.[67] She has a lot of work to do to properly host Jesus; Mary should help her get everything done. The specific verb, συναντιλαμβάνομαι, is a fairly rare verb, used only one other time in the New Testament (Rom 8:26), and it means "to come to the aid of, be of assistance to, to help (someone)."[68] In Exod 18:22 (LXX), the judges who are selected by Moses to lead the people are called on to help Moses by lightening his caseload. Similarly, in Rom 8:26, Paul writes that the Spirit helps us in our weakness.[69] The use of this verb conveys the sense that Martha is dealing with a great burden that Mary should help support. Furthermore, the narrative can be structured in such a way as to evoke sympathy for the overwhelmed hostess. After all, as we have already seen, she has acted hospitably, in the manner that followers of Jesus are supposed to act. This is further emphasized if one reads her distraction as inevitable when faced with a number of tasks.

---

65. It is interesting that in Luke 8:24, which is Luke's account of that same story, he does not use that construction but rather ἐπιστάτα ἐπιστάτα, ἀπολλύμεθα.

66. See Luke 12:13, where Jesus is asked to intervene in another domestic dispute, this time between two brothers and their inheritance. Another domestic dispute is depicted in Luke 15:11–32 in the parable of the prodigal son. In that narrative, it is an older brother who is upset about his younger brother's behavior and the treatment he is receiving despite that behavior. It should also be noted that in neither of these examples is the gender of the sibling pair a primary point of discussion.

67. Alexander, "Sisters in Adversity," 210.

68. BDAG, s.v. "συναντιλαμβάνομαι," 965.

69. A final reference can be found in Ps 88:22 LXX: ἡ γὰρ χείρ μου συναντιλήμψεται αὐτῷ, καὶ ὁ βραχίων μου κατισχύσει αὐτόν.

On the other hand, however, her request and accusation reveal that she is improperly focused on her sister instead of the one she is serving. Furthermore, it is her accusation that forces the tension between the two different types of discipleship (represented by the sisters' behavior) to escalate. Without her complaint, the two forms could have existed alongside each other, but she forces Jesus to essentially choose between her serving and Mary's listening. Her distraction and frustration at her sister has not allowed her to focus on what is ultimate, forcing her service to become a burden to her. Thus, she demands that Jesus intervene and force her sister to stop listening and help her. By seeking to be vindicated, she has placed the burden on Jesus to decide between the two.

"And the Lord, Answering Her, Said": Jesus's Paradoxical Response

The most difficult interpretive questions in this story concern Jesus's response to Martha's request in verses 41–42. At this point, as we have seen, Luke has set up two good behaviors. But Martha has put them at odds with each other, and Jesus must choose the correct one. Martha has been showing Jesus hospitality and serving him, while Mary has been listening to his teaching; narratively, either sister or both could be in the right. Martha, through her accusation and request, has now demanded that Jesus decide between the two forms, by either telling Mary to stop listening and go help her sister or by rejecting Martha's request. However, Jesus responds in such a way that leads to more questions than answers. In this section I carefully examine each part of Jesus's response in order to highlight these questions and the ambiguity they create in the text itself.

Μάρθα Μάρθα, μεριμνᾷς καὶ θορυβάζῃ περὶ πολλά

Jesus, who is referred to by the title κύριος,[70] begins his reply with a doubling of Martha's name in the vocative case. This doubling reflects a Semitic

---

70. In fact, Jesus is referred to as κύριος throughout this pericope. In 10:40, Martha calls him "the Lord" in her address, and in both 10:39 and 10:41 the narrator refers to him as such. By solely referring to Jesus in this way, Luke is creating a scene that appears to move beyond the immediate dispute occurring between two sisters and their guest. By only presenting Jesus as the κύριος, the narrative moves into a more direct conversation with the early church, offering them instruction and guidance from the Lord himself on how to participate in discipleship, forcing them to engage

influence on Luke's writing style.[71] It is meant to relay an affectionate relationship and is seen frequently in the Old Testament when the divine is directly engaging with a character in the story (i.e., Gen 22:11; Exod 3:4; 1 Sam 3:10). In Luke, however, it also often carries the tone of a mild rebuke, one that reflects genuine concern for the addressee.[72] For instance, in Luke 22:31, Jesus begins his prediction of Simon Peter's betrayal with Σίμων Σίμων. Similarly, in Acts 9:4, Jesus addresses Saul on the road to Damascus with another doubling: Σαοὺλ Σαούλ, τί με διώκεις. Thus, when Jesus addresses Martha with the doubling of her name, it prepares the reader for Jesus to correct Martha's thinking.

He tells her that she is μεριμνᾷς καὶ θορυβάζῃ περὶ πολλά, worried and troubled about many things. Μεριμνάω is best translated "to be worried, anxious" and is used throughout Luke to describe the state of worrying that hinders the development of faith. As Bovon observes, "It pertains to someone or something, looks on the future with anguish, either blocking or precipitating action. Theological meaning was added to this secular one, discreetly in the LXX and then more openly in the Gospels; insofar as worries are oppressing … they can be entrusted to God."[73] In Luke, one can see this concept fleshed out more fully in Luke 8:14, in Jesus's interpretation of the parable of the sower: one type of soil is choked by the worries and riches of life, and thus the word of God does not thrive (ὑπὸ μεριμνῶν καὶ πλούτου καὶ ἡδονῶν τοῦ βίου πορευόμενοι συμπνίγονται καὶ οὐ τελεσφοροῦσιν). Likewise, Jesus instructs his disciples not to worry about their lives in 12:22 (μὴ μεριμνᾶτε τῇ ψυχῇ τί φάγητε, μηδὲ τῷ σώματι τί ἐνδύσησθε). Worry is something that is both unnecessary and distract-

---

with the tension between the two types. However, it should be noted that both narrative occurrences have well-supported textual variants that switch κύριος with Ἰησοῦς. In 10:39, τοὺς πόδας τοῦ κυρίου is switched to τοὺς πόδας τοῦ Ἰησοῦ by several manuscripts, mostly notably 𝔓[45], 𝔓[75], and A. In 10:41, ὁ κύριος is switched to ὁ Ἰησοῦς by the majority of manuscripts again, but this time 𝔓[45] and 𝔓[75] support the κύριος reading along with ℵ and 𝔓[3]. These variants are illustrative of the larger textual issues in this passage, since many early and usually reliable manuscripts often disagree. I think it is more likely that κύριος was the original reading, but it shows the way in which this story has clearly moved out of the immediate literary context and into the broader discussion on discipleship in the church early in its transmission.

71. See Str-B 2:258. It is a common construction in later rabbinic work.
72. Walter Grundmann, *Das Evangelium nach Lukas*, THKNT 3 (Berlin: Evangelische Verlagsanstalt, 1971), 227. See also Bovon, *Luke 2*, 72 n. 33.
73. Bovon, *Luke 2*, 72.

ing from the pursuit of discipleship.[74] Particularly when noting Martha's distraction in verse 40, one can see that Jesus is drawing a comparison. Martha is distracted and worried, reflecting her incorrect orientation to following Christ. This has allowed the word of the Lord to pass by her.

The second verb, θορυβάζω, is the third New Testament *hapax legomenon* in this short passage. It is defined as "to cause trouble."[75] It is a rare verb even in the larger context of Greco-Roman writings. The passive construction of the word in this verse emphasizes how Martha has allowed herself to be troubled by outside sources (her service and her sister), which have led to her internal distress as she seeks to force Jesus to right her sister's behavior. She is worried and troubled by many things, and she has allowed these external factors to bring her grief.

However, the "many things" that Jesus says have troubled her present the beginnings of an interpretive problem. Are the many things that Jesus mentions specifically the dishes she is attempting to prepare, or are the many things a less specific references to the many distractions that Martha has encountered with her hosting? Marshall argues that it "clearly refers to the excessive preparations for a meal."[76] Bovon takes a broader view to argue that this response points to Jesus's concern that Martha is allowing worldly worries to impede her own encounter with him and does not discuss dishes.[77] The contrast between how these two scholars discuss this verse reveals a larger disagreement in the interpretation of the passage. Another option, however, is to focus not on the external factors that might lead to distraction but rather on the internal factors that are leading her to worry. She is frustrated by her sister. She is overwhelmed by her act of hospitality. She is distracted by her service. Which raises the question: Is Jesus talking literally about food and external issues, or is he talking on a deeper, spiritual level? The scholarly disagreement on this point shifts more into focus when one examines the next part of this phrase.

---

74. Another potential parallel is found in 1 Cor 7:32–35, which discusses how unmarried men and women are not worried about worldly things but rather only about the things of God.

75. The strangeness of the verb has led the majority of manuscripts (A, K, P, Γ, 565, 700, 892, 1241, 1424, 2542) to exchange it for the more common verb, τυρβάζω, which has a similar meaning.

76. Marshall, *Gospel of Luke*, 453.

77. Bovon, *Luke 2*, 72.

ἑνὸς δέ ἐστιν χρεία

Part of the difficulty of interpreting this phrase is the complete lack of textual stability. There are six variants of this phrase, and most of them are well attested. This makes coming to a conclusion about the meaning difficult, since there is still disagreement among scholars about the actual words in the phrase. The four major versions of the phrase are given in the following table.

Table 2.2. Textual Variations in Luke 10:41/42[78]

	Version	Translation	Sources
1	ἑνὸς δέ ἐστιν χρεία	One thing is needed	𝔓⁴⁵ 𝔓⁷⁵ C W Λ Ψ Θ 69 157 1071 1424
2	ὀλίγων δέ ἐστιν χρεία	Few things are needed	38 sy^pal arm geo
3	ὀλίγων δέ ἐστιν χρεία ἢ ἑνός	Few things are needed, indeed only one.	𝔓³ ℵ B L f1 33, sy^h mg bo
4a	Omission 1 (after περὶ πολλά)	... many things, Mary has chosen the better part	Clem, Ambr
4b	Omission 2 (entire phrase after Μάρθα)	Martha, Mary has chosen the better part	it^a b e ff i l r sy^rs
4c	Omission 3 (Μάρθα, θορυβάζῃ, Μαριάμ)	Martha, you are troubled, Mary has chosen the better part	D

As one can see, the difficulty centers on whether Jesus tells Martha that a few things (ὀλίγων) or only one thing (ἑνός) is necessary. Several early manuscripts even attempt to include both words, though it leads to an almost nonsensical answer. Metzger argues that this conflation leads to the omissions, which are "a deliberate excision of an incomprehensible

---

78. Chart adapted from Marshall's presentation of the variants and Metzger's discussion of the issues. See Marshall, *Luke*, 452–53; Metzger, *Textual Commentary*, 154. For another breakdown of the variants, see Fee, "One Thing Needful?," 4–5.

passage."⁷⁹ The instability reflects a disagreement among scribes about what Jesus actually refers to when he responds to Martha. Some scribes clearly believe Jesus is referring to the specifics of the meal itself, and thus the few things are dishes that need to be prepared. Jesus is reassuring Martha that she does not need to outdo herself in her preparations. Other scribes see Jesus's answer as a reference to a deeper point about the difference between the serving and listening to the word, and thus the one thing is listening to Jesus. The combined variants reflect the observation that even if Jesus is referring on one level to specific dishes, he is also addressing the deeper concern as well, which leads to the combination variant. The question remains which one reflects the earliest tradition. It is a difficult problem to solve, however, and this instability led Fee to argue that "the final resolution [of this exegetical crux] is inextricably bound to textual criticism."⁸⁰

Each of the different variants has found support in modern textual criticism. The reading most scholars believe to be original is variant one, in which Jesus says that only one thing is necessary. Fee observes that in the history of interpretation this variant is the most frequent reading in both the Christian East and West and still enjoys the support of most of the critical editions.⁸¹ Metzger also supports this reading, arguing that the other variants are caused by a misunderstanding of Jesus's claim: "The variations seem to have arisen from understanding ἑνός to refer merely to the provisions which Martha was preparing for the meal. The absoluteness of ἑνός was softened by replacing it with ὀλίγων.⁸² This variant also has strong textual evidence, with two early papyri and manuscripts supporting it. The second variant (version 2), which only includes ὀλίγων, is less popular among scholars, but Monika Augsten argues that it is original for two reasons: first, Augsten sees this as the most difficult reading, and second, it provides an explanation for how ὀλίγων is found in so many of the later manuscript traditions.⁸³ G. B. Caird, on the other hand, following the tradition of early textual critics, argues that the omissions (versions 4a–4c) reflect the earliest tradition surrounding the story, with the other readings

---

79. Metzger, *Textual Commentary*, 154. Bovon similarly argues that it would seem that the scribes refused to transmit that which they did not understand (*Luke 2*, 74).
80. Fee, "One Thing Needful?," 3.
81. Fee, "One Thing Needful?," 7.
82. Metzger, *Textual Commentary*, 153–54.
83. Monika Augsten, "Lukanische Miszelle," *NTS* 14 (1967–1968): 581–83.

being later glosses intended to flesh out what Jesus means by claiming that Mary has chosen the better part.[84]

Variant three of this verse is perhaps the most interesting because it appears to reflect a combination of variants one and two. Fee argues that this variant is likely to be the earliest, arguing that it is not actually a conflation, but rather the other readings are deviations, attempting to correct a difficult reading.[85] He presents evidence that it would be highly unlikely for this version to be created by a second-century scribal revision. After all, it too has strong textual evidence with early papyri and manuscripts. He argues that the sense of version three is this: "There needs but a little (for the body), or even but one thing (for the soul)."[86] This subtlety could easily have been misinterpreted by later scribes, leading to redactions.

Thus, one can see that we have two variants (1 and 3) that have strong textual evidence and scholarly support, making a decision between the two of them difficult.[87] In my opinion, reading three is the *lectio difficilior prior*, and I personally find Fee's argument compelling. But as we will see, variant one is the predominant reading for most of Christian history. However, we can see that both versions circulated throughout the early church, regardless of which is earliest. Furthermore, the conflict reveals the level of ambiguity that is embedded in the transmission of the story itself. If version one was the earliest, clearly several scribes thought it needed clarification, leading to a variety of different readings. A similar argument can be made about reading three. In part, this contributes to the diversity of interpretation we will see in later chapters, because it is clear that there is a lack of clarity surrounding the basic point being made by Jesus. Thus, some focus on the logistics of hospitality; others focus on the spiritual tension between service and devotion. Both readings are created out of a close reading of the text, depending on the source used. The interpreters are not

---

84. G. B. Caird, *Saint Luke* (Baltimore: Penguin, 1963), 149–50. For earlier voices who share this position, see Julius Wellhausen, *Das Evangelium Lucae* (Berlin: Reimer, 1904), 54; Erich Klostermann, *Das Lukasevangelium*, HNT 5 (Tübingen: Mohr, 1919), 485; J. M. Creed, *The Gospel according to Luke* (London: Macmillan, 1930), 154.

85. Fee, "One Thing Needful?," 8–16.

86. Fee, "One Thing Needful?," 13.

87. Fitzmyer argues that the discovery of $\mathfrak{P}^{75}$ conclusively decided the matter in favor of the first variant (*Gospel according to Luke*, 2:894). However, I agree with Wasserman ("Bringing Sisters Back Together," 439–41) that Fee's detailed work leaves the question still open and not as decided as Fitzmyer argues.

careless readers of Scripture, but the interpretations rise out of this point of confusion in the text itself.

Μαριὰμ γὰρ τὴν ἀγαθὴν μερίδα ἐξελέξατο ἥτις οὐκ ἀφαιρεθήσεται αὐτῆς

Jesus concludes his response to Martha by informing her that her sister has chosen the better part (or more literally the good part),[88] which will never be taken away from her. On the surface, τὴν ἀγαθὴν μερίδα refers to Mary's decision to sit and listen to the words of the Lord rather than to help her sister serve. It is also used in Luke-Acts to refer to a share or portion of the specific ministries of the church. In particular, in Acts 1:17, it is used in reference to the ministry of the Twelve when they are choosing a replacement for Judas. It can also be used to discuss a portion of a meal, which led some early biblical interpreters to assume that this too could be referring to a meal and the number of dishes in some way.[89] However, μερίς can also contain a deeper eschatological or more spiritual meaning, particularly when one examines its use in the LXX, where, following Bovon's observation, it "suggests the idea of eschatological retribution, expressed [originally] in terms of the dividing up of the land.... It also recalls the part that God himself represents for those who do not receive their share in land."[90] The good part represents an eschatological reward, given to those who choose God. There are three particularly illustrative examples of this type of usage in the Psalms:

> Κύριος μερὶς τῆς κληρονομίας μου καὶ τοῦ ποτηρίου μου· σὺ εἶ ὁ ἀποκαθιστῶν τὴν κληρονομίαν μου ἐμοί.
> The Lord is the portion of mine inheritance and of my cup: you are the one that restores my inheritance to me. (15:5)

---

88. As Fitzmyer observes, "The positive degree of the adjective is often used in Hellenistic Greek for either the superlative or comparative" (*Gospel according to Luke*, 2:894). The use of ἀγαθός here could also be an echo of the good soil in 8:8.

89. See notes under BDAG, s.v. "μερίς," 632. For an LXX citation that uses μερίς in this way, see Gen 43:34: ἦραν δὲ μερίδας παρ' αὐτοῦ πρὸς αὐτούς ἐμεγαλύνθη δὲ ἡ μερὶς Βενιαμιν παρὰ τὰς μερίδας πάντων πενταπλασίως πρὸς τὰς ἐκείνων ἔπιον δὲ καὶ ἐμεθύσθησαν μετ' αὐτοῦ. See also Deut 18:8; 1 Sam 1:4.

90. Bovon, *Luke 2*, 73. Fitzmyer refers to this as the "higher sense" of this word (*Gospel according to Luke*, 2:894).

ἐξέλιπεν ἡ καρδία μου καὶ ἡ σάρξ μου, ὁ Θεὸς τῆς καρδίας μου καὶ ἡ μερίς μου ὁ Θεὸς εἰς τὸν αἰῶνα.
My heart and my flesh have failed: [but] God [is the strength] of my heart, and God is my portion forever. (72:26)

Μερίς μου εἶ, Κύριε, εἶπα τοῦ φυλάξασθαι τὸν νόμον σου.
You are my portion, O Lord: I said that I would keep thy law. (118:57)

In these verses, one can see that a place with God is the ideal reality for the psalmist. His μερίς is in God, which will not be taken away from him; it is an eternal inheritance that represents both a future and present experience. God is with him now, and God will be with him forever. One can also see this eschatological meaning elsewhere in the New Testament and in Luke-Acts (Luke 12:46; John 13:8, 1 Cor 13:9, Eph 1:18; Col 1:12). For instance, Col 1:12 reads εὐχαριστοῦντες τῷ πατρὶ τῷ ἱκανώσαντι ὑμᾶς εἰς τὴν μερίδα τοῦ κλήρου τῶν ἁγίων ἐν τῷ φωτί (giving thanks to the Father, who has enabled you to share in the inheritance of the saints in the light). Thus, when Jesus tells Martha that Mary has chosen the better part that will not be taken away from her, it could be that the part that is secured is her share of the eternal reward. This also echoes Luke 8:18, where Jesus says those who listen well and receive the word will be given much, while those who do not listen are at risk of having even more taken away from them. This is the sort of eschatological conclusion that Bovon notes often suddenly appears at the end of Jesus's teaching.[91] This eschatological conclusion then shapes how the story should be read.

Ultimately, Luke's conclusion to the story provides a noteworthy reversal of expectations. The story ends without the audience hearing Martha's response to Jesus, and in this way the narrative once again moves out of the dinner-party setting to leave Jesus's statement before Luke's audience. Mary, who we might anticipate would be told to help serve, is instead said to have chosen the better part. Martha is mildly rebuked for being distracted and worried about things that are not of ultimate concern. However, the nature of her rebuke remains open to a number of interpretations, reflected in its textual instability. Either Jesus is reassuring her that she only needs to prepare a few things, or he is telling her that only one thing is ultimately needed and it is not her service but rather Mary's

---

91. Bovon, *Luke 2*, 73.

A Step Back and a Conclusion:
Examining Again the Context of Luke 10:38–42

Having examined the entire passage in detail, we must now step back and examine the whole once more in its Lukan context. The story presents two sisters characterized as engaging in praiseworthy behavior, embodiments of two different forms of Christian discipleship. Martha is actively practicing hospitality, welcoming the Lord into her house, and should receive the blessings promised by Jesus in 10:6–9 to those who welcome him and his disciples. Furthermore, her characterization immediately follows the parable of the good Samaritan in 10:25–37. In this story the Samaritan embodies the love of neighbor by taking care of an injured stranger. His service is physical and radical in its nature. He is the hero of the narrative, and when we transition to Jesus's arrival in Martha's home, this emphasis on service as the proper way to love one's neighbor cannot be ignored.

The text that immediately follows Jesus's response to Martha finds Jesus alone with his disciples, praying and teaching his disciples how to pray in 11:1–13. Here we see Jesus emphasizing the importance of prayer and of searching after God. For instance, in 11:10, Jesus teaches: "For everyone who asks receives, and everyone who searches finds, and for everyone who knocks, the door will be opened." Read against the backdrop of Jesus's response about Mary's good choice in 10:41–42, it is clear that this side of discipleship is central as well. Note that Jesus is said in Luke 11 to be alone in a certain place (ἐν τόπῳ τινί), which echoes Jesus's entrance in 10:38 to a certain village (εἰς κώμην τινά). Similarly, the parable of the good Samaritan starts by introducing a certain man (ἄνθρωπός τις), while the story of Mary and Martha begins by introducing a certain woman (γυνὴ δέ τις). Donahue points out that this linguistic parallel represents Luke's desire to underscore the paradigmatic nature of the story that follows.[92] In this way,

---

92. Donahue, *Gospel in Parable*, 135. However, I think Donahue stretches this point too far by claiming that the linguistic parallel between 10:25–37 and 10:38–42 clearly means that Luke intended these two stories to be read as a couplet, illustrating love of God and love of neighbor. The stories are interrelated, to be sure, but to claim that Luke intentionally constructed two narratives to flesh out Jesus's twofold love command seems to push the connection too far.

the lack of specificity is meant to imply that these stories are intended to illustrate an important point about faith and discipleship.

So one can see that the story of Mary and Martha exists in the intersection between the concerns discussed in the surrounding pericopes: discipleship as radical love and hospitality for one's neighbor (10:25–37) and discipleship as prayer and seeking after God (11:1–13). Similar to the way in which Jesus's response to Martha exists on multiple layers, moving from the immediate context of a dinner party into a deeper conversation about decisions with eternal implications, this story easily moves out of its immediate setting into that broader conversation in Luke about the best ways to engage in Christian discipleship. In my view, a close reading of these stories illustrates the concern of the Christian to listen to Jesus's words but to also do them. Blessed are those, Jesus says in 11:28, who listen to his words and who obey them. By reading these stories together, one can see that these two forms of discipleship are inherently connected. One cannot discuss Christian service without Christian devotion and vice versa. Donahue correctly argues that for Luke one form cannot authentically exist without the other.[93]

However, our story illustrates the occasional tension between these two good behaviors and raises the question of ultimacy. For Luke it is clear that, despite the ambiguities in the story, devotion to God is the better part. Listening to the word of the Lord is the primary, but not the sole, practice of a Christian. To not be focused on the Lord can lead to an incorrect orientation of one's service, allowing one to be distracted and worried about the wrong things, like Martha. It is this disorientation, not her service or her hospitality, that leads to Jesus's gentle rebuke. Mary has chosen God as her portion, and that will never be taken away.

That Jesus's rebuke of Martha can be read on the level of the number of dishes she needs to prepare is a legitimate option, and we will see that option entertained by later interpreters. But to ignore the deeper spiritual conversation about the tension between service and devotion and the eschatological implications that accompany it is also to ignore the context of both the immediate surrounding passages in 10:25–37 and 11:1–14 and the larger context of the travel narrative and its emphasis on the teaching of disciples.

---

93. Donahue, *Gospel in Parable*, 135.

2. A Literary Approach to Luke 10:38–42   69

That Luke 10:38–42 operates both on the spiritual and the practical level has led Donahue to argue this story is better classified as a parabolic narrative, as it contains a surprising twist "in Jesus's enigmatic saying which has caused more than sufficient doubt to commentators over the centuries."[94] Donahue does not mean that the story is a literal parable in the strict sense, but rather that the ambiguous nature of Jesus's response, combined with the fact that the story appears to operate on numerous levels, allows the story to operate parabolically. It challenges its readers to wrestle with Jesus's response. As we will see, interpreters of Luke throughout the centuries have read this story in light of their own concerns about discipleship. Alexander, while not labeling the story parabolic, also points out that like most dinner-party stories in Luke (7:36–50; 11:37–52; 14:1–6, 7–11, 12–14, 15–24), this story contains an element of unexpected reversal typical of parables: "Reading Martha's story alongside these co-texts suggests that here too we may be operating on two levels. On the surface, Martha's behavior is a mistake common to hosts.... To that extent, the story works simply as a piece of advice on etiquette. When the guest is Jesus, however, the mistake assumes cosmic proportions. Martha is in danger of 'missing the point' which of all points must not be missed."[95] Alexander and Donahue both emphasize that Jesus's response operates on multiple levels. This, as we have seen, is supported by the number of textual variants found in 10:41–42 as scribes have attempted to reconcile these levels.

Strangely, however, both Alexander and Donahue push back against patristic and medieval readings that attempt to further unpack the implications of Luke's claims about listening and serving for their own communities. Alexander argues that by reading this story as a paradigm for Christian behavior, one does damage to the text by misreading it.[96] Similarly, Donahue argues that "though in the history of interpretation, this passage has often been used to exalt the contemplative life over the

---

94. He argues that it shares many of the same characteristics of parables in Luke, such as realistic and human with dramatic interaction, the "certain woman" construction, little information on background characters, a surprising twist, and an ending with an enigmatic saying, which follows the law of "end stress" (Donahue, *Gospel in Parable*, 134–35).
95. Alexander, "Sisters in Adversity," 209.
96. Alexander, "Sisters in Adversity," 212.

active, the Lukan context precludes such an interpretation."[97] Their resistance to the paradigmatic way of reading seen in earlier interpretations ignores the way in which the ambiguity in the text itself opens itself up for a number of different readings.

If the text does indeed exhibit a parabolic intent, then the variety we find in the history of interpretation should not be surprising. Rather, it is the natural effect of different readers who have approached the story with their own set of questions and concerns about discipleship and hospitality, which in turn allow them to see different things. The Lukan context does not preclude this sort of reading. The intersectional nature of the story combined with its textual instability naturally leads to a plurality of potential interpretations of the passage. Thus, as we turn to study the long and complex history of interpretation on this passage, we will see that the interpreters were not simply bad readers, overspiritualizing and carelessly allegorizing. On the contrary, they attempted to unravel the complexity embedded in the narrative, using their own exegetical tools and cultural contexts, in order to make claims about the proper way for disciples to achieve the better part.

---

97. Donahue, *Gospel in Parable*, 136.

3
Origen and Early Monastic Interpreters

> That great scholar used to say that inspired Scripture taken as a whole was on account of its obscurity like many locked-up rooms in one house. Before each room he supposed a key to be placed, but not the one belonging to it; and that the keys were so dispersed all round the rooms, not fitting the locks of the several rooms before which they were placed. It would be a troublesome piece of work to discover the keys to suit the rooms they were meant for. It was, he said, just so with the understanding of the Scriptures, because they are so obscure; the only way to begin to understand them was, he said, by means of other passages containing the explanation dispersed throughout them.
> — Origen, *Philocalia* 1.10, translated by George Lewis

Introduction

The most influential figure in the history of interpretation is Origen, whose reading made this story a focal point in monastic interpretations for centuries. Unfortunately, in most recent scholarship, discussions on this point lack nuance. It is often claimed within the New Testament guild that Origen read the two sisters as action and contemplation and that this allegorical reading was accepted whole cloth by the monastic tradition.[1] The reality, however, is more complicated. As we will see in this chapter,

---

1. This claim is the mostly succinctly stated by Heller in "Sibling Rivalry," 246. It is more important to note that many New Testament scholars have been quick to criticize this reading as overly allegorical and thus are mostly dismissive of it. For instance, see Schüssler Fiorenza, *But She Said*, 54–55; Fitzmyer, *Gospel according to Luke*, 2:892–93. Within monastic studies, there has been more careful work done, but even within that field generalizations about Origen's interpretation can still be found. For the primary example of careful patristic scholarship on this topic, however, see Csanyi, "Optima Pars," 5–78.

Origen's own interpretation(s) of the passage are multifaceted, and in fact he offers several different readings of Luke 10:38–42, which move beyond the simple claim that he saw Mary as contemplation and Martha as service. The first section of this chapter focuses on these readings in order to better understand how Origen uses the story of the two sisters to illustrate several key tenets of his own view of Christian discipleship. The evidence further shows that his view was not simply adopted in its entirety into the monastic tradition. Rather, it was used as one reference point in a larger discussion about the best ways to live out the Christian faith. In fact, Origen's views were expanded, adapted, and even contradicted by monastic writers who followed him. The second section of this chapter illustrates this point by examining the Liber Graduum, Pseudo-Macarius, John Cassian, Basil, the desert fathers, and Ephrem.

The goal of this chapter is to show how the story of Mary and Martha functioned within Origen's work and within the monastic communities that developed in the fourth and fifth centuries. As we will see, there is no single reading of Luke 10:38–42 that can be labeled "the monastic interpretation." Rather, Luke 10:38–42 is a biblical witness around which various theories could be developed concerning Christian discipleship. The monastic readers wrestle with the paradoxical nature of the story and the tension between active service and listening to God's word. They dedicate almost no space to discussing the implications of Mary and Martha's gender. Instead, they focus on the implications of the story for the practice of Christian discipleship.

Origen

Origen's Life and Work

Origen was born in approximately 185 CE in Alexandria and died in Caesarea around 254 or 255 CE, possibly as a consequence of the torture he endured during the Decian persecution a few years prior. Most of what is known about Origen's life comes from two ancient sources: Gregory Thaumaturgus's *The Address of Thanksgiving to Origen* and Eusebius's *Ecclesiastical History*, book 6.[2] From these texts, we learn that Origen's

---

2. For more information about the scholarly debate on the reliability of these sources, see Peter Martens, *Origen and Scripture: The Contours of an Exegetical Life* (Oxford: Oxford University Press, 2015), 15 n. 36.

father died as a martyr when Origen was a teenager and that this led him to become an instructor, in order to support his family, teaching Greek literature and philology (Eusebius, *Hist. eccl.* 6.2.15). He also taught catechetical classes in Alexandria, and after a wealthy man named Ambrose converted to the faith and became his patron, Origen was able to stop teaching secular subjects and focus solely on studying and teaching the Bible. This was his focus for the rest of his life. Before his death, he delivered over a thousand homilies and published dozens of commentaries and other works on the Christian faith. As Jerome later observed after discussing all of these works, "Who of us can read everything he wrote? Who can fail to admire his enthusiasm for Scripture?" (*Ep.* 84.8 [Martens]).

Origen adopted an intense asceticism in order to focus more fully on the study of Scripture. As Eusebius describes:

> Through the entire day he endured no small amount of discipline; and for the greater part of the night he gave himself to the study of the Divine Scriptures. He restrained himself as much as possible by a most philosophic life; sometimes by the discipline of fasting, again by limited time for sleep.... With a zeal beyond his age he continued in cold and nakedness; and, going to the very extreme of poverty, he greatly astonished those about him. And indeed he grieved many of his friends who desired to share their possessions with him, on account of the wearisome toil which they saw him enduring in the teaching of divine things. (*Hist. eccl.* 6.3.9–11 [trans. Arthur Cushman McGiffert, *NPNF* 2/1:252])

Such asceticism is indicative of Origen's belief that things of the world can distract from spiritual development. As Peter Martens argues, Origen was concerned with the moral dilemma between focusing on the world or focusing on the things of God. He writes, "it only follows, then, that it is a mark of progress or advancement in Christianity when the individual transforms his interests away from the distractions of the world to loftier, spiritual matters."[3] For Origen, focus on spiritual things came through studying and teaching Scripture, which led him to create the vast amount of work Jerome observed.

Origen's exegetical tendencies in these works, and the pros and cons of his approach, have been the frequent point of discussion in modern studies. Previously dismissed as an allegorist, it is only in the last fifty years that

---

3. Martens, *Origen and Scripture*, 97.

Origen's actual interpretive project has begun to be taken more seriously.[4] While he does use allegory, he does not do so arbitrarily, but rather his interpretations are shaped by his belief that everything in Scripture, no matter how obscure, was placed there by the Holy Spirit for specific purposes. Thus, he often uses passages of Scripture to interpret other, more complicated passages. Furthermore, he argues that Scripture operates on different levels, which serve different purposes. In *On First Principles*, he argues that "just as the man consists of body, soul and spirit, so in the same way does Scripture" (*Princ.* 4.2.4 [Butterworth]). Henri De Lubac argues that these different levels are represented in Origen's exegetical work in several ways.[5] The historical sense, or the literal sense, is the body of Scripture. It is the surface meaning, and while it has value, Origen does not think the biblical interpreter should be content to remain on this level. The soul of Scripture consists of the moral sense. The spirit of Scripture refers to the mystical sense, in which the realities of Jesus Christ are revealed to the church. For Origen, therefore, the ultimate goal of reading Scripture is to encounter Jesus and to be transformed by that encounter.

Because Scripture can operate on these distinct levels, each passage can have a number of valid meanings existing alongside one another. Because of Origen's immense knowledge of Scripture and the fact that he viewed all Scripture to be connected, he explores different threads in this vast tapestry, allowing his mind to make different connections to words and themes in each passage.

Fragmenta in Lucam 171

This is certainly true when one turns to study his discussion of Luke 10:38–42, found in *Fragmenta in Lucam..* (171). While not much is known about the Lukan fragments, it is believed that they come either from his

---

4. This has led to a more nuanced approach to Origen's interpretive works in recent years. For three important discussions of Origen's exegetical project, see Henri de Lubac, *History and Spirit: The Understanding of Scripture according to Origen*, trans Anne Englund Nash (San Francisco: Ignatius, 2007); Jean Danielou, *Origen*, trans. Walter Mitchell (New York: Sheed & Ward, 1955); Richard P. Hanson, *Allegory and Event: A Study of the Sources and Significance of Origen's Interpretation of Scripture* (London: SCM, 1959). For a treatment of Origen's audience and goals, see Karen Jo Torjesen, *Hermeneutical Procedure and Theological Method*, PTS 28 (Berlin: de Gruyter, 1986); Martens, *Origen and Scripture*.

5. De Lubac, *History and Spirit*, 139–50.

lost commentary on Luke or from some of his missing Lukan homilies.[6] It is believed that both the commentary and homilies were composed after Origen's move to Caesarea in 233 CE. In particular, the commentary was likely composed after he wrote his commentary on Matthew in 244 CE, placing the fragments near the end of his life and scholarly career. As such, Joseph Lienhard observes, these works reveal "a shift from cosmological interests to mystical and pastoral interests ... with a clear and ever present concern for the spiritual progress of his hearers."[7] This can be seen clearly in his treatment in *Fr. Luc.* 171.

While most of the attention on this passage has focused on Origen's introduction of Martha and Martha as the paradigm for a life of service and a life of contemplation, this is only one of many readings Origen offers for this story. In reality, he presents his readers with five different options for interpretation, and we will see that in none of those options is the gender of Mary and Martha highlighted.[8] Rather, each interpretation revolves around Origen's understanding of the proper way to engage in the Christian life and the stages of spiritual development Christians undertake on their journey toward perfection. Origen is able to see in the story of Mary and Martha several of his core beliefs about the nature of Christian discipleship. I now examine each of these interpretations in turn before stepping back to analyze them as a whole.

Reading One: Martha as Action, Mary as Contemplation

The fragment begins with Origen offering the famous comparison that Martha stands for action and Mary for contemplation: "You might reasonably take Martha to stand for action [πρᾶξις] and Mary for contemplation

---

6. For more background on the composition and translation of the Lukan fragments and homilies, see Joseph T. Lienhard, "Introduction," in Origen, *Homilies on Luke*, FC 94 (Washington, DC: Catholic University of America Press, 1996), xv–xxxix; Max Rauer, "Einführung," in Origen, *Die Homilien zu Lukas in der Übersetzung des Hieronymus und die griechischen Reste der Homilies und des Lukas Kommentars*, trans. Rauer, GCS, Origenes Werke 9 (Berlin: Akademie, 1959), vii–lxii. While it is impossible to prove irrefutably that these fragments are authentic, most scholars agree that they are likely genuine.

7. Lienhard, "Introduction," xxiii.

8. Bovon (*Luke 2*, 75) and Csanyi ("Optima Pars," 10–27) both argue that there are three interpretations offered here in this fragment. I think it is better to separate them into five different interpretations, following the logic of Origen's own divisions.

[θεωρία]. For, the mystery of love is lost to the active life unless one directs his teaching, and his exhortation to action, toward contemplation. For, there is no action without contemplation or contemplation without action" (*Fr. Luc.* 171).[9] The two sisters represent two types of behavior in the life of Christians. As Csanyi notes, Origen is the first to introduce this important comparison: "Er ist der erste bei dem—allerdings offensichtlich allegorsierend—die Deutung Maria/Marta = θεωρία/πρᾶξις auftaucht, eine Deutung die im Laufe der jahrhunderte bis zum heutigen Tag immer wieder aufgegriffen wird."[10] However, the comparison is more nuanced than usually assumed, because the active life and the contemplative life are not presented here as oppositional or even as hierarchical.[11] They are two sides of the Christian life. One cannot properly exist without the other. One's actions should be propelled by one's learning, and that action in turn propels one back to more contemplation. Martens contends that this concept reflects Origen's most central idea about Scripture: "At its core, the Scriptures repeatedly advocated action and thought, twin facets of the Christian way of life. Christianity for Origen was quintessentially 'practical' and 'contemplative.'"[12] The interconnectedness between the two ideas is elsewhere developed in his writings.[13] It is worth briefly exploring two of those other discussions in order to further understand Origen's claim about Mary and Martha here. In his first homily on Luke 1:1–4, he presents the relationship between action and contemplation as similar to the relationship between the theory of medicine and the practice of medicine:

> For example, the science of geometry has as its goal only the science and discipline itself. But the goal of another science, like medicine, includes its application. I ought to know the theory and principles of medicine not

---

9. Translations of *Fragmenta in Lucam* from *Homilies on Luke*, trans. Lienhard. Origen writes almost the exact same line in *Fr. Jo.* 80: "Mary symbolizes the contemplative life and Martha the active life" (all *Fragmenta in evangelium Joannis* quotations are based on Crouzel's French translation). The rest of this fragment and how it diverges from the Lukan one will be discussed later.

10. Csanyi, "Optima Pars," 10.

11. For the philosophical background surrounding this claim, see Nicholaus Lobkowicz, *Theory and Practice: History of a Concept from Aristotle to Marx* (Notre Dame: University of Notre Dame Press, 1967).

12. Martens, *Origen and Scripture*, 206.

13. For other discussions of the relationship between practice and contemplation in Origen, see *Hom. Judic.* 1.4; *Hom. Exod.* 8.1, *Fr. 1 Reg.* 2.

merely to know what I should do, but to do it. In other words, I should incise wounds; prescribe a regulated and controlled diet ... and restrain an excess of humors. If someone merely knows these principles and does not follow them up with an application, his knowledge is pointless. There is a relation like that of the science of medicine to its application in the knowledge and service of the Word. Hence Scripture says, "Just as those who from the beginning saw and were ministers of the Word." We should realize that the words "they saw" indicate a discipline and a science, while the words "they were ministers" refer to applications. (*Hom. Luc.* 1.5)

Encountering the word is not knowledge gained for its own sake. Rather, the goal is to apply that knowledge through service, like the eyewitnesses in Luke 1:2. Using this analogy, knowledge comes first and is followed by practice. Henri Crouzel argues that one can clearly see that, for Origen, the knowledge given by God will be used to further develop good behavior in the life of the Christian. Knowledge of God is used then to serve God.[14]

Origen also explores this relationship in book 1 of his *Commentary on John*. However, there he argues that sometimes the practical life can lead to the contemplative life: "The beginning of a good way is to do justice. For since a 'good way' is very great, we must understand that the practical, which is presented by the phrase 'to do justice,' relates to the initial matters, and the contemplative to those that follow" (Origen, *Comm. Jo.* 1.91).[15] One is guided by one's correct actions to an experience with God, which in turn leads one to grow in knowledge and contemplation. Origen then continues with another analogy. Ethical teaching and practices represent the bread of life, and they sustain the Christian who follows them. Contemplation of the mystical is the fruit of the vine, and this wine allows Christians not only to be nourished but to delight and revel in the Lord (1.208). For Origen, contemplation and practice are the bread and the wine of the Christian faith. Both are needed in order to be nourished.

Thus, when he compares Martha and Mary to these two practices in *Fr. Luc.* 171, he appears to be highlighting their intertwined nature. As monasticism developed, there were debates surrounding which is better, activity or contemplation, but in this first interpretation, Origen does not

---

14. Henri Crouzel, *Origene et la "Connaissance Mystique,"* MLST 53 (Paris: de Brouwer, 1961), 435.

15. Translations from *Commentarii in evangelium Joannis* come from *Commentary on the Gospel according to John, Books 1–10*, trans. Ronald E. Heine, FC 80 (Washington, DC: Catholic University of America Press, 1989).

view them as separate.[16] As Crouzel argues, "Mais si Origene fut le maitre en spiritualite des debuts du monachisme, il n'a jamais envisage serieusement une vie d'anachorestisme et de contemplation pure."[17] They are not different lifestyles but rather two different practices that flow into each other in the Christian life. This belief was mirrored in Origen's own life and teaching, as he remained connected to the everyday life of the church through his preaching and commentaries, while at the same time engaging in ascetic practices. The contemplative life only flourishes when it is practicing and sharing that which was learned, and the active life, if it is not rooted in contemplation, will be without any benefit. For Origen, Luke's account of Mary and Martha demonstrates the interconnectedness of two aspects of the Christian life.

Reading Two: Mary and Martha at Different Stages of Spiritual Development

After presenting the two sisters as contemplation and practice, Origen shifts his focus to discuss other details in the story. His next interpretation, which is the most complicated, focuses on the fact that Martha received Jesus into her house, while Mary sat at his feet: "But we should rather say that Martha received the word more somatically, in her house—that is, in her soul—whereas Mary heard it spiritually, even if she sat 'at his feet.' This means that she [Mary] had already passed beyond what was handed down by way of introduction according to the plan of salvation, since she 'had put aside the things of a child' but had not yet received what is perfect" (*Fr. Luc.* 171). The language of this passage is confusing. Usually when Origen refers to something being achieved somatically, he means a lower stage of spiritual development. By analyzing some of the other Lukan fragments more closely and by analyzing Origen's view on the spiritual development of Christians, we can see that Origen is actually presenting Mary and Martha in different stages along their spiritual journey, with Mary further along in her spiritual progress.

---

16. Walter Volker first observed this trend in Origen's writings, arguing that practice and contemplation are the two distinct but inherently interconnected concepts that dictate Origen's understanding of the properly lived Christian life. See Volker, *Das Vollkommentheitsideal des Origenes: Eine Untersuchung zur Geschichte der Frömmigkeit und su den Anfängen christlicher Mystik* (Tubingen: Mohr, 1931), 76–79.

17. Crouzel, *Origene et la "Connaissance Mystique,"* 437.

Part of the difficulty of unpacking this particular interpretation is the fragmented nature of the work. As previously mentioned, it is thought to consist of Origen's lost commentary on Luke. From the fragments that remain of this commentary, one can see Origen drawing connections between concepts that appear frequently in Luke. Specifically, from the surrounding fragments, we can see that Origen has been developing an argument based on the concepts of the οἰκία and περὶ πόδας, which, as I noted in chapter 2, appear repeatedly throughout Luke-Acts.

In *Fr. Luc.* 114, 120, and 121, Origen discusses the importance of receiving Jesus into a house. In *Fr. Luc.* 114, Origen interprets Luke 8:4, focusing specifically on Jesus teaching the crowds. Drawing on Matthew's reference in 13:1, he argues that those who are outside the house can only receive Jesus's teaching in parables, but that those within the house (the disciples) can have those parables fully explained to them. In *Fr. Luc.* 120–21, he discusses Luke 8:16: "No one after lighting a lamp hides it under a jar, or puts it under a bed, but puts it on a lampstand, so that those who enter may see the light." He argues that the vessels of the house are the powers of the soul. The body is represented by the bed and the lampstand is the intellect (120). He argues that the church are those who are in the house: "Let 'all those in the house'—that is those in the Church—look upon the brightness of the lamp placed on the lampstand, which draws them into clear knowledge by the Word" (174). By placing one's light on the lampstand and not hiding, the church is able to encourage one another to shine brightly (174). Thus, when Martha receives the word into her house, which represents her soul, one could argue that it is a marker that she has been granted similar knowledge of the word.

But it is still unclear what Origen intends by saying she received the word more somatically. Often the bodily reception of the word implies a less perfect understanding. For instance, in *Fr. Luc.* 122, Origen argues that the Jews, through their somatic worship, placed a bushel over the word of God, blocking those who are in the house (in this instance the house represents the world) from being able to receive the divine knowledge. As we will see later, Origen compares Martha to the synagogue of the circumcised, which receives Jesus but does not fully understand. Thus, one can argue that Martha's reception of the word into her soul does not imply that she has achieved perfect knowledge. The best reading of the evidence, when taking in Origen's larger view of the somatic, suggests that Martha is at an earlier stage of Christian progress because she only grasps somatically. Unfortunately, this reading of Martha is underdeveloped because

Origen is not really concerned with her in this particular interpretation; his primary focus is on Mary and her spiritual development.

Origen states that Mary has received the word spiritually while sitting at Jesus's feet. Origen argues repeatedly throughout *Fragmenta in Lucam* that sitting at the feet of Jesus reflects a specific stage of spiritual development. For instance, in *Fr. Luc.* 113 on Luke 7:37, Origen presents the woman washing Jesus's feet as representative of a less perfect soul, because she starts at Jesus's feet:

> But the less perfect woman—that is, soul—is at the feet and occupies herself with humbler things. We are near her, for we have not turned from our sins. Where are our tears? Where is our weeping, so that we can approach at least Jesus' feet? We cannot go first to the Head himself. After our sins, it is enough to be able to bring the good odor of repentance, so that we can be the second one, the woman who anoints the feet, but not the head, that is, the woman who touches not what is more perfect and exalted, but the lowest and the least.

From this, one can see that the soul who sits at Jesus's feet has begun their spiritual journey by participating in the act of repentance, but they have not yet achieved what is perfect, like the "soul that serves the Word of God well" (113). This soul has the freedom to go right to the head of Christ.

Similarly, in *Fr. Luc.* 124, which focuses on the healed demoniac in Luke 8:39, Origen argues that Jesus sent the man away because he "did not have enough power to go and sit 'clothed at Jesus's feet.' ... He did not have the capacity for more." He continues by arguing that the man was still in need of learning temperance, having only recently been freed by Jesus from the power of sin. He concludes that the one who has not only moved away from sin but is moving toward temperance is the one who is able to be at Jesus's feet (124). In both of these passages, one can see that sitting at the feet of Jesus represents an early (but not the earliest) stage of spiritual progress. When Origen describes Mary as one who sits at Jesus's feet in this passage, then, he presents her as one who is moved beyond the initial stages of Christianity, but she has not achieved what is perfect.

He fleshes out this argument by drawing a comparison to the one who puts aside childish things, quoting 1 Cor 13:11. Origen uses this verse frequently to explain his understanding of the stages of spiritual development. In his homilies on Ps 36, he argues that the follower of Christ progresses as on a journey toward perfection: "Every individual who makes his way toward virtue makes progress by walking, so that through many stages of progress along the way little by little he arrives at virtue" (*Hom. Ps. XXXVI* 4.1 [trans. Heintz]).[18] The end goal is to see God with a completely pure heart, which involves a long journey and many potential pitfalls, which can be avoided only by focusing on Christ and his teachings:

> Blessed then, is the one who opens his mouth to the Word of God and who, growing in age following Christ, will grow also in wisdom.... All of us will become—if, however, we will be deserving of it—disciples of Wisdom. If, here in this life, one is educated and instructed in these things to which one was able to attain while in the flesh, there he will then be enlightened by a more perfect training and those things which are pursued here by effort and exertion will there be part of the abbreviated course of the education to come. But the one who has not yet put aside the elementary subjects but still speaks as a child and thinks as a child, there too he is taught as a child so that at a certain point, having become a grown man through progress in wisdom, he might put aside those things proper to a child. (5.1)

From this, one can see that Origen recognizes that one will need to progress in wisdom in order to advance along one's spiritual journey. Origen believes that the proper way to progress in this wisdom is to spend time in contemplative practices (frequent prayer, devoting oneself to Scripture, and dwelling in the psalms, hymns, and spiritual songs; 5.1). Such Christian practice enables one to avoid the pitfalls of worldly evils. Mary participates in these practices by sitting at the feet of the Lord, and thus, this reading of Luke 10:38–42 implies that she will continue moving toward perfection.

This second interpretation shows that Origen is concerned with the spiritual progression represented by Mary sitting at Jesus's feet. She has progressed past the initial stages of repentance, but she is still trying to grow in wisdom, to "the contemplation of the Godhead with pure and spiritual love" (*Comm. Cant.* prol.).[19] Martha, on the other hand, appears to have received the word already, but the ambiguity of the terms used

---

18. For another discussion of the spiritual progression in Origen's work, see *Princ.* 4.4.10: "Here we are clearly shown that in God all these virtues exist forever and that they can never come to him or depart from him, whereas men acquire them gradually and one by one" (Butterworth). See also *Hom. Num.* 27 and *Comm. Cant.* prol.

19. Translations of Origen's *Commentarius in Canticum* come from *The Song of Songs: Commentary and Homilies*, trans. R. P. Lawson, ACW 26 (Westminster, MD: Newman, 1957).

makes her spiritual progression unclear.[20] There are two potential readings: either (1) she is further ahead of her sister, if she has already received full knowledge of the word, or (2) her somatic understanding of the word means that her knowledge is still incomplete. Origen's consistent use of somatic as a lesser state of being suggests the latter is the correct reading. Either way, however, one can see that in this reading Origen sees Luke 10:38–42 as a way to discuss the different stages of Christian development, with Mary representing a more advanced stage.

Reading Three: Martha as the Jewish Synagogue, Mary as the Gentile Church

In a third interpretation of the story, Origen uses the story of the two sisters to discuss another important theme in his writings: the proper interpretation of the Scripture. Origen compares Mary and Martha to the "synagogue of circumcision" and the gentile church with regard to their understanding of the law:

> Martha can also be the synagogue of circumcision, which received Jesus in his own territory, because it was engaged in worship according to the letter of the Law. But Mary is the Church of the Gentiles, which has chosen the good part, the "spiritual law," which is not to be taken away from her and cannot be destroyed, like the glory upon the face of Moses. From the Law she takes the few beneficial things, or rather, she sums them all up in one commandment: "You shall love."… And, corresponding to the expression, "there is need of few things," you understand the commandments: "You shall not commit adultery. You shall not murder," and what follows. (*Fr. Luc.* 171)

This interpretation focuses on what Origen understands to be the correct way to interpret and follow the law, which is an important theme

---

20. It is worth noting that in Origen's Johannine fragments, he presents a more definitive statement on the spiritual development of Mary and Martha in John 11–12. In this story, it is Martha who goes out to receive Jesus, whereas as Mary waits to receive him in their house, a detail Origen uses to suggest that Mary is more perfect: "Martha seems to have more zeal than Mary, because she runs to meet Jesus, while Mary sits at home. There are people, like the centurion, who are not capable of receiving Jesus, others who are worthy of them, as the chief of the synagogue; it is because she is less perfect that Martha runs to Jesus, Mary, waiting for him at home, to welcome him, for she can receive him" (*Fr. Jo.* 80).

throughout his writings. Martha represents the Jews, who have insisted on following the letter of the law. Mary has a better understanding of the law and thus has chosen the better part. By keeping the spiritual law, she represents the gentile church. It is in this third interpretation that Origen offers a reading of Jesus's response to Martha in 10:41–42.

Here, once again, Origen draws on imagery found elsewhere in the fragments. In *Fr. Luc.* 122, Origen compares the synagogue to a figurative bushel that is placed over the light of Christ: "[Luke] means the somatic worship prescribed by the Law, and the old symbols of the letter of the law; for the synagogue was wholly unable to discern the light of true knowledge contained in the concepts."[21] This is one of Origen's primary critiques of the Jews, repeated in both *Fr. Luc.* 122 and 171: they keep the law to the letter, following all the liturgical and ceremonial customs.[22] By worshiping somatically, they are unable to understand the spiritual law and the "light of true knowledge," which comes from properly understanding who Jesus is. We remember that Origen believed the Bible to consist of three different senses, directed to the body, the soul, and the spirit: "One must therefore portray the meaning of the sacred writing in a threefold way upon one's own soul so that simple man may be edified by what we call the flesh of scripture (this name being given to the obvious interpretation); while the man who has made some progress may be edified by its soul as it were and the man who is perfect.... This man may be edified by the spiritual law which has a shadow of the things to come" (*Princ.* 4.2.4 [Butterworth]). Martha represents those who have not fully understood the full meaning of Scripture and thus are still focused on only the bodily nature of the law. Mary, on the other hand, has grasped the spiritual law, which is a lighter burden (*Fr. Matt.* 10). For Origen, Jesus summed up the spiritual law with the twofold love command. Mary sets aside the details of the Old Testament law, and she has chosen the better part, which is the spiritual sense. Origen argues that this choice will never be destroyed but rather will be an eternal glory, unlike the glory that shone on the face of Moses after his encounters with the Lord (2 Cor 3:18). Origen states the point more fully in his *Commentary on Romans*: "[The letter of the law] possesses a certain glory in its commands, nevertheless it is not capable of being glorified. There exists another glory which remains and is glorified

---

21. See discussion on p. 79 on how this represents a negative use of somatic and how it relates to the first interpretation.

22. See Martens, *Origen and Scripture*, 140–41.

in Christ. This shows that when Jesus was transformed into glory … the glory of the law could be understood in the Spirit" (*Comm. Rom.* 2.5.4).[23] He later writes, in the same work, that the person who has grasped this spiritual sense and contemplates the Lord, unfettered by the literal sense of the law, will be transformed into a future glory, one that cannot be taken away (4.9.8). This reading displays Origen's eschatology. With access to the spiritual nature of Scripture comes a transformation that has eternal implications. One will be in the presence of the glorified Lord and will be made even more into his likeness. Origen's Mary has grasped this, but Martha is still focused on the physical level of Scripture.

It can be noted here that Origen again exhibits a close attention to the text in front of him, by attending to all the literary details, when he turns to discuss "a few things are necessary."[24] We meet here the text-critical issue in 10:41–42. If the text of Luke 10:41–42 Origen knew had only said "one thing is necessary," he would have been set with his reading that the spiritual law can be encapsulated by the claim "you shall love." However, since Origen is a careful exegete, he has to attend to the phrase "a few things are necessary," and thus he discusses the basic summary of law that Jesus gives the young ruler in Luke 18:19, which becomes "the few things." It seems highly likely, then, that Origen was familiar with a version of this story that used "a few necessary things," because in his exegesis he directly engages with what the few things might be. While this is not a direct quotation of the text itself, I think it provides another important data point concerning which versions of Jesus's response were known in the early church. At least in third-century Alexandria, the "few things" version of the text existed. Origen takes that detail and uses it to interpret the few things, not as literal dishes or acts of service but rather as representing the Ten Commandments.

Reading Four: Martha as "the Judaizers" and Mary as the "Jews in Secret"

In his fourth interpretation, Origen further expands on the analogy comparing Martha to those who keep the letter of the law and Mary to those

---

23. Translations of Origen's *Commentarii in Romanos* come from *Commentary on the Epistle to the Romans, Books 1–5*, trans. Thomas P. Scheck, FC 103 (Washington, DC: Catholic University of America Press, 2001).

24. See previous discussion of the textual variant and its influence on interpretation in ch. 2.

who understand the spiritual law. However, in this interpretation, instead of the synagogue and the church, Martha and Mary represent the Judaizers and the gentile Christians: "Still another interpretation: Martha can be the believers from among the circumcised, and the Judaizers, who keep the precepts of the Law in Jewish fashion, while Mary can be those among them who have been evangelized and are 'Jews in secret.' They sit only at Jesus' feet, and 'seek the things that are above, not the things upon the earth'" (*Fr. Luc.* 171). Here Origen connects Martha and Mary to a larger debate in the New Testament between Jewish Christians and gentile Christians. Martha no longer represents Jews more broadly but specifically those Jewish Christians who believed that all converts to Christianity should also convert and follow the Jewish law. Drawing on the imagery in Romans 2:28–29, Origen argues that Mary is like those who are secret Jews, or put another way, those who are spiritual Jews despite externally appearing to be gentiles.

In particular, the phrase "Jews in secret," a variation of a phrase taken from Rom 2:29, is an important concept for Origen's interpretation of the Law. In his *Commentary on Romans*, he focuses on this phrase extensively.[25] He argues repeatedly that those of the gentile church are circumcised spiritually and as such have a spiritual understanding of the law, which frees them from the somatic elements of the law. In this way, the mystical meaning allows the gentile church to excel beyond their Jewish counterparts who are still bound by the law: "He will also discover that he who is a Jew in secret and who has been circumcised in the inner man excels and surpasses the one who is a Jew according to the flesh to the same degree that Judah, who is praised by his own brothers and who slept like a lion and arose like the whelp of a lion, excels and surpasses the Judah who was born from the loins of Jacob according to the flesh" (*Comm. Rom.* 2.14.4; 2.13.36). By comparing Mary to those who are Jews in secret, he is once again comparing her to those who have the deeper understanding of the Scripture and thus are able to advance further in their knowledge of God. This is heightened by the fact that Origen compares her to those who seek the things above and not the things below, a quotation from Col 3:1–2. Only those who have received this spiritual circumcision are able to properly do this. God has "opened up a road in which anyone who longs to train himself in the Holy Scriptures may more extensively pro-

---

25. See Origen, *Comm. Rom.* 2.7.2; 2.11.4; 2.13.34–36; 2.14.4; 3.2.8; 4.1.4; 4.2.6.

ceed" (4.7.10). Through this training they are able to grow in knowledge of the Lord and move closer to perfection. Mary and those who sit at Jesus's feet are able to train in this way. In his *Commentary on the Song of Songs*, Origen praises Mary and those like her who always show this commitment: "Blessed are his servants, who stand ever in his sight: it is not those who sometimes stand and sometimes do not stand who are truly blessed, but those who always and unceasingly stand by the Word of God. Such a one was that Mary who sat at Jesus's feet, hearing him. And the Lord himself bore witness to her saying to Martha: 'Mary has chosen the best part, which shall not be taken away from her'" (*Comm. Cant.* 10.1).[26] Mary's commitment to learning from the Lord sets her apart from her sister and is the better part that will not be taken away from her. In both of these interpretations and the one that preceded them, one can see that Origen is using the two sisters to draw a comparison between those who understand the spiritual sense of Scripture and those who understand only the physical sense. Mary represents Christians who are committed to studying and understanding the word of God on its deeper level. For Origen, this is the better part because this knowledge will lead her closer to perfection.

In both the third and fourth interpretations, Origen does not have an overtly negative view of Martha. Rather, he presents her as lagging behind Mary: she does not have a proper understanding of the law and thus is not as far along on her spiritual journey. In fact, in *Fr. Luc.* 226, Origen argues (in his interpretation of the young ruler in 18:21) that those who follow the law and the old covenant are still worthy of God's love but are held back from perfection because they have not fully embraced that love.[27]

---

26. It is interesting to note that in the *Commentary on the Song of Songs* Origen represents Mary's sitting as representative of the fact that she was standing unceasingly before the Word. In *Fr. Luc.* 171, he discusses her sitting at his feet as representative of the fact that she had not yet progressed to Christian perfection. This is another example of the fluidity in which Origen uses terms. Like his use of *house* in the Lukan fragments, it would appear that sitting at the feet also has different connotations depending on context. We will see in ch. 4 that Augustine similarly discusses Mary's sitting and how it connects to standing before the Lord.

27. It is worth briefly mentioning whether these two interpretations of Mary and Martha suggest actual hostility to Jewish people. Origen repeatedly, throughout several of his works, contends that the Jews have misunderstood the Scripture by reading it too literally. However, in other places he clearly assumes Jewish allegorical interpretation to interpret difficult passages. Peter Martens argues that this seeming disconnect centers on the fact that Origen does not broadly reject Jewish interpretation

Similarly, Martha lacks the proper understanding to truly progress in her spiritual journey.

Reading Five: Martha as Busy with Somatic Things, Mary as Focused on Spiritual Things

Origen makes a final turn to address Martha's distraction with "many things." This allows him to discuss another important theme in his writings: the competition of the incorporeal and corporeal world for the attention of the mind, and the dangers of worldly distractions.[28] The two sisters are examples of two different ways of living: "For, interpreting the passage in another way, you will find that Martha is more somatic and busy 'with many things' while Mary is concerned only with contemplation and spiritual things" (*Fr. Luc.* 171). The corporeal world, despite being good and created by God, is constantly placing demands on and distracting people away from a focus on their Creator.[29] He argues that "everyone who is concerned about the affairs of the world, about money, about profits ... who is tied up with concerns for possessions and distracted for riches, who is zealous for glory of this age and honors of the world is turned away" (*Hom. Exod.* 12.2).[30] On the other hand, the one who is completely devoted to the contemplation of God, who meditates on God's word day and night, is turned toward God (12.2). In order to accomplish this, Christians must be willing to rid themselves of all worldly distractions. This means selling their possessions, setting aside responsibilities of the household, and embracing an ascetic lifestyle. Origen favors this interpretation of Mary and Martha in his homily on Gen 1: "For either we come to him with the crowds and he refreshes us by parables to this end only, lest we faint 'in the way' from many fasts, or, of course, we sit always and incessantly at his

---

whole cloth but rather that he rejects those interpretations that focus on the practice of the law specifically. Origen is concerned with those readings that focus on following the letter of the law, which he argues prohibit one from being able to experience the spirit of the law. See Martens, *Origen and Scripture*, 136–46.

28. See Martens, *Origen and Scripture*, 94–100, for a fuller discussion of the relationship to the mind and the corporeal and incorporeal worlds.

29. For the goodness of creation, see Origen, *Princ.* preface 1; 1.1.6; 4.1.7. For the dangers of being attracted to it at the expense of losing focus on God, see *Princ.* 1.1.6.

30. Translations from Origen's *Homiliae in Genesim* and *Homiliae in Exodum* come from *Homilies on Genesis and Exodus*, trans. Ronald E. Heine, FC 71 (Washington, DC: Catholic University of America Press, 1982).

feet, being free for this alone, that we might hear his word, not at all disturbed about much serving, but choosing the best part 'which shall not be taken away' from us. And certainly those who thus approach him obtain much more of his light" (*Hom. Gen.* 1.7). Those who are still focused on this world, like Martha, can be followers of Christ, but their distractions mean they will not be as far along on the journey to perfection, whereas those who are ready to sit constantly at his feet like Mary will receive more of Christ's light.

Origen seems to be building here on Clement of Alexandria's reading of Luke 10:38–42. Clement was an important influence on Origen's writings, and he was his instructor while Origen was based in Alexandria. Clement only mentions the story of Mary and Martha in one place, during a long discussion of the rich young ruler and the relationship between possession and salvation.[31] Specifically, Clement argues that Martha and the young ruler in Luke 18 are both unable to progress in their spiritual journey and achieve perfection because they are still distracted by earthly things:

> And he was capable of busying himself about many things; but the one thing, the work of life, he was powerless, and disinclined, and unable to accomplish. Such also was what the Lord said to Martha, who was occupied with many things, and distracted and troubled with serving; while she blamed her sister, because, leaving serving, she set herself at His feet, devoting her time to learning: "You are troubled about many things, but Mary has chosen the good part, which shall not be taken away from her." So also he bade him leave his busy life, and cleave to One and adhere to the grace of him who offered everlasting life. (*Quis div.* 10 [trans. A. Cleveland Coxe, *NPNF* 1/2:594)

According to Clement, Martha's core problem is her distraction. Her busy life hinders her from being able to choose the better part. Origen appears to follow suit with his final interpretation. In many ways, this reading echoes the concerns of Epictetus (discussed in ch. 2). The world will inevitably distract her from being able to fully focus on God. This became a central aspect of later monastic readings. One must set aside the distractions of this life by selling one's possessions and giving up familial relationships in order to truly be able to live a contemplative life that is spent constantly at

---

31. This is the earliest reference in patristic literature to the two sisters.

the feet of Christ. Origen embodied this in his own life when he sold all he had and dedicated his life to learning and teaching about Scripture.

This last interpretation appears more hierarchal than his first. Mary clearly makes the better decision by pursuing spiritual and contemplative things. The comparison here is not between action and contemplation, but rather between distraction and contemplation. This is an important distinction, because it is an easy mistake to assume that, since in this final reading Mary as contemplation is placed above Martha, we should also read Mary as contemplation above Martha as action. Indeed, within later monastic interpretations, this reading flourished. However, since Origen himself makes a distinction between these two interpretations, it naturally follows that we should as well and be careful not to conflate them.

Summary: Analyzing Origen's Reading of the Two Sisters

Having analyzed each interpretation in its own right, we can now turn to examine how we should understand the fragment as a whole. When one places these readings beside one another, one could see them as contradictory. However, for Origen, the text is always capable of holding multiple meanings simultaneously, depending on which aspect of the text one is focusing on.[32] After all, Scripture is a living document, one that the Holy Spirit can use for different ends. Origen views the job of the biblical interpreter as exploring these different meanings. With each reading, he shifts his view slightly to focus on a different detail, which leads to a slightly different reading. He does not seem concerned with the fact that one reading places Mary and Martha as equals and another elevates Mary above Martha. Rather he appears to recognize a potential tension within the story itself, allowing this tension to work itself out in multiple ways as he attempts to discover the text's spiritual meaning.

---

32. Csanyi draws a slightly different conclusion:"Wir müssen uns daher nach den grossen Linien der besprochenen Texte orientieren, und diese Linien konvergieren alle ein Richtung. Nirgends sagt er das ganz eindeutig und offen. Wer aber deshalb die nachgewiesene Einheit aller einschlägigen Stellen ignoriert, der ignoriert Origines eigentliche Marie-Marte Deutung" ("Optima Pars," 27). He repeatedly argues that all of the interpretations are intentionally connected if we read them carefully enough. I think this move is unnecessary, however. The five interpretations can be variations on a theme. As I argue above, one can see that there are minor differences in his interpretations without claiming that Origen is contradicting himself.

As de Lubac argues, Origen recognizes that his readings might not reflect the spiritual meaning of a text given from the Holy Spirit, and thus "he makes attempts, outlines; he gives his opinion … he proposes one explanation, then another, equally competent or even better; he floats hypotheses to see if they will succeed … but he does not claim that he has earned the understanding of everything enclosed in the Holy Books."[33] This tendency is on full display in this fragment as Origen explores the literary details of this text. He gives his readers multiple ways into the story so that the Spirit might speak.

It should also be noted that Origen arrives at his different meanings by paying close attention to the text itself. He focuses on Martha's reception of Jesus "in her house" and Mary's sitting at Jesus's feet. He discusses Mary's choice of the better part and the few things that are necessary and Martha's distraction at many things. Furthermore, since all of Scripture is connected, he traces these details at the level of the words themselves back to their other appearances in Scripture. Thus, he can use other places in Luke, but also Romans, 1 Corinthians, and Colossians in order to interpret this passage. At times, this can make it difficult to follow, as he seemingly holds all of Scripture in his head, and it is not always easy to trace his train of thought. Furthermore, at times, he takes the same word and uses it for different meanings, as I noted in his use of the term *house* in his second interpretation. However, while this can be frustrating to the modern reader, it does not appear to break any of Origen's own exegetical rules as he attempts to uncover the spiritual meaning of a text.

Within these five different readings, there are shared thematic elements that were further developed by later writers. All of these readings revolve around discipleship and the proper ways to be engaged in the Christian life. More specifically, there is a theme of spiritual development, as the two sisters represent two different stages of Christian progress toward perfection. Also, there is a continual focus on the spiritual nature of the Scripture. This appears to be a key aspect of being able to move closer toward perfection. The somatic readings and the somatic ways of life can ultimately distract one from the "better part." From this passage, one can see that Origen clearly believes the story of Mary and Martha is paradigmatic for understanding how Christians should live.

---

33. De Lubac, *History and Spirit*, 370.

Later writers further developed the paradigmatic character of the passage by combining different aspects of Origen's multilayered interpretations and rejecting others. Origen does not solve the tension in the text between the types of Christian practice that the sisters seem to embody. In some of his readings, Mary is clearly favored, but in others Mary and Martha are equals, and in one reading, Martha perhaps could even be seen as further along in her development, depending on one's interpretation of the house. This tension continues in later interpretations.

Ultimately, Origen's interpretation(s) of Luke 10:38–42 are important in the history of interpretation because he emphasizes multiple themes that were taken up by later monastic interpreters in the fourth century and beyond: namely, the language of contemplation and action and the concept that the sisters represent different stages of a spiritual journey. However, since he offers multiple readings, we will see that the interpreters who follow him choose to emphasize different options in order to create their own exegetical arguments about Mary and Martha and their contributions to Christian discipleship.

Monastic Interpreters

Having shown the complexity of Origen's reading of the Luke 10:38–42, I now turn to examine the monastic interpreters who are traditionally understood as being dependent on his work. In particular, I choose to focus on fourth- and fifth-century readings because during this period monasticism began to take a more defined shape within the Christian tradition. The story of Mary and Martha became a focus point for fleshing out concerns over the best practices of Christian living, with multiple interpretations circulating. The majority of these interpretations prefer Mary and her perceived asceticism over her sister, though Martha is also frequently depicted positively. This tendency can be found in the anonymous Book of Steps or the Liber Graduum, Pseudo-Macarius's Spiritual Homilies, and John Cassian's *Conferences*. Each of these texts adapts and expands Origen's stages of Christian development and the pursuit of perfection, while also using the story as a prime biblical example for its own understanding of the relationship between contemplation and physical service. The texts appear to use Origen's reading as a starting point to interpret the passage, but ultimately their interpretations address the concerns within their own communities. Not all monastic voices, however, follow this path. A second tendency counters the predominant view and interprets Luke 10:38–42 by focusing entirely on Martha, even favoring her. This can be seen most clearly in Ephrem's *Commentary on the Diatessaron* and Basil's *Long Rule*.

The Liber Graduum

The Liber Graduum is a little-known collection of thirty Syriac homilies (called Memre, or "words," in Syriac)[34] that depict an early stage of Syrian monasticism.[35] Little attention has been given to this source in modern scholarship, in part due to early twentieth-century claims that it was produced by the Messalians, a misunderstood heretical movement that focused on constant prayer at the expense of all other Christian practices.[36] When the Liber Graduum was first published in a critical edition in 1926 by Michael Kmosko, he labeled the text Messalian, pointing out its emphasis on prayer and other popular Messalian themes.[37] This opinion was soon accepted throughout the guild, with several other scholars examining the text in light of its supposed heretical affiliation.[38] This thesis was challenged in 1954 by Arthur Vööbus when he argued that while the Liber Graduum does discuss prayer, it also affirms the importance of baptism, of worshiping in the larger church community, and of participating in the

---

34. This work is also sometimes referred to as the Kthaba demasqatha, its Syriac name.

35. For an introduction to the text, see Robert A. Kitchen and Martien F. G. Parmentier, "Introduction," in *The Book of Steps: The Syriac Liber Graduum*, CSS 196 (Kalamazoo, MI: Cistercian, 2004), xiii–lxxxiii.

36. Messalianism was a heresy found in northern Mesopotamia and Asia Minor during the fourth and fifth centuries. It was condemned by the Council of Ephesus in 531 CE. Its primary focus was on complete and constant prayer to the degree that all other aspects of Christian life were forsaken, including the sacraments. Followers mostly slept (as dreaming was seen as a type of prayer) and relied on the support of others to survive. However, there is much debate surrounding it, since, as Marcus Plested summarizes, "We know *that* Messalianism was; we do not know *what* it was"("The Christology of Macarius-Symeon," in *Cappadocian Writers, Other Greek Writers*, ed. M. F. Wiles and E. J. Yarnold, StPatr 37 [Leuven: Peeters, 2001], 595). For a full discussion of the complexities of this heresy and whether it actually existed, see Columba Stewart, *"Working the Earth of the Heart": The Messalian Controversy in History, Texts and Language to AD 431* (Oxford: Clarendon, 1991).

37. Michael Kmosko, "Prefatio," in *Liber Graduum*, PatrSyr 3 (Paris: Didot, 1926), i–cccvii.

38. See, for instance, Irenee Hausherr, "L'erreur fondamentale et la logique de Messalianisme," *OCP* 1 (1935): 328–60.

visible church.[39] Vööbus pointed out that the author of the Liber Graduum even argues that those who withdraw and do not participate in the larger church have gone astray and have not achieved Christian perfection.[40] Vööbus's argument, that the Liber Graduum should be studied not for its potential insight into a fifth-century heresy but rather for its potential contribution to our understanding of Syrian monasticism more broadly, paved the way for a more balanced discussion of this text, but it remains an understudied resource in monastic studies.

The location, date, and authorship of the collection are difficult to determine. The most widely held opinion is that it was written in Mesopotamia (perhaps near the River Zab) sometime during the mid- to late fourth century.[41] This places this work as a near contemporary to the work of Aphrahat, another important Syriac monastic figure. Furthermore, there appears to have been some persecution in the surrounding area in recent decades, and the community appears to be composed of rigorous and less rigorous groups of believers.[42] The author, though unknown, was clearly a spiritual leader over this mixed group, with some of his flock ascribing to radical asceticism while others continued to hold secular jobs, marry, and run households. Parmentier and Kitchen describe him as a spiritual leader of a precenobitic era of spiritual asceticism. There is a strong tension between these two groups throughout the text, and the author navigates this tension constantly, often alternating between harsh declarations and pastoral encouragement.

In order to understand how the author interprets Luke 10:38–42, it is important to understand the core concept driving the ecclesiology of the Liber Graduum. Essentially, there were two different types of Christians, which he labels the Upright and the Perfect. Describing the ministries of these two groups and their relationship to each other is a recurring theme throughout the homilies. The Upright were those Christians who engaged in physical ministries of the church and who still lived fully in the secular

---

39. Arthur Vööbus, "Liber Graduum: Some Aspects of Its Significance for the History of Early Syrian Asceticism," *PETSE* 7 (1954): 108–28.

40. Arthur Vööbus, *History of the Asceticism in the Syrian Orient*, CSCO 184 (Leuven: Secrétariat du Corpus, 1958), 182.

41. D. J. Lane, "Book of Grades, or Steps," *The Harp* 14 (2001): 82. Lane sees several comparisons between this work and the work of Aphrahat (81–88).

42. Kitchen and Parmentier ("Introduction," xxiv) connect this persecution to the Persian ruler Shapur II, who persecuted Christians between 340 and 372.

world. They took care of the poor and visited the sick. They had households and families and could collect wealth (as long as they used it wisely). They avoided the sins of pride, lust, and greed and tried to love their neighbors as themselves. They even fasted twice a week and prayed three times a day. They are to strive to one day achieve Perfection.

The Perfect were those who embraced an ascetic lifestyle. They had sold all their possessions and had fully renounced the world. They had chosen a lifestyle of the cross, fasting, praying constantly, and practicing celibacy. They were called to a radical love of God and neighbor, embodying Christ's love for the world. They had received a full measure of the Holy Spirit. Because of their renunciation of all worldly things, they had become united with God. Their primary ministry was to teach those who had not achieved this goal and to pray for others that they might also arrive at Perfection. They were ministers of the word, prayer, and the Spirit. There were stages even of Perfection, however, and by practicing the command of love one could progress even closer to God. It was also possible to lose focus and regress to the stage of the Upright if one was tempted by the things of the world. It was even possible to lose any measure of the Spirit and be rejected by the Spirit and the church (Lib. Grad. 3.11).

The relationship between the Upright and the Perfect was one of interdependence. The Upright were called to support the Perfect, and in turn, the Perfect were expected to teach the higher things of God to the Upright. An Upright person was to always be striving toward Perfection, and this development was marked by the pledge of the Spirit. As a person gradually renounced earthly things, she was able to push out the "pledge of Satan" and was thus able to more fully receive the Spirit. When one was finally perfect, one received the full measure of the Spirit. However, not everyone would be able to achieve this goal, and thus God provided a means of grace for them too. As Kitchen and Parmentier note: "God recognizes that not all persons are capable of the same standards and so provides a means of salvation for all."[43] It is important to note that both of these groups were authentic Christians. The difference in the end is the reward. The Perfect will reach Zion fully, dwell there, receive a full portion of the Spirit, and have a greater reward, whereas the Upright will only barely reach Zion and only receive a portion of the Spirit (Lib. Grad. 14.2).

---

43. Kitchen and Parmentier, "Introduction," xxxviii.

The author has an elevated view of Scripture, and Kitchen and Martien describe him as "living in a thought-world saturated with the Bible."[44] Almost all of his illustrations and arguments come from the biblical text, and he often engages in long exegetical discussions of entire biblical narratives. Furthermore, throughout the Liber Graduum, he is careful to address potential contradictions within the Bible. For instance, he adjudicates between the command to take care of the poor and the command to sell all one has and live without goods, by arguing that these are commands directed at different people (Lib. Grad. 3.15).[45] He ultimately argues that there are major commandments, which are directed toward the Perfect, which include such commands as loving one's enemy, selling all one's possessions, and forsaking marriage, and there are minor commandments, directed toward the Upright, which include commands such as the golden rule, giving to the poor, and being faithful in marriage.[46] He wants to ensure that no one accuses the Perfect of disobeying Scripture by not having alms to give to the poor. Rather, the Perfect have a different set of commands, which they are following. The good interpreter of Scripture will be able to decipher which commands are intended for which group. This reflects a core belief of the author: everything in the Scriptures is either meat for the Perfect or vegetables and milk for the Upright: "Now let us expound the major commandments through which a person is made Perfect: that is to say, those commandments that were given by the Lord and his apostles to the Perfect and that distinguishes them from the 'vegetables and milk.' … It was necessary to write them down so that even simple people may attain insight and everyone may struggle to enter by the narrow gate of Perfection or inherit the place of Uprightness below it" (Lib. Grad. 2.1).[47] Thus, God gave the lesser commands so that the Upright could still receive God's blessings and participate in the physical ministries of the church. This view

---

44. Kitchen and Parmentier, "Introduction," l.

45. Another example of his concern for biblical unity is found in Lib. Grad. 9, where he tries to unpack how the Old Testament prophets could be viewed as part of the Perfect, as they are often described as having a close relationship with God and yet still do terrible things, such as Elisha calling the bears to kill the children who mocked his baldness.

46. See Lib. Grad. 1, 2, 19, 20 for descriptions of the minor and major commandments and the different journeys the two groups take by following them.

47. The reference to meat, vegetables, and milk is an allusion to 1 Cor 3:2. All translations of the Liber Graduum come from Kitchen and Parmentier.

of Christian development is the lens through which the author approaches the Bible, as seen in his interpretation of Mary and Martha.

The author turns to discuss Mary and Martha in the third *memre*, in which he explores the different ministries and gifts of the Upright and the Perfect. He uses the biblical examples of Mary and Martha and Moses, Aaron, and Miriam to expand his discussion of those gifts: "We must distinguish better the greater gifts and from the lesser ones and the pledge from the full blessing. The Lord said this in connection with Miriam and Aaron, their gifts were smaller than those of Moses.... In the same way the portion of Martha was smaller than that of Mary. Although the Lord has communicated with all of them, only his pledge was in Miriam and Aaron and Martha. In this respect they were different from Moses and Mary, the sister of Lazarus" (Lib. Grad. 3.13). Here we see that the author is setting up a dichotomy between Mary and Moses on one hand, and Martha, Miriam, and Aaron on the other. Mary and Moses have both been granted the greater gifts, while the others have received lesser gifts, despite the fact they have all communicated with God. Martha, Miriam, and Aaron have this so-called pledge of the Spirit.[48] As he previously explained: "There are also people in whom is only a little of our Lord; it is the so-called 'minor blessing,' the minor portion which is called the pledge of God" (3.12).

---

48. The translation here of "pledge" is complicated. It comes from a Syriac word, *'ūrbānā*, which is only found in the Liber Graduum and nowhere else in Syriac literature. Tracing back its potential origin from the *'rab*, Michael Kmosko concludes that it should either be translated as "to pledge" or as "to mix, to mingle." In his parallel Latin version, he chooses *commixtio*, implying that we should understand that Martha, Aaron, and Miriam have a co-mixing of the Spirit and not the full portion. They are still mixed with God and with sin. This usage of co-mixing is similar to what we will see in Pseudo-Macarius when he discusses this passage. That said, there is also strong evidence for "to pledge" being the better translation, as the "pledge of the Spirit" (from 2 Cor 1:22; Eph 1:14), from ἀρραβών, is translated in the Peshitta as *rāhbūnā*, which appears to be the noun form of *'ūrbānā*. For this argument, see Antoine Guillaumont, "Les 'arrhes de L'Esprit' dans le Livre des degres," in *Memorial Mgr Gabriel Khouri-Sarkis* (Leuven: Secrétariat du Corpus, 1969), 107–13.

Columba Stewart, however, argues for the definition of "to mix, to mingle" but concludes that ultimately the evidence remains ambiguous (*"Working the Heart of the Earth,"* 199–203). He does note that it is important that even if one decides to define it as "to pledge," this pledge must be understood in material terms. It is a present reality: "But one can say that the significance of the *'ūrbānā* of the Spirit is the same as that of the presence of sin in the human person: vivid, active and real. Whether it be commixture or pledge or both, it is certainly presence" (203).

Mary, however, has been granted the greater gift, "which is called the Spirit, the Paraclete. They [the Perfect] are fulfilled and replenished so that Christ dwells in them completely" (Lib. Grad. 3.12). Then follows a long discussion of why Mary was able to receive this greater gift: "This is how Mary's portion came to be larger than Martha's, as our Lord testified about her, 'Mary has chosen the better part': It was Mary who took up the Cross, which consists in practicing lowliness, the major commandments. She died to the world and its business and spiritually lived in our Lord; served him in the Spirit, was bound to him and glorified him all day, and she instructed and taught women and made them disciples for our Lord, receiving the Paraclete and serving our Lord in Perfection" (3.13). As we can see, Mary is the ideal representative of the Perfect. The better part that Jesus commends her for choosing is that she imitated the Lord by taking up the cross, being humble, following the major commandments, practicing asceticism, and serving the Lord spiritually by making disciples of other women.[49] Like Origen in his third interpretation, the author of the Liber Graduum sees Mary as following the major commandment to love God and neighbor.

He then discusses Martha's behavior and ministry, which he describes as Upright and in keeping with the minor commandments: "At the same time, Martha served our Lord with clothing and food, for himself and for the crowd that was with him, as she had a house and possessions, like Abraham and she led an Upright life. But Martha did not go so far as to take up the Cross.... So no one receives the Paraclete as long as his ministry is physically oriented, [if] he engages in taking and giving and his mind is tethered to the earth" (Lib. Grad. 3.13–14). Martha serves the Lord, meeting his physical needs. She supports him out of her own household, and he describes her as living an Upright life, meaning she follows the minor commandments. However, she has not taken up her cross like her sister has, and thus she has not received the major gift of the Spirit. She is still focused on physical ministries and has not embraced an ascetic life.

Before continuing, it is important to note another key difference between Mary and Martha for this author. Mary takes up the cross, and

---

49. This reference to Mary being in ministry to other women is one of a small number of texts (as we will see) that explicitly reference some sort of women's ministry. Here the author seems to depict a historical reality in which Mary ministered to other women. That said, being Perfect is not a gendered construct, as it appears the author of the Liber Graduum sees both men and women as capable of achieving this state.

Martha does not. The imitation of Christ through taking up the cross is an important theme throughout the Liber Graduum. As Renato Roux argues, this imitation takes the form of embracing Christ's humility in all things, sharing in his sufferings, and renouncing the things of the world.[50] In particular, this means the Upright one will be inferior to the Perfect one, "who has been nailed to the Cross, who cannot move hands or feet, not being able to conduct business with the earth, but who contemplates, searches, and meditates on what is above ... and who has died to this world" (Lib. Grad. 3.14). It is ultimately both the asceticism and the spiritual ministries of Mary and the Perfect that differentiate them from Martha and the Upright. And while there is potential for spiritual progress, and the Upright should aspire to become Perfect, the author recognizes that not everyone will be able or willing to accomplish this, and thus they will stay on the easier path and focus on the lesser commandments. Their reward in heaven will be lesser than for those who achieve perfection (Lib. Grad. 19.40).

The author, therefore, uses the sisters to illustrate some of his central themes and to highlight the differences between the two groups of Christians in his community. He also pays close attention to the details of the text in front of him. Martha participates in a physical ministry of serving and hospitality, and she is the head of the household. Mary, through listening to the Word and sitting at his feet, is seen by the author as one who then engages in a spiritual ministry, teaching and making disciples. Furthermore, from this one can see that he expands on the idea, seen earlier in Origen, that the two sisters are two different types of disciples. He presents the two sisters as real people who are part of the two categories, like the members of his own congregation, not simply as metaphors of the Upright and the Perfect. They are not only metaphors for the Upright and the Perfect; they are Upright and Perfect.

From this brief analysis, one can see that the author's use of Mary and Martha is intended to highlight the differences in the ministries of the Upright and Perfect and their spiritual progress. He further adapts the concept of the stages of Christian development first discussed in Origen. He also follows Origen in that he does not focus on their gender but on their roles as disciples. Unlike Origen, however, who argues that Mary has

---

50. Renato Roux, "The Doctrine of the Imitation of Christ in the Liber Graduum," in *Biblica et Apocrypha, Ascetica, Liturgica*, ed. Elizabeth A. Livingstone, StPatr 30 (Leuven: Peeters, 1997), 263.

not achieved Perfection, the author of the Liber Graduum sees Mary's act of sitting at Jesus's feet as indicative of her having already achieved the full measure of the Paraclete. He also expands Origen's reading by adding the concept of taking up the cross as the central difference between the two sisters. Martha, by engaging in primarily physical ministries, is further behind her sister despite living an Upright life because she has not taken up her cross. The author of the Liber Graduum does not depict Martha negatively; she is merely someone who has further to travel before reaching that which is full communion with God. Clearly, however, there is a hierarchy of Christian behavior, and the author views living like Mary as the better option.

Pseudo-Macarius's Spiritual Homilies

The theme of spiritual progress toward perfection is also at the center of Pseudo-Macarius's discussion of Mary and Martha in the Spiritual Homilies. The homilies were written anonymously in the fourth century, but within a few centuries, many well-known monastic figures, such as Macarius the Egyptian, Macarius the Alexandrian, and Symeon of Mesopotamia, were named as the text's author, perhaps to lend credibility to the work.[51] While significant scholarship has been done in an attempt to uncover the identity of the author, George Maloney accurately notes that "as yet there has not been a convincing conclusion that has been accepted by all patristic scholars."[52] From the text itself, however, we can derive some information about the author. First of all, geographical and cultural references imply the author had familiarity with both Asia Minor and Syria. He wrote in Greek but clearly was shaped in significant ways by Syriac Christianity, since he often uses Syriac vocabulary and imagery throughout the homilies, leading many scholars to assume that he was a monk located in northeast Syria during the middle of the fourth century.[53] He likely finished writing around the 380s, since Gregory of Nyssa shows

---

51. Stewart, *"Working the Earth of the Heart,"* 70.
52. George A. Maloney, "Introduction," in Pseudo-Macarius, *The Fifty Spiritual Homilies and the Great Letter* (New York: Paulist, 1992), 6. See also Hermann Dörries, *Symeon von Mesopotamien: Die Überlieferung der messalianischen "Makarios" Schriften*, TUGAL 55.1 (Leipzig: Hinrichs, 1941), 6–8. Dorries first discovered the manuscripts that attributed the works to Symeon, a known Messalian.
53. Maloney, "Introduction," 7.

familiarity with Pseudo-Macarius's Great Letter, which is thought to be his last work.[54]

Like the Liber Graduum, the Spiritual Homilies have been often associated with Messalianism, and there continues to be scholarly debate as to whether the author was connected with that movement. Some have claimed that the original author was Messalian but that the work was attributed to a non-Messalian author (i.e., Macarius the Egyptian) so that it could continue to circulate. Others have argued it was actually anti-Messalian only to be later used by Messalians as a core text.[55] However, Columba Stewart's argument that most of the Messalian controversy and Pseudo-Macarius's place within it comes out of the misunderstanding of Syrian imagery and language is compelling.[56] Furthermore, by stepping back and examining the text on its own terms, rather than against the backdrop of an obscure heretical movement we know little about, we can learn a significant amount about monasticism in Syria and Asia Minor during the fourth century.

The Spiritual Homilies do not systematically present the author's theology and practice. They reveal a more paraenetic approach, focusing on the instruction of fellow monks on a variety of issues. As Maloney summarizes it, the author of the homilies embodies a "practical monastic pedagogy."[57] The details of the text show that he led a type of cenobitic community, though one that was less regimented than the communities that developed in later centuries. It had, for example, no fixed times for prayers. There is a repeated focus on the call to serve God through renouncing all one's possessions and familial relationships, and adopting a life of asceticism. Having done this, the monk should no longer be distracted by the world and so should be able to better focus on the word of God. The text itself can be divided into three types: questions and answers, discourses on theological topics, and the Great Letter (containing a fuller discussion of the Christian life).

---

54. Stewart, *"Working the Earth of the Heart,"* 70.

55. See Andrew Louth, *The Origins of the Christian Mystical Tradition from Plato to Denys* (Oxford: Oxford University Press, 1981), 114; Kallistos Ware, "Preface," in Pseudo-Macarius, *Fifty Spiritual Homilies and the Great Letter*, xii. For a summary of the various positions of Pseudo-Macarius and Messalianism, see Hannah Hunt, *Clothed in the Body: Asceticism, the Body and the Spiritual in the Late Antique Era* (Abingdon: Ashgate, 2012), 126–28.

56. Stewart, *"Working the Earth of the Heart,"* 70–84.

57. Maloney, "Introduction," 12.

One of the primary themes discussed throughout the homilies is the idea of spiritual progress. For Pseudo-Macarius, there are three stages of every Christian's spiritual journey.[58] First, the heart is completely controlled by evil, caused by the sin of Adam. Next, one enters into a time of spiritual battle where the heart is struggling between sin and grace, which he summarizes in Hom. 17.4: "There are some persons in whom grace is operative and working in peace. Within, however, evil is also present hiddenly and the two ways of existence … vie for dominance within the same heart."[59] Most of his audience appears to be at this stage. The final stage is when the heart becomes completely controlled by God, sin has been totally thrust out, and the heart has been freed from all passions. At this stage, the heart is now fully united with God, mixed with the Holy Spirit, so that they can become one spirit. This is a stage of perfection even greater than that perfection embodied by Adam before his fall. While one can experience this perfection during this life, one will still be at risk of returning to an earlier stage, since evil still attempts to pull one back into sin. Complete and final perfection can only be experienced after death.

Pseudo-Macarius's interpretation of Mary and Martha appears in Homily 12 in the form of a question: "What is the meaning of Martha saying to the Lord about Mary: I am busy about many things and here she sits at your feet?" (Hom. 12.16).

> Answer: What Mary ought to have said to Martha, the Lord, anticipating her remark, said to her, that Mary had left everything to sit at the feet of the Lord and to bless God throughout the whole day. You see the value of her sitting came from love. To understand more clearly God's Word, listen. If anyone loves Jesus and really gives oneself attentively to him and not in a superficial way, but also perseveres in love, God is already planning to reward that soul for that love, even though the person does not know what he is about to receive or what portion God is about to bestow on him.
>
> Indeed when Mary loved Jesus and sat at his feet, Jesus did not merely place himself alongside her, but he endowed her with a certain hidden power from his very own being. For the words which God spoke to Mary in peace were an in-breathing and of a certain power. And these words penetrated her heart and brought his soul to her soul, his Spirit

---

58. For a good summary of the stages, see Ware, "Preface," xiii.
59. Translations of Pseudo-Macarius's Homilies and Great Letter come from *Fifty Spiritual Homilies and the Great Letter*, trans. Maloney.

to her spirit and a divine power filled her heart. The power necessarily wherever it is released, remains there as a possession which cannot be taken away. For this reason the Lord, who knew what he had given to Mary said, "Mary has chosen the good part." But not long after, the works of service that Martha kindly performed, brought her also to that gift of grace. She also received the divine power in her soul. (12.16)

In this answer, Pseudo-Macarius presents Mary as having left everything in order to pursue Christ. This is a key step in one's spiritual battle against the spirit of evil. As he writes in the Great Letter, "What does it means to renounce one's own self except to give oneself completely to the fraternity … and be totally available to the Word of God?" Mary has made herself completely available to listening to God in order that she might learn from him always. In this way, Mary exemplifies the asceticism aspired to within Pseudo-Macarius's community. He emphasizes, however, that her primary motivation for this behavior is rooted in love of God. Here he seems to argue that renunciation of the world is not enough; it must be motivated by a desire to persevere in loving God. He writes in Homily 10:

> Persons who love truth and God, who thoroughly wish to put on Christ with great hope and faith, do not need so much encouragement or correction from others. They never give up their longing for Heaven and their love of the Lord.… Such persons that pursue the Lord with such ardent and insatiable love are worthy of eternal life. For this reason they are deemed worthy also to be freed from passions and obtain fully the illumination and participation with the fullness of grace of the hidden and mystical communion with the Holy Spirit. (Hom. 10.1–2)

In fact, Mary's love leads to God rewarding her by filling her soul with the power and peace of God's own Spirit, "his soul to her soul, his Spirit to her spirit and a divine power filled her heart." This statement appears to reflect Pseudo-Macarius's understanding of the stage of Christian development when one's soul mingles with God's soul. In the next paragraph, Pseudo-Macarius explicitly uses this language: "How much more in the case of the Lord speaking to Mary or Zaccheus or the sinful woman … or with the Samaritan woman or the good thief? Did not power go out and the Holy Spirit mingle with the souls?" (Hom. 12.17).

This mixing/mingling language, drawn originally from Stoic philosophy, is important imagery for Pseudo-Macarius's understanding of one's relationship with God. As Stewart observes, "Ps. Macarius's distinction is to have made mixing language a central metaphor in his portrayal of the soul's involvement with both sin and with the Holy Spirit and to have done so with little apparent interest in the nuances of philosophical or theological vocabulary."[60] In his work, *mixing* is primarily used to state how the believer's soul has a real union with the Spirit of God.[61] In this union, the Holy Spirit enters the soul of the believer and makes it possible for sin, which was once mixed in the soul, to be cast out. In Hom. 24.4, Pseudo-Macarius compares this mixing to leavening dough and salting meat:

> Take the example of a person kneading flour without putting into it a leaven. However much effort he makes, turning it over and over and thoroughly working it up, still the lump remains unleavened and unfit to eat. But if the leaven is put into the dough, it draws to itself the mass of dough and works into all the leaven.... If there were some meat and someone were to take great pains with it but did not salt it with the salt that kills the worms and destroys foul odors, the meat would smell and decay and become unfit for men.
> In this same way, picture yourself as meat and unleavened dough. Realize that the salt and the leaven belong to another world, the divine nature of the Holy Spirit. If therefore the heavenly leaven of the Spirit, this good and holy salt of the Godhead be not mixed and inserted into the lowly nature of men, a person ... will not be leavened to put away the heaviness and be freed from the unleavened state of evil. (Hom. 24.4)[62]

At this stage of mixing with the "heavenly leaven of the Spirit," sin can no longer have a place in the heart of the Christian, and through this grace sin is slowly excised from the believer's life. Through the practice of the fruits of Spirit and the pouring out of God's grace, the Christian is able to "become more like and mingled with the good and divine nature" (Hom. 24.6). Eventually, the believer will be able to "become totally one with the

---

60. Stewart, *"Working the Earth of the Heart,"* 171. For a more in-depth look at mixing imagery in Pseudo-Macarius and Syriac writings, see 170–202. For the role of mixing imagery in the christological debates more broadly, see Aloys Grillmeier, *Christ in Christian Tradition*, trans. John Bowden (New York: John Knox, 1965), 129–32. For the potential relationship between Pseudo-Macarius and Stoicism, see Joseph Stoffels, *Die mystische Theologie Makarius des Aegypters: Und die Ältesten Ansätze Christlicher Mystik* (Bonn: Hanstein, 1908), 57–71.

61. Stewart, *"Working the Earth of the Heart,"* 171. See also 173–78 for a discussion of the different terms Pseudo-Macarius uses in his metaphors for mixing.

62. See also Hom. 18.10, 9.12, 46.3 for more examples of mixing imagery.

Spirit and thus is rendered holy and pure by the Spirit forever" (24.6). This is the final stage of Christian perfection and the goal of the Christian life.

Mary receives this gift of grace as a result of her love of God, which compels her to listen to the Word of God. But Pseudo-Macarius argues that Martha too receives this gift of the spirit as a result of her physical service. One sees in Pseudo-Macarius's writings a tendency to privilege the ascetic lifestyle and spiritual practices as the best way to battle the sin in one's heart and to achieve perfection, but he is clear that it is not the only way, since there is freedom through God's grace:

> Some of them do not wish to be a burden to others, while others carry on for themselves. Others receive gifts from those in the world and distribute them to the poor. *This latter is better.* Certain persons endowed with grace have only one concern about their own affairs. Others seek to help others. Others expose themselves to insults for the name of God.... In contrast, others strive to hide themselves even from encountering the world. These latter are more outstanding than the former.... These excel by far the first. Do you see how in the matter of perfection, good will towards God is found superior and richer? (Hom. 17.7–8)

Even within ascetic practices, there are behaviors and practices that are better than others as one strives toward perfection. What counts is not necessarily the action but rather the motivation. Martha, according to Pseudo-Macarius, is driven in her service by her love of the Lord. Because of this love, he argues, the Spirit will also be granted to her and will be mixed with her soul. This leads him to conclude: "Whoever, therefore, dedicates themselves to different forms of service and eagerly perform all such activities, motivated by zeal, faith, and love of God, that very service, after a while, leads them to a knowledge of truth itself. For the Lord appears to their souls and teaches them how the Holy Spirit operates" (Hom. 16.18). Thus, we can see that while Mary reaches this stage first through her ascetic practices, Martha also reaches the final stage. While their ministries were different, Pseudo-Macarius sees both as being recognized by God as forms of love and commitment. In this reading, Martha is still seen as a positive figure.

When we place Pseudo-Macarius's reading beside Origen's and the Liber Graduum, a few aspects of his reading stand out. First, like in the Liber Graduum, Pseudo-Macarius draws on Origen's stages-of-development interpretation and the paradigm of contemplative and active lives. Unlike in the Liber Graduum, however, Martha does not need to walk the same spiritual journey as Mary, but rather there can be multiple paths to spiritual perfection and receiving the Spirit, if one's actions are rooted in love of God. Love appears to be ultimately more important than specific practices. In this sense, Mary and Martha appear more like equals, even if Mary's way does lead her to progress more quickly. The hierarchy is less defined than the hierarchy in the Liber Graduum between the Perfect and the Upright.

Furthermore, Pseudo-Macarius adds a new dimension when he emphasizes that one cannot know when or how God is going to send the Spirit. It is a gift, a view shared by the author of the Liber Graduum. Pseudo-Macarius casts the better part as this eternal gift, rooted in his eschatological vision of the future and connected to the reception of the Holy Spirit. This is an important expansion from Origen's reading of the passage, because while Origen does discuss spiritual progression to perfection, he does not introduce the role of the Holy Spirit in that journey, nor does he emphasize the eschatological nature of this perfection. By incorporating the reception of the Spirit as the ultimate goal and gift of the faith, Pseudo-Macarius and the author of Liber Graduum both leave their own mark on the tradition of interpretation that began with Origen.

John Cassian's *Conferences*

Our third monastic author, John Cassian, wrote in the early fifth century. As Colm Luibheid notes, "He was a monk writing for monks. But in a more profound way, he was a salient example of the problem faced by any Christian who is somehow obliged to reconcile an admired past with the needs and burdens of his own day."[63] Unlike the previous two authors, who remain mostly unknown to us, John Cassian is a well-known monastic figure. Between 420 and 430 CE, he wrote two influential works in Latin: the *Institutes* and the *Conferences*. He joined a monastery in Bethlehem in 392, when he was still young, and after several years of monastic living, he journeyed to Scete in Egypt to learn from the Pachomian monastic community, which was seen as the heart of monasticism at this time. During this time, he was exposed to the teachings of Evagrius of Pontus and, through him, Origen as well. He also formed his basic doctrine of monas-

---

63. Colm Luibheid, "Preface," in John Cassian, *Conferences*, trans. Luibheid (New York: Paulist: 1985), xi.

tic life, which was highly influenced by Evagrius. He left Egypt around 400 CE and continued traveling, ending up in Marseilles and founding his own monastic community there. There he wrote the *Conferences* and the *Institutes*, both intended to help shape the monastic life by drawing on the practices of Egyptian monasticism.[64]

The *Conferences* is structured as a collection of wisdom from the desert fathers whom Cassian met while traveling around monastic communities in Egypt. It is uncertain how much of the *Conferences* should be attributed to Cassian's own voice and how much is attributable to the men whose discourses he reports.[65] The *Conferences* were written two decades after his time in Egypt, and so it is unlikely that they are direct quotations, but rather the *Conferences* are Cassian's way of bringing Egyptian monasticism into the West. As Owen Chadwick argues, "Nothing in the Conferences suggests that they are not an authentic presentation of moral and ascetic ideals practiced in Egypt."[66] That said, Cassian is the author of these discourses, and he clearly composed them in such a way that they reflect his own worldview. This is particularly important for our purposes since it gives us further insight into how Luke 10:38–42 was functioning in monastic communities in Egypt through the interpretive lens of John Cassian. As Columba Stewart argues, within the *Conferences* Cassian attempts to weave together the past wisdom of the abbas in order to chart out a path for the future of monastic living. This path depicts the spiritual journey of one seeking to see God.[67]

Cassian discusses the story of Mary and Martha twice: in *Conf.* 1 and 23. In *Conf.* 1.8, which Cassian presents as wisdom collected from the abbot Moses, he offers this interpretation: "To cling always to God and to the things of God—this must be our major effort, this must be the road that the heart follows unswervingly. Any diversion, however impressive, must be regarded as secondary, low-grade, and certainly dangerous. Mary and Martha provide a most beautiful scriptural paradigm of this outlook

---

64. For three thorough introductions to John Cassian, see Jean-Claude Guy, *Jean Cassian: Vie et doctrine spirituelle* (Paris: Lethielleux, 1961); Owen Chadwick, *John Cassian*, 2nd ed. (Cambridge: Cambridge University Press, 2008); Columba Stewart, *Cassian the Monk* (New York: Oxford University Press, 1998).

65. See Chadwick, *John Cassian*, 18–22, for a discussion of the evidence surrounding the *Conferences* as a historical source.

66. Chadwick, *John Cassian*, 22.

67. Stewart, *Cassian the Monk*, 40.

and of this mode of activity."⁶⁸ He explicitly names the story of Mary and Martha as functioning paradigmatically to illustrate a larger point about the importance of clinging to God always. The goal is to be able to achieve purity of heart. He argues in 1.7: "Everything we do, our every objective, must be undertaken for the sake of purity of heart ... to hold our hearts free of the harm of every dangerous passion and in order to rise step by step to the high point of love." Perfection, for Cassian, means having a completely pure heart, free of worldly distractions and secondary virtues and dedicated fully to the love of God.

Mary and Martha, then, offer him the perfect opportunity for discussing this journey and the potential dangers on the path. He continues:

> In looking after the Lord and His disciples Martha did a very holy service. Mary, however, was intent on the spiritual teaching of Jesus and she stayed by His feet, which she kissed and anointed with oil of her good faith. And she got more credit from the Lord because she had chosen the better part, one which could not be taken away from her.
>
> For while Martha was working hard, responsibly and fully intent on her job, she realized that she could not do all the work by herself and demanded help of her sister from the Lord.... Certainly, she summons Mary to a task that is not inconsequential but is a praiseworthy service. Yet what does she hear? "Martha, Martha you are full of worry and are upset over many things when actually you should be focused on a few or even one thing. Mary has chosen the good part and it will not be taken away from her." (1.8)⁶⁹

Even though Martha's service and hospitality to the Lord was good, it was not the ultimate good. The secondary virtues can serve as distraction from that which is more important. He argues that even though service is good, "the Lord establishes as the prime good contemplation, that is, the gaze turned in the direction of God. Hence we say that the other virtues, however useful or good, must be put on a secondary level" (1.8).

In this argument, we hear an echo of Origen's discussion in *Fr. Luc.* 171 of contemplation and activity. As in Origen's first interpretation, it appears that these two types of behavior, activity and meditation, are

---

68. Unless otherwise specified, translations of Cassian's *Conferences* come from *Conferences*, trans. Luibheid.

69. It is worth noting here that Cassian is clearly familiar here with the longer textual variant of 10:41–42, since he references "a few or even one thing" as being necessary.

found within the same person and not to be understood as two different groups of people. Instead of placing them as equal parts of the believer's life, however, Cassian argues that contemplation is actually the higher good. Activity can distract from that higher good. He continues: "In saying this, the Lord locates the primary good, not in activity, however praiseworthy ... but in the truly simple and unified contemplation of himself" (1.8). One does not need both, because contemplation is the final and ultimate goal of the Christian: it turns one's gaze toward God in all things. In this way, Cassian appears to draw from Evagrius, who briefly discusses this passage in his *Foundations of the Monastic Life*:

> And if the thought of expensive foods should arise at all for reasons of hospitality, leave it there and give it no credence at all, for the adversary is setting a snare for you; he is setting a trap trying to dislodge you from your stillness. You know how the Lord Jesus blames the soul that busies itself with such things, namely Martha: "Why are you concerned and troubled by many things? There is need for one thing," namely, he says, to listen to divine word, and after that everything follows along easily. (Evagrius, *Rer. mon. rat.* 3 [Sinkewicz])

Evagrius clearly focuses on hospitality as a distraction, and potentially a trap, that pulls the Christian away from the goal of listening to the divine word. Cassian, however, thinks that hospitality and service are virtuous acts, though he notes that these acts fall short of the primary good. In order to turn one's sight to God and fully achieve purity of heart, one must be fully focused on contemplation.[70] As Stewart observes, while Evagrius was concerned about the soul's pilgrimage through the world and Cassian shared that concern, "for him the dominant issue was gathering fractured intentions and scattered energies into the singleness of purpose in 'contemplation alone.' For the monk, as for Mary of Bethany, this means the contemplation of Christ."[71]

Cassian gives his reasons for why contemplation is ultimately better than service in the last part of *Conf.* 1.8 and in 23.3. In *Conf.* 1.8, he concludes: "But one must look carefully at this. In saying, 'Mary chose the good part,' He was saying nothing about Martha and in no way was He

---

70. For further discussion between the differences between Origen, Cassian, and Evagrius on the relationship between action and contemplation and the journey of the soul, see Chadwick, *John Cassian*, 82–109.

71. Stewart, *Cassian the Monk*, 49.

giving the appearance of criticizing her. Still, by praising the one, He was saying that the other was a step below her. Again, by saying it will not be taken away from her, He was showing that Martha's role could be taken away,—since the service of the body can only last as long as the human being is there—whereas the zeal of Mary can never end." Here Cassian makes an important distinction. He is careful to state that Jesus is not criticizing Martha in this story but rather ranking their behaviors. The reason that Mary's choice will never be taken away from her is that her choice is eternal, whereas Martha's choice is rooted in her physicality, which will ultimately pass away. This reveals that the primary difference between the two types of actions is eschatological in nature. Mary's behavior, that is, contemplation, means that she will come to see God, which is the eternal goal of the Christian.

For Cassian, such contemplation is a foretaste of the eternal kingdom of heaven. It is the quest for the vision of God. Finishing that quest and seeing God means that one now has knowledge of both of God and of the things of God and that this knowledge and blessing will never pass away with the physical things of this world. To see God is to have complete purity of heart and to have reached perfection. As Stewart argues, "Martha's corporeal ministry will come to its inevitable end with her death. Cassian works through a series of other biblical texts to argue that works are useful but cannot produce the perfection of love that is God's promise of life now and forever."[72] Since Mary's behavior is rooted in the spiritual, it will not pass away when her physical body has died. This is why she has made the better choice.

Cassian further expands this argument between the two types of behavior in *Conf.* 23.3, when he again turns to discuss the two sisters and the nature of Mary's "better part":

> What then is that one thing which is so incomparably above those great and innumerable good things, that, while they are all scorned and rejected, it alone should be acquired? Doubtless it is that truly good part, the grand and lasting character of which is thus described by the Lord, when Mary disregarded the duties of hospitality and courtesy and chose it: Martha, Martha, you are careful and troubled about many things: but there is but need of but few things or even of one only. Mary has chosen the good part which shall not be taken away from her. Contemplation

---

72. Stewart, *Cassian the Monk*, 55.

then, i.e., meditation on God, is the one thing, the value of which all the merits of our righteous acts, all our aims at virtue, come short of. (trans. Alexander Roberts, *NPNF* 2/11:520)

He continues with the illustration of different metals being of different worths. A basic "alloy metal," he argues, is often considered valuable unless one places it beside silver. Furthermore, silver is considered very valuable, but its value diminishes in its owner's sight when it is placed beside gold. Gold is outshone by precious stones, and so on. In same way, the other virtues, hospitality, service, acts of holiness, "are not merely good and useful for the present life, but also secure the gift of eternity, yet if they are compared with the merit of Divine contemplation, will be considered trifling and so to speak, fit to be sold" (23.3 [Roberts]). The other virtues, as part of God's creation, are very good. All things have their proper time and place. Creation is nothing compared to heaven, however, and contemplation of God is comparable to dwelling in heaven, while the other virtues are rooted firmly in this earth (23.3). Thus, Mary has made the better choice in forsaking the other virtues in order to pursue meditating on God.

Cassian is aware, though, that is impossible to always make that choice and that no one can constantly meditate on God while living on this earth.[73] He continues in *Conf.* 23 by making the point that even the apostle Paul often had to turn his heart away from his contemplation to serve the many needs of his communities:

> Further we confidently assert that even the Apostle Paul himself who surpassed in the number of his sufferings the toils of all the saints, could not possibly fulfil this, as ... when in writing in the Thessalonians he testifies that he worked in labour and weariness night and day. And although for this there were great rewards for his merits prepared, yet his mind, however holy and sublime it might be, could not help being sometimes drawn away from that heavenly contemplation by its attention to earthly labours. (23.5 [Roberts])

---

73. See Cassian, *Conf.* 23.5: "Who when ministering support to the poor, or when receiving with benevolent kindness the crowds that come to him, can at the very moment when he is with anxious mind perplexed for the wants of his brethren, contemplate the vastness of the bliss on high, and while he is shaken by the troubles and cares of the present life look forward to the state of the world to come with a heart raised above the stains of earth?" (Roberts).

Thus, Cassian acknowledges that even the most faithful Christians cannot always choose the better part, but sometimes acts of hospitality and ministry are necessary in this life. Martha showed hospitality to Jesus; Paul provided spiritual guidance to his congregations. These are valuable and necessary actions, but the Christian should not mistake them for the best actions. This is why Cassian can say that Jesus is not criticizing Martha when he rebukes her. Her actions are good and in fact even righteous. Mary's choice to contemplate God was the better choice, because she chose the eternal act. Turning one's sight to God is always better than choosing to focus on the things of this earth.

Stewart argues that Cassian's reading of Mary and Martha accomplishes three goals within his larger theological project.[74] First, Cassian is able to use the story of the two sisters as a biblical paradigm to divide human existence into two different aspects: active and contemplative. Second, he is able to demonstrate how contemplation bridges the temporal divide between earthly life and eternal life. Third, he is able to discuss the relationship between present action and present contemplation and their relationship to the hope for the future. Stewart is correct in these claims, because it does seem that Mary and Martha serve as the ideal biblical paradigm for these arguments. Furthermore, Cassian's discussion shows that, while he draws on the interpretations of Origen and Evagrius, he is not limited to them.

In summary, Cassian uses the story of Mary and Martha as a paradigm to discuss his understanding of the relationship between action and contemplation. Unlike the authors of the Liber Graduum and the Spiritual Homilies, he does not refer to different types of people, ascetics and nonascetics. Instead, he draws from Origen's first interpretation of contemplative and active practices as different dimensions of the same person to argue that physical service and contemplation are behaviors in which all Christians participate. However, unlike Origen's first reading, in which the two virtues are mutually dependent, Cassian is clear that contemplation is best. Mary's choice was that she chose contemplation, which is the ultimate good. Contemplation allows one to focus on the eternal things of God. It is through contemplation that one is brought to finally see God and therefore truly reaches perfection. On the other hand, Cassian acknowledges that Jesus was not criticizing Martha. He recognizes that acts of hospitality and

---

74. Stewart, *Cassian the Monk*, 49.

service are good and sometimes necessary actions. They are not ultimate, however; these acts will not last into eternity. Cassian's practical concern is that on this earth, no one can constantly turn one's gaze to God, and that human needs and the concerns of one's community will at times dictate that one participate in those lesser virtues. It is not until one passes into eternal life that one will be able completely to meditate on God. Similar to Pseudo-Macarius and the author of Liber Graduum, eschatology shapes how Cassian interprets this passage.

Silvanus in the Sayings of the Desert Fathers

The first three monastic texts we examined repeatedly emphasized Mary's behavior as the more praiseworthy choice. They present her as the sister who is further along on her spiritual journey. The author of Liber Graduum, Pseudo-Macarius, and Cassian all conclude that Mary's decision to focus on the spiritual and the eternal means that she should be elevated. As Hellen Dayton notes, this strand of interpretation places Mary as spiritually higher and more advanced than her sister.[75] Even though all the authors also grant that Martha's behavior should be seen as good, and even in some circumstances that it ultimately will be rewarded, it is clear that they each favor Mary. Furthermore, even though they adapt and expand Origen's interpretations, they still follow his basic interpretation of the passage, with Mary representing contemplation and Martha representing action. Without a doubt, this is the predominant trend of monastic interpretation of Luke 10:38–42.

However, the next text I examine shows that there is an awareness that this interpretation could be taken too far. Silvanus, in the Sayings of the Desert Fathers, offers an alternate reading, addressing potential concerns that this passage might downplay the necessity of work. Silvanus clearly holds (like Cassian) that work is at times both necessary and good. In doing so, he appears to pick up a different thread of Origen's interpretation, in which both the active and contemplative forms of discipleship can and should be part of the Christian life.

---

75. Hellen Dayton, "On the Use of Luke 10:38–42—Jesus in the House of Mary and Martha—for Instruction in Contemplative Prayer in the Patristic Tradition," in *Archaeologica, Arts, Iconographica, Tools, Historica, Biblica, Theologica, Philosophica, Ethica*, ed. J. Baun et al., StPatr 44 (Leuven: Peeters, 2010), 207.

The Sayings of the Desert Fathers, in which our text is found, is a collection of the wisdom attributed to the desert fathers and mothers, who moved out into Egyptian wilderness in order to practice rigorous asceticism. The collection circulated in different arrangements and in different languages throughout the fifth and sixth centuries, revealing its popularity, particularly among the Eastern church.[76] The Sayings, each attributed to a various father or mother, mostly contain short apothegms but also some short moral narratives, intended to reveal how a particular virtue could be practiced. The collection offers an important look into the teachings and lives of the desert monks and the monasticism they practiced during this time period. The father Silvanus was, according to tradition, a Palestinian who led twelve disciples into the Sinai region in 380 CE.[77] Twelve sayings are attributed to him in the Alphabetical Collection of Sayings. In the fifth one, the story of Mary and Martha begins and ends a particularly amusing story: "A brother went to see Abba Silvanus on the mountain of Sinai. When he saw the brothers working hard he said to the old man, 'Do not labour for the food which perishes (John 6:27). Mary has chosen the good portion.' The old man said to the disciple, 'Zacharias, give the brother a book and put him in his cell without anything else'" (Silvanus, APalph 5 [Ward]). The brother remains in his cell all day and after dinner wonders why no one has come to get him for a meal. He eventually wanders out to ask Abba Silvanus why this happened. Abba Silvanus responds to him: "'Because you are a spiritual man and do not need that kind of food. We, being carnal, want to eat and that is why we work. But you have chosen the good portion and read the whole day long and you do not want to eat carnal food.' When he heard these words, the brother made a prostration, saying 'Forgive me, Abba.' The old man said to him 'Mary needs Martha. It is really thanks to Martha that Mary is praised'" (APalph 5 [Ward]). Abba Silvanus reversed the usual way of reading the story of Mary and Martha.

---

76. In particular, there were two popular collections: the alphabetical collection known as the Apophthegmata patrum alphabetica (APalph) and the later systematic collection, which was categorized by theme, known as the Apophthegmata patrum systematica (APsys). See John Wortley, "Introduction," in *The Book of the Elders: Sayings of the Desert Fathers, the Systematic Collection*, CSS 240 (Collegeville, MN: Liturgical Press, 2012), xiii–xxi, for a discussion on the different manuscript traditions of the text.

77. *The Sayings of the Desert Fathers*, trans. Benedicta Ward (Kalamazoo, MI: Cistercian, 1975), 222.

In the beginning of the story, we see the newly arrived brother offer the interpretation of the story that we have come to expect. One should not be distracted by earthly work; one should be engaged constantly in prayer and study of the word of God. Silvanus, however, rejects this reading and elevates Martha's behavior as necessary for sustaining Mary, and he presents his disciple with the impossibility of always choosing the act of contemplation.

In the systematic collection of the sayings, this story is found in the chapter on the monastic virtue of discretion or discernment (APsys 10.99). This chapter begins with the assertion from Anthony that "There are some who wore their bodies away with askesis but became far from God because they did not have discernment" (10.1 [Wortley]). This is one of the longest chapters in the entire collection, with example after example of the desert fathers and mothers attempting to instruct their disciples on the importance of properly discerning situations as they arise. One abba, Achilles, denies two men a net but grants the third one's request of a net, because of the specific condition of that man's soul (10.18). Another, Abba Poemon, instructs some disciples to fight their passions, whereas others he instructs to flee from them (10.38). All of these reflect a concern for ultimatums that could lead to the destruction of the souls of their followers.

In Silvanus's interpretation on Mary and Martha, we see such a concern for proper discernment in his rejection of an extreme reading of Luke 10:38–42 that would view any work at all as inherently negative. Taking it to its logical conclusion, Silvanus points out that no one would be able to eat if the monastic community never engaged in physical labor. In a way, this seems similar to Cassian's argument that no one is able to sit and contemplate God all the time, but Silvanus takes the point even further when he makes an exegetical point that has mostly been ignored. If Martha had not been the one serving and hosting Jesus, Mary would not have been able to sit at his feet in the first place. He aptly observes that it is only because of Martha's service that Mary is able to choose the better part, earning her Jesus's praise. Silvanus shows that while contemplating God is indeed a worthy goal, one still needs to eat. Physical service is necessary and not something that should be condemned by those who think they have achieved a higher level of spirituality. In this argument, Silvanus mirrors Origen's claim that both the active and contemplative life are valuable and necessary to the Christian. With his focus on discernment, he represents a break with the interpretations we have seen so far, however, because he does not present the two sisters on a spiritual journey. His focus seems to be on the realities of the Christian life in the present, and as such his reading does not reflect any eschatological concern. His message is practical and offers a warning against monastic readings that would take the story of Mary and Martha to a dangerous extreme.

Ephrem and Basil: Different Directions

Each of the above authors expands on ideas found in Origen's interpretation of Luke 10:38–42. Even though they each use his ideas in different ways and to create their own theological arguments, they are still focused on the two sisters as a way to discuss the relationship between service and contemplation. There are other voices within the monastic tradition, however, that reflect different interpretive concerns other than the ones introduced by Origen. While these voices reflect a minority position within monastic literature, they are important to note briefly. Ephrem's *Commentary on the Diatessaron* and Basil's *Long Rule* show these alternative readings.

Ephrem

In his *Commentary on the Diatessaron*, Ephrem's interpretation of Luke 10:38–42 represents a notable departure from the readings we have studied so far. Ephrem lived and wrote in the fourth century, spending most of his life in the caves close to Edessa.[78] While he did not adopt a completely eremitic lifestyle like the desert fathers, he did appear to practice a strict form of asceticism near Edessa. He wrote homilies, poetry, hymns, commentaries, and treatises, and his works are some of the most important Syriac texts from the fourth century. He interprets the story of Mary and Martha briefly:

> *Mary came and sat at his feet.* This was as though she were sitting upon firm ground at the feet of him who had forgiven the sinful woman her sins. For she had put on a crown in order to enter into the kingdom of the First-Born. *She had chosen the better portion,* the Benefactor, the Messiah

---

78. Carmel McCarthy, "Introduction," in *Saint Ephrem's Commentary on the Diatessaron*, JSSSup 2 (Oxford: Oxford University Press, 1993), 10. For a discussion of the degree that Ephrem practiced asceticism and the ways his lifestyle might have been embellished by later biographers, see Joseph P. Amar, "Christianity at the Crossroads," *RelLit* 43.2 (2011): 1–21.

himself alone as it is said, *It will never be taken away from her.* Martha's love was more fervent than Mary's, for before he had arrived there, she was ready to serve him, *Do you not care for me that you should tell my sister to help me?* When he came to raise Lazarus to life, she ran and came out first. (*Diat.* 8.15 [McCarthy])

Ephrem makes the surprising claim that Martha actually loved Christ more than Mary for two reasons. First, she was ready to serve him even before he arrived. Second, after the death of Lazarus and Jesus's subsequent arrival (in John 11:20), she ran out to meet him first when her sister stayed behind at home. For Ephrem, this is evidence that Martha actually loved Jesus more, despite the fact he still grants that Mary has received the "kingdom of the First-Born." The surprise is that he begins his interpretation in such a way that one expects him to claim that Mary loved Jesus more. He connects Mary sitting at the feet of Jesus to the story of the sinful woman who washes Jesus's feet (Luke 7:36–50), but it should be noted that he does not confuse the two.[79] They are still separate characters, and he states that by doing what she does, Mary of Bethany is able to receive a crown.[80] Furthermore, he grants that her portion will never be taken away, and that portion is the Messiah himself. Only then does he claim that Martha actually loved more.

Regrettably, he does not develop this interpretation any further. We have no more information about Martha's reward or any other comparison to her sister that would give us insight into how his view aligns or diverges from the other readings we have seen. It is enough for our purposes, however, to note that he does in fact place Martha's love for Christ above her sister and that this is a distinctive perspective, particularly in the fourth century.

Basil

Basil of Caesarea takes an entirely different approach in his interpretation of Mary and Martha. Basil was a fourth-century theologian and monk who became one of the most important figures in the development of cen-

---

79. Origen also has a connection to the sinful woman in Luke 7:38 in his interpretation in *Fr. Luc.* 171. See the above section on Origen's second interpretation.

80. The conflation of Mary with other biblical Marys and women will be discussed in more depth in ch. 5.

obitic life. Coming from a devoutly Christian family (which eventually produced three bishops, a monk, and a nun), he studied rhetoric, theology, and the arts. He traveled widely, most notably to Athens and Caesarea. Eventually he felt compelled to forsake the secular and adopt the ascetic lifestyle. Drawing on his own experience of the desert fathers, he adapted the monastic system into what monasticism would come to look like in the West. He created a strict and detailed set of guidelines for how monasteries should function, called the *Long Rule*, and wrote many other ascetic discourses and homilies. He discusses the story of Mary and Martha in two locations: the *Long Rule* 20.3 and *Moral Rule* 38.1. Uniquely, he does not focus on Mary at all, but rather focuses specifically on Martha and the proper way to show hospitality to one's guests.[81]

First, in the *Moral Rule* 38.1, he states: "The Christian should offer his brother simple and unpretentious hospitality."[82] He follows this with scriptural warrants and quotes John 6:8–11 and Luke 10:38–42 in full with no additional comment.[83] He fleshes out this interpretation in more detail in the *Long Rule*, however, where he argues that Martha's problem was that she was too focused on preparing a multitude of dishes for her guests:

> If you also change your daily fare, then, for rare quality or abundance in food to please a brother's palate, you imply that he takes delight in sensual pleasure and you heap reproaches upon him for his gluttony by the very preparations you make, since you thus accuse him of finding pleasure in such things. In fact, have we not often guessed who or what sort of guest was expected, upon seeing the appearance and quality of the preparations? The Lord did not praise Martha for being anxious about much serving, but He said: "Thou art careful and art troubled about many things; few things-nay, one thing only is necessary": "few things"—that is, for the preparation of the meal, and "one thing"—that is, the purpose, namely, to satisfy need. (*Long Rule* 20.3)

---

81. Evagrius also discusses hospitality in his interpretation, but he also pulls in other themes such as listening to the word of God. Basil ignores those other themes.

82. Translations of Basil come from Basil of Caesarea, *Ascetical Works*, trans. M. Monica Wagner, FC 9 (Washington, DC: Catholic University of America Press, 1962).

83. It should be noted that he quotes the longer variant of Luke 10:41–42: "Martha, Martha, you are careful and are troubled about many things: few things, nay, one thing only is necessary."

118   Beyond Mary or Martha

As one can see, Basil does not discuss Mary at all in this passage. Instead he uses the story of Martha to discuss the kind of hospitality one should prepare for visitors. He argues that by preparing too many dishes, one misses the point of hospitality, which is simply to satisfy the immediate needs of one's guests. If a person prepares too many or too extravagant of dishes, then he could actually insult his guests, because it could be inferred that he believes them to be gluttonous. The reason behind Jesus's reproach of Martha is not rooted in her dismay over her sister's behavior, but instead is rooted in her concern about the appearance and quality of her preparations. This anxiety meant she could not focus on the one necessary thing: meeting the basic needs of her guest, Jesus.

Basil's interpretation of the passage is a departure from the interpretations of Origen and other monastic interpreters.[84] There is no mention of Mary's behavior and the importance of contemplation over action.[85] There is no spiritual hierarchy or discussion of the journey toward Christian perfection. That said, Basil offers an interpretation that is still rooted in the details of the text itself. He interprets the "many things" not as a reference to earthly things more broadly but rather as a specific reference to the amount of dishes Martha is preparing, and thus the passage offers insight into Jesus's view of proper hospitality. Martha's story becomes a prime example for the monastic community on how to prepare for guests, serving as warning not to overdo it.

These two works are important because they reveal that there was a diversity even within the ascetic tradition over how to properly interpret

---

84. An interpretation that is more line with predominant interpretive tendency can be found in Monastic Constitution 1.1. This text was originally attributed to Basil, but most scholars today agree that it was not written by him. It is suggested, however, that the author of this text (perhaps Eustathios of Sebastia) was highly influenced by Basil and his form of monasticism. For our purposes, the monastic constitutions presents a view highly similar to Cassian on the topic of Mary and Martha, concluding: Ἡ γάρ θεωρία τῶν μαθημάτων ἀναδέδηκε τοῦ σώματος τήν διακονίαν. This has led Hellen Dayton to claim that the Monastic Constitution contained a summary of the orthodox interpretation of Luke 10:38–42 ("On the Use of Luke 10:38–42," 208). The dating and the authorship being so uncertain, however, places it beyond the scope of this chapter.

85. Bovon (*Luke 2*, 76) argues that this reading shows Basil's appropriation of Origen's reading about the primacy of the contemplative life, but I disagree. Basil does not seem to be concerned with Origen's interpretation here. This is not to say that Basil would disagree with Origen about the contemplative life, but rather to state that Basil highlighted a different part of the passage in order to discuss a different issue.

the story of Mary and Martha. As seen, both of these texts diverge from the themes introduced by Origen. Moreover, each text is clearly rooted in an close exegetical reading of the story itself, but focusing on different details. Ephrem focuses on Martha's preparedness to serve, while Basil focuses on the theme of hospitality. While the major part of early monastic tradition treated the two sisters as paradigms the stages of the Christian spiritual journey, it is important to recognize that other interpretations existed as well.

Conclusion

This overview of early monastic interpretations of Luke 10:38–42 leads to several conclusions. First, Origen was undeniably an influential interpreter of the passage, and his interpretation in *Fr. Luc.* 171 set the stage for the direction of interpretations in the centuries to come. Origen introduced the paradigm of Martha and Mary representing action and contemplation as two different virtues needed for a Christian life. His interpretation does not end with that distinction, however. He also introduces a hierarchy between the two sisters being at different stages along their respective spiritual journeys, with Mary having a deeper understanding of the essentials of the Christian faith. Origen is also responsible for presenting the interpretation that Martha is somatic and distracted by worldly things, whereas her sister is focused on only the spiritual. As we have seen, these interpretations in different ways were adopted, expanded, and occasionally ignored or contradicted by the readers who followed, but Origen's reading is clearly the lens through which many monastic interpreters viewed the story.

For many scholars, the claim that Origen's reading of contemplation and action became the monastic reading ends the discussion.[86] But Origen himself contains more than just one reading, and by focusing on this one, the other interpretations are ignored. Origen's multifaceted reading holds together a tension between the two different types of behavior represented by the two sisters, and he deals with that tension in multiple ways. An overconcentration on Origen's first reading, however, has led to a lack of serious scholarship on how the different monastic readers interpreted this text, and consequently the complexity and creativity of later monastic interpreters has been overlooked.

---

86. See 71 n. 1, above.

Even the writers who follow Origen's general interpretive structure often diverge and expand on it in some important ways. For instance, in the Liber Graduum, the author uses Mary and Martha to represent the Perfect and the Upright, using the idea of spiritual development seen in Origen to argue that Mary is further along her journey. He expands it, however, by introducing the concept of taking up the cross as a way to further explain their differences. Pseudo-Macarius uses a similar metric to argue that Mary's behavior and her focus on the spiritual ultimately leads her to perfection, the mingling of her soul with God's soul. Interestingly, however, Martha's physical service will ultimately also lead her to the same goal, only later than her sister. Cassian focuses on Mary's behavior as contemplation and how this meditating on God ultimately leads her to see God. Martha's behavior, while also good, is rooted in the physical and eventually will pass away. Cassian, like Origen, holds both behaviors as part of the same person, only instead of seeing them as equally important, Cassian ranks them, with contemplation always being preferable. These authors are influenced by Origen in their readings but do not simply repeat him.

All three of these writers also introduce an explicitly eschatological reading of this passage lacking in Origen. They are concerned with the eternal consequences of the different behaviors. Each author uses the story to discuss what the better part, that which will never be taken away from Mary, actually is. For the author of the Liber Graduum, being one of the Perfect means that one receives the Spirit of God, and this is the better part. For Pseudo-Macarius, Mary's soul becomes mingled with God, and this is the eternal goal. For Cassian, one sees God and the eternal, and this will be more fully known after all the physical things of this earth have passed away. This focus on the better part and its eternal implications is a core theme shared by most monastic readers that is mostly absent in Origen's interpretations.

Beyond expanding on Origen's reading, there are also significant pieces of Origen's multipart interpretation that are not focused on by later interpreters. For instance, many of the Scriptural parallels he attaches to Luke 10:38–42 are not used by the later readers. Romans 2:29 and the concept of "Jews in secret" drops out of the later interpretations. Similarly, the comparison between the gentile church and Jewish synagogue disappears. In part, this reflects the different contexts of the writers. Origen lived in Alexandria, a diverse cultural community where it is clear that he engaged with Judaism. Cassian, on the other hand, does not have the same concern, having lived in a much different cultural context, in a cenobitic Christian community. These different contexts affected which interpretations were useful for later interpreters, and therefore several pieces of Origen's interpretations ultimately fell out of the conversation.

Furthermore, we can see that some monastic writers diverge from or even disagree with the basic roadmap Origen introduced. In the Sayings of the Desert Fathers, Silvanus pushes back against the prevalent monastic reading that contemplation like Mary's should be practiced all the time at the expense of any physical work. He shows the impracticality of such a reading and offers that Mary is only capable of listening to Jesus because her sister had already done all the work. Ephrem argues that Martha's behavior shows that she actually loved Jesus more than her sister because she was willing to serve him. Basil ignores the larger argument entirely and instead uses the story to argue for modest practices of hospitality. This shows that while Origen did inform the direction most monastic interpreters took in their readings, his reading was not the only reading, and in fact other important monastic figures exegeted the story in other ways. There is a plurality of monastic interpretations in the fourth and fifth centuries.

Sweeping claims about the so-called monastic reading of this story should therefore be avoided, but some generalizations can be made. First, this overview shows that the monastic interpreters understood this story to be an important text for understanding the newly developing monastic world. The tension between Mary and Martha reflected monastic concerns between the different types of Christian behavior, and thus the story is interpreted through that lens, even though the specific monastic contexts shaped the way the story is ultimately read. The author of the Liber Graduum, for instance, is wrestling with two different groups of believers (the Upright and the Perfect) under his care with very different ways of practicing their faith. Luke's story of Mary and Martha allows his use of Scripture to further explore the implications of those differences and the eternal distinction between the two. The Perfect and the Upright is a central theme for this author, and Luke 10:38–42 is one of the core biblical examples that he turns to in order to explain it.

Similarly, we see that Pseudo-Macarius is concerned with the idea of souls mingling with God's soul as the ultimate goal of Christianity. In Luke 10:38–42, he finds two biblical examples to discuss the different journeys believers take to reach that goal. Cassian uses the story when he is discussing what it means to cling to God always and how Christians should turn their gaze to God. This is a core theme throughout the *Conferences*, and the story of Mary and Martha is used to further explicate his understanding of contemplation. The two sisters are an important scriptural reference for each of these authors as they turn to discuss central themes of their understanding of discipleship. Their readings are not simply reheated ideas inherited from Origen but rather creative interpretations that speak to their specific concerns.

Second, in none of these interpretations is there a focus on the gender of Mary and Martha. They are primarily viewed as disciples, and as such their story is used to instruct both male and female believers. Other than one reference in the Liber Graduum to Mary instructing other women, gender is never even mentioned. While many feminist readers have viewed this as an unfortunate abstraction that ignores the reality of their genders, I would argue that by presenting the two women as disciples of Christ and highlighting this as their primary identifying marker, the monastic interpreters are actually elevating them.[87] Mary and Martha become key figures in the discussion of how best to practice the faith alongside other biblical heroes such as Moses and Paul. Their discipleship is not diminished because they are women.

Third, the tension and paradoxical nature of the story that we discussed in chapter 2 still exists in these interpretations as well. The monastic authors wrestle with how to understand Martha and Jesus's response to her. While we find that Mary is viewed in a better light in most of these stories, Martha is never viewed negatively. Her service can never be fully dismissed. Martha also receives the same reward as her sister, though in a different way. Physical service is still seen as necessary, even if it is not as desirable as contemplation. We see it in the fact that the Perfect need the Upright and in the fact that even Cassian acknowledges that no one can meditate all the time. Mary's way might be better, but Martha's is acceptable too. This reveals that these interpreters recognize that this story gets to a core tension with the Christian faith more broadly. They are careful readers who understand that there is a complicated relationship in Christianity between physical acts of service and spiritual practices.

In conclusion, the monastic interpreters of Luke 10:38–42 highlight concerns they notice in the text itself. While Origen introduces a basic roadmap for interpretation, different authors writing in specific monastic contexts interpret the passage in a such way that it speaks to the needs of

---

87. Schüssler Fiorenza, *But She Said*, 54–55.

each community. Their readings elevate Mary and Martha as disciples of Christ and reflect a concern for how to best practice the Christian faith. By escaping overly simplistic claims about how monastic readers engaged with this text, we are able to better see how their interpretations highlight concerns embedded in the text itself that have often been missing from modern discussions of Luke 10:38–42.

4
Patristic Preachers

> Even now, you see, we do enjoy something of that [better part]. You've left your shops and offices, you've laid aside your family matters, you've gathered here, you are standing still and listening; insofar as you are doing this, you are like Mary. And it's easier for you to do what Mary does, than for me to do what Christ does. However, if I do say anything that is Christ's, that's why it nourishes you, because it is Christ's, because it's our common bread, which I too live on, if in fact I live.
> — Augustine, *Sermo* 103.4

Introduction

In this chapter, I focus on a selection of early Christian preaching on Luke 10:38–42. My attention to these sermons, however, does not imply a hard and fast line between monastic writers and preachers. After all, many monastic figures were also preachers, and many ecclesial leaders were deeply influenced by monasticism. But in this chapter, I want to show that the passage was being received beyond the walls of the monastery by various congregations in the early Christian world. After the legalization of Christianity in the fourth century, larger numbers of people were coming to hear the Scriptures being preached, and lectionary readings and homilies were the primary means through which ordinary people encountered the biblical narratives, since they had very little access to the Bible as a written text.[1] This leads us to the question: How was the Bible heard by these diverse groups, by the men and women, rich and poor, lay and

---

1. James O'Donnell notes that "the average Christian of [this] age, including those in congregations, was less attached to the written form of the word and encountered it more through the formal oral presentation of liturgical readings and preaching." See O'Donnell, "Bible," in *ATA*, 100.

ordained, who made up the congregations? Homilies on Mary and Martha's encounter with Jesus can give us a unique insight into how this story was being interpreted for congregations in the fourth and fifth centuries.

While the passage is featured by a number of important Christian figures during this period, I have chosen to focus on three: Augustine of Hippo, John Chrysostom, and Cyril of Alexandria. Each preached one or more sermons on Luke 10:38–42, and, importantly, they arrive at three distinct interpretations, offering us insight into the variety of interpretations that coexisted during this period. Augustine interprets the two sisters entirely in light of the present and future church. Chrysostom interprets the passage as a story ultimately about the necessity of having discernment, while explicitly rejecting certain monastic interpretations. Cyril interprets the passage entirely as a story about proper practices of hospitality. Such diverse readings further support my claim that there were diverse traditions of interpretation on this passage during the fourth and fifth centuries that move far beyond the contemplation/action dichotomy. Each preacher uses the passage to instruct his congregation in how they should embody different aspects of their Christian faith. At the core, each sermon is practical, offering concrete advice on how to apply the story to life. Once again, the gender of Mary and Martha is never a central theme in interpreting the passage; each preacher presents the lessons he finds in the story as relevant for disciples more broadly, not just women.

The Sermon in the Early Christian Church

Before turning to discuss each bishop and the specifics of his congregational setting, however, it is helpful to begin with a brief overview of the nature and function of the sermon more broadly. While the early church was diverse and existed within many different cultures, there were general trends surrounding the practice of early Christian worship and the sermon in particular. Traditionally, it is thought that the genre of the early Christian sermon evolved out of two types of speech in the ancient world: the Jewish synagogue sermon and Greco-Roman rhetorical discourse (particularly the form found within the Stoic tradition).[2] While there is

---

2. Thomas K. Carroll, *Preaching the Word*, MFC 11 (Wilmington, DE: Glazier, 1984), 12–13.

still much scholarly uncertainty about the development of the synagogue sermon, most agree that it developed over time into an lesson given by a rabbi in order to interpret the text at hand.[3] To the synagogue sermon the Christian sermon owes two things: first, its focus on specific biblical texts, and second, its location within a liturgical setting.

The fourth- to fifth-century sermon was also influenced by Greco-Roman rhetoric. Thomas Carroll points to Cynic and Stoic speeches to show how these diatribes were specifically constructed to be informal speech, one that "had the pose of informal plainness, an intimate and confidential tone and divagations from and returns to the main theme."[4] These speeches followed specific rules of rhetoric and as such were intended to both persuade and to entertain. Many of the great preachers in the fourth century were trained as rhetoricians, and many Greco-Roman rhetorical techniques made their way into the Christian sermon.[5] Thus, the Christian sermon became rooted specifically in a liturgical setting and based around a sacred text like the Jewish synagogue sermon, but it was also delivered in a specific rhetorical style, intended to persuade and engage its listeners, similar to the Stoic diatribes of Epictetus.

While the sermon was a part of Christian worship as early as the first century, it became a central part of the service in the fourth and fifth centuries for a few different reasons. First, the legalization and subsequent rise in popularity of Christianity in this century led to larger crowds. This in turn led to the building of larger and more elaborate church buildings and the development of pulpits and platforms from which preachers could speak to larger crowds. Second, in the fourth century, the liturgical year was being finalized, along with a rise in festivals around saints and martyrs, which led to more opportunities for worship services (making more opportunities for sermons). Third, skilled rhetoricians were in great demand, allowing for preachers, who were trained in rhetoric, to become extremely popular.[6] These changes led to the sermon becoming a central part of the worship.

Thus, in the fourth century, the sermon was a core part of the liturgical life of the church. Within the sermons, which are rooted in the exegesis of

---

3. Otis Carl Edwards, *A History of Preaching* (Nashville: Abingdon, 2004), 11.
4. Carroll, *Preaching the Word*, 12.
5. Edwards, *History of Preaching*, 12.
6. Edwin Charles Dargan, *History of Preaching*, 2 vols. (New York: Hodder & Stoughton, 1905), 1:65–67.

specific biblical passages, important theological ideas were being fleshed out in practical and pastoral ways. The preacher of this time period was concerned with interpreting the text in clear and accessible ways for his specific setting.

Augustine

Augustine is universally regarded as one of the most prolific and talented thinkers in the Western church. Because of Augustine's own memoir, the *Confessions*, and an early biography written by his companion, Possidius, much of Augustine's life and work is known.[7] He was born in the city of Thagaste in 354 and studied in Carthage during his late teens. During this time he had a son, Adeodatus, with an unnamed common-law wife, and converted to Manichaeism. He became a professor in rhetoric, teaching in Thagaste, Carthage, and Rome, before finally coming to teach in Milan in 384, where he met Ambrose (Possidius, *Life* 1). His conversion occurred in 386. After living a semimonastic life, he was ordained a priest in 391 despite some initial hesitation (*Life* 4).[8] In 395 he was appointed to the episcopacy. He began preaching after his ordination to the priesthood (which was unique because only bishops were permitted to preach in that region). He died in 430, after almost forty years of ministry. During his ministry, he discussed the story of Mary and Martha frequently, since he viewed the two sisters as representative of the present and future life of the church. His figurative interpretation of the passage marks a departure from the interpretations we have studied so far. Before turning to his analysis, however, I first discuss Augustine's view of preaching and his view of Scripture.

---

7. See Possidius, *Life of St. Augustine*, trans. Herbert T. Weiskotten (Princeton: Princeton University Press, 1919), which offers a contemporary account of Augustine's life. For a thorough piece of secondary scholarship on Augustine's life and work, see Frederick van der Meer, *Augustine the Bishop: The Life and Work of a Father of the Church*, trans. Brian Battershaw and G. R. Lamb (London: Sheed & Ward, 1961).

8. This is also supported by Augustine's own account in *Serm.* 355.2, where he mentions that he used to avoid cities without sitting bishops, lest he be forced into an office. For a more recent discussion of Augustine as preacher, see William Harmless, *Augustine in His Own Words* (Washington, DC: Catholic University Press of America, 2010), 122–55.

Augustine as Preacher

Augustine likely preached over four thousand sermons during his thirty-nine years of ordained ministry. Only around eight hundred of those are still known to us today.[9] He regularly preached multiple times a week and continued preaching until his last illness.[10] Augustine quickly became well known for his sermons throughout North Africa and beyond. Even today, he stands as one of the most important preachers in Christian history. As Frederick van der Meer observes:

> In [Augustine's] genius for the right word, he surpasses all the church fathers. Never once does he fail to make an idea unforgettable. Never once does he fail, when he desires so, to turn a simple statement into an aphorism. He never uses the sharpness of his mind to wound; on the contrary, every word he says carries its conviction by reason of an irresistible tenderness. Everyone who reads a number of his sermons will carry away the same impression as the men of his day, for no words from the pulpit have ever so fully come from the heart or combined that quality with such brilliance as did the words spoken by this one man in this remote corner of Africa.[11]

What is perhaps even more remarkable about Augustine's sermons is that, following the custom of his day, they were not written out beforehand but rather were delivered extemporaneously. *Notarii* or scribes were present for the sermon and took detailed notes while he was speaking for the purpose of circulation.[12] After his sermons were transcribed, they were eventually placed in collections, which Augustine had originally intended to edit before circulation. He was unable to complete this task before his death, however, meaning the sermons we do have represent a

---

9. Hildegund Müller, "Preacher: Augustine and His Congregation," in *A Companion to Augustine*, ed. Mark Vassey (Chichester: Wiley-Blackwell, 2012), 301.

10. Possidius, *Life* 31.4: "Up to his very last illness he preached the word of God in church incessantly, vigorously, and forcefully, with clear mind and sound judgment." Translation from "Life of St. Augustine," in *Early Christian Biographies*, trans. Roy J. Deferrari, FC 15 (Washington, DC: Catholic University of America Press, 1952).

11. Van der Meer, *Augustine the Bishop*, 412.

12. Possidius observes, however, that no matter how good a preacher Augustine appears on paper, the scribes were unable to capture the actual skill of Augustine. See *Life* 31.

fairly clear look at what Augustine actually preached to his congregation in Hippo.[13]

There is much to be learned about Augustine's congregational setting from the sermons themselves. Though we know little about the standards for preaching in North Africa because no sermons remain from the time before Augustine, we do know that before him only bishops were permitted to preach in Hippo. Augustine, however, was uniquely called to this task while still a presbyter after the elderly bishop in Hippo requested his service (Possidius, *Life* 5). Thus, we know that his preaching career began early in his ordained ministry. Augustine does not often remark in his sermons on specific social or political events, however, making individual sermons difficult to date, as they focus more on universal Christian concerns and less on localized issues.[14]

From his sermons, one can see that there was a sort of lectionary already in place in Hippo with an Old Testament passage, an epistle, and a gospel reading being read during each service.[15] There also appears to have been set readings for feast days as well. Augustine usually began preaching after one of these readings, referencing the passage just read. His congregation stood, while he sat.[16] Augustine often addresses the noise level, noting that he has a weak voice, and he repeats things if necessary to ensure important points were better received (*Enarrat. Ps.* 50.1). He often comments on the fact when he feels he has his congregation's full attention, and he makes disparaging comments about poor attendance or compliments high attendance, particularly if a pagan festival was going on elsewhere (*Serm.* 198.1).

---

13. See George Lawless, "Preaching," in *ATA*, 676, for the remarkable claim: "the fact that the bishop was prevented by his death from revising his complete homiletic corpus, as he had intended, preserves virtually everyday discourse. Thus we possess it in a form which approximates its original composition and delivery while allowing for the errors of copyists in their subsequent transcriptions through the centuries."

14. Müller, "Preacher," 298. Though this could be a side effect of the fact that only his more generalized sermons were copied; after all, there are 3,200 sermons that we do not have.

15. Van der Meer notes: "Augustine is anxious that the Bible should be read in the traditional sequence, which in the year 400 already corresponded to the ecclesiastical year and included some arrangement of which we know very little, for a *lectio continua* of the most important books" (*Augustine the Bishop*, 344).

16. For instance, Augustine makes an observation about them standing in *Serm.* 103.4.

Augustine was flexible, adapting to the various circumstances before him. This can be most clearly seen on those occasions when the lector would read a different passage from the one Augustine was expecting. Augustine took this as a sign from the Spirit and then would begin preaching on this new passage instead.[17] That said, he acknowledged that he was often unhappy with the end result of his sermons: "Indeed, in my case, too, my own discourse nearly always displeases me. For I am covetous of something better, which I frequently enjoy inwardly before I begin to express it in intelligible words; and then, when my capacities of expression prove inferior to my inner apprehensions, I grieve over the failure which my tongue has manifested in co-operating with my heart, for I desire that my auditor should have the same complete understanding of the subject which I myself have" (*Catech.* 7 [trans. Arthur West Haddon, *NPNF* 1/3:284]). Furthermore, he would at times acknowledge when a specific detail in the text in front of him was causing him some difficulty, acknowledging that some details were difficult to unravel correctly.[18] He would then readjust his interpretation, coming at the text from a different angle, revealing his immense talent at interpreting Scripture.

Augustine believed that improvement in preaching came not from increased rhetorical skill but through increasing one's knowledge of the Scripture. Rhetoric was still an important skill, but ultimately, for Augustine, having the wisdom that comes from knowing the word was ultimately more important for one's congregation. Augustine rejects rhetoric for rhetoric's sake throughout his sermons, and he exhorts others to do the same in his handbook *On Christian Doctrine*: "He helps his hearers more by his wisdom than his oratory; although he himself is less useful than he

---

17. For examples of the wrong passage being read, see *Enarrat. Ps.* 138.1 and 50.1.

18. See, for instance, this selection from *Serm.* 265.9: "Many exegetes have given a variety of interpretations and have sought ways of approaching their listeners. They have said things not opposed to faith: one man this, another that, without departing from the rule of truth. If I were to say that I know why the Lord gave the Spirit twice, I would be lying.... Therefore I profess before you the fact that the Lord did give the Holy Spirit twice, but I am still searching and longing to achieve greater certainty on the why. May the Lord help me through your prayers.... I do not know the answer, therefore, but I can conjecture [*existimem*] without yet knowing, without yet having an answer that is certain (though I do most certainly know that he did give the Spirit twice), nor will I hide my lack of knowledge as long as I am still conjecturing. If the answer I suggest is true, may the Lord confirm it; if another answer appears truer, may the Lord give it" (unless otherwise indicated, Augustine quotations from Ramsey).

would be if he were eloquent speaker also. But the one to guard against is the one whose eloquence is no more than empty words.... Such eloquence is mistaken for truth.... Furthermore, a man speaks more or less wisely in proportion as he has made progress in the Holy Scriptures" (*Doctr. chr.* 4.5). Ultimately, for Augustine, the preacher's own life was the best sermon; thus, the preacher should always strive to fully embody the Scriptures he has studied.[19] Augustine believed preaching was not a task that should be undertaken lightly. In *On Christian Doctrine* he offers eight goals that he thinks the preacher should be intent on accomplishing. The Christian preacher should (1) interpret and teach the Scriptures, (2) defend the right faith, (3) teach everything that is good, (4) unteach anything that is evil, (5) endeavor to win over the individuals hostile to truth, (6) arouse careless individuals, (7) impress on ignorant people what is happening, and (8) impress on them what to expect (*Doctr. chr.* 4.46).[20] Throughout his sermons, we can see how he attempts to accomplish these goals.

Preaching was a draining task for Augustine, though, and at times he even admits his own exhaustion. On the anniversary of his ordination, he delivered a sermon about how he did not wish to preach and that he tried to avoid it, and yet, he said: "But to preach, to refute, to rebuke, to build up, to manage for everybody, that's a great burden, a great weight, a great labor. Who wouldn't run away from this labor? But the gospel terrifies me" (*Serm.* 339.4). That said, he continued to do it, because he believed the Lord had called him to this work. He viewed himself as a servant simply trying to convey through his sermons what he had learned: "I am just a waiter, I am not the master of the house; I set food before you from the pantry which I too live on, from the Lord's storerooms, from the banquet of that householder who for our sakes became poor, though he was rich, in order to enrich us from his poverty" (*Serm.* 339.4).

Augustine and Scripture

Intersecting Augustine's approach to preaching is his view of Scripture. For our purposes, there are three key points.[21] First, unlike modern ser-

---

19. Augustine, *Doctr. chr.* 4.29: "Let the beauty of his life be as it were a powerful sermon."

20. See Lawless, "Preaching," 675.

21. See William Harmless, "Augustine the Exegete," in *Augustine in His Own Words*, 156–201.

mons that mostly focus on one specific passage at a time, Augustine was comfortable moving between passages he felt illustrated the same point. This was because, for him, there is complete unity in Scripture between the Old and New Testaments.[22] As Michael Cameron observes: "Augustine came to think of the Scriptures as just such a unified body, which replicates the body of Christ. After rereading the books of the prophets and apostles, which he once thought were contradictory, Augustine suddenly found peering back at him a single divine Face."[23] For Augustine, each book, despite being written at a different time, reflects the same work of the Spirit and a single hypothesis. As he once summarized, "There is but a single discourse of God amplified through all the scriptures, dearly beloved. Through the mouths of many holy persons a single Word makes itself heard" (*Enarrat. Ps.* 103.4.1).

Second, because of the hand of the Spirit at work in the Scriptures, passages can have both literal and figurative meanings. Throughout his sermons Augustine engages in both types of interpretation. He often appears to prefer figurative readings, viewing them as more beneficial to his hearers, but he also engages in literal interpretations.[24] For Augustine, it is the job of the interpreter to discover which one is the most useful for fostering a fuller love of God and neighbor. This can be difficult, and many go astray trying to interpret the literal as figurative and vice versa:

> To this warning against treating figurative expressions, that is metaphorical ones, as though they were meant in the literal, proper sense, we also have to add this one, to beware of wanting to treat literal, proper statements as though they were figurative. So first of all we must point out the method for discovering if an expression is proper or figurative. And here, quite simply, is the one and only method: anything in the divine writings that cannot be referred either to good, honest morals or to the truth of the faith, you must know is said figuratively. Good honest morals belong to loving God and one's neighbor, the truth of the faith to knowing God and one's neighbor. As for hope, that lies in everybody's own conscience,

---

22. See Augustine, *Faust.* 4.2–9; 7.2–48, for a discussion on the unity of the two Testaments.

23. Michael Cameron, "Augustine and Scripture," in *The Cambridge Companion to Augustine*, ed. David Vincent Meconi (Cambridge: Cambridge University Press, 2014), 205. See Augustine, *Conf.* 3.4.9, for Augustine's original view of Scripture before his conversions.

24. See his literal reading of Gen 1–3, for instance.

to the extent that you perceive yourself to be making progress in the love of God and neighbor, and in the knowledge of them. (*Doctr. chr.* 10.14)

An interpreter adjudicates between the figurative or literal meaning by asking which meaning points to an increase in love of God and neighbor. This brings us to the third point: at the core of his hermeneutics is his belief that a good reading points to a greater love of God and neighbor. If a reading does not point to this, then the passage has not yet been properly understood.[25] As we turn to analyze his preaching on Mary and Martha, we see that charity is a driving force behind his interpretation.

Augustine on Mary and Martha

Augustine discusses Luke 10:38–42 and the story of Mary and Martha repeatedly. He devotes two sermons specifically to Luke 10:38–42 (*Serm.* 103–4), but he also discusses the two sisters in a number of other sermons (*Serm.* 169, 179, 255, 352; *Tract. Ev. Jo.* 15.18). Augustine contributes a thread of interpretation that we have not before seen. His primary thesis is that the two sisters represent two different types of life: Martha corresponds to the life of the present church, and Mary corresponds to the life of the future church. His interpretive approach, however, is nuanced, and, in order to correctly unpack all of his claims about how we should read this passage, we must work carefully through each of his main points.

Martha and the Nature of Her Service

Like many of the interpreters we have examined so far, Augustine has a consistently positive view of Martha's activity. Martha is taking care of the poor, welcoming the stranger, and doing the works of service that all Christians should be practicing. As he says in *Sermo* 255: "So Martha was doing what was required by the needs of hungry and thirsty men; she was preparing, with all the trouble she was taking, something for the saints,

---

25. See Augustine, *Doctr. chr.* 1.35.39: "So anyone who thinks that he has understood the divine scriptures or any part of them, but cannot by his understanding build up this double love of God and neighbor, has not yet succeeded in understanding them." See Luke Timothy Johnson, "Augustine and the Demands of Charity," in *The Future of Catholic Biblical Scholarship*, by Johnson and William S. Kurz (Grand Rapids: Eerdmans, 2002), 93–121.

and for the Saint of saints himself, to eat and drink in her house" (*Serm.* 255.2). In *Sermo* 103.2, he presents her as literally serving her Lord and Creator, something that Augustine does not think should be overlooked. Furthermore, more than simply participating in good work, Martha is an example that all Christians should follow:

> Services performed for the poor are good, and specially so are the offices duly performed for God's saints, the religious respect that is owed them. These are rendered as a duty, you see, they are not just optional gifts, as the apostle tells us: If we have sown spiritual goods for you, is it a great thing if we reap your material benefits? They are good. I am encouraging you in their performance, and building you up in the word of God: do not be slack about welcoming the saints. Sometimes, by welcoming those they did not know, people have welcomed angels without knowing it. (*Serm.* 103.5)

Martha's behavior indicates how all Christians should behave, meaning that her service was not only good, but it was also necessary. After all, works of service are not just optional gifts. Christians are commanded to welcome those in need of hospitality.

Connected to this good and necessary service, Augustine argues that one can see that Martha is blessed because of it. Jesus, according to Augustine, did not actually need any physical care. He could have had angels come to take care of his physical needs, but instead he chose to let Martha care for him: "Still, it was a maidservant receiving the Master, a sick woman receiving the Healer and Savior, a creature receiving the Creator. Needing to be fed in spirit herself, she received him to be fed in the flesh. The Lord, you see, wished to receive the form of a slave, and having received the form of a slave to be fed in that form by slaves, thus doing them a favor, not seeking one" (*Serm.* 103.2). This was a specific favor that Martha received from the Lord when she was permitted to "serve him in the flesh." Augustine says that his audience might be tempted to grieve the fact they are not able to serve the Lord in this way. He imagines that they might be envious of her, saying, "We might be able to welcome people into our homes, but we could never welcome the Lord in his physical form." Augustine rejects this potential complaint by reminding his congregation in multiple sermons, whenever the topic turns to Martha's service, that when a person welcomes "the least of these" they are physically welcoming Jesus himself. As he says in *Sermo* 103: "Don't be disappointed, don't grumble because you were born at a time when you could not now see the Lord in the flesh. He hasn't, in fact, deprived you of this privilege and honor: when you did it, he says, to one of the least of mine, you did it to me" (*Serm.* 103.2). This should encourage the Christian to welcome anyone in need of hospitality, because she can receive the same blessing that Martha received.

The main problem with Martha's service, however, is that it is fleeting. One day there will be no need for the services that she provided. As Augustine concludes in *Sermo* 255.2, it was a great service that she provided, but it was a passing one. In the coming kingdom, there will be no more mouths to feed, no more people to welcome and serve, and thus no need for the type of service that Martha provides. Augustine turns to address Martha directly in *Sermo* 169.17: "You are serving the hungry, serving the thirsty, making beds for people to sleep on, offering your house to those who wish to stay there. All these things come to an end. The time will come when nobody's hungry, nobody's thirsty, nobody sleeps. So your concern will be taken away from you." In the kingdom of God, all of the forms of Martha's service will no longer be needed.

This is Augustine's most important point about Martha's service: it was good and necessary, yes, but her service will pass away, because one day there will be no one needing hospitality; everyone will be home. Similarly, it is important for Augustine's audience to have that perspective about their own acts of service:

> Let us consider, then, our busy involvement with many things. Service is needed by those who wish to restore their tissues. Why is this? Because people get hungry, because they get thirsty. Distress calls for compassion. You break your bread to the hungry, because you have found him hungry. Abolish hunger; whom will you break your bread to? Abolish traveling; to whom will you offer hospitality? Abolish nakedness; for whom will you find clothes? Let sickness be no more; whom will you visit? No more captivity; whom will you redeem? No more quarreling; whom will you reconcile? No more death; whom will you bury? In that age, that world that is to come none of these evils will exist, and therefore none of these services. (*Serm.* 104.3)

No evil will exist when the kingdom of God is fully known, and therefore one day, all acts of service that keep Christians busy in the present will not be necessary. Moreover, they will not even be able to be performed, because there will be no one left to serve. This is why, according to Augustine, while Martha has chosen a good part, Mary has chosen the better part.

Mary and the Better Part

Augustine's discussion of Mary focuses on three things: (1) the better part as the eternal part, (2) the nature of the one thing that was necessary, and (3) whether we can participate in this eternal better part in the present. First of all, Augustine repeatedly emphasizes that the better part is inherently so because it is eternal. Unlike Martha's part, which will eventually pass away, Mary's choice to sit at the feet of the Word will last forever: "So, Mary has chosen the better part, and it shall not be taken away from her; what she chose, you see, will abide forever, and that's why it shall not be taken away from her. She wished to busy herself with the one thing; she was already in possession of it: 'For me it is good to cleave to God'" (*Serm.* 104.3, quoting Ps 73:28). Mary's choice was to be with God, and that is something that will last for eternity.

In this sense, the one thing necessary is to be united with God. In *Sermo* 103, this is a major theme: the one thing necessary is complete unity with God. Augustine draws on the example of the Trinity to further flesh out what he understands this one necessary thing to be:

> So, magnify the Lord with me, and let us exalt his name together as one. Because there is one thing necessary, that one supreme thing, that oneness where Father and Son and Holy Spirit are one. Just see how unity is commended to us. Certainly our God is a trinity, a threesome. The Father is not the Son, the Son is not the Father, the Holy Spirit is neither the Father nor the Son, but the Spirit of them both; and yet these three are not three gods, not three almighties, but one almighty God, the trinity of persons, one God; because there is one thing necessary. To this ultimate oneness nothing can carry us through, unless being many we have one heart. (*Serm.* 103.4)

Augustine understands this complete unity with God and with one another as the ultimate goal. Martha is distracted by many things, which we have already established are good and necessary, but the ultimate goal is oneness rather than multiplicity. Eventually there will only be one thing, and that thing is to worship with one mind and heart the Creator.

The question remains, however, whether this is something that can be accomplished in the present or whether it must wait until the end of time. To answer this question, Augustine turns to Paul in the letter of Philippians. According to his reading of Phil 3, not even Paul has attained this one thing, though he was striving to one day attain it:

> Mary has chosen the better part, which will not be taken away from her. She has chosen to contemplate, chosen to live on the Word.... That was the one and only life, to contemplate the delight of the Lord (Ps 27:4). This we cannot do, though, in the dark night of this world.... "Therefore, I," he says, "do not consider myself to have grasped this one thing. So what am I to do? Forgetting what lies behind, stretched out to what lies ahead, I follow the direction—I'm still following—toward the palm of God's summons up above in Christ Jesus. I am still following, still forging ahead, still walking, still on the road, still extending myself; I haven't yet arrived." (*Serm.* 169.17)

Augustine does not think this is something that we can fully attain here "in the dark night of this world." It is something that Christians are currently journeying toward, but no one will arrive there during this life. Living on the word alone and therefore spending all one's time contemplating the Lord is an eternal reward.

That said, Augustine does believe that occasionally we are able to achieve glimpses of this future life. For instance, he points out that when Christians celebrate the feast days after Easter, they are celebrating a past event, but also a reality that has not yet happened. By partaking in those festivities and subsequent rest from their labors, they are glimpsing a small piece of what is to come (*Serm.* 255). Similarly, when people come to church and listen to the sermon, they are participating in a glimpse of what heaven will be:

> But now, what share have we got of that one, insofar as we have any at all, as long as we are here? How much is it that we already have from that one? What is it that we have from there? Even now, you see, we do enjoy something of that sort. You've left your shops and offices, you've laid aside your family matters, you've gathered here, you are standing still and listening; insofar as you are doing this, you are like Mary. And it's easier for you to do what Mary does, than for me to do what Christ does. However, if I do say anything that is Christ's, that's why it nourishes you, because it is Christ's, because it's our common bread, which I too live on, if in fact I live. (*Serm.* 104.4)

Thus, gathering for worship and listening to the word read and discussed in the sermon is a foretaste of what is to come. Augustine is clear, however, that it is not something we can fully attain. Not even Mary could fully attain it during her lifetime. It can be increased over time, but it is not until the next life that "it will be perfected, it will never be taken away" (*Serm.* 103.5).

This is similar in some ways to what we have seen already in monastic writers such as Cassian and Pseudo-Macarius. Martha's actions are good but fleeting, whereas Mary's actions are eternal. Christians are on a journey toward this eternal vision of being one with God. Where Augustine differs strongly is on the point of whether the glimpses of eternity should be the focus of the Christian in the present. For Augustine, acts of service are necessary for the Christian to do. They are not simply inevitable distractions. All Christians are called to do them.

In fact, Augustine is critical of the idea that Martha was reprimanded for her service or that some might suggest because of this that we should ignore the needs of our neighbor and instead sit and contemplate the word all day:

> If that's really the case, let people all give up ministering to the needy; let them all choose the better part, which shall not be taken away from them. Let them devote their time to the word, let them pant for the sweetness of doctrine, let them busy themselves with theology, the science of salvation; don't let them bother at all about what stranger there may be in the neighborhood, who may be in need of bread or who of clothing, who needs to be visited, who to be redeemed, who to be buried. Let the works of mercy be laid aside, everything be concentrated on the one science. If it is the better part, why don't we all grab it? (*Serm.* 104.2)

Augustine continues that, of course, we cannot all focus solely on the one thing because there are sick people in need of healing; there are hungry people; there are people in prison and in need of hospitality. Because of this, all Christians must necessarily be focused on many things here in this life. Even though we might get glimpses of eternity by attending worship and listening to the word, as Augustine concludes: "But how much really is it, that by listening and understanding you derive and grasp of that life which Mary represented; how much really is it?" (*Serm.* 104.2). How Augustine resolves this tension is by focusing on the two sisters as not representative of different types of followers in this life, but rather as representative of our present and future selves. In this way, Augustine departs from a dominant trend in monastic interpretation.

Martha as the Present Church; Mary as the Future Church

Augustine's point about the nature of Mary and Martha is most clearly presented in *Sermo* 104. For him, the two sisters always represent two different lives: "So you see, beloved, and as far as I can tell you now understand, that in these two women who were both dear to the Lord, both lovely people, both disciples of his; so you see, and understand something of great importance, those of you who do understand, something even those who don't understand ought to hear and to know; that in these two women two kinds of life are represented: present life and future life, toilsome and restful, miserable and beatific, temporal and eternal life" (*Serm.* 104.3). Augustine believes that both women are disciples and worthy of praise. The difference between them is not one of kind but rather of time. Martha represents the church, which is currently on a journey. Her work is the work of the faithful, who are still struggling along the road. She is doing journey work, not at-home work, as he preaches in *Sermo* 255. Mary, on the other hand, represents the church in the life to come. She has arrived at home, and there is no more service to be done. Only those who have finished their earthly journey can sit always at the feet of the Lord, listening to the Word. In fact, Mary's life represents the eventual reward that Christians will receive after having run their races well. This is the reward of rest and contemplation that will be given Martha and to all believers after a life of service (*Serm.* 104.6).

Anne-Marie La Bonnardiere argues that it is fitting that Augustine would present this reading during this stage in his own life.[26] Augustine, she notes, states often that he wished to remain in a monastic life instead of being called to ordained ministry and eventual appointment to the episcopacy. He would have certainly preferred to sit and contemplate the word all day, and yet he says, in his sermon on the anniversary of his ordination, that he felt he had no choice. The gospel compelled him to serve in this way (*Serm.* 339.4). Thus, Augustine served the church and was dedicated to its service, looking forward to that time when he could sit in eternal rest, contemplating the Lord.

While Augustine might appear to have a certain personal connection to the service of Martha, however, it is important to state that he does not interpret this passage on the individual level. Martha represents the life of the church communally as it exists here on earth. Mary represents the church in the life to come, when the kingdom of God will be made fully known. When Augustine stops to address Martha directly in his sermons, encouraging her that she should remember that one day she will receive the reward of rest and that she need only continue to run her race well, he was actually speaking to his whole congregation, as well as himself,

---

26. La Bonnardiere, "Les deux vies," 424.

because they were all Marthas. It is through this form of service that eventually they would get to partake in the work of Mary, as La Bonnardiere summarizes it: "C'est par le Verbe fait chair qu'on parvient au Verbe Principe; par Marthe qu'on s'efforce de devenir Marie."[27]

This view is concisely summed up in his *Questions on the Gospels*, in which he responds to a question about the nature of the better part:

> That Martha received him into her home signifies the Church that exists now, which welcomes the Lord into her heart. Her sister, Mary, who sat at the Lord's feet and listened to his words signifies the same Church but in the age to come, when she ceases work and service to the needy and enjoys wisdom alone. Martha, therefore, is occupied with much service, because the Church is now burdened with such works. Her question about why her sister does not help, however, provides an occasion for the Lord's statement in which he shows that this Church is now worried and bothered about many things, although only that one thing is necessary, which it attains through the merit of this service. But he says that Mary chose the better part, which will not be taken away from her and it is understood to be the best because, through this present part one tends to that which is to come, and it will not be taken away. (*Quaest. ev.* 2.20)

Martha and Mary are both the church, and the church will only get to the life of Mary after performing all the necessary service of Martha. It is a communal experience, not an individual one.

There is one interpretive problem that Augustine still must solve, however, and that is Jesus's seeming critique of Martha in his response to her complaint. First of all, he notes that the doubling of her name seems to imply the affection Jesus holds for her (*Serm.* 103.3). Jesus does not condemn Martha, and more importantly, Jesus does not attempt to diminish her work, saying he finds no fault in it (*Serm.* 104.2). Rather, Augustine believes that Jesus is making a distinction between two acts so that Martha will have the proper orientation toward her work. One day, all that troubles her will pass away, and she too will be given the reward of rest: "But it will be taken away for your benefit, so that the better part may be given you. Toil, you see, will be taken away from you, so that rest may be given you. You, my dear, are still on the high seas; she is already in port" (104.2).

La Bonnardiere argues that there is a similarity between how Augustine discusses Mary and Martha and how he discusses Peter and John in

---

27. La Bonnardiere, "Les deux vies," 424.

John 21.[28] According to Augustine, in John 21, Jesus seems to imply that he might love John more than Peter despite Peter's constant affirmations that he does love Jesus. In Augustine's reading, Peter also represents the present church, like Martha, while John parallels Mary in representing the future life of the church (*Tract. Ev. Jo.* 124.5).[29] In analyzing his discussion of this duo, one can see how he understands Jesus's response to Martha, since initially it seems unfair that Jesus would seem more harsh both toward Martha and toward Peter: "But in this active life the more we love Christ, the more easily we are delivered from evil. But he loves us less as we now are, and from this, therefore, he delivers us in order that we may not always be such. But there he loves us more fully because we shall not have what would displease him and what he would remove from us…. Therefore let Peter love him so that we may be delivered from this mortality; let John be loved by him so that we may be preserved in that immortality" (124.5). Augustine believes that Christ loves John and Mary more than Peter and Martha only because they have achieved perfection in immortality and are fully restored to their relationship with God. There is no more sin, temptation, or evil weighing them down. Martha and Peter are still on that journey, and Christ is working alongside them to bring them to the place of Mary and John. Mary and John are both able to focus on the one thing of loving God, while Peter and Martha are still held back by a multiplicity of necessary actions.

---

28. La Bonnardiere, "Les deux vies," 420.

29. As one can see, the language is very similar: "And so the Church knows two lives, preached and commended by Divinity to her, of which one exists in faith, the other in direct vision; one in the time of sojourning abroad, the other in an eternity of dwelling; one in toil, the other in rest; one in the way, the other in one's homeland; one in the effort of action, the other in the reward of contemplation … one comes to the aid of the needy, the other is there where it comes upon no one in need; one forgives another's sins that its own may be forgiven it, the other neither suffers what it may forgive nor does what it may ask to be forgiven it; one is scourged by evils that it may not be exalted in its goods, the other by so great a fullness of grace lacks every evil so that without any temptation to pride it adheres to the highest good; one sees the difference between goods and evils, the other sees things which are only good; therefore, one is good but still wretched, the other is better and happy. This [first life] has been signified by the Apostle Peter, that other by John. This one is wholly spent here up to the end of this world and finds its end there; that other is put off to be completed after the end of this world, but it does not have an end in the world to come."

Thus, by holding to his view of Martha and Mary as the present and future church, Augustine differs from many of the readings we have seen so far, in two important ways. First, Augustine does not view Mary and Martha as representative of different types of Christians or as representative of different types of Christian behavior in this lifetime. Mary is not the contemplative Christian while Martha practices physical acts of service. Unlike many monastic readings, Augustine does not believe that the church could be like Mary in the present age. While there might be glimpses of this behavior at times, where one can practice contemplation or listen to the word, inevitably every Christian will be (and should be) busy with much serving. The better part that Mary has chosen will only be made known in the age to come, and that is when Martha will be given that better part. While many previous interpreters, such as Cassian, for instance, acknowledge that Mary will only fully achieve perfection in eternity and that some distractions are inevitable, Augustine wants to draw a firmer line, saying that her better part is something we experience in eternity, not something that we can partially attain here in the present age.[30] The best one can hope for is glimpses of it. Mary's better part is the reward of rest given to the church for having run the race well. It is the one thing that Paul considered himself not to have attained and would not attain until he was with Christ.

Second, Augustine's overall approach to Martha is even more sympathetic than the most positive treatment of her that we have seen so far. She has not chosen the wrong sort of life, but rather she is doing what is necessary for all Christians to do. She is not a less mature Christian than her sister, choosing less important acts. Rather, she is serving the poor and showing hospitality to saints. She is troubled and weighed down by all her labors, but one day she will receive the reward of rest. Augustine implores his congregation to act similarly and continue to strive, while hoping for the same reward, as he concludes in his message in *Sermo* 104:

---

30. It has often been discussed that Cassian was familiar with Augustine's work more broadly. This, however, leads to the question of whether he knew Augustine's interpretation of Luke 10:38–42. As one can see, having now seen both, their arguments are similar in nature, but it is impossible to determine whether Cassian was repackaging Augustine's idea for his own context. For a discussion of Cassian's relationship with Augustine, see Boniface Ramsey, "John Cassian: Student of Augustine," *CS* 28 (1993): 5–15.

> So, beloved, I beg you, I urge you, I warn, command, implore you, let us desire that life together, let us run together toward it as we go, so that we may stop in it as a reward for our perseverance. The moment is coming, and that moment will have no end, when the Lord will make us recline, and will wait on us.... Toil passes, and rest will come; but rest only through toil. The ship passes, and you arrive home; but home only by means of the ship. We are sailing the high seas, after all, if we take account of the surges and storms of this world. The reason, I am convinced, that we are not drowned is that we are being carried on the wood of the cross. (*Serm.* 104.6)

Augustine is endlessly compassionate to Martha, speaking only words of encouragement to her and through her, to his entire congregation.

Similar to the interpreters we have studied so far, however, Augustine's reading is not gendered in such a way that he focuses on their tasks as only tasks women can do. This is not a story about women for women. Rather, Martha's hospitality is something that everyone should do so that they can also receive the blessing of welcoming Christ into their homes. Every Christian, man or woman, is actually Martha on this side of eternity as they are part of the *ecclesia*. Furthermore, every Christian will, in the life to come, receive the reward of Mary, that is, to sit forever at the feet of God. Augustine only focuses on the gender of the two sisters when their gender overlaps with his understanding that the church, the *ecclesia*, is a woman. Thus, in Augustine's reading, the exegetical move from Martha and Mary, two female disciples, to the present and future church, which is also depicted in female terms, is a natural one.

Ultimately, Augustine's preaching on Luke 10:38–42 is both practical and pastoral. He does not condemn the physical work of his congregation and in fact encourages them to continue doing it. While he acknowledges that listening to the word of God is a good thing, he is aware that to truly live a faithful life one cannot do only that, because there are people who need to be served. In his approach toward Martha, he is encouraging the members of his congregation, who are similarly distracted and busy with many necessary things, to continue to serve as Christ commanded them to serve. Following his overall commitment to loving God and neighbor, Augustine seems to recognize that if one only sat in prayer, then the hungry would not get fed and the sick would not be healed. It would be selfish and impossible to ignore them in pursuit of contemplation. Thus, he encourages them to run the race and continue in their works of service, so that one day their hard work will lead to the eternal reward of rest.

Excursus: Mary's Sitting and Standing in Augustine and Origen

Before discussing Chrysostom and Cyril, it is worth mentioning a specific digression that Augustine makes in numerous sermons when discussing Mary's sitting, since it parallels claims we previously saw in Origen. Both thinkers describe Mary as both sitting and standing before the Lord. Where they differ, however, is that Augustine dedicates space in his homilies to explain the difference in the postures in order to alleviate any confusion, whereas Origen presents the two images without additional comment. As previously discussed, Origen makes an important interpretive argument in *Fr. Luc.* 171 based on the fact that Luke depicts Mary sitting at Jesus's feet, because her location points the reader to her specific place in her faith journey. In his *Commentary on the Song of Songs*, however, he makes an extended point that Mary represents the one who is always standing before the Lord:

> Solomon's women: for this doubtless means the souls who are partakers of the Word of God and of his peace. Blessed are his servants, who stand ever in his sight: it is not those who sometimes stand and sometimes do not stand who are truly blessed, but those who always and unceasingly stand by the Word of God. Such a one was that Mary who sat at Jesus's feet, hearing him. And the Lord himself bore witness to her saying to Martha: "Mary has chosen the best part, which shall not be taken away from her." (*Comm. Cant.* 2.1)

Origen quotes from 1 Kgs 10:8 (LXX) to make his argument: "Blessed are your women, blessed are your servants who stand before you continually, listening to all your wisdom." Mary is like Solomon's wives in that by her sitting, she is standing always before the Lord. This could potentially be viewed as a contradiction in his reading, since sitting in *Fr. Luc.* 171 implies that she is not yet able to stand before the Lord. Furthermore, how can Mary represent a servant who always stands, not one who "sometimes stands and sometimes does not stand," when she is described as sitting in Luke 10:39? Origen is not concerned with this question: he is clearly comfortable with her sitting representing her metaphorical standing before the Lord. As I have noted previously, Origen frequently explores different avenues of interpretation in his commentaries, so for him, Mary's sitting can mean one thing in one place (her sitting representing an early state in her progression in the faith) and another thing somewhere else (that she stands before the Lord forever).

Augustine similarly interprets Mary's sitting as meaning that she stands before the Lord, though he quotes Ps 5:3 ("In the morning I will stand before you and gaze") and not 1 Kgs 10:8. He recognizes, however, that this could be a point of confusion for his congregation when he is arguing that by sitting Mary is actually standing before the Lord. So in two different sermons, he dedicates time to explaining how one can both sit and stand. In *Sermo* 104, he presents the problem:

> She was sitting down; so what's this I've just said, In the morning I will stand up and gaze? How can sitting down be like standing up, if morning stands for the age to come? When the night of the present age has gone, I will stand up, he says, and see; I will stand up and gaze. He didn't say, "I will sit down." So how can Mary, by sitting down, provide the image of this tremendous reality, if, I will stand up and gaze? Well, don't let all this bother you; it's a matter of physical limitations; both things cannot be demanded of the human body, that it should simultaneously both stand and sit.... But if I prove to you that the mind can do both at once, will there be any grounds left for hesitation? Because if it can do such a thing now, it will be much easier to do it then, when all difficulties will be at an end. (*Serm.* 104.5)

He then sets out to prove, by using different Scriptures (Ps 66:9; 86:11; 121:3; 1 Cor 9:24; Phil 3:16), that though the body is limited, the mind can be said to sit, stand, and walk or run before the Lord. He concludes: "So don't be too surprised, brothers and sisters; there you are; what the body can't do, the mind can. As far as the body is concerned, when you walk you don't stand; when you stand you don't walk. As far as the mind is concerned, as far as faith, as far as your intention is concerned, both stand and walk, both remain true and make progress" (*Serm.* 104.5).

This allows him to transition into discussing what it means for Mary and for all Christians to be said to sit and to stand before the Lord. Sitting, for Augustine, represents humility. One approaches the Lord only from a place of humility as one "beholds the Creator from a lowly position" (*Serm.* 104.5). Similarly, in *Sermo* 179, he argues that Mary's sitting means that she was listening to the Word from a place of humility. Because of this, she was also standing: "John the Baptist was standing, she was sitting; yet she in her heart was standing, and he in his humility was sitting. Standing, you see, signifies perseverance; sitting, humility" (*Serm.* 179.3). Standing, for Augustine, means being able to have run the race well and now being able to stand before the Lord for eternity.

That Augustine stops to address that he has presented Mary as both sitting and standing reflects his pastoral concern and the difference in preaching a homily and writing a commentary. He is directly aware of his audience and that he is using potentially contradictory metaphors if someone chooses to take those metaphors literally. He even points out that they are physically standing while listening to his sermon, and yet because they are listening to the Word, they are mentally sitting in humility. Through this, he is pushing them beyond a literal reading of the Scripture to see how potentially contradictory images can point to complementary truths about the word of God.

John Chrysostom

John Chrysostom was one of the most prolific and popular early Christian preachers, known for his rhetorical skill and his sometimes divisive sermons. Thomas Carroll argues that Chrysostom "was the very embodiment of his age and place, and in him all the tensions meet—East and West, Hellenism and Christianity, asceticism and hierarchy, ethical heroism and ecclesiastical intrigue."[31] Chrysostom was born between 344 and 347 CE and raised by his mother when his father died shortly after his birth. He lived during a particularly tumultuous time. Christianity was adapting to being a legal religion within a religiously diverse empire.[32] As Wendy Mayer and Pauline Allen note, Christianity was on the rise but still struggled with Judaism and with the imperial cult of Rome. Furthermore, as Christianity grew, internal conflicts also grew as Christianity became a part of the political landscape.[33] Chrysostom was baptized in 369 and served as an aide to the Antiochian bishop Meletius for several years. He then spent a number of years studying under a Syriac ascetic, living a strict lifestyle and learning the Scriptures. After seriously damaging his health

---

31. Carroll, *Preaching the Word*, 97.
32. Wendy Mayer and Pauline Allen, *John Chrysostom* (London: Routledge, 2000), 3. This book offers a substantial introduction to both Chrysostom's life and his most important works. See also J. N. D. Kelly, *Golden Mouth: The Story of John Chrysostom, Ascetic, Preacher and Bishop* (Ithaca, NY: Cornell University Press, 1995); Chrysostomus Baur, *John Chrysostom and His Time*, 2 vols., trans M. Gonzaga (Westminster, MD: Newman, 1959).
33. Mayer and Allen, *John Chrysostom*, 3.

as a result of this regimen, he returned to the city of Antioch.[34] He was ordained a deacon in 381 by Meletius and was ordained a priest in 386 by Flavian, Meletius's successor.

After his ordination to the priesthood, Flavian recruited him to preach, and thus he began preaching multiple times a week. He became beloved in Antioch, and his preaching skills made him well-known in the surrounding regions. In 397 he was nominated to the episcopacy in Constantinople. There were considerable fears that his local congregations in Antioch would rebel if they heard their priest was being taken from them, so he was taken abruptly and brought to Constantinople while on a journey to a neighboring town.[35] After he became bishop of Constantinople, he made a number of political enemies for his condemnations of wealth and his fight against corruption in the priesthood. He was sent into exile and died as result of harsh conditions in 407.[36]

In his *Homilies on the Gospel of John*, he twice preached on the story of Mary and Martha. His primary exegetical discussion comes in *Hom.* 44, where he warns against harmful interpretations of Jesus's praise of Mary. He also briefly discusses Luke 10:42 in *Hom.* 62, though its mention is tangential to his larger discussion of John 12. Before analyzing those references, however, I briefly consider Chrysostom's approach to preaching and Scripture.

Chrysostom as Preacher

Chrysostom (literally "golden tongue") is best known as a preacher. His popularity led to many of his sermons being collected and distributed to churches across the empire; over nine hundred of those sermons are extant.[37] While this number in no way represents the entirety of Chrysostom's sermons, it provides a good base from which to determine certain things about his preaching style, his audience, and his approach to Scripture.

---

34. Kelly, *Golden Mouth*, 32. Kelly cites Palladius's account of this time period: "His gastric regions were deadened and the functions of his kidneys were impaired by the intense cold. As he could not doctor himself, he returned to the haven of the church" (Palladius, *Life of Chrysostom* 5).

35. See J. N. D. Kelly, "Unexpected Promotion," in *Golden Mouth*, 104–14. See also Johannes Quasten, *Patrology*, 4 vols. (Westminster, MD: Newman, 1960), 3:425.

36. Mayer and Allen, *John Chrysostom*, 15.

37. For a concise summary of these sermons, see Quasten, *Patrology*, 3:433–59.

The themes of Chrysostom's sermons varied as he preached on specific topics (*On the Statues*, *Against the Jews*), on liturgical events (*Sermons for Liturgical Feasts*), and on entire biblical books, moving verse by verse in an almost commentary-type style (*Homilies on Genesis, John*, etc.).[38] It is believed that he preached from the middle of the nave instead of from the front so that his congregation could better see him. He was well-known for his skill as a rhetorician, and it is believed that sometimes his homilies lasted as long as an hour.[39] He, like Augustine, is believed to have preached extemporaneously, with his words recorded by scribes in attendance.[40] In contrast to Augustine, many of Chrysostom's sermons draw on current political and social issues. In fact, he first became well-known for his preaching skills when he preached an extended series on repentance after Antioch rioted and destroyed several imperial statues (*Ad populum Antiochenum de statuis* [*On the Statues*]).[41] He also repeatedly preached on the dangers of wealth in both Antioch and Constantinople, condemning ostentatious displays of wealth and calling for the care of the poor in his communities.[42]

There is some debate over the exact makeup of his congregation, particularly in Antioch, which is our focus. Antioch was a diverse city with large Jewish, Christian, and pagan populations.[43] It was a city of both great wealth and extreme poverty. Chrysostom's congregation in Antioch clearly included the wealthy and prominent, but there is some debate over whether the poorest in the community were permitted to attend the same services, even though there was some range of wealth represented.[44] Besides disparities in wealth, the congregation also consisted of both men and women, as well as Christian and pagan. Chrysostom became very popular in Antioch throughout his years as a presbyter, and large groups of people traveled to hear him preach. He frequently mentioned the people's affection for him and their love of good preaching (see *Stat.* 2.4).[45]

---

38. Quasten, *Patrology*, 3:433.
39. Mayer and Allen, *John Chrysostom*, 30.
40. Mayer and Allen, *John Chrysostom*, 31.
41. For more details, see Quasten, *Patrology*, 3:457–58, .
42. Mayer and Allen, *John Chrysostom*, 35.
43. See Chrysostomus Baur, "Antioch, the City and Its People," in *Chrysostom in His Time*, 29–44.
44. Mayer and Allen, *John Chrysostom*, 36.
45. See also Chrysostom, *Terr. mot.* 15: "For just as you are hungry to listen to me, so too I am hungry to preach to you. My congregation is my only glory and everyone

Chrysostom believed, however, that praise was not something the preacher should seek. He knew that good rhetoric was popular in Antioch and that people sought it. He also knew the dangers of seeking after those crowds: "And equally the man who is carried away with the desire for eulogies may have the ability to improve the people, but he chooses instead to provide nothing but entertainment. That is the price he pays for thunders of applause" (*Sac.* 5.2).[46] The preacher, according to Chrysostom, should despise praise. This is not to say that Chrysostom believed one should not be concerned with rhetorical skill. On the contrary, the preacher should always strive for eloquence, not for the sake of praise but for the sake of people's souls. Throughout books 4 and 5 of *On the Priesthood*, his manual for priests, Chrysostom discusses the importance of rhetorical skill. The priest should be able to inspire his congregation to good deeds and greater faith. It is a mark of shame for a priest to leave his audience bored: "How, then, can anyone endure the deep disgrace of having his sermon received with blank silence and feelings of boredom, and his listeners waiting for the end of the sermon as if it were a relief after fatigue; whereas they listen to someone else's sermon, however long, with eagerness, and are annoyed, when he is about to finish, and quite exasperated when he decides to say no more" (5.8). Not only should the preacher be concerned with keeping his audience's attention, but he should also be concerned with being able to resist false teaching. Chrysostom argues that many heretics and false teachers will be persuasive and have great rhetorical skill. Thus, the priest must be able to combat that with talent of his own, lest his congregation think that orthodox doctrine is flawed and not simply the priest's skills (4.8). The role of rhetoric is to defend orthodoxy.

The belief that preachers should be skilled but wary of praise can be seen throughout Chrysostom's preaching. For instance, in one sermon in *On the Statues*, he remarks: "What is the benefit of this applause to me, or what does the praise and fuss profit me? It will be my praise if you transmute all my words into deeds" (*Stat.* 2.4). Furthermore, Chrysostom repeatedly uses his preaching to condemn what he views as unorthodox

---

of you means much more to me than anyone of the city outside" (Carroll, *Preaching the Word*, 107).

46. Quotations from Chrysostom's *On the Priesthood* come from *Six Books on the Priesthood*, trans. Graham Neville (Crestwood, NY: Saint Vladimir's Seminary Press, 1964).

positions.[47] For him, the sermon is important because through preaching, the "doors of [God's] house are opened" to his congregation (*Anna* 5.1). He is turning people away from their sins and from false teachings and compelling them to live as Christ taught. He views the act of preaching as one of the most important tasks of the priest. Not only did he find it to be important, but Chrysostom also found preaching to be one of things he enjoyed most: "Preaching improves me. When I begin to speak weariness disappears; when I begin to teach fatigue too disappears. Thus neither sickness itself nor indeed any other obstacle is able to separate me from your love.... For just as you are hungry to listen to me, so too I am hungry to preach to you" (*Terr. mot.* 15). Chrysostom's love of preaching stands in contrast to Augustine, who repeatedly presents the act of preaching a draining but necessary task. Both men, however, despite their different styles and appreciation for preaching, rooted their preaching in their interpretation of the Bible.

Chrysostom and Scripture

As Carroll observes, "For Chrysostom, preaching was essentially the interpretation of a text from Scripture and its application to a particular congregation. Exegesis is, therefore, the starting point of his preaching as exhortation is its conclusion."[48] Chrysostom generally preferred to interpret Scripture in a literal fashion. For instance, in his homilies on the *Sermon on the Mount*, he pushes back against readings that would interpret the phrase "give us our daily bread" as something other than actual daily sustenance: "'Daily bread.' What is this? Bread for one day because he was preaching to men of flesh and blood who were subject to the laws of nature and its every need.... It is neither for riches, for delicate living, not for costly garments, not for any other such thing, but for bread only" (*Hom. Matt.* 19.5 [trans. Pelikan]). This tendency has led many scholars to label Chrysostom as one of the most famous members of the so-called Antioch school, which focused on a more literal interpretation of Scriptures. These interpreters stood in contrast to interpreters from the Alexandrian school, who preferred to interpret texts more allegorically.[49]

---

47. For instance, we see this tendency in *Hom. Jo.* 44.
48. Carroll, *Preaching the Word*, 114.
49. For the more traditional analysis of the Antioch school and the Alexandrian school, see Robert M. Grant and David Tracy, *A Short History of the Interpretation of*

We should be careful, however, when drawing such a hard line between the two school of exegesis. At times, members of each school draw on different exegetical methods when interpreting difficult passages, particularly when preaching. Theodore of Mopsuestia, another member of the Antioch school, argues in his preface to his *Commentary on John's Gospel* that while the exegete's task is to clear up obscure content in the Bible, it is the preacher's job to present the message of the Bible for the purpose of edifying his hearers. Chrysostom appears to follow this approach. He avoids heavily allegorical readings, but he uses metaphors or typology occasionally within his sermons if he believes they will benefit his hearers.[50] As J. N. D Kelly argues, "far from being a dry as dust academic lecturer, [Chrysostom] is always striving to make the Bible come alive for his hearers."[51] That said, Kelly also notes that Chrysostom usually finds the most benefit in the literal sense of the text.[52] These tendencies, both his desire to make the Bible useful for his congregation and his preference for this literal sense of the text, are important to remember when examining his interpretations of Luke 10:38–42.

Interpreting Mary and Martha

Chrysostom's eighty-eight homilies on John were likely delivered in Antioch after 391. They are considerably shorter than most of his homilies, lasting only ten to fifteen minutes. They are also frequently polemical as he confronts Arian interpretations of John, particularly relating to the relationship between the Son and Father.[53] Chrysostom wants to clarify for his audience how John's Gospel differs from the other gospels because of its more spiritual character. Each homily includes a close verse-by-verse exegetical treatment. He usually begins his homilies with a close exege-

---

the Bible (Minneapolis: Fortress, 1988), 52–72. For more recent scholarship questioning the standard narrative surrounding the two schools, see John J. O'Keefe, "'A Letter That Killeth': Toward a Reassessment of Antiochene Exegesis, or Diodore, Theodore, and Theodoret on the Psalms," *JECS* 8 (2000): 83–103.

    50. For instance, see *Catech. ult.* 3.17: "Blood and water flowed from his side.... Beloved, do not pass over this mystery without thought. It has yet another hidden meaning, which I will explain to you. I said that water and blood symbolized baptism and Holy Eucharist. From these two sacraments the Church is born" (trans. Harkins).

    51. Kelly, *Golden Mouth*, 60.

    52. Kelly, *Golden Mouth*, 60.

    53. Quasten, *Patrology*, 3:439.

sis of the passage at hand before discussing an ethical or moral issue that arises from the text. The conclusion usually includes some sort of parable or a summary of the moral of each story.[54] Such is the structure of *Hom.* 44, to which I now turn.

Homily on John 44

Chrysostom's homily focuses on John 6:26–27: "Amen, I say to you, you seek me not because you have seen signs but because you have eaten of the loaves and have been filled. Labor not for the food that perishes, but for that which endures for the life everlasting."[55] Chrysostom argues that Jesus says this so that his audience will recognize that it is not the fact that Jesus can supply physical food that matters but rather that they should be looking for spiritual nourishment.

Chrysostom is concerned, however, that some are misusing Jesus's statement: "However since some who wish to live without working misapply this statement by saying that Christ was renouncing manual labor, it is timely to speak also against them. They are slandering the whole of Christianity, so to speak, laying it open to be ridiculed for laziness."[56] That Chrysostom knows of people making this exegetical argument leads him to look at what the Bible actually says about physical work.[57]

He presents different examples, which he grants on the surface appear to contradict one another. First, he presents Paul saying that it is better to give than to receive, noting that if one does not work it would be impossible to have anything to give and the fact that Paul himself worked as a tentmaker. Second, he presents Luke 10:41–42 and Matt 6:34: "How is it then, that Jesus said to Martha: 'You are anxious and troubled about many things; and yet only one thing is needful. Mary has chosen the best part?' And again, 'Do not be anxious about tomorrow?' It is indeed necessary to explain all these texts now, not only in order that we may cause those who are lazy to cease to be so—if they should be so open to persuasion—but also that we may prove no statements made by God contradict one

---

54. Carroll, *Preaching the Word*, 119.
55. This is Chrysostom's translation of John 6:26–27 in *Hom. Jo.* 44.1, trans. G. T. Stupart, *The Homilies of S. John Chrysostom on the Gospel of St. John* (Oxford: Parker, 1848–1852), 1:442.
56. Carroll, *Preaching the Word*, 119.
57. These opponents will be discussed in the following section.

another" (Chrysostom, *Hom. Jo.* 44.1 [trans. Stupart]). Chrysostom holds that this cannot be an actual contradiction. Because God's word cannot contradict itself, he turns to examine each of these passages in greater depth. He grants that at the level of the letter they might be in tension, but when the careful reader pays attention to the context, he will clearly see that Jesus never says to stop working. In particular, Chrysostom argues that Jesus's saying that Mary has chosen the better part does not mean that he is telling Martha that all her work is worthless:

> And what was said to Martha did not refer to work and daily labor, but to the necessity of knowing the proper time for it and of not spending the time, intended for listening to Him, on more material occupations. Well, then, He did not say these things to encourage her to idleness, but to compel her to listen to Him. "I have come," He meant to say, "to teach you the things necessary for salvation and are you busying yourself about a meal? Do you wish to make me welcome and to prepare a lavish table? Prepare another kind of refreshment by making yourself an attentive and enthusiastic listener and imitating the loving attention of your sister." It was not, then, to forbid hospitality that He spoke as He did to her: perish the thought! How, indeed could He do so? But it was to show that one must not be preoccupied with other things when it is the time to listen to Him. (*Hom. Jo.* 44.1)

Chrysostom argues that Martha's problem was not that she worked, but rather that she worked when she should have been listening. She was busy when she should have been focused on Jesus's teaching. Martha's problem, therefore, was not her work or her hospitality, but rather her lack of proper discernment. She did not recognize in that moment that preparing a meal should have been less important than paying attention to Jesus.

Chrysostom then turns to connect the passage to John 6:26–27. He argues that despite the impulse of some interpreters to argue that spiritual food is what Martha should always be focusing on, working for spiritual food "that does not perish" does not always mean sitting in prayer. Sometimes working for spiritual food means engaging in physical service, such as caring for the poor. Like Augustine, he quotes Matt 25 to show that when people take care of the poor, feed the hungry, or care for the sick, they are working for Christ and thus for the food that does not perish. On the contrary, he argues it is the lazy, who only sit around and pray, who are seeking the food that perishes: "And if some lazy fellow should glut himself and exert every effort for nourishment, he is working for the food that perishes; whereas if a working person should feed Christ and give him drink and clothe Him, no one would be so dull and ignorant as to say that such a laboring is for food that perishes since in return for this there is the promise of the Kingdom to come and of the well-known rewards. This food indeed endures forever" (*Hom. Jo.* 44.1). Chrysostom argues that laziness (and therefore only being concerned for oneself) ultimately produces the food that perishes, because the lazy person will not reap any eternal rewards. Physical work is important when it allows the Christian to follow the spiritual commands of Christ, such as caring for the poor. Martha and her acts of hospitality were good actions, but in her specific case, she did not show proper discernment because in that moment she could have chosen not to prepare what he describes as a lavish meal and instead listened to the Word of God, who was in front of her. His overall argument, however, suggests that at times showing discernment and choosing the better part might mean taking care of the poor and vulnerable.

Recent scholarship has been divided over who exactly Chrysostom is targeting with this homily. Some scholars hold that those monks who interpreted John 6:27–29 and Luke 10:38–42 as prohibitions of all work must have been Messalians.[58] Others hold that Chrysostom's critiques are too vague to allow us to make claims about the offending party.[59]

---

58. See Csanyi, "Optima Pars," 34–47. Csanyi was the first to argue that Chrysostom is specifically engaging with the Messalian interpretation of the story of Mary and Martha. His argument is rooted in two claims. First, he argues that Messalians were known to be in Antioch when Chrysostom was beginning his ministry there. Specifically, he points to Chrysostom's mentor, Flavian, who oversaw the Synod of Antioch, which condemned a monk named Adelphius who was accused of being Messalian. Second, he argues that the three passages that Chrysostom addresses in this sermon, John 6:27; Luke 10:41–42; and Matt 6:34, were important texts for the Messalian community, since these verses formed the basis of their refusal to work: "Diese zwei Stellen beweisen uns, dass alle drei Texte, die Chrysostomus als von seinen Gegnern missbrauchte Herrenworte bezeichnet zu den beliebtesten Waffen aus dem Arsenal der Messalianer gehörten." He bases his argument on Epiphanius's refutation of the Messalians (38).

59. More recent scholarship has challenged this reading, particularly as more attention has been paid to Messalianism. In particular, see Klaus Fitschen, *Messalianismus und Antimessalianismus: Ein Beispiel ostkirchlicher Ketzergeschichte* (Göttingen: Vandenhoeck & Ruprecht, 1998). He argues that that there is not enough information within the homily to justify Csanyi's claims; he points out that the only critique here against them is "idleness," which is not enough to link them to Messalianism. He argues this is a vague criticism that could be applied to many groups. Furthermore,

While there do appear to be monks who were accused of Messalianism in Antioch, we know that Chrysostom interacted with several different monastic leaders and groups during his time as a priest and as a bishop, and he often had a complicated relationship with monastic orders.[60] Klaus Fitschen correctly observes that the homily itself does not provide us with much information other than that this group used these texts to justify what Chrysostom condemns as "idleness" (ἀργία).[61] Chrysostom's primary concern is defending the church against charges of idleness rather than fighting off a clearly defined opponent.[62]

In fact, the sin of idleness (ἀργία) and its dangers is a recurring theme in his homilies: "Work without ceasing, because idleness is an incurable vice. Among you, 'If anyone does not work, let him not eat.' For even the Lord our God hates idle people. None who serve God should be idle" (Const. App. 2.63.1-6). Throughout his career, Chrysostom repeatedly condemned monks who refused to work, yet insisted on receiving alms from people in order to survive. In both Antioch and Constantinople, Chrysostom, while praising monks who lived out their philosophy in seclusion, had concerns over certain monks who came into the cities for support.[63] These monks, he worried, were scandalous to non-Christians: "These find grounds for countless jabs and accusations when they see a healthy man who is capable of supporting himself out begging, seeking his support from others.... They are even calling us 'Christmongers' [Χριστεμπόρους]" (Chrysostom, *Hom. 1 Thess.* 6.1 [trans. Caner]).

---

as we already seen, the Messalian heresy is a unique phenomenon to study because the Messalians were likely not a sect of unorthodox Christians that existed as "Messalians," but rather charges of Messalianism evolved out of misunderstandings of Syriac asceticism (134).

60. For two examples of Chrysostom's encounters with monastic figures and communities, see Daniel Caner, "John Chrysostom and the Christmongers of Constantinople," and "John Chrysostom and the Monks of Constantinople," in *Wandering, Begging Monks: Spiritual Authority and the Promotion of Monasticism in Late Antiquity* (Berkeley: University of California Press, 2002), 169–76, 190–98, .

61. Fitschen, *Messalianismus und Antimessalianismus*, 134.

62. See Caner, *Wandering, Begging Monks*, 176, for his conclusion that while some of Chrysostom's critiques do mirror critiques that will later come to be identified with the Messalian heresy, the primary issue for Chrysostom in his homily is not a specific heretical group but rather to counter the use of Scripture to justify idleness.

63. Caner, *Wandering, Begging Monks*, 169–77.

Chrysostom believed that the reputation of the church was at stake when certain monks refused to work, and he believed that the arguments that justify their lack of work were linked to their poor interpretations of Luke 10:38–42 and John 6:26–27 (*Hom. Jo.* 44). It is clear that he was familiar with interpretations of the story that prioritize not engaging in any physical labor, and Chrysostom represents a significant rejoinder to these interpretations. He rejects any monastic reading that would claim that ascetics have achieved the better part because they have abandoned physical work. In the previous chapter, we saw some monastic authors have Mary represent the monastic lifestyle, focusing all her time on praying and listening to the word. The author of the Liber Graduum, for instance, uses the text in this way. The Perfect, whom Mary represents, do not participate in physical service or any type of earthly work because the Upright, such as Martha, are expected to support them.[64] Chrysostom attempts to correct such an interpretation, arguing instead that Martha's problem was her lack of discernment, which led to her good service to be improperly oriented. In this way, Chrysostom appears more in line with Silvanus in the Sayings of the Desert Fathers, who also rejected extreme readings that prohibited any work. Both Silvanus and Chrysostom argue for proper discernment over when one should work and when one should listen, and both men argue that physical labor is an important act of service.

---

64. It should be noted that Chrysostom's critique, if he was aware of the Liber Graduum, would not hold together, because the Perfect were responsible for teaching, which, according to Chrysostom, would qualify as work in a way that only fasting and praying does not. See Caner on this potential inconsistency in *Wandering, Begging Monks*, 177: "There was, however, another side to Chrysostom's troubles with the wandering monks of Constantinople, which neither he nor Palladius discloses. While criticizing other members of the church for skimming 'fatty droppings' off tables of the rich and advising Olympias to refrain from lavishing wealth on these (including not only clergy but 'innumerable ascetics' as well), Chrysostom himself continued to rely on the deaconesses' wealth and services to supply his own needs. Although Palladius defends this, saying Chrysostom 'did not have to touch church funds and took his daily food as it came, ever eluding this sort of anxiety,' it evidently raised talk of double standards. Moreover, Chrysostom's justification for such support, based as it was on teaching, could only have sparked animosity among the city's ascetics, as it implied that they were not teachers themselves."

Homily on John 62

Before concluding this section on Chrysostom, I turn briefly to his second reference to Luke 10:41–42, also found in *Homilies on John*. In this homily he exegetes the story of Jesus raising Lazarus from the dead (John 11–12), and he follows the narrative closely, moving from verse to verse. He makes three claims about the two sisters that are worth noting. First, he resists harmonizing Mary in John 12 and the sinful woman who anoints Jesus's feet in Luke 7:36–50. He wants his audience to know that the anointing of the sinful woman in Luke is a different incident, because he does not want them to assume that Mary is a sinful woman. Mary is "devout and zealous. And I say this because she used to show much concern for the hospitable reception of Christ" (*Hom. Jo.* 62 [Goggin]). This conflation of Mary of Bethany with the sinful woman who anoints Jesus's feet and other Marys in the gospels became a more substantial problem during the medieval period, as we will discuss in the next chapter, but it is important that Chrysostom recognizes this danger and intentionally addresses it.[65]

Second, Chrysostom enters into a discussion about whose love for Christ was stronger. He appears to be aware of an argument that says Martha's love is more fervent because she ran out to meet Jesus, similar to the one we saw in Ephrem's *Commentary on the Diatessaron*. He argues, however, that Mary is the sister whose love is greater because she does not question Jesus at the tomb like Martha does when she points out that Lazarus had been dead four days:

> Do you perceive how ardent her love of Him was? She it was of whom he said: "Mary has chosen the best part."
> "How is it, then," you will ask, "that Martha seems more fervent?"
> She was not more fervent, for it was not Mary who heard [His words about the resurrection] since Martha was the weaker. Indeed, though she had heard such sublime words, she said afterwards: "He is already

---

65. For instance, Gregory the Great states in his homily on Luke 7 that he does believe that the sinful woman is clearly Mary Magdalene: "This woman, who Luke calls a sinner, John names Mary. I believe that she is the same Mary of whom Mark says that seven demons had been cast out." Gregory the Great's interpretation was particularly important to medieval interpreters, and the idea that Mary of Bethany, Mary Magdalene, and the sinful women were the same became an almost universally agreed-on reading during that period. See Gregory the Great, *Hom.* 33, in *Forty Gospel Homilies*, trans. David Hurst, CSS 123 (Kalamazoo, MI: Cistercian, 1990), 269.

decayed, for he is dead four days." Mary, on the contrary, though she had listened to no instruction, said nothing of the kind, but merely declared at once with faith: "Master, if thou hadst been here, my brother would not have died." (*Hom. Jo.* 62 [Goggin])

So Mary's love is more fervent, yet Chrysostom then immediately pivots to discuss how both women were praiseworthy, virtuous, and wise, despite the fact that they had not received the full measure of truth about Christ. Both sisters are beloved disciples and friends of Christ.

Third, Chrysostom uses Mary's and Martha's reaction to their brother's death and their overall love of Christ to address the women in his congregation directly. He uses them as an example of how to properly grieve and then rebukes the women in attendance for improperly grieving by making a scene and carrying on: "What are you doing, O woman? Tell me, do you who are a member of Christ, shamelessly strip yourself in the middle of the market-place.... Do you tear your hair, and rend your garments … and act like a mad woman … ? What great insanity is this?" (*Hom. Jo.* 62 [Goggin]). While at first, this seems like an exegetical departure, Chrysostom argues that the overall purpose of the story of Lazarus is to teach Christians how to grieve properly: "Why did the Evangelist tell us this story? … That we ought not to complain and bear it hard if those who are exemplary men and friends of God become sick" (*Hom. Jo.* 62 [Goggin]). This is notable for our purposes because Chrysostom uses Mary and Martha here as examples specifically for women and how they should act when someone they love dies. This is one of the first times we have seen the two sisters used in such a specifically gendered way, though within a few paragraphs he turns again and addresses both the men and women on how to grieve, using Mary and Martha as an example for both genders about the nature of Christian grief.

Conclusion

In many ways, Chrysostom represents the counterpoint to many of the interpretations we have seen so far. He resists a reading of Luke 10:38–42 in *Hom. Jo.* 44 that leads to the rejection of all physical work. Like Augustine, he argues that physical service is good because it allows one to follow the commands of Christ to take care of the poor, but he resists any sort of typological interpretation. Rather, he engages in a careful literal reading that privileges the context of specific passages. He concludes that Martha's problem is not her service but rather her lack of discernment. She should have recognized that when the Lord is present, she should privilege listening to him over being distracted by preparing an extravagant feast. The better part is not always sitting and listening to the word. Sometimes serving the poor is the better part.

Chrysostom was clearly aware of monastic readings that used this passage to justify never working and depending on the support of others to survive, and his interpretation attempts to correct their misreading. In *Hom. Jo.* 62, he rejects a reading that might privilege Martha's faith over Mary's because Martha ran out to meet the Lord. He flips this story to argue that actually her actions show that Mary had a greater faith because she does not question Jesus. He also wants to ensure no one is in danger of conflating Mary of Bethany with the sinful woman in Luke 7. This is further evidence of the multiplicity of interpretations surrounding Mary and Martha in the late fourth century as Chrysostom offers his reading in direct response to these other interpretations.

Furthermore, it is important that Chrysostom, like Augustine, also adapts a pro-work reading of this passage. Physical work is necessary to fulfill Christ's commandments. In this way, the fact that he is speaking before a group of laity is important. He encourages their service and work as being a way for them to fulfill their Christian duty, while also pointing them to having proper discernment over when one should pray and when one should work. Both by seeking to correct what he sees as misreadings of the story and by his explicit endorsement of physical work, Chrysostom reveals pastoral and practical concerns for his congregation that appear to drive him as much as his theological concerns.

Excursus: Gendered Readings in Chrysostom

Before fully concluding this section on Chrysostom's interpretations of Mary and Martha of Bethany, it is worth briefly engaging with the ways in which he does offer gendered reading in these homilies in order to highlight the ways in which gender was being discussed during the ancient world. The biblical text throughout the precritical period (just as in many Christian communities today) was certainly used to justify and enforce specific gendered expectations. Chrysostom is a good example of the ways in which this occurs, because he often preached to mixed-gender congregations. That said, a similar analysis could be done with any number of our patristic authors.⁶⁶ Patristic writers and later medieval writers, after all, were not blind to gender, meaning their exegesis was not always gender neutral.

For Chrysostom, this gendered reading sometimes occurs in the actual exegesis of a text. Take, for instance, one of his sermons on John 20, which focuses on Jesus's resurrection appearance to Mary Magdalene in the garden (*Hom. Jo.* 86). He begins his sermon by reflecting on why Mary remains and cries when Peter leaves, seemingly emotionally unfazed. He concludes that Mary weeps because she is of the weaker sex: "Full of feeling somehow is the female sex, and more inclined to pity. I say this, lest you should wonder how it could be that Mary wept bitterly at the tomb, while Peter was in no way so affected. For, 'The disciples,' it says, 'went away unto their own home'; but she stood shedding tears. Because hers was a feeble nature, and she as yet knew not accurately the account of the Resurrection; whereas they having seen the linen clothes and believed, departed to their own homes in astonishment" (86.1 [trans. Charles Marriott, *NPNF* 1/14:321]). His exegetical decision here is based on his understanding of women and in what he sees as their inherent nature. Peter and the beloved disciple are able to simply believe that the empty tomb means Jesus had been raised, whereas Mary's gender (and thus her emotional state) keep her from being able to accept the same truth. This begins his exegesis of what follows as Mary encounters Jesus. It is a brief moment in the sermon, to be sure, but it reveals to us the ways in which assumptions about gender informed his understanding of specific biblical scenes.⁶⁷

His gendered interpretations also come to the forefront when he is discussing the nature of marriage versus celibacy with the pros and cons

---

66. There have been whole books written on Augustine's treatment of women throughout his works. For instance, see Kim Power, *Veiled Desire: Augustine on Women* (New York: Continuum, 1996). A similar excursus could have been written about him. As we will see with Chrysostom, many of his gendered readings surround the issue of marriage, widowhood, and celibacy. In particular, Augustine returns exegetically again and again to Mary the mother of God to make his arguments. See, for instance, *Virginit.* 20, where he compares Mary as virgin with Susanna as widow. See also Augustine, *Of the Good Marriage*, for further discussion.

67. One can also see this exegetical tendency in *Hom. Phil.* 9, where he discusses the widow who lives for pleasure (1 Tim 5:6): "But if she's a widow in that case it's a question of being old, for the aged need much attention, and its her nature too. I mean, the female nature needs more rest because it's weak, so if here you have both old age and female nature, he won't let her be self-indulgent" (trans. Allen).

of each.[68] Within in his argumentation, many of his assumptions about the nature of women are at the forefront when he is wrestling with Paul's statements on marriage. For instance, he discusses how a wife is an impediment to her husband being able to obtain perfection and the biblical tension that women are created to be a helper to their husbands:

> How then, you will say, could have God called this impediment a helper? Indeed, he says: "Let us make for him a helper like himself." Yet, I ask you how does he help who deprives her husband of so much security who banished him from that splendid life in Paradise, and who has thrown him into the confusion of the present life? This is not help but treachery. Scripture says, "In woman was sin's beginning, and because of her we all die." Saint Paul says: " … it was not Adam who was deceived by the woman." (*Virginit.* 46.1)[69]

He continues on by pointing to biblical after biblical example of women who attempted (and sometimes succeeded) in destroying their husbands (Job's wife, Delilah, Jezebel, Solomon's wives, etc.). He then argues that women still today cause their husbands to offend God. He concludes this section by arguing: "For this reason does not the sage say: 'There is scarce any evil like that in a woman'" (46.2). Chrysostom, in this argument, once again shows his ability to read female biblical characters in a very gendered way by focusing on their relationship to the men in their stories.

Finally, we see how Chrysostom interprets certain passages through a gendered lens when he discusses wealth and women who wear jewelry, fine clothing, gold, and ostentatious behavior. In doing so, he often turns to address women directly or sometimes their husbands. As we already saw, he briefly does addresses the women in his audience near the end of *Homily on John* 62, but this is something one can find throughout his col-

---

68. For a full discussion of Chrysostom's understanding of the relationship between marriage and ascetism, see Peter Brown, "Sexuality in the City," in Brown, *The Body and Society: Men, Women and Sexual Renunciation in Early Christianity* (New York: Columbia University Press, 2008), 305–22. In this chapter, Brown discusses Chrysostom's complex understanding of the purpose of marriage and how it actually intersects with his understanding of taking care of the poor.

69. Translations of Chrysostom's *De Virginitate* come from *On Virginity; Against Remarriage*, trans. Sally Rieger Shore, SWR 9 (Lewiston, NY: Mellen, 1983).

lection of work.[70] He was deeply concerned about ostentatious displays of wealth that he often saw in women in his congregations. For instance, in his *Hom. Phil.* 11, he attacks men who insist on giving their wives and their horses fine jewelry to wear. He remarks that it is particularly stupid to give a horse gold, but then turns to discuss the dangers of women dressing in a way that reveals their wealth: "I mean, along with the rest, possessing wealth makes them stupid as well. They consider both their women and their horses worthy of the same honor.... And the women want to appear finer than the vehicles and the fur coverings on which they ride.... What extra does a woman have who wears such a great mass of gold and stones?" (*Hom. Phil.* 11). He continues by arguing that these women and their insistence on fine things actually hurt their husbands' businesses because instead of being able to spend money on useful things, their husbands are forced to spend it on gold and stones, which are ultimately worthless. Chrysostom makes a similar argument in *On Virginity* (62). In this he turns and directly addresses women: "'Another man has noticed me,' you say, 'and has been impressed.' But he admires the ornaments, not the woman wearing them; she is often reproached by because of them as if she were adorned by them contrary to her true worth. If she is beautiful, they violate her true beauty.... However, if she is misshapen and ugly, it sets off her unattractiveness even more" (*Virginit.* 62.1). He then turns to argue about the ridiculousness of gold and fine jewels, arguing instead that a woman should pursue the ornament of virginity because virginity can transform even the ugliest woman by surrounding with her irresistible spiritual beauty. Virginity adorns the soul and cannot perish.

Chrysostom could have chosen to read the story of Mary and Martha through the lens of their inherent weakness as women and their struggle against their evil natures, or he could have even chosen to praise them for their lack of spouses. These were all gendered readings that existed within his exegetical framework. He did not choose to do so, and instead he focuses on this question of proper discernment in discipleship. This is worth pointing out before we continue to other patristic and medieval

---

70. There is another example about his concern about women's emotions during grieving found in *Hom. Phil.* 4: "Those lamentations in the marketplace come not from sympathy but from ostentation and ambition and vainglory. Many women do this as an art. Weep bitterly, groan at home, when no one is watching." As in *Hom. Jo.* 62, he then turns to address both genders on how to properly grieve and for whom they should be grieving.

writers, as some might argue that the lack of gendered reading during these periods sprang up from gender not being a subject of much concern. This is clearly not the case with Chrysostom. This excursus is also serves as an important reminder that patristic authors often held deeply misogynistic views toward women, and these views often influenced their writings and their biblical interpretations. Thus, it is even more interesting that when we study their interpretations of Mary and Martha, they do not view their characters through the lens of their understanding of women but rather through their understanding of disciples.

Cyril of Alexandria

Cyril of Alexandria was one of the most important theologians of the patristic period.[71] He is a complicated figure, however, as his episcopal career was one marked by many political and theological controversies.[72] In particular, he is known for his feud with Nestorius on the nature of Christ and whether Mary could properly be called the Theotokos, culminating in the condemnation of Nestorius at the Council of Ephesus.[73] The majority of scholarship on his life and work focuses on his contributions to Christology. In recent years, more attention has been paid to Cyril as biblical exegete,[74] but little work has been done on Cyril as preacher.[75] I will be

---

71. For a more in-depth look at Cyril's life, see Norman Russell, *Cyril of Alexandria* (New York: Routledge, 2000); John Anthony McGuckin, *St. Cyril of Alexandria: The Christological Controversy, Its History, Theology and Texts* (Crestwood, NY: Saint Vladimir's Seminary Press, 2004). The most thorough biography of Cyril's life, however, is over a century old: Joseph Kopallik, *Cyrillus con Alexandrien, eine Biographie nach den Quellen* (Mainz: Kircheim, 1881).

72. Many scholars have depicted Cyril as being a violent and selfish man. For instance, Edwin Dargan introduces Cyril in the following way: "He succeeded his evil uncle as patriarch of Alexandria about the year 412 and was an apt pupil of his predecessor in selfishness, intrigue and even violence," and concludes in the following way: "How true it is that the evil traits of a man's character may hinder and even ruin his influence, although he be gifted with unusual talents" (*History of Preaching*, 1:117, 119).

73. Quasten, *Patrology*, 4:117.

74. See Lois Farag, *St. Cyril of Alexandria, a New Testament Exegete* (Piscataway, NJ: Gorgias, 2007); Alexander Kerrigan, *S. Cyril of Alexandria: Interpreter of the Old Testament* (Rome: Pontifical Biblical Institute, 1952); Matthew Crawford, *Cyril of Alexandria's Trinitarian Theology of Scripture* (Oxford: Oxford University Press, 2014).

75. A notable exception is John Anthony McGuckin, "Cyril of Alexandria:

discussing Cyril's *Homilies on Luke*, which were originally published as a commentary. Here we find his fullest interpretation of Luke 10:38–42.

Cyril was born in 378 in Theodosiou, and little can be said conclusively about his life before 403 CE, when he was present at the Synod of Oaks with his uncle Theophilus, who preceded him as bishop of Alexandria.[76] In 412, following his uncle's death, Cyril assumed the episcopate, serving in this capacity until his death in 444.[77] During this period Cyril delivered his *Homilies on Luke*. While there is no definite dating for the sermons, they contain a few polemical references to Nestorius, leading most scholars to argue Cyril must have preached them after 430, which is when the Nestorian controversy began.[78] As Robert Payne Smith notes, however, one "will find the commentary written, as might be expected in homilies by a teacher directed to his own people, far from the baleful atmosphere of controversy."[79] They were originally composed in Greek, but the only extant version is in Syriac.[80] Smith translated the collection from the Syriac into English in the mid-1800s, but little attention has

---

Bishop and Pastor," in *The Theology of Cyril of Alexandria*, ed. Thomas G. Weinandy and Daniel Keating (London: T&T Clark, 2003), 205–36. His work, however, focuses on how Cyril made use of episcopal authority to address monastic communities and liturgical issues.

76. This council deposed John Chrysostom.

77. The beginning of this time was marked by controversy as Cyril attempted to consolidate power and engaged in several fights with others in Alexandria. There were three days of rioting before he took over his uncle's seat, as many secular authorities supported the archdeacon Timothy. Furthermore, he immediately ejected the Novatianists from the city and took their churches and then moved against the Jews. Also during this early period, Hypatia, an important pagan mathematician, was murdered by a Christian mob, which led to outrage. Russell argues that overall Cyril used this early period to consolidate his power through the use of ecclesiastical politics (*Cyril of Alexandria*, 6).

78. Adolf Rücker, who translated several of the Syriac fragments into German, argues that in *Hom.* 63 one can see an allusion to one of Cyril's Nestorian anathemas, meaning the homilies must have been written after 430. See Rücker, *Die Lukas Homilien des hl. Cyrill von Alexandrien: Ein Beitrag zur Geschichte der Exegese* (Breslau: Drugulin, 1911), 33–34.

79. Robert Payne Smith, "Introduction," in Cyril of Alexandria, *A Commentary upon the Gospel according to Saint Luke*, trans. Smith (Piscataway, NJ: Gorgias, 2009), xi (some of fragments of the homilies exist in Greek in larger collections of patristics writings).

80. Quasten, *Patrology*, 4:123–24.

been paid to this work overall, with many favoring Cyril's *Commentary on John* instead. It is relevant that this work is usually labeled as a commentary, and as such it has often been grouped with other commentaries. Originally, however, this work was delivered as sermons to his congregation in Alexandria.

A large portion of Cyril's work remains extant, second only to John Chrysostom among Eastern patristic figures, and 75 percent of his works consist of scriptural exegesis.[81] Cyril clearly has memorized large portions of both Testaments and, like most patristic interpreters, moves among them freely, believing that while each book was written by an individual author, they were all linked together by the inspiration of the Spirit and properly understood only through the lens of Christ as the Word of God.[82] Moreover, Cyril frequently engages in allegorical and typological readings of biblical passages, for the Scriptures contain mysteries. For instance, in his *Commentary on John*, he argues that the blind man healed by mud in John 9 signifies the nations:

> It is not possible in any other way for the nations to throw off blindness that laid upon them and to behold the divine and holy light, that is to receive the knowledge of the holy and consubstantial Trinity, except by becoming partakers of his holy body and by washing off the sin that darkens ... through holy baptism. And when the Savior engraved on the blind man the type that anticipated the mystery, he at that time fulfilled the power of participation by anointing him with the spittle. Indeed as an image of holy baptism, he commands him to run and wash. (*Comm. Jo.* 9.6–17 [Pusey])

As Farag argues, each story can have a literary and a spiritual meaning.[83] In John 9, the blind man represents all the nations who are currently in darkness, and the spittle from Jesus represents partaking of the body of Christ, and washing in the pool of Siloam represents baptism. Throughout his scriptural exegesis, Cyril follows this pattern, leading Dargen to describe him as an "able exponent of the Alexandrian school who ... pushes very far his allegorical interpretations."[84]

---

81. Farag, *St. Cyril of Alexandria*, 24.
82. Crawford, *Cyril of Alexandria's Trinitarian Theology*, 67.
83. Farag, *St. Cyril of Alexandria*, 149.
84. Dargen, *History of Preaching*, 1:118.

His *Homilies on Luke*, however, reveal a different approach to Scripture. Smith notes that within the New Testament, Cyril "chiefly follows the obvious meaning and considers each parable, discourse, narrative as a whole, the key of which he usually finds in the occasion which gave rise to it."[85] His *Homilies on Luke* were delivered in this more literal style of exegesis. Each sermon begins with a reading from the Gospel of Luke, which Cyril then interprets for his congregation. Rarely does he explicitly engage in polemical discourse or overtly allegorical readings. Instead he focuses on exegetical, moral, and practical concerns.

A Lesson in Hospitality: *Homily* 69

His literal approach is particularly evident when Cyril interprets Luke 10:38–42 in *Hom.* 69. As we have seen, the story of Mary and Martha had frequently been interpreted through an allegorical lens. Yet Cyril does not draw from any of these readings in his interpretation. Instead, his approach is similar to Basil's, because he reads the entire passage as being a lesson in proper Christian hospitality. In contrast to Basil's brevity, Cyril expands his interpretation into an entire sermon on hospitality. In fact, immediately after the passage itself, he begins: "Ye who love the virtues which adorn piety, and carefully practice every art which becometh the saints, again come and listen to the sacred doctrine, and let not the method of hospitality be unknown to you."[86] He then cites Heb 13:1, reminding his congregations about its command not to forget hospitality. Cyril then calls for an imitation of Mary, with the hope that by carefully listening to the Lord (and to his sermon), the congregation will be taught more about Christ and the virtue of hospitality:

> Let us learn therefore of Christ, the Saviour of all, this also, as well as all other things. For it would be a disgrace to us, that while those who desire worldly wisdom, and gather written learning, select the best teachers for their instructors; we who are encouraged to pay earnest heed to doctrines of such surpassing value, and may have as our instructor and teacher Christ the Giver of all wisdom, do not imitate this woman in

---

85. Smith, "Introduction," ix.
86. Translations from Cyril's *Homilies on Luke* come from *A Commentary upon the Gospel according to Saint Luke*, trans. Robert Payne Smith (1859, repr., Piscataway, NJ: Gorgias, 2009).

her love of learning, even Mary, who sat at the Saviour's feet, and filled her heart with the doctrines He taught, feeling as if she could never have enough of what so profited her.

This is an interesting rhetorical move because instead of setting up a contrast between Martha and Mary and comparing their behaviors, he calls his congregation to be like Mary, sitting and listening so that they can learn from the passage about how to be hospitable. After this introduction, he actually moves entirely away from Mary, choosing to focus instead on Jesus and Martha. In particular, he wants to focus on how Jesus and Martha are presented in the story as examples of how to receive and give hospitality.

As Cyril moves into the core of his argument, he states at once that both Mary and Martha were holy women, but Mary received a spiritual and thus eternal blessing. He then shifts to the example that he sees Jesus intentionally setting for his disciples on how to properly receive hospitality. Cyril observes the main thing Jesus does upon entering the home of Martha is to teach and to focus on offering those present spiritual doctrines and blessings. Similarly, any holy men who travel should have a similar focus: "For they must not immediately on entering indulge themselves in relaxation, or suppose that this is the reason why they lodge with men, but rather that they may fill them with every blessing, and the divine and sacred doctrines." These holy men he addresses are the religious teachers and authorities, though it is unclear whether he is referring only to priests and deacons or whether monks are also included. The saints, as he also calls them, are to only eat small amounts as to not be tempted to eat out of concerns for earthly pleasure. Rather, their entire focus should be on imitating Christ and offering their hosts spiritual blessings: "Thou therefore wilt give things more valuable than those thou receivest from men: for things temporal Thou wilt give things eternal: for earthly things things heavenly: for the things of sense, things intellectual: for the things that perish, things that endure."

After discussing how to receive hospitality, Cyril turns to discuss how to offer it. He is clear that Martha's problem in Luke 10 is not that she was being hospitable, but rather that she was going about it incorrectly: "Does any one then blame [Martha] for being occupied with careful service? By no means. For neither does the Saviour chide her for having proposed to herself the discharge of this duty; but rather He blamed her, as one who was labouring in vain, by wishing to procure more than was necessary. And this He did for our benefit, that He might fix a limit to hospitality." Martha's problem, according to Cyril, is that she was overly generous in her hospitality. Only a few things are necessary, and Cyril repeatedly returns to the fact that one should avoid excess. It is clear that he has shifted to address men and women who might be in the position of showing this hospitality. After all, he argues that the ones being welcomed only need a little to be sustained. If the host prepares too much, she is placing a stumbling block before them, because they might be tempted to indulge. Furthermore, the host is limiting her own spiritual blessings, because the guests will not be able to focus on what they need to be teaching. He then offers specifics on how the host should prepare her table. She should only have a plain table with a limited amount of food that is extremely simple; he describes it as "meager and scant," with only enough to drink to satisfy thirst.

Cyril is concerned that people believe they should prepare their tables like the rich: "For the rich in this world delight in costly banquets; and in many kinds of viands, prepared curiously often with sauces and flavours; a mere sufficiency is utterly scorned, while that which is extravagant is praised, and a profusion beyond all satiety is admired, and crowned with words of flattery. The drinkings and revellings are excessive; and the draining of cups, and courses of wines, the means of intoxication and gluttony." Such excess should be avoided at all costs. Furthermore, he argues that if people believe their hospitality should mirror that of the rich, then those without much means will never be willing to host a stranger or offer any hospitality to their neighbor. He rejects this belief. Because hospitality should always be simple, anyone, even the poor, can afford to offer it. No one should be unable to participate.

Anyone who participates in this act of hospitality, he argues, receives a double blessing. First, they receive the spiritual blessing of being taught by the holy men, which, as he has established, is a blessing that will never pass away. Second, they win the reward of hospitality. He points to the biblical examples of Abraham and Lot, who were both blessed because of their hospitality to strangers. Cyril concludes with a call for all Christians to engage in this practice: "Very great therefore is the virtue of hospitality, and especially worthy of the saints: let us therefore also practise it, for so will the heavenly Teacher lodge and rest in our hearts."

Cyril's version of Luke 10:38–42 includes the longer textual variant of 10:41–42: "There are few things necessary, indeed only one." The few things that Jesus mentions Cyril interprets to be the few dishes that Martha was supposed to prepare. This is the core of his entire interpretation. It is unclear whether Cyril is aware of other interpretations, but his reading is far removed from debates about contemplative versus active living. We note again the importance of the textual variants in Luke 10:41–42. Like Basil before him, Cyril appears to be using a different base text from either Augustine or Chrysostom, and it shifts how he reads the story entirely. In his reading, there is no comparison between Mary and Martha; in fact, Mary is almost a side note in his sermon. There is no concern over monastic behavior or the role of physical work in Christianity. For him, this story is a lesson intended to instruct followers of Christ about how to both properly receive and give hospitality.

It is also notable that in this sermon, Cyril reflects many pastoral concerns. His is an extremely practical sermon. He lays out how and why people should welcome religious teachers and other authorities into their homes, offering specific suggestions and discussing potential pitfalls. He even addresses concerns about wealth and the lack thereof that might keep people from being able to be hospitable. He gives the religious authorities under his authority specific instructions on how to behave in the home of a host, placing Jesus as the ideal guest, whom they should imitate.

Conclusion

Various homilies on Luke 10:38–42 highlight different concerns, though each concern can be found in the text itself. Augustine approaches the two sisters as representative of the present life of the church and the future life. Chrysostom explicitly rejects readings that prioritize contemplation at the expense of working, arguing the passage illustrates the need for proper discernment. Cyril uses the text to present his vision for giving and receiving hospitality. These three preachers and their sermons on this passage reveal that any claims about uniformity of interpretation in the early Christian world are clearly misguided.

It is relevant that each of these sermons was delivered to a mixed audience, including lay and clergy, men and women, rich and poor, perhaps even pagan and believers. Unlike the passages discussed in chapter 3, where most of the texts were directed to ascetics, these homilies are directed toward people practicing and discovering Christianity in the midst of busy lives, filled with children, businesses, civic duties, and other responsibilities. The preachers and their congregations are not separated from the problems and tribulations of the world, such as poverty and political unrest. As such, these sermons reflect practical and pastoral concerns. Augustine wants his congregation to be encouraged to keep doing the work of Martha, even though he knows it is difficult, so that they can one day have the better part of Mary. Chrysostom is worried that his congregation will believe certain monastic interpretations of this passage and think that Jesus is condemning work of any kind. Cyril wants his congregation to practice hospitality, and he believes everyone should be able to do it, no matter their personal wealth. Ultimately, the pastoral context of these sermons, all of which were delivered in major cities, make them notably different from most of the monastic interpretations of the same passage.

It is worth noting again how even in mixed groups with women present, this story does not become a story about women for women. Rather, Mary and Martha continue to be discussed in the context of discipleship more broadly. Only Chrysostom briefly turns to address the women in his congregation directly when discussing Mary and Martha (in John 12), and even then he shifts quickly to discussing how their behavior is an example for men as well. Finally, it is relevant that at this stage in the fifth century, Mary had not yet been conflated with other Marys in the New Testament, though Chrysostom clearly knows that this conflation is a possibility. This conflation was not solidified until the Middle Ages. Right now, in each of these contexts, Mary and Martha are two holy disciples of Christ whose encounter with Christ is intended to teach all Christians important lessons in hospitality, discernment, the importance of service, and the nature of the life to come.

5
Medieval Readers

In this respect, the story of Mary and Martha is a microcosm of the difficulty in distinguishing between old and new elements of interpretation. Very few [medieval] interpretations, except perhaps in detail, were absolutely new.
— Giles Constable, "The Interpretation of Mary and Martha"

With the sign of the cross, Martha subdued the dragon's wildness and with her own girdle bound its neck as the people looked on intently from afar. "What is it," she asked, "that you fear? Here I am holding this serpent and still you keep back."
— The Life of Saint Mary Magdalene and of Her Sister Saint Martha, translated by David Mycoff

Introduction

The medieval period continued the conversation concerning Mary and Martha of Bethany and their place within the construction of Christian discipleship. The patristic threads of interpretation are rewoven as medieval theologians expand, adapt, and resist earlier readings. Debates over whether one can be fully Mary in this life and questions about the value and necessity of Martha's service were rehashed in different religious communities. As Giles Constable observes, while there were changes in emphasis and tendency within Western medieval interpretations, very little was actually new.[1] In the first section of this chapter, we will examine

---

1. Constable, "Interpretation of Mary and Martha," 14. In this extended essay, which is over 140 pages, Constable walks through almost every reference to Mary and Martha in the medieval period, translating a number of important references that otherwise do not currently exist in any translation. Unless otherwise noted, all medieval translations in this chapter come from him.

his claim by examining a number of commentaries, sermons, and art from the medieval West.[2]

While much of the theology surrounding Luke 10:38–42 remained familiar, new elements of interpretation did appear during the Middle Ages. These new elements make up the second section of this chapter. The first element is the tendency to conflate Mary of Bethany and Mary Magdalene. The merging of these two biblical characters led to Mary receiving new characteristics, which in turn shaped understandings of Luke 10:38–42. One can also see the Virgin Mary introduced into the narrative, as she became representative of the one who is both Martha and Mary. The introduction of other Marys into the story in turn affected interpretations of Martha's character. Particularly in the late Middle Ages, one finds interpretations around her shift to include new elements. The rise of religious artwork allowed for a form of visual exegesis that highlights many of the common interpretative threads as well as the conflation between Mary and Mary Magdalene. Finally, during the Middle Ages, certain religious women were interpreting this passage, providing new perspectives on the story. Their interpretations allow us to understand the ways in which female interpreters both aligned with and diverged from the formerly exclusive male conversation on Luke 10:38–42.

Throughout this chapter, I show that Mary and Martha continued to be important as examples of discipleship for both men and women. Their lives represented the actions that all Christians should practice.

Interpreting the Bible in the Medieval World

I begin with some observations on how the Bible was read and interpreted in the Middle Ages. Though the medieval period stretches over a millennium and includes many different traditions throughout the church in the East and the West, the Bible was a universal influence, affecting intellectual, moral, and aesthetic dimensions of life. As Francis van Liere argues, "One cannot understand the medieval world without appreciating the scope of medieval people's engagement with biblical stories, characters

---

2. Due to space constraints, this chapter will focus primarily on the medieval West, meaning there is no discussion of Mary and Martha in icons or within prominent Eastern writers.

and images."³ Medieval scholarship has still not uncovered all the nuances of medieval exegesis throughout these centuries. In fact, some have even claimed that the study of exegesis is the "last great unexplored frontier" of the medieval period.⁴ That said, there have been several important works published on this topic over the past fifty years, and it is possible to outline some general beliefs and practices that shaped medieval interpreters and their approach to reading Scripture.

The first is the central belief shared by all medieval and patristic exegetes alike that the Bible is entirely composed of God's words, with the biblical authors serving more as scribes than interpreters. It is not just that the Bible is a story about God; it is the story of God by God and thus is entirely true and consistent.⁵ This commitment to the inherent truth of the Bible was central to medieval exegesis, as even difficult or seemingly contradictory passages had to be found to be in line with the overall principles of Christian faith.

Intersecting with this belief about the truth of the Bible was a belief that the Bible is not a foreign book, studied from afar. Rather, the Bible and its characters were always near to the readers. As Beryl Smalley notes, "Sacred history unrolled itself before [the reader], the Old Testament characters were living and near to him.... It was a familiar procession of patriarchs and prophets, the Savior and his Apostles."⁶ Medieval exegetes were fully enmeshed in the world of the Bible. This is not to say that they

---

3. Frans van Liere, *Introduction to the Medieval Bible* (Cambridge: Cambridge University Press, 2014), xi.

4. E. Ann Matter, review of *L'Exégèse chrétienne de la Bible en Occident médiéval*, by Gilbert Dahan, *Speculum* 77 (2002): 1272–74. For an overview of scholarship on this question over the last thirty years, see in particular Christopher Ocker and Kevin Madigan, "After Beryl Smalley: Thirty Years of Medieval Exegesis, 1984–2013," *JBRec* 2 (2015): 87–130.

5. See, for instance, Hugh of Saint Victor, who wrote: "Only that scripture is rightly called 'sacred' that is inspired by the Spirit of God, make the human person holy—reforming him, according to the likeness of God, instructing him to know God, and exhorting him to love Him, whatever is taught in it is truth; whatever is prescribed in it is goodness; whatever is promised in it is happiness. For God is truth without falsehood, goodness without malice, happiness without misery." See *On Sacred Scripture* 1, in *Interpretation of Scripture: Theory; A Selection of Works of Hugh, Andrew, Godfrey and Richard of St Victor, and Robert of Melun*, ed. Franklin Harkin and Frans van Liere, VTT 3 (Turnhout: Brepols, 2012), 213.

6. Beryl Smalley, *The Study of the Bible in the Middle Ages* (Notre Dame: University of Notre Dame Press, 1952), 24.

believed interpreting the Bible was simple, but they did not see themselves as outside observers. For them, the biblical world was still the same world as their own. Thus, we will see that when they discussed Mary and Martha, they were not concerned with historical questions, but rather they continued to ask questions about what Mary and Martha could teach them about living faithful lives in the present.

A second core tenet of medieval exegesis is that the Bible contains multiple levels of meaning. This, of course, is another trait that medieval exegesis shares with its patristic predecessor, though it became more formulaic during this period. Each passage can have multiple levels of meaning. While different medieval scholars discuss these levels differently, they can be broadly described as literal (or historical), moral, allegorical, and anagogical, as summarized by Augustine of Dacia:[7]

> Littera gesta docer, quod credas allegoria; Moralia quid agas, quid speres anagogia.
> The letter teaches the facts; allegory what you should believe; the moral what you should do and anagogy what you should hope for.

Often modern scholars have been focused on identifying the nuances of the different levels.[8] But for our purposes, it is important to understand that interpretation always began with the literal and then moved into the various spiritual interpretations.[9] These other interpretations involved uncovering the deeper, often hidden, meaning of the text. The allegorical meaning of the text was usually found in a line-by-line spiritual interpreta-

---

7. Augustine of Denmark, "Augustinus de Dacia, Rotulus Pugillaris," as quoted in van Liere, *Introduction to Medieval Exegesis*, 121. Van Liere refers to this phrase as being best understood as a medieval jingle written to help train biblical scholars.

8. Henri de Lubac, in his important work on medieval exegesis, argues that often modern scholars spend too much time trying to uncover whether there were three or four levels of Scripture, but he concludes that in actual practice, there is no real difference in interpretation, regardless of whether a medieval author describes three or four levels when discussing Scripture in the abstract. See de Lubac, *Medieval Exegesis*, trans. Mark Sebanc, 4 vols. (Grand Rapids: Eerdmans, 1998), 1:91.

9. See Hugh of Saint Victor again: "I wonder how some people dare to present themselves as scholars of allegory when they do not even know the first meaning of the letter. They say: 'We read Scripture, but we do not read the letter. We do not care about the letter, for we teach allegory.' How can you read Scripture and not read the letter? If we take away the letter, what is Scripture?" (*On Sacred Scripture* 5, in Harkin and van Liere, *Interpretation of Scripture*, 216).

tion of the text, with particular sensitivity to imagery and numbers. The allegorical level teaches the reader who discovers it about the mysteries of faith. The moral meaning in turn offers readers instructions on how they should live their lives. The anagogical level focuses on what the text teaches about the life to come. It should be noted that not every passage contains every level.

Medieval exegesis, however, was not meant to be a free-for-all, where one could make any far-reaching claim about a text. As de Lubac observes, "Students of Scripture were not allowed to betray spiritual understanding to imaginary fancies and they were not allowed, moreover, to make spiritual understanding a rhetorical or improvisational enterprise."[10] There were limits to spiritual exegesis put in place by the rule of faith and the literal level of the text. Scripture could not mean something that contradicted the foundation of Christian faith, nor could a reading blatantly contradict the literal level.

A third recurring theme of medieval exegesis was that their interpretations were often built on patristic interpretations. As John Contreni, Richard Mardsen, and E. Ann Matter observe: "The fathers loomed large over almost the entire field of scriptural exegesis, especially those scriptures that meant the most to the early Middle Ages—the Pentateuch, Psalms and the Gospels."[11] Many medieval writers had access to earlier patristic readings, and so they drew on those as their starting point in many cases.[12] As we will see, this is certainly true of medieval exegesis on Mary and Martha.

A final characteristic is the influence of monasteries on medieval exegesis. Van Liere argues that after the late antique period, the monastery

---

10. De Lubac, *Medieval Exegesis*, 1:16.

11. John J. Contreni, Richard Marsden, and E. Ann Matter, "The Patristic Legacy to c. 1000," in *From 600 to 1450*, vol. 2 of *The New Cambridge History of the Bible*, ed. Richard Marsden and E. Ann Matter (Cambridge: Cambridge University Press, 2012), 507.

12. Because of this dependency on the patristic writings, many medieval scholars argue that the medieval writers of simply regurgitated old readings. Smalley rejects this oversimplified reading. She argues, "A book as central to medieval thought as the Bible was must necessarily have been read and interpreted rather differently by different generations. There may be underlying continuity; there are bound to be changes in emphasis." Smalley has shown throughout her work that while there is significant dependence on patristic thinkers in medieval interpretations, oftentimes there are differences in emphasis as cultural concerns and other changes forced different questions to be highlighted (*Study of the Bible*, xiii).

shifted from an ascetic refuge, away from the world, "to a school and a scriptorium, a place where biblical texts were read, studied, preserved and reproduced. Although one should not underestimate the role that bishops played ... the monastery would remain a place of biblical study for years to come."[13] For most of the medieval period, monasteries were the central location of biblical interpretation. This means that the Bible was being read and interpreted within a community of faith whose members were constantly immersing themselves in Scripture, in liturgy, daily readings, prayers, and so on.[14] The monastic setting of medieval exegesis cannot be ignored, particularly when it comes to interpretations of Luke 10:38–42.

Picking Up Familiar Threads

In light of these common factors, it should not be surprising that most medieval interpretations of Luke 10:38–42 are built on patristic treatments of the passage. The medieval writers were concerned with the same interpretative issues that Origen, Augustine, and others had already highlighted. Medieval interpreters were heavily influenced by the idea that Mary represented contemplation while Martha represented action, models of discipleship for both men and women. The relationship between Mary and Martha, and by extension the relationship between contemplation and action, is a primary focus of medieval interpretation, but as in patristic interpretation, this relationship is discussed in different ways.

In this section I identify these common threads. None of these interpretations are unfamiliar to us, and yet they often carry different emphases and expand on patristic concerns. First, a substantial number of medieval exegetes focus on Mary and Martha as illustrative of different behaviors within individual Christians. At different times in one's faith journey, one can practice contemplation, while at other times one can practice acts of service. As in the patristic period, medieval interpreters offer different answers as to the correct balance between these two, which life should come first, and whether one can achieve perfect contemplation in this life.

---

13. Van Liere, *Introduction to the Medieval Bible*, 144.

14. See Derek Olsen, *Reading Matthew with Monks: Liturgical Interpretation in Anglo-Saxon England* (Collegeville, MN: Liturgical Press, 2015). Olson presents an argument for how the structure of the monastic life influenced the interpretation of the biblical texts.

A second thread is that Mary and Martha represent two fundamentally different types of Christians: the contemplative Christian and the active Christian. Martha comes to represent laity and clerics, whereas Mary represents those who have chosen the monastic life. A third familiar thread is an ongoing dispute over which sister is to be preferred: Mary and her acts of contemplation or Martha and her acts of service. While Mary is continually said to have chosen the better part, we will see that Martha has a large number of defenders, particularly during the later Middle Ages.

Despite their lack of overall agreement on the relationship between Mary and Martha, interpreters consistently focus on the two women as models for all Christians, not solely as models of their gender. As Constable states in his thorough overview of medieval interpretations of the two sisters: "The fact that Mary and Martha were related as sisters was more important at that time than that they were women, and their models were applied to men as well as women."[15] Finally, we see that some patristic interpretations dropped out of the conversation, most notably those interpretations that present the story as a lesson in proper hospitality.

Mary and Martha as Different Types of Christian Behavior

The most frequent reading of Luke 10:38–42 has Martha representing acts of service and Mary representing acts of contemplation. The contrast often draws explicitly on patristic authors, particularly Augustine and Origen.[16] However, as we have seen, even within Origen and Augustine there are different nuances. Likewise, within medieval interpretation, one finds different perspectives on the relationship between those two types of

---

15. Constable, "Interpretation of Mary and Martha," 4.
16. Another important patristic figure for medieval interpretations of Luke 10:38–42 is Gregory the Great, who mostly follows the interpretation of Augustine. Space did not permit a further discussion of him in previous chapters, but Gregory states that Christ praised Mary but also showed Martha to be praiseworthy, "because the merits of the active life are great but those of the contemplative life are preferable" (*Moral.* 6.37 [Constable]). In a homily on Ezek 1:8, he depicts Mary and Martha as the creature described there. Martha and the active life are the hands of a man on the creature, while the Mary and the contemplative life are the wings. He concludes: "Although we do some good by the active, we fly to heavenly desire through the contemplative" (*Hom. Ezech.* 1.3 [Constable]). For a brief overview of Gregory's interpretation, see Constable, "Interpretation of Mary and Martha," 20–22.

actions. In this section, I outline the three major directions this interpretation takes.

Practicing Contemplation and Action in This Life

Patristic interpretations of Mary and Martha were introduced into the Middle Ages in the writings of Bede and Isidore of Seville.[17] Isidore of Seville, writing at the turn of the seventh century, discussed Mary and Martha. In *Allegories*, he presents Martha and Mary as images of the present and future church. In *Sentences*, he argues that Christians begin as Marthas, living an active life, but should then aspire to live lives of contemplation like Mary: "The active life is the innocence of good works. The contemplative life is the vision of heavenly things; the former is common among many people, but the latter among few.... Someone who is proficient first in the active life does well to ascend to contemplation" (*Sent.* 3.15). That said, Isidore insists that one cannot permanently remain in a state of contemplation during this life. One must return to acts of physical service. In the *Book of Various Questions against the Jews and Other Unfaithful*, which has been attributed to Isidore, one finds this idea further fleshed out:

> Both [the active and contemplative] are so connected with each other that one cannot suffice without the other, since neither can the love of neighbor be of any use without the love of God nor can the love of God become perfect without the love of neighbor.... Those men known to be perfect who, at a distinct time within the church, know how to rise from the active life to the contemplative and how to descend by brotherly love from the contemplative life to the active. If active action is well-maintained, as is fitting, it wins eternal life for its adherents. Contemplative action confers not only the life, however, but also the reward. (*Lib. var. quaest.* 49)

In this passage, one can see several of the interpretations we have already discussed stacked on top of each other. First is the idea that the lives of action and contemplation are connected, and both are needed in Christian faith. Second is the idea that even Christians who are pursuing the perfect life of contemplation must at times participate in action of service. The

---

17. Constable, "Interpretation of Mary and Martha," 23.

truly wise Christian can discern when this should happen. While Cassian and Augustine both argue for this view, such discernment became a major theme throughout medieval exegesis. Third, Isidore argues that the active life will also lead a Christian to eternal life, but that the contemplative life is ultimately better, as we have already seen in the writings of Pseudo-Macarius, the Book of Steps, and Cassian. Such a combination of ideas is frequent as authors take interpretations from previous authors and combine them to create their own view. Overall, though, it seems that Isidore believes the contemplative is ultimately the best life, while still acknowledging a role for the active life.

Bede, writing in Northumbria in the eighth century, takes a similar approach. He argues in his *Commentary on Luke* that "these sisters who were dear to the Lord show the two spiritual lives with which the holy church is concerned in the present. Martha is the active life by which we are associated with our neighbor by charity; Mary is the contemplative by which we aspire in the love of God" (*Luc. evang.* 3.10).[18] He goes on to the describe the two lives and to argue that the contemplative life is better because, while the active life will end in this life, the contemplative life "begins here in order to be perfected in the heavenly homeland" (3.10).[19] Bede's interpretation is quoted in Grimlaicus's *Rule for Solitaries*, written by a monk living at the turn of the tenth century. Chapters 8–12 have a discussion of the natures of the active and the contemplative lives, followed by an overview of the future rewards of each. He summarizes his view by quoting Bede:

> Some people think that the contemplative life is nothing else but acquaintance with things hidden and in the future, or leisure from all worldly occupations, or the study of Sacred Scripture. When we visit the sick, bury the dead, and correct the erring then we are in the active life. But when we shed tears in the sight of God and set ourselves to consider how great is the blessedness, the light, and the glory of the saints in heaven, then we are in the contemplative life. Whereas the active life begins with the body and finishes here below with it, the contemplative life begins here and reaches fulfillment in the age to come. Of these two lives, the

---

18. Translation from *Homilies on the Gospels*, trans. Lawrence T. Martin and David Hurst (Kalamazoo, MI: Cistercian, 1993). This interpretation clearly presents an argument for the dual love of God and neighbor.

19. This is pulled almost word for word from Gregory the Great's *Hom. Ezech.* 2.2.7.

active is signified by Martha, and the contemplative by Mary. But there is no doubt that Mary needs Martha.[20]

Embedded in this description of the active and contemplative lives is the tension that will be discussed again and again throughout the Middle Ages. The acts of Martha are good actions and in fact are necessary actions. Grimlaicus sums it up by saying, "There is no doubt that Mary needs Martha." This is the same tension we saw in Silvanus when he says that it is because of Martha that Mary is praised, or when Cassian discusses how one cannot always live a contemplative life because of the realities of living in this world (APalph 5). Taking care of the sick, burying the dead, and correcting those who err are all necessary. Furthermore, many bishops and other leaders lead contemplative lives but are then called into the active life again. Bede and Isidore bring this tension, already seen in the patristic period, into monastic conversations.

"Descending" to Action

This language of ascent and descent now began to appear frequently in discussions of Mary and Martha. A person ascends to the contemplative life of Mary, and then descends to the active life of Martha, according to the needs of the church. We have already seen this in Isidore's *Book of Various Questions*: "Those men known to be perfect who at a distinct time within the church know how to rise from the active life to the contemplative and how to descend by brotherly love from the contemplative life to the active" (*Lib. var. quaest.* 49). The Christian pursuing perfection will have the wisdom to know when she should descend to action.

The same idea is also expressed in Bruno of Segni's *Commentary on Luke*, written in the latter half of the eleventh century. He argues: "Although the contemplative life is better than the active life, yet the active life is necessary and never deceives.... The contemplative life could not exist without

---

20. Grimlaicus, *Rule of Solitaries*, trans. Andrew Thorton, CS 200 (Collegeville, MN: Liturgical Press, 2011), 42–43. Grimlaicus often just repackages ideas from previous thinkers such as Bede, Isidore, and Augustine, but occasionally he adds his own voice. For instance, in ch. 10 he writes: "Further if I may add something of my own, those who are living the active life are eager to forgive someone who sins against them; those who pursue the contemplative life are more ready to ignore injuries as though no blow had been struck at all" (44–45).

it in this life. Martha is more useful than Mary in churches.... Martha helps everyone; Mary helps herself" (*Comm. Luc.* 1.10.22).[21] Bruno is explicit that the work of the contemplative does not benefit the church in the same way as the work of the active person. He emphasizes that Jesus's response to Martha does not mean that her sister will never get up and help her again. Mary will have the proper discernment to know when to help, concluding: "Martha's care is good provided she ministers not to the world but to God. Mary should at times rise to help her caring sister.... For when solitary and peaceful men of religion dedicated to divine contemplation take on the rule of the churches at the request of many people, then Mary certainly rises and comes to help her careful sister" (1.10.22). Isidore and Bruno, like most medieval interpreters, acknowledge that Mary's part is better, but they want to emphasize the necessity of the active life and the inability to always remain in the state of contemplation. The need for discernment reflects the same concern that Chrysostom exhibited in his interpretation of the passage. One needs to be able to recognize when one should be contemplative and when one should be active.

Balancing the Two Lives

Other medieval interpreters consequently argue that Mary should not always be privileged over Martha, but the best Christian life is one that balances both. This reminds us of Origen's claim that "there is no action without contemplation, or contemplation without action" (*Fr. Luc.* 171). This point is made especially by Bernard of Clairvaux, the twelfth-century abbot who helped form the Cistercian Order. Bernard was fiercely committed to the monastic life and a strong advocate for the contemplative life.[22] Yet he argues that one should strive to cultivate a life of both contemplation, which he equates with freedom for oneself, and action, which is service to others. He claims: "He who is properly free for God may have the better part, but he who is perfect in both has the best part" (*Serm.* 2.2.5–6).[23]

---

21. See here that Bruno reverses the standard idea that Mary descends to help because here she rises to help, by standing up from her seated position at the feet of Christ.

22. G. R. Evans, *Bernard of Clairvaux* (New York: Oxford University Press, 2000), 3.

23. Translations of Bede's works come from *Selected Works*, trans. G. R. Evans (New York: HarperCollins, 2005).

Bernard elsewhere uses the metaphor of night and day to make a similar argument. The day is the time for action and service, while the evening is the time for contemplation (*Serm.* 3.4). While contemplation may be preferable, one cannot sleep forever. In this life, one must get up and serve: "As often as the mind falls from contemplation, it recovers itself in action, whence it will return more familiarly to the same thing, as from a nearby place, since these two are companions living side by side, as Martha is indeed the sister of Mary" (*Serm.* 51.2.2). Like Augustine, Bernard believes that in the life to come, one will be able to remain permanently in a state of contemplation, but in present human existence, the perfect life embodies the characteristics of both Mary and Martha (*Serm.* 57).[24]

Richard of Saint Victor, also writing in the twelfth century, held a similar view, arguing that the contemplative life must alternate with the active life. He wrote in his treatise on the rule of Saint Augustine, while reflecting on Mary's need for Martha: "[The contemplative] ceases from time to time to do even good things in order meanwhile to be free for divine contemplation.... The two lives are indeed separate but cannot properly be separated, for the contemplation of God is required in action and the utility of the neighbor must be considered in peace. They differ, however, in that the love of truth seeks holy quiet and the need for fraternal love undertakes just activity" (as quoted in Robert of Brindlington, *The Brindlington Dialogue*). Richard clearly thinks that contemplation is the better part, but like Bernard and Augustine, he recognizes that one cannot remain in the contemplative state forever. There must be a balance. He offers a practical example of what it means to embody both action and contemplation when he discusses preaching, which he labels as the highest form of action. In order to preach, one must practice internal contemplation and prayer over the Scripture at hand before going out and proclaiming the message. He holds that the entire biblical narrative, not only the story of Mary and Martha, supports this reading because, he argues, it never presents just one type of life without the other. After all, he writes, "No one can persist in the application of contemplation for a time without the exercise of

---

24. See also *Serm.* 71. Bernard often includes Lazarus in his discussion of the better part and action and contemplation, an inclusion that had not appeared that frequently in previous interpretations. Interestingly, he argues that Lazarus cleaned the house before Christ came to visit, while Martha prepared it and Mary completed it. All three siblings were necessary (*Serm.* 2.7). See also Constable, "Interpretation of Mary and Martha," 65–76.

action just as action itself without contemplation is equally less agreeable, less discrete, less useful" (*Serm.* 33).

Hugh of Saint Cher, a Dominican friar, also describes good preaching as the result of both contemplation and action in his commentary on Luke written in 1235. He argues that the preacher who manages both is like Mary and Martha combined. He grants that contemplation is better than action, but ultimately the best life is the one that combines them both. The preacher who manages to do that is "truly the bride of Christ."[25] Constable observes that for Hugh, "There was a progression and overlap between the two loves, and no one could live an exclusively contemplative or an exclusively active life. Hugh distinguished the office from the persons and the parts and properties of each life and concluded that contemplation though more worthy was reciprocal with action in the life of the church, religious order and individuals."[26] Hugh also explicitly connected the story of Mary and Martha to the story of the good Samaritan, which precedes it, arguing that Mary and Martha represented the love of God, while the good Samaritan represented the love of neighbor (*Comm. Luc.* 10).[27] Both are needed.[28]

---

25. Constable, "Interpretation of Mary and Martha," 110.

26. Constable, "Interpretation of Mary and Martha," 111. See also Beryl Smalley, "The Gospels in the Paris Schools in the Late 12th and Early 13th Centuries: Peter the Chanter, Hugh of St. Cher, Alexander of Hales, John of La Rochelle," *FS* 39 (1979): 249-51.

27. It should be noted that this reading, which draws on Bede, is similar to Donahue's modern interpretation, which we discussed in ch. 2, showing that even new, modern interpretations are rarely new and that medieval scholars, despite their reputation for being haphazard in their interpretations, are close readers.

28. This particular view can also been seen in the writings of Thomas Aquinas, Thomas à Kempis, Robert Pullen, and many more important medieval thinkers. However, the above review is enough to show how prevalent the interpretation that Mary and Martha were two aspects of Christian behavior that needed to be properly balanced was during this period. As one can see, while the medieval interpreters mostly drew on patristic writers for their own readings, the emphasis has shifted slightly to focus on how one can achieve that balance between the two. For more examples, see Thomas Aquinas, *ST* 2.2 q. 182; Aquinas, *Impugn.* 1, 4; Thomas a Kempis, *Imitatio Christi* 2.8, 11; Robert Pullen, *Sent.* 7.23-25. (Pullen in particular summarizes this view when he writes: "Contemplation is suitable for those [who are] removed from the world; action suits those involved [in the world], but both are required of the prelate who by contemplating learns what he should for those who are beneath him" [Constable]).

Mary and Martha as Different Types of Christians

A second thread of medieval interpretation focuses on the two sisters as different types of Christians. There are Christians who are Marys and Christians who are Marthas. Marys are monks and other cloistered Christians, whereas Marthas are laity and clergy. While we have seen this idea already, it was expanded during the Middle Ages. As Constable notes, "The tendency to combine the lives of Mary and Martha in this world and to find the highest example of the Christian life ... was paralleled, sometimes in the works of the same writers by a tendency to separate the two lives and to associate each with a distinct social or religious group or category."[29] Thus, the comparison appears as the authors discuss different groups of Christians and their interactions with each other. For instance, Geoffrey of Saint Thierry, a twelfth-century French Benedictine abbot, described people who separate themselves and call themselves contemplatives as Marys, and the "two orders of rectors and married men" as Marthas (*Serm.* 2). Usually the comparison is that basic, so much so that "choosing the better part" becomes shorthand for choosing the monastic life.[30]

Joachim of Fiore, who discusses Luke 10:38–42 at great length in his *Concord of the New and Old Testament*, presents a similar parallelism. He argues strongly that Mary and Martha represent monks on one side and laity and clergy on the other. Only certain people are able to attain the life of a contemplative, only those who are "spiritual," but the life of Martha is still a good one and should be practiced by the more "fleshly and weak" (*Conc.* 5.16). Such completely different lives cannot mix. He uses the analogy of speech and silence, arguing that each life was the alternative of the other, as speech and silence cannot exist in the same space. Furthermore, you cannot leave one and become the other. You are a Mary or a Martha; there is no switching between them: "For just as it is impossible for Martha to be changed into Mary so it is impossible for the church of laymen to be changed fully into the churches of clerics or for the body to be changed into souls.... For the mystery of Martha is one thing and the contemplation of Mary another" (5.71). Joachim is certain that these two groups are separate, even if they hold complementary roles in Christian faith, and

---

29. Constable, "Interpretation of Mary and Martha," 72.
30. See later discussion of Hildegard of Bingen and her letters for examples of this shorthand.

that they are arranged hierarchically, with Mary and the contemplatives clearly holding the higher place.

Stephen of Murot, the founder of the Grandmont Order, also drew a sharp distinction between Marys and Marthas. He rejects the idea that once one has been called to the life of Mary, God would then call one to descend again to the life of Martha: "When a man leaves himself and throws himself at the feet of Jesus in order to hear His words and do His will, the Lord never orders him to return to the care of Martha, that is, to the good which he could do in the world. For the Lord praised Mary, who was sitting at His feet and listening to his words, more than Martha, who served and thought that her sister was doing nothing" (*Sent.* 10.4). His monastic order, which was one of the strictest of its kind, had rules that ensured members were not to associate with people outside the monastery to show any desire for outside work or concern for earthly matters. Exegetically, Stephen draws on Jesus's response to Martha to show that Jesus does not command Mary to help her sister (*Regula* 35). In the same way, members of the Grandmont Order did not work on temporal issues. They were to spend all their time in contemplation. Lay brothers were the ones who worked on external cares and who kept the monastery functioning, with the choir monks themselves praying, reading Scripture, and ministering to each other.

Other theologians did not make such strong divisions. In fact, the archbishop of Magdeburg in 1107 argued that Marys (monks and hermits) are required to come and help the Marthas at certain times out of Christian love: "You most holy fathers, monks, hermits and recluses have chosen the best part with Mary, but the present time requires you to rise with Martha from the peace of contemplation, because Mary is essential to your brothers who have been greatly troubled with Martha. We speak to you and indeed Christ speaks to you in us saying, 'Arise and make haste my love, my dove, and come.'"[31] He argues that the two groups should live in harmony with the Marys of the faith (who have achieved the better part) and should help the Marthas who are struggling. There was never to be any sort of discord between the two sisters or the two groups. For instance, Stephen of Tournai writes: "Martha does not complain at the silence of Mary, and it is wonderful to say, Mary seated at the feet of the

---

31. Otto Posse, ed., *Urkunden der Markgrafen von Meissen und Landgrafen von Thuringen 1100–1195* (Leipzig: Gieseke & Devrient, 1889), 19.

Lord does not leave Martha alone to serve. Between them there is constant joy and communal exaltation" (*Ep.* 1).

It does seem, however, that there was occasionally discord between the two groups, a tension that can be seen even as early as the Liber Graduum. For instance, Robert Pullen writes in his *Sentences*, Christians should grieve whenever they see active and contemplative men not living in harmony together. He argues that the fact that Mary and Martha were called sisters reinforces the fact that active and contemplative men are supposed to show each other brotherly love (*Sent.* 7.23–25).[32] He argues that people do not understand the proper relationship that Marys and Marthas are supposed to have. Hugh of Fouilloy also seems to know of issues between Marys and Marthas. He argues, however, that those who complain about Marys (monks) are false Marthas and vice versa: "So Mary, who should be silent and was accustomed to hear the Lord's word, detracts from Martha and serves verbosity. This is the false Mary. For there is a true Mary and a false Mary, a true Martha and a false Martha" (*Claustr.* 2.10). One of the main critiques he levels against false Marys is that they are those who criticize people for engaging in pastoral practices. Other practices of false Marys include being involved with external matters and complaining about being unable to go out into the world. False Marthas, on the other hand, complain not because they are doing the Lord's work but because of worldly things. Interestingly, he concludes that "since like seeks like, however, [the false Martha] wishes to have the false Mary as a companion" (2.10). Similarly, true Marys and Marthas live in harmony together.

The distinction between Mary and Martha was used polemically in monastic rivalry. Monks often accused other orders of being Marthas, while they were the true Marys. This can be seen throughout the Middle Ages, particularly among the Cluniacs and Cistericians, but for our purposes two examples will suffice. First, Archbishop Siegfried of Mainz describes his transfer from the house of canons to the Order of Cluny in the following way: "When I considered with myself that although Martha was busy about with much serving to the Lord, Mary, however, who was sitting quietly listening to his words, chose the best part, I transferred what I had started into the more excellent rule of monks according to the

---

32. Pullen himself holds that the two groups should not be so sharply divided and that the best life is one that exhibits both.

venerable habit and sacrosanct custom of the monastery of Cluny and Hirsau" (*Mainz.* 1). Siegfried joined the order of the Cluniacs because he believed they were the true Marys, who have chosen the better part.

In the *Dialogue of Two Monks* by Idungus of Regensburg, a Cluniac and a Cistercian are in conversation with each other. The Cluniac monk accuses the Cistercians of being Marthas since they are willing to engage in physical labor: "Just as your order is active because it chooses for itself righteous labor with Martha, so our order is contemplative because it chooses for itself the holy tranquility with Mary. I do not doubt that our order is of greater dignity than yours because it chose for itself, as Christ is witness, the better part" (*Dial.* 1.5). This was a frequent complaint by the Cluniacs to the Cistercians, since they were permitted to work. The monk in this dialogue says this proves that they were actually Marthas. The Cistercian monk responds, however, that they have chosen the better part, like Mary, because Mary recognized her freedom to sometimes work and to sometimes listen. He argues: "Someone is called a contemplative because he is free from works of mercy, owing to his desire for contemplation, not from manual labour which helps rather than hinders contemplatives" (1.5). He concludes that this makes them the true contemplatives (the true Marys). These two examples show how different monastic orders attempted to embody the real Mary, the one who has chosen the better part of contemplation.

In this thread of interpretation, there are sharp distinctions between the two sisters, putting them in contrast to each other. This tension, of course, was present in the patristic period, in particular in the Liber Graduum and in John Chrysostom's sermons, but in the medieval period the tension was elevated as Luke 10:38–42 was used more polemically as a scriptural warrant to justify distinct classes among Christians.

Which Sister Is to Be Preferred?

A final common thread, picked up from the patristic period and carried into the Middle Ages, concerns which sister is to be preferred. On one hand, Mary was repeatedly affirmed as the sister to emulate, since Jesus says she has chosen the better part. On the other hand, Martha experienced a surge in popularity during the medieval period, and more interpreters argued that she was the better sister, presenting the better way to live.

The predominant reading was still that Jesus chose Mary over Martha. Mary is perfect and spiritual, and Martha, while still having value, is viewed as physical and less than perfect. The notion that one must descend to the acts of Martha implies that the higher place is held by Mary. Sometimes, the praise of Mary is explicit, particularly among monastic writers. For instance, Hugh of Pontigny, in a sermon on the assumption, describes Martha as representing a human traveler, but Mary is a heavenly resident: "a traveller engaging with the enemy; a resident established on the seat of his realm. A man as traveller; an angel as resident.... The man is careful and busy about many things with Martha; the angel imparts one thing with Mary."[33] Mary's part is clearly better. In his commentary on the Rule of Benedict, he makes the more standard argument for preferring Mary: "The wise man will put an end also to honest things in favour of more salutary things. The part of Martha is good, but that of Mary is best. Even Christ at the end of his life stopped preaching and was free for prayer."[34] Hugh, like most monastic writers, is clear that Mary's is the life that should be emulated.

That said, particularly as the Middle Ages progressed, Martha began to be more elevated. Constable argues that this made certain monastic thinkers defensive about Mary, leading to more explicit arguments in her favor.[35] For instance, William of Thierry asks in his *Meditations*: "Where today is Martha's complaint that she alone is sent away to service? Does not rather Mary's concern that she be allowed to sit at the feet of the Lord fill the house more strongly today?" (*Med. or.* 11.19). He believed more people were privileging works of service over acts of contemplation.[36] This elevation of Martha and her life of service can be seen in the following three examples of medieval writers: Pope Innocent III, Simon of Tournai, and Meister Eckhart. Each writer takes a different exegetical approach to make his argument in favor of Martha.

---

33. Hugh of Pontigeny, unpublished sermon, selections published by Jean Leclercq in *Bibliotheque national: Catalogue generale des manuscrits Latin* (Paris, 1966), 136. For more information about the transmission history of this homily, see Constable, "Interpretation of Mary and Martha," 46 n. 178.

34. See Constable, "Interpretation of Mary and Martha," 47.

35. Constable, "Interpretation of Mary and Martha," 91.

36. For another example of this overt privileging of Mary, see Petrarch, *On the Solitary Life*, who writes that while Martha was holy, Mary was much more so: "If it true, as learned men assert that in addition to the truth of history, the mystery of the double life is also contained under the cover of the two sisters, then there is no doubt that the contemplative was preferred to the busy and active life by the judgement of Christ and should be preferred in the choice especially of Christ's faithful followers."

First, Simon of Tournai, a twelfth-century theologian, argues in *Disputations* that the "active man is more meritorious than the contemplative man" (*Disp.* 4.1). He allows for the fact that contemplation is a more joyful and sweeter act, but argues that this is irrelevant to the discussion. It is irrelevant, because ultimately what matters is not what is more joyful but what is most advantageous. He argues that action is better than contemplation because contemplation only helps the contemplative, but the active man helps many more people. He resists the standard reading of Luke 10:42, "the best part, which shall not be taken away from her," as proof of contemplative superiority. Instead, he argues this phrase should be read instead as "the best part, that is, because it will not be taken away from her." Constable argues that this discussion of the grammar of the phrase, which seems minor, is intended to show that Jesus's response is not absolute statement about Mary being the best, and thus Simon is able to build an argument for Martha's superiority.[37] Ultimately, Simon concludes, "For to him administration is a merit so that he may see contemplation as a prize in the future, whereas for the contemplative, contemplation is a prize in the present rather than a merit" (*Disp.* 4.2). Simon holds to his argument about action being better but in reality has to do some exegetical sleight of hand to get his argument to align with Luke 10:38–42. Nonetheless, instead of simply dismissing the text, he finds a way to work within it.

Pope Innocent III takes a different approach in his treatment of Mary and Martha. Constable describes the pope as a "vigorous proponent of Martha."[38] Innocent III, in particular, was concerned with being able to recruit enough bishops out of the monasteries, and thus his advocacy of Martha is no surprise. In his letter *On Renunciation*, which was addressed to a monk who had recently been brought into the episcopacy, Innocent III argues:

> You should not think that Martha, who was busy with many things chose a bad part because Mary chose the best part, which would not be taken away from her, since the former is more fruitful though the latter is more secure. Although Mary is sweeter, Martha is more useful since the production of children of Lia's bleary eyes are preferable to Rachel's beauty.... We therefore advise you not to reject the work of pastoral

---

37. Constable, "Interpretation of Mary and Martha," 91.
38. Constable, "Interpretation of Mary and Martha," 97.

rule lest perchance he refuse to receive you with Mary at his feet if you refused to minister to Him with the careful Martha when he visited you.[39]

Here Innocent III does not reject the idea that Mary has chosen the best part, but he reinforces the idea that Martha's role is more useful and more fruitful. He also expands his reading to offer a warning to the new bishop that to reject this part of Martha and not minister when he has been called might lead to Jesus rejecting him and not allowing him to sit at his feet with Mary. In another letter a few years later, Innocent III reiterates the idea that Martha's work is ultimately more useful and fruitful, arguing that Jesus loved the ministries of both Mary and Martha. Like Simon of Tournai, he also acknowledges that the ministry of Mary was sweeter but that Martha's was harder won: "For where the battle is harder, the victory is more glorious, as the Apostle says that he 'is not crowned except he strive lawfully'" (*Ep.* 8.15). Innocent III seems to imply here that Martha's part is more notable because of the struggle. As Constable notes, "Innocent was a trained lawyer and skillful advocate.... He did not deny the traditional recognition of the superiority of Mary, but he softened the terms and put it in an almost selfish light."[40] In Innocent's work, to ignore the call of Christ to serve in order to sit in solitude was a dangerous decision because one ran the risk of being rejected by Christ.

Meister Eckhart, our third example, was similarly favorable to Martha. In one of his sermons, he presents a case for privileging Martha over Mary. Eckhart, a fourteenth-century Dominican friar, presents a full exegetical argument for why Martha is the more advanced sister. He begins by arguing that Martha, whom he says is older and more spiritually mature, does not ask Jesus to get Mary to help out of anger, but rather out of concern and love for her sister. Martha knows Mary better than Mary knows herself, and she is worried that she is sitting at the feet of Christ for her own happiness and not for her own spiritual gain:

---

39. It should be noted that Rachel and Leah, Jacob's wives, are also frequently linked to Mary and Martha, as they are another biblical pair of women who come to represent the lives of action and contemplation. Mary and Martha are frequently linked with other biblical pairs of both genders, as we have seen: Moses and Aaron, Peter and John, and others. That said, Rachel and Leah became a popular comparison, as we can see in Innocent's argument cited above.

40. Constable, "Interpretation of Mary and Martha," 99.

> Thus it was with Martha. Hence her words, "Lord, tell her to help me," as if to say, "my sister thinks she is able to do what she wishes to do, as long as she sits and receives solace from you. Let her see if it is so: bid her get up and go from you." The latter part was kindly meant, though she spoke her mind. Mary was filled with longing, longing she knew not why and wanting she knew not what. We suspect that she, dear Mary, sat there a little more for her own happiness than for spiritual profit. That is why Martha said, "Bid her rise, Lord," fearing that by dallying in this joy she might progress no further. (*Serm.* 86)[41]

According to Eckhart, Martha is not upset about not having anyone to help her, and therefore her motivation is pure. Christ's response to her, then, is not a rebuke but intended to be reassuring. Eckhart considers what the doubling of her name signals: "Why did he name Martha twice? He meant that every good thing, temporal and eternal, that a creature could possess was fully possessed by Martha" (86). He discusses at length what Martha's maturity looks like and how Martha has full understanding of what it means to be grounded in the love of God. Her work brings her close to God. Unlike previous authors who stated that Martha ascends to Mary, he counters that Mary actually ascends to Martha. Martha wants her sister to learn the things that she has. Jesus reassures her that Mary will one day have what she has and that Martha has no reason to be worried. Eckhart points to the later traditions that developed around Mary to point to the fact that she eventually goes and serves like her sister: "And so, when Mary sat at the feet of our Lord, she was learning, for she had just gone to school to learn how to live. But later on, when Christ had gone to heaven and she received the Holy Ghost, she began to serve: she traveled overseas and preached and taught, acting as a servant and washerwoman to the disciples" (86). According to Eckhart, one begins with contemplation and then ascends to action, like Mary eventually ascended to the acts of service like her sister. Eckhart's interpretation flips the usual script about the two sisters by elevating Martha. She is the one who is closer to perfection than her sister, who is still learning and only just beginning her spiritual journey.

In these three authors, one can see the different ways that Martha is elevated. They stand as an important counternarrative to the more dominant theme of elevating Mary. The lack of consensus in the Middle Ages

---

41. Translations of Eckhart's sermons come from *The Complete Mystical Works*, trans. Maurice O'C Walshe (New York: Crossroads, 2009).

about Mary and Martha is, in many ways, more pronounced than it was in the patristic period, where those who clearly favored Martha were few in number. It suggests an ongoing debate during the medieval period about the relationship between works and contemplative practices.[42]

The More Things Change …

Mary and Martha remained in the center of an ongoing debate over how one is supposed to actually practice Christianity. Is it through prayer and monastic living, is it through ministering, or is it holding the two together? The tension over the necessity of service during this life, however, moved more into the center of the debate than in previous generations. Chrysostom's arguments about the need for discernment are rarely quoted but are clearly behind many medieval interpretations: a faithful disciple knows when to be contemplative and when to be active. Furthermore, now more scholars were willing to argue in favor of Martha than we saw previously. As biblical interpretation moved away from the realm of the monastery and back into the broader Christian world, contemplation no longer stood as the pinnacle of Christian behavior, because service is ultimately more useful.

Some threads of patristic interpretation dropped out entirely. The argument that the passage concerns the proper methods of hospitality, which we saw in Basil and Cyril, all but disappeared in the Middle Ages. In part this can be attributed to a general agreement over the textual variant in Luke 10:41–42. Due to the influence of the Vulgate, most medieval theologians read the passage as "one thing is necessary," rather than "a few things," and thus, the reading that Martha is concerned over the number of dishes she is preparing was no longer relevant. As Constable observes, "It is obviously of importance to biblical scholars whether one or a few things were necessary … but in the medieval West, in spite of the wide diffusion

---

42. This tension leads some to argue, such as Stephen Langton, that the sisters are equally good and that which one should be preferred depends on one's specific point of view: "The best works of the active life, such as martyrdom and preaching are better than the best works of the contemplative life, but the contemplative life is more excellent because it is purer. The two lives are better than the other in its own type." See Stephen Langton, *Summa* in Félix Ravaisson-Mollien, *Rapports ou Ministre de l'Instruction Publique sur les Bibliothèques des Départements de l'Ouest: Suivis de pièces inedites* (Paris: Schneider & Langrand, 1841), 407–9.

of the works of Jerome and Cassian, the short Vulgate version was universally accepted."[43] The one thing necessary refers to something spiritual, and most medieval interpretations focus on what that spiritual thing is.

Distinctive Elements of Medieval Interpretation

The medieval period did not simply copy the patristic period. There were new developments in interpretation that go beyond the mere shifts in emphasis that we have surveyed. These elements include the conflation of Mary of Bethany with other Marys (both Magdalene and the mother of God), a proliferation of visual depictions of Luke 10:38–42, and the appearance of female theologians interpreting the story alongside their male counterparts. While there were surely women interpreting the story before the Middle Ages, it is only during this period that we have access to their words. All of these factors led to new contributions for interpreting and understanding the two sisters from Bethany and their role in the lives of Christians.

Mary, Martha, and Other Marys: Conflation, Absorption, and Adoption

One cannot get very far into the medieval material without noticing that Mary of Bethany is often referred to as Mary Magdalene and that Mary and Martha are both often discussed in the same breath as Mary the mother of God. These two other Marys are important for understanding the ways Mary and Martha are sometimes discussed during this period.

By the eleventh century, Luke 10:38–42 was the standard lectionary passage for Mary's assumption on August 15.[44] At first glance, this can seem like an unlikely text to highlight Mary's assumption into heaven. However, Bruno of Segni argues in a sermon on the assumption that "the holy fathers rightly established that this Gospel text should be read on this solemnity of the Virgin who is signified by these two women" (*Hom.* 117). For Bruno and many other medieval interpreters, the text is a perfect fit because the Virgin Mary was said to embody the characteristics of Mary and Martha perfectly. In her, the active life of Martha and contemplative life of Mary find their proper balance. She hosts and serves

---

43. Constable, "Interpretation of Mary and Martha," 5.
44. Diane E. Peters, "The Life of Martha of Bethany by Pseudo-Marcilia," *TS* 58 (1997): 450.

Jesus like Martha, only instead of solely welcoming him into her home, she welcomes him into her womb. She listens and meditates like Mary, focusing on his great divinity. She is both sisters rolled into one. Bruno argues that Jesus's mother is both sisters, but also greater than both. She embodies the intersection between the two lives of action and contemplation (117).

The argument appears also in the writings of Odo of Canterbury. He states that the Virgin Mary embodies both Mary and Martha, except her action and contemplation were even greater than Mary and Martha (*De assumptione*). This is because Martha was only able to serve Christ externally, whereas the Virgin was able to serve him "from her own substance." She surpasses Mary because "in the person of the Son of God she had the very divinity of His flesh in her uterus." Thus, her contemplation of Christ's divinity was deeper than Mary of Bethany's.

Thus, by studying Luke 10:38–42 some believed one could better understand the nature of Mary the mother of God, as we see in the anonymous work Monastic Distinctions: "Although by Mary and Martha we can understand the two lives, that is, active and contemplative, since the blessed mother of God was without doubt most perfect in both lives, I think that by these two sisters the body and spirit of the blessed Virgin can be more properly understood." From this, one sees how Mary is depicted as the Virgin's soul, and Martha is her body. They are still being cast in their familiar roles of contemplation and action, but now Jesus's mother is introduced to represent their perfect balance, which many medieval theologians argued should be the goal for all Christians. Bonaventura, for instance, constructs this exact argument in his *Commentary on Luke*. When he discusses Luke 10:42, he argues that, while it was literally said to Mary of Bethany, it is better suited to the Virgin Mary, since she was perfect in action and contemplation. He concludes: "What was given to these sisters in parts, was given in its entirety and integrally to [the Virgin] Mary" (*Evang. Luc.* 71–75). He continues this same argument in a sermon on the assumption, saying that the best part is specifically about the Virgin, since Mary of Bethany only achieved part of perfection through her pursuit of contemplation. He believes that this entire story in Luke 10:38–42 points to Jesus saying that the perfect life can only be found in the practice of contemplation and action (*Serm.* 6). Bernard of Clairvaux, in his sermon on the Feast of the Assumption, argues: "Martha decorates the house; Mary fills it. The busyness of Martha and the 'not idle leisure' of Mary are both united in the Blessed

Mother Mary. The 'best part' belongs to her, who is simultaneously a mother and a virgin."[45]

This combination of Mary and Martha into the Virgin Mary provided theologians with more evidence that the combination of the two lives is actually the better way of understanding Luke 10:38–42. In the debate between which life is better, many theologians turned to Mary the mother of God as proof that the best life is the one that embodies both the lives of action and contemplation. It is worth noting that while bringing the Virgin into the conversation was new, it did not introduce a new interpretation of the passage. Mary and Martha were still being identified with action and contemplation. Furthermore, all of these figures are undeniably women, and yet the conversation never strayed into overt conversations about their gender. The Virgin with her balance between action and contemplation is an example for all Christians in the same way that Mary and Martha are.

Somewhat more problematic is the conflation of Mary of Bethany and Mary Magdalene. Furthermore, this conflation was much more widespread. Almost all Western medieval writers conflated the two sisters.[46] This was not necessarily a new problem. As we saw back in the fourth century, Chrysostom seems to have knowledge of people conflating Mary of Bethany with the sinful woman who anoints Jesus's feet, who in turn is conflated with Mary Magdalene. In the Middle Ages the conflation of the three biblical women became nearly universal. As Elisabeth Moltmann-Wendel observes, "The shadow of [Mary Magdalene] has almost overwhelmed Mary of Bethany from the middles ages down to the present."[47] In interpretations of Luke 10:38–42, Mary of Bethany is seen as the former sinner who repented and ended up sitting at Christ's feet.

Such conflation, however, hardly affected the overarching arguments of most interpreters. Often it is merely that Mary is named Mary Magdalene with little expanded discussion about it because Mary still represents contemplation. Sometimes, though, Mary Magdalene's characteristics are added to further emphasize her contemplative nature. For instance, Hugh

---

45. As quoted in Heffner, "Meister Eckhart," 175.
46. Constable makes the important point that not all medieval writers make this exegetical mistake. The Eastern writers mostly separated the sisters, and several important Western medieval writers such as Bernard of Clairvaux and Joachim of Fiore kept the two apart ("Interpretation of Mary and Martha," 6–7).
47. Moltmann-Wendel, *Women around Jesus*, 53.

of Fouilloy in his work *On the Cloister of the Soul* writes about the true and false Mary and Martha. In it he notes how false Marys criticize Marthas for doing pastoral work. The false Mary complains about her silence and being unable to go out into the world, whereas the true Marys keep silent, listen, weep, and repent. She goes out to buy ointment for the purpose of visiting the tomb out of her great devotion. These are clearly elements of Mary Magdalene's story that he uses to emphasize the nature of the true Mary's contemplation. Repentance of the kind Mary Magdalene exhibits when she washes Jesus's feet became a significant part of the contemplative life.

Another aspect of this conflation can be seen in Richard of St. Victor's argument discussed previously. He conflates Mary of Bethany and Mary Magdalene in his argument that Mary achieved both the roles of action and contemplation, saying: "Martha worked with her body about a few things, in one place, Mary [Magdalene] with her love about many things in many places. In her contemplation and love of God, she saw everything, extended herself to everything, understood and embraced everything" (*Cant.* 8). Mary Magdalene, after all, did a lot more than simply sit at Jesus's feet. She proclaims, she anoints, she serves the gospel actively.[48] This aspect of the conflation mostly served to stretch what might be considered a contemplative act and was used by many theologians to justify more active behaviors by those pursuing a contemplative life.

In some instances, however, Mary of Bethany's conflation with Mary Magdalene led to many negative and overtly sexist interpretations of Luke 10:38. This particularly became true in the late medieval period as Mary Magdalene's "sinful past" was continually highlighted. Mary is emphasized repeatedly as a vain and sexually promiscuous sinner who, yes, eventually cries tears of repentance but is still somewhat stained by those sins. This depiction of Mary serves to elevate Martha as the patient, plain, and holy sister. Mary is vain, selfish, and often cruel, but because the pious Martha brings her to sit at the feet of Jesus, she is saved. For instance, in the fifteenth century, Valeriano da Socino, a preacher from Bologna, expanded on Luke 10:38–42 with the following backstory:

> When Christ was preaching in Bethany, he came to the attention of saint Martha and she conceived the idea that "O if only I could take Mary

---

48. Mary Magdalene's more active role expanded beyond the bounds of the canon, as she is a frequent character in the apocryphal gospels as a key figure in the early church.

to his preaching. Then perhaps she would give up her vanities of hers." With these ideas she went to Mary, saying, "O Mary," who said, "What do you want?" Then Martha said, "Do not you know that the great prophet who is called Jesus is preaching tomorrow in the square and that everyone is going Do you want us to go tomorrow? We may see a miracle." But Mary was completely worldly and said to her sister, "Do not bother me with your talk; I have other things to do." Then Martha, seeing that was not a good time for this matter, waited until after dinner and again urged her to go. And Martha spoke so well that the Magdalene agreed and said "Very well, I want to please you; tomorrow we shall go together."

And behold in the morning, Martha came at the right time to Mary's room and said "Get up, because it's time." And when she got up she adorned herself like a queen. Then Martha went first and she followed. And as they went Martha said in her mind, "I pray God that you give her such a thrashing that you will make her give up such vanity." When Mary came to the preaching, do you think she put herself in a lowly place for the sake of devotion? O no, but what? She put herself in a prominent place so that she might be enlivened and seen by everyone.[49]

This extended excerpt is a good example of the qualities that Mary began to take on during the late medieval period. Da Socino depicts her as worldly and vain, primarily concerned with her own appearance. She is at first rude to Martha and has to be convinced to go hear Jesus. Martha is the better sister because she is so concerned for her sister's well-being. In other sermons from this same time period, Mary, consumed by her own vanity, goes to Jesus because she believes she can make Jesus fall in love with her.[50] After her encounter with Jesus, she is repentant and transformed, though her sins are still constantly mentioned.

Thus, one can see that the conflation of the Marys shifts interpretations of Luke 10:38–42. Mary is given new characteristics. She is a vain and worldly person who becomes penitent, and because of this she embraces acts of contemplation. It also provides evidence that Mary does not only sit at Jesus's feet, because the story of Mary Magdalene continues with her proclamation of the risen Jesus. This conflation allows interpreters more leeway in expanding the boundaries of the contemplative life.

---

49. As quoted in Constable, "Interpretation of Mary and Martha," 128–29. This sermon was originally delivered in a mix of a Latin and Italian, with the preacher switching back and forth between the two.

50. See, for instance, Michel Menot, *Sermons choisis*, ed. Joseph Nève (Paris: Librairie spéciale pour l'histoire de France, 1924), 148–50.

While this conflation seems particularly strange to modern readers, it is worth momentarily stepping back to discuss how this came to be. It was caused in part by the complicated relationship of several stories in the gospels themselves. As Chrysostom notes in his interpretation of the passage, Luke draws a clear demarcation among the sinful woman who washes Jesus's feet in Luke 7:36–50; Mary Magdalene, who is cleansed from seven demons in Luke 8:2; and Mary of Bethany in Luke 10:38–42. Within Luke's Gospel, these three scenes depict different women. That said, the introduction of Mary Magdalene immediately follows the story of the parable of the sinful woman, which led to interpretative overlap between these two stories.

The situation becomes more complicated, however, when one looks at these scenes in the other gospels. In the scene where Jesus's feet are washed, which occurs in all four gospels, Matthew, Mark, and John all place this scene at Bethany (Matt 26:6–13; Mark 13:3–9; John 12:1–8). Matthew and Mark leave the woman unnamed, but John explicitly names the woman as Mary of Bethany, sister of Martha and Lazarus (John 12:3). It is important to note that in these three other accounts, the woman is not described as a sinner but rather as someone who has done a beautiful act to anoint Jesus before his burial.

Over time, Luke's demarcation of the three women as separate characters got lost in favor of harmonizing the story. As we saw, this mixing began happening as early as the fourth century, as Chrysostom was clearly aware of it (*Hom. Jo.* 62).[51] Thus, Luke's details about the woman in Luke 7 and her sinfulness remain, but the location of Bethany in Matthew and Mark and John's explicit identification of her as Mary of Bethany got absorbed into the narrative. The final piece is the connection between Luke 7 and 8, where Luke introduces Mary Magdalene. All of this led to Mary Magdalene becoming the sinful woman who washes Jesus's feet, who in turn became Mary of Bethany.

A side effect of the combination of the Marys is that Martha began to gain new characteristics as well.[52] As we saw in the quote from da Soncino,

---

51. For a brief example of the overlap between Mary Magdalene, Mary of Bethany, and the sinful woman in the fifth century, see 158 n. 65, above.

52. There was a less popular conflation with Martha and the one who was healed from chronic bleeding from Matt 9:20. For a fuller discussion of its roots, see Diane E. Peters, "The Legends of St Martha of Bethany and Their Dissemination in the Later Middle Ages," *ATLASP* 48 (1994): 152.

she is the patient, virtuous sister. She does not complain out of envy. She acts solely out of concern for her sister's soul. Beyond becoming more loving and long-suffering, Martha also began to develop her own legend alongside Mary Magdalene. She became a popular and beloved figure, particularly in the late Middle Ages.

See, for example, the medieval biography The Life of Saint Mary Magdalene and Her Sister Martha. The authorship is unknown, though originally it was attributed to Rabanus Maurus, a ninth-century Carolingian monk. More recently it has been argued that it is a late twelfth-century work compiled by a monk influenced by Bernard of Clairvaux.[53] The biography begins: "The contemplative life of that sweet lover of Christ, dearly loved by him and worthy to be named with reverence, the blessed Mary Magdalene; the active life of her glorious sister, the servant of Christ, Martha."[54] It claims to be recording the "authentic testimony of the four Gospels," but the story begins well before the biblical text and follows both sisters until their deaths. Many of the elements in the conflation between the Marys exist here: Mary begins vain and worldly, repents, and begins a life of contemplation. She is the first to see the risen Christ and brings the "first draught of life to the apostles which cancels out the potion of Eve."[55] Martha, on the other hand, is described after the resurrection as having "incomparable devotion in rendering the holy services to the Saviour and providing all for his necessities with a liberal spirit and a benevolence full of grace."[56] After the ascension, Mary and Martha both begin spreading the gospel. Mary lives a particularly ascetic life, eating very little food and preferring to spend time alone in the wilderness (though this does not exclude her from serving when necessary).[57] Martha, while also living frugally, begins to preach to all people about the Lord and performs miracles: "The gift of healing came to her so that when the occasion demanded, by prayer and by the sign of the cross, she healed lepers, cured paralytics,

---

53. David Mycoff, "Introduction," in *The Life of Saint Mary Magdalene and of Her Sister Saint Martha*, trans. David Mycoff, CSS 108 (Kalamazoo, MI: Cistercian, 1989), 9–10.

54. Mycoff, *Life of Saint Mary Magdalene*, 27.

55. Mycoff, *Life of Saint Mary Magdalene*, 70.

56. Mycoff, *Life of Saint Mary Magdalene*, 89.

57. In this section the author of the biography notes that he has heard some people claim that Mary lived in the desert naked because of her isolation and that once a priest visited her and she had to borrow clothes. He argues this is not true (Mycoff, *Life of Saint Mary Magdalene*, 97).

revived the dead and bestowed her aid on the blind, the mute, the deaf, the lame, the invalid and the sick. Thus did Martha do."[58]

At this point, the biography shifts to record the miracles of Martha, including most notably a story about Martha defeating a dragon:

> One day, as the holy woman Martha preached the word of God to a crowd that had gathered, breaking off the talk, which was, as usual, about the dragon, some people out of devout humility and some out of a desire to test her said: "If the power which this blessed woman shows us is of Christ, is it not possible that she could do what no human efforts can do and remove this dragon from our midst?" To this she answered: "I can if you are ready to believe for all things are possible to those who believe."
>
> At once, the people pledged their faith and followed her gratefully to the dragon's lair. With the sign of the cross, she subdued the dragon's wildness and with her own girdle bound its neck as the people looked on intently from afar. "What is it," she asked, "that you fear? Here I am holding this serpent and still you keep back. Approach bravely in the name of our Lord and Savior and tear this venomous beast to pieces."[59]

After they finish killing the dragon, everyone in the town (called Tarascon, after the dragon) is baptized, and Martha decides to live there, teaching and preaching the gospel. During her ministry in Tarascon, she continues performing miracles, such as raising people from the dead, including a young boy who drowns while trying to hear her preach, a story that clearly echoes of Paul's raising of Eutychus (Acts 20:7–12). She is repeatedly called the most holy servant of Christ, and at the moment of her death, Christ appears to her and says: "Behold, here I am, to whom you once ministered with great devotion out of your own means; to whom you showed a most gracious hospitality, for whom you have done many good deeds since my Passion in the person of my people.... Come, then, my hostess, come out of your exile and receive your crown."[60]

In this legend Martha becomes a powerful preacher and miracle worker who wins a whole town over to the gospel. Her story is told in the same way as the apostles' stories are told. She is a holy woman, loved by Christ. She is not depicted as whiny or bossy. Rather, she is the epitome of a disciple of Christ, and when she dies the whole region mourns her

---

58. Mycoff, *Life of Saint Mary Magdalene*, 97.
59. Mycoff, *Life of Saint Mary Magdalene*, 99.
60. Mycoff, *Life of Saint Mary Magdalene*, 109–10.

death.[61] Most of these accounts are attributed to the twelfth and thirteenth centuries and appear to share sources. In particular, each version highlights her battle with the dragon of Tarascon.[62] In each account she is able to subdue the dragon with a sign of the cross. Some also include her use of holy water. Moreover, Martha's characterization is often rooted in her identity as the active life, just as Mary remains the representative of the contemplative life. For instance, in Pseudo-Marcillia's account, Martha is summed up in the following way: "Thus Martha, the hostess of Christ, is a form of the active life in the present and for the future, for she will receive the needy who come to her home in the kingdom of heaven, as it was said to her by the Lord."[63] Her legends serve to give her more opportunities for this active life. She preaches, heals, makes disciples, and performs miracles.

Alongside these legends of her bravery and miracles, Martha is also depicted frequently within the context of the household, leading her to become the patron saint of housework and cooking.[64] This is mostly depicted not through written texts but rather imagery. As we will discuss in the following section, she is often depicted holding a soup spoon, broom, cooking pot, or keys. In other images she is depicted as the dragon slayer, with a dragon in the background and the aspergillum (a liturgical instrument used for dispersing holy water) and a pot of holy water in her hand. She is depicted as both a dragon slayer and a housekeeper.

Louis Réau, in particular, observes this discrepancy and argues that Martha's association with cooking comes from people misidentifying the container of holy water as a normal cooking pot, labeling it an icongraphic misinterpretation: "Peut-être y a-t-il aussi à l'origine de ce patronage un contre-sens iconographique: le seau d'eau bénite qu'elle tient à la main pour

---

61. For a critical introduction to and translation of the four accounts, see Diane Elizabeth Peters, "The Early Latin Sources of the Legend of St Martha: A Study and Translation with Critical Notes" (MA diss., Wilfrid Laurier University, 1990).

62. This is not the only account of her heroics. A similar outline of her story is preserved in four medieval Latin texts: the text discussed above, *Vita Pseudo-Marcilia*; *Interprete Pseudo-Syntyche*, a text composed from the perspective of Martha's servant, Marcella; the *Speculum Historíale* by Vincent of Beauvais; and, most famously, the *Legenda Aurea* by Jacobus de Voragine. For a brief outline of Martha in these accounts and their relationship between the texts, see Peters, "Legends of St Martha of Bethany," 156–58.

63. As quoted in Peters, "Life of Martha of Bethany," 452.

64. Peters, "Legends of St Martha of Bethany," 160.

asperger la Tarasque à pu être pris pour un ustensile de menage."65 While I disagree with his overall conclusion, since Martha is actually depicted as serving and leading a household in the biblical text, I understand Réau's confusion over these two seemingly contradictory images that seem to exist side by side in the Middle Ages. However, they are both extensions of Martha's active life. As we will see, in the Reformation, the legends surrounding Martha disappeared as her skills as a housekeeper came to the forefront and her dragon-taming skills were forgotten.

Like her sister Mary's, Martha's character was expanded in the Middle Ages, and she gained new attributes in line with her overall depiction as the active Christian. Some of this development was a direct response to Mary's conflation with Mary Magdalene, but other aspects of it came from a fleshing out of her activity. She no longer only hosts and serves Jesus, but she continues the life of the active Christian by preaching the gospel and performing miracles. Discussions about Mary and Martha shifted due to the combination and conflation of the characters with other biblical women, notably the Virgin Mary and Mary Magdalene. In some instances, this led to Mary being given many more negative qualities, while Martha was elevated. However, at its core, the conversation still revolved around Mary representing the contemplative life and Martha representing the active life.

Mary and Martha in Art: Visual Exegesis

We cannot discuss distinctive elements of medieval exegesis without briefly mentioning visual depictions of Luke 10:38–42. In contrast to the patristic period, where we rely solely on texts, beginning with the eighth century, we actually have access to artwork. To leave visual material culture out of our discussion would be to miss a significant way people accessed this story.66 It is particularly important to discuss during the medieval period because, as Diane Peters notes: "The majority of people in the Middle Ages were illiterate, and their ideas regarding theology and history were obtained not from reading but through art. Many of the manuscripts and early editions

---

65. Louis Réau, "Sainte Marthe," in *Iconographie de l'Art Chretien*, 3 vols. (Paris: Presses Universitaires de France, 1959), 3:893.

66. Vernon K. Robbins, "New Testament Texts, Visual Material Culture, and Earliest Christian Art," in *The Art of Visual Exegesis: Rhetoric, Texts, Images*, ed. Robbins, Walter S. Melion, and Roy R. Jeal, ESEC 19 (Atlanta: SBL Press, 2017), 21.

of saints' lives were illuminated or decorated with woodcut illustrations. Churches also contained paintings and sculptures which brought the lives and works of the saints before the eyes, and into the imaginations, of the general populace."[67] Through such artwork, many of the same themes we have already discussed are also portrayed visually. In various pieces, we see the two sisters depicted as equals, some works in which Mary is privileged, and still others clearly conflate Mary with Mary Magdalene. Because the story became ever more popular, we cannot discuss every appearance, but in the following section I highlight the most common themes as well as the most famous images.

First, the earliest preserved image of Mary and Martha is from the eighth century. It is a small engraving of Mary and Martha embracing each other with their names written beside them. It is one of the biblical scenes found on the Ruthwell Cross, located in Northumbria. The cross also includes images of crucifixion, John the Baptist, the annunciation, Mary Magdalene, and others. For many years, a popular argument was that these two women, who appear nearly identical, were intended to be Elizabeth and Mary, since the image is similar to other visitation scenes, but the inscriber made a mistake when writing the names.[68]

This theory has recently fallen out of favor, since it seems unlikely that someone would make such a severe mistake. In light of the monastic setting of the cross, Paul Meyvaert argues that the embrace of the two sisters was intended to signify the relationship between the active and the contemplative life. [69] Constable argues more explicitly that the image represents the idea that the perfect Christian is one who embodies both the lives of action and contemplation. They are intended to be held together. One is not elevated over the other. He compares it to Bede's interpretation, which was written in the same area

Fig. 5.1. The Ruthwell Cross. Eighth century. Source: Wikimedia.

---

67. Peters, "Legends of St Martha of Bethany," 160.
68. Paul Meyvaert, "A New Perspective on the Ruthwell Cross: Ecclesia and Vita Monastica," in *The Ruthwell Cross*, ed. Brendan Cassidy (Princeton: Princeton University Press, 1992), 138.
69. Meyvaert, "New Perspective on the Ruthwell Cross," 140.

around the same time.[70] Bede, as we mentioned earlier, argues that both action and contemplation are a part of the life of a monk. This idea that Mary and Martha are embracing as representatives of the active and contemplative life, thus showing the need for unity between the two, seems to fall in line with many monastic writers who constantly reiterated the need for some balance between the two.

Other depictions of Mary and Martha in Luke 10:38–42 can frequently be found in illustrated Bibles and evangelaries. For instance, the Gospel Book of Henry the Lion, sometimes referred to as the Gmunden Gospels, created in the late twelfth century, has a double panel of the story. The first depicts Mary alone at the feet of Jesus, washing his feet and receiving forgiveness of her sins.[71] The bottom panel is a depiction of Luke 10:38–42 with Jesus seated in the center and Mary seated at his feet. On the other side, Martha is holding up one finger toward Jesus, holding her complaint: "Tell her to help me." Jesus is holding two scrolls, one of which reads, "Mary has chosen the better part"; the other reads, "Martha, you are careful and troubled." In many ways, this scene is a very literal depiction of the passage. Martha appears particularly grumpy toward Jesus, but otherwise it stays very close to the text. This image, like many, makes it difficult to deduce any allegorical meaning.[72]

That said, some depictions explicitly favor Mary as the more beloved sister. Take, for instance, the Evangeliary of St. Martin, an early thirteenth-century work. Like the Gospel Book of Henry, this also contains a double panel. The top panel depicts both Mary and Martha welcoming Jesus into Bethany, while the bottom panel depicts the usual scene from Luke 10:38–42. What is particularly interesting about this scene is that Mary is the only sister to have a halo. Martha holds a jug and a scroll asking Jesus to tell her sister to help her, while Mary, with a halo, kneels at Jesus's feet. Jesus declares that Mary has the better part. A similar depiction is found in a moralized Bible from the late thirteenth century. Here too, only Mary is given a halo. The inscription on this image reads: "This is the sign that whoever will do well in the contemplative life will be saved and whoever will do well in the active [life] will be blessed, and this is figured by Mary and Martha" (MS Bodl. 270b, fol. 91v [Constable]). This interpretative statement next to the image is particularly notable, as it directly states,

---

70. Constable, "Interpretation of Mary and Martha," 25–26.
71. Note the conflation of the accounts of the woman who washes Jesus's feet.
72. Constable, "Interpretation of Mary and Martha," 56.

like so many of our authors, that Mary and Martha represent the active and contemplative life. The fact that Mary is saved while Martha is blessed seems to suggest a hierarchy between the two sisters. Combined with the fact that only Mary has a halo, this implies that Mary is higher than her sister Martha.

The passage presents a popular scene for painters during the late Middle Ages and throughout the Renaissance. Frescoes, altarpieces, and paintings depicting Christ in the house of Martha and Mary began to appear in the fourteenth century and beyond as the story presented a good opportunity for still life.[73] Usually Martha is painted holding keys or serving ware, wearing an apron, representing her role as the house owner/housekeeper, while Mary is seated, often dressed more finely, sometimes seen holding a book. For instance, in the Rinuccini Chapel in Church of Sta Croce in Florence, there is a fresco of *Christ in the House of Mary and Martha*, painted by Giovanni da Milano in 1365.[74] In this painting, both Mary and Martha have halos, and Martha is wearing an apron, while her servant (likely Marcella, Martha's servant in apocryphal accounts) is cooking the meal in the background.

As time progresses, we see the conflation of Mary and Mary Magdalene appear more blatantly in the artwork. In particular, throughout the Renaissance, one finds scenes of Mary's vanity and her sister's attempts to save her. For instance, in Caravaggio's painting *Martha and Mary Magdalene* in 1598, the focus is on Mary, who is seen sitting in front of a mirror, very finely dressed. A comb and powder sit on the table in front of her. Martha is seen entreating Mary, though her face is almost entirely turned away. The scene has no biblical basis, but it evokes the accounts of Martha bringing Mary Magdalene to Christ. The most shocking image of this conflation comes from Guido Cagnacci in his sixteenth-century painting *Martha Rebuking Mary for Her Vanity*. In this painting, Mary is depicted mostly undressed on the floor, while her sister sits by her head, talking to her. Behind them an angel is shown fighting off a demon. This is clearly a depiction of the seven demons that Jesus exorcised from Mary Magdalene, which was discussed in great detail during this period.

We also find images of Martha holding holy water with a dragon in the background. For instance, in the Church of Saint Laurence in

---

73. Stephano Zuffi, *Gospel Figures in Art*, trans. Thomas Michael Hartmann (Los Angeles: Getty Publications, 2002), 192.

74. Constable, "Interpretation of Mary and Martha," 124.

Nuremberg, there is a scene on the Mary Altar from 1517 titled *Martha Defeating the Dragon* that depicts Martha subduing the dragon of Tarascon with a cross or a similar image found in Chambery that depicts Martha with holy water in hand and a dragon at her feet. There are also statues, paintings, and icons with similar images. On the other hand, one can also find depictions of Martha as a housekeeper, such as Lucas Moser's *Martha Serving at the Table*, which is found on the Magdalene Altar in Tiefenbronn from 1431. Thus, we can see both aspects of her personality are being depicted visually. As Elisabeth Moltmann-Wendel observes, in medieval art we see Martha in both familiar and unfamiliar guise as she is both housewife and dragonslayer.[75]

Fig. 5.2. *Martha Defeating the Dragon*. Nurumberg altar. 1517. Source: Wikimedia.

Overall, the art shows how ideas about Mary and Martha that were being written and preached about were also being painted and sculpted throughout this era. Mary and Martha were popular biblical figures throughout the Middle Ages, and various forms of artwork made them accessible to a wider public. Sometimes they are depicted as equals; in others Mary is clearly preferred; in still others Martha is depicted more favorably. One can also see how as time progresses Mary was more heavily painted with the flaws and virtues of Mary Magdalene and how Martha stood alone with her own characteristics.

New Voices: Women Interpreting Luke 10:38–42

A final distinctive element of medieval interpretation is the introduction of women who interpreted the story of Mary and Martha. In this section I briefly discuss three women who discussed Luke 10:38–42: Hildegard of Bingen, Birgitta of Sweden, and Teresa of Ávila. Despite living in a patriarchal society that minimized women's voices, these women were able to gain enough renown that their works were published, and even men sought their advice. Because of their authors' piety and skill, their

---

75. Moltmann-Wendel, *Women around Jesus*, 17.

works were preserved, giving us access to their opinions on the biblical text. Perhaps surprisingly, their interpretations mostly fall in line with the threads we have already seen: they locate Mary and Martha as representing the contemplative and active life. They do not interpret the story as being particularly gendered, but rather see it as instructive for both men and women.

Hildegard of Bingen

Hildegard of Bingen, recently declared a doctor of the church, was born in 1098, the tenth child to a noble family in Bermerseim, a medieval town located in what is now Germany.[76] Partially due to having so many siblings and partially due to visions she began to receive at a young age, her family sent her to become a nun when she was eight.[77] There she was taught Latin and received a rudimentary education. She spent the rest of her life in this Benedictine religious community, eventually becoming the head of her convent in 1136. In the 1140s she began to record her visions. These became her most famous work, the *Scivias*. These were eventually approved by Pope Eugenius III with some prompting from Bernard of Clairvaux.[78] Most of her public ministry took place after this point. Hildegard wrote several more books, preached, composed music, and offered advice to bishops, abbots, popes, and nobility. As Joseph Baird and Radd Ehrman observe, despite starting all this at the age of forty-nine: "She produced six major written works, she founded two flourishing monasteries, she wrote music, she gave birth to the earliest full-fledged morality play, she became the correspondent—and advisor—of popes, kings, emperor. It was a full life indeed."[79] She died in 1179.

Hildegard is not normally discussed as a biblical exegete because of the emphasis she placed on visions she receives from the Spirit. But Hil-

---

76. She was declared a doctor of the church in 2012 by Pope Benedict XVI. See "Proclaiming Saint Hildegard of Bingen, Professed Nun of the Order of Saint Benedict, a Doctor of the Universal Church," https://tinyurl.com/SBL4824a.

77. Abigail Young, "Hildegard of Bingen," in *Handbook of Women Biblical Interpreters*, ed. Marion Ann Taylor and Agnes Choi (Grand Rapids: Baker Academic, 2012), 259.

78. Joseph L. Baird and Radd K. Ehrman, trans. and ed., "Introduction," in *The Letters of Hildegard* (New York: Oxford University Press, 1994), 1:5.

79. Baird and Ehrman, "Introduction," 6.

degard was clearly steeped in the biblical world, and all of her works draw from biblical imagery. The charismatic nature of her writing allows her to insist that her interpretations are not her own but rather are given to her directly from God. As she writes in one letter, she is merely sharing what is being revealed to her: "And just as the sun, moon and stars appear reflected in water, so the Scriptures, sermons, virtues shine in it for me."[80] Still, people reached out to Hildegard to ask questions about difficult scriptural issues in her letters, and she published a work called *Answers to Thirty-Eight Questions* after a monk from Gembloux sent her a number of biblical questions. Thus, one can see that despite Hildegard's own claims to the contrary, she should be studied as an important biblical interpreter from the Middle Ages.

Hildegard does not discuss Mary and Martha in her books, but they appear frequently throughout her letters. Over four hundred of Hildegard's letters are extant, revealing the remarkable nature of her correspondence, and these letters offer modern readers insight into the practical side of Hildegard's ministry. As Baird and Ehrman argue: "In these letters, instead, we find the practical abbess, as above, concerning herself with the pragmatic details of religious ceremony, a ritual modeled, to be sure, on her ethereal visions of the celestial virtues but worked out nonetheless on an earthly plane."[81] In these letters, almost every paragraph contains biblical echoes, images, and sometimes even direct quotations.

Luke 10:38–42 often appears in this fashion. In particular, Hildegard frequently refers to the better part that Mary chose in the middle of larger arguments. Frequently she uses it almost as shorthand for describing the monastic life. For instance, in a letter to Abbot Helengerus that reads more like a sermon than an epistle, she describes "how their [monastics'] way of religious life began, what its status is now, and how it will be in the future" (*Letter* 77r).[82] She depicts what these future religious men and women do after they turn their gaze to heaven: "Afterward, like a hart to the fountains of waters, *they ran to the better part*, ascending from virtue to virtue , and in the light of divine love they shone for God and for men" (77r). She uses the phrase in a similar way when responding to an abbess

---

80. As quoted in Young, "Hildegard of Bingen," 261.
81. Baird and Ehrman, "Introduction," 4.
82. Translations of Hildegard's letters come from *Letters of Hildegard*, trans. Baird and Ehrman.

who asked for advice: "I see also that [the nuns] are rising up strenuously into *the better part* and that although they are not fully established in the religious way of life, they are nevertheless growing vigorously" (94r). Here one can see that Hildegard is using the "better part" to affirm that the women under the abbess's care are, despite their shortcomings, living the contemplative life.[83]

Sometimes Hildegard uses it not for the monastic life more broadly but for specific behaviors. For instance, Hildegard wrote to a congregation of nuns, rebuking them for vain and worldly practices. She begins: "Surely, you do not suppose that you will receive the kingdom of God by feasting and drinking and wanton morals? No! You will receive the kingdom of God through denial of body and contrition of mind" (*Letter* 194). She then continues to describe the ways in which this community was failing to do these things. She writes about the coming judgement for this behavior before stating: "For it is necessary that they *arise to the better part* because it is God's will that they not abandon His law" (194). She then reminds them of what happens to people who abandon their covenant with God. Here Hildegard is trying to convince the women to choose the better part, by which she means the practices of bodily denial and repentance. A similar use of the phrase appears in her letter to a priest named Werner, condemning what she saw as wicked behavior in the church. She concludes the letter: "Now, may the unquenchable fire of the Holy Spirit so infuse you that *you will turn to the better part*" (*Letter* 149r). She hopes he will be able to resist the evils of extravagance and choose to live a simple life.

Further proof that Hildegard views the "better part" in terms of monastic and contemplative living can be found in her sole reference to Martha. In a short letter to a rich noblewoman, the Countess Irmintrude of Widen, she writes, "Your soul is diligent in its foresight and its heartfelt solicitude through the grace of God. And you sigh to God which is good.... It is good also for you to be Martha, but to love Mary" (*Letter* 329). It is only to a layperson that Hildegard invokes Martha. This reflects the familiar dichotomy in which Martha was said to represent laity while Mary represents monastic men and women. Hildegard further encourages the countess to continue to give alms as those "who walk in the wide ways

---

83. For another example of this type of usage, see *Letter* 113r (2.58), in which she compares those who have chosen the better part to decorations on a tower built by wisdom.

of God." She assures her that God loves those who serve in this way, while also encouraging her to love those who are "closely gathered to God's bosom" (monks/nuns; *Letter* 329). Hildegard clearly reiterates the theme that the laity should be assured that being Martha is good, while also being charged to love those who have chosen the life of Mary.[84]

Following the broader medieval trend, Hildegard in several places also conflates Mary of Bethany with Mary Magdalene, particularly in the way she associates repentance with the better part. For instance, in a letter to a prior, in which she is describing a certain vision she had: "The fourth living creature, like a flying eagle, reveals certain people who refrain from sin and, coming forth from among the aforementioned secular people, rise up to self-restraint. One of these was Mary Magdalene, who, regarding her sins as filth, cast them off, and thereby choosing the best part, she sat in the dawn of holiness" (*Letter* 84r). Here Mary chose the better part, by choosing to repent and refrain from sin. By casting off her sins, Mary is able to sit before Christ. This link between the better part and repentance can also be found in her letters that focus on turning away from sins in order to embrace the better part, but this is her only instance of naming Mary of Bethany as Mary Magdalene.

---

84. Constable notes that it was fashionable to link great women with the traits of Mary and Martha, either on their own or combined ("Interpretation of Mary and Martha," 39). This trend can be seen throughout Hildegard's correspondence, as seen above. Furthermore, those seeking her advice frequently offer her greetings that name both Mary and Martha. For instance, an unnamed monk wrote: "To the lady Hildegard, his spiritual mother, Brother S., least of the brothers of the church at Otterberg and darkened with the filth of sin beyond all others, with a prayer that she serve the spiritual banquet with Martha, and sigh with Mary for the joys of life in heaven" (Baird and Ehrman, *Letters of Hildegard*, 2:139; for more examples of this trend, see also 1:54, 83, 130; 2:12). Most frequently, Mary and Martha are both mentioned, though occasionally a writer will invoke only Mary. There are no examples of only Martha being mentioned in connection to Hildegard, which further supports the above argument that laity were primarily connected to Martha, not those living cloistered lives. That said, one would be wrong to assume that only women were greeted in this manner. During this period, men were occasionally greeted and discussed in the same manner, particularly bishops and abbots. See, for instance, this description of Bishop Woldbodo of Liege (d. 1021): "He did not neglect the care of internal things for the care of external things ... devoting himself in a practical way like Martha and in a theoretical way like Mary" (Reiner of St. Laurence, *Wolbod.* 3). For more examples of this trend, see also Rudolf, *Liet.* 7; Herbord of Michelsberg, *Dial. Ott. Bamb.* 1.41–42.

Birgitta of Sweden

Birgitta of Sweden (sometimes called Bridget or referred to as the Bride) was born in 1302 in Finsta, Sweden.[85] She was married to Ulf Gudmarrson in 1316 and had eight children before Ulf died in 1344. While she was said to have had visions and been extremely pious while she was a wife and mother, it was after she became a widow that she began to publish her visions.[86] She also began her own monastic order alongside her daughter Catherine after her husband's death. The Birgittine Order, also known as the Order of the Holy Savior, was founded in 1346, with Birgitta writing the Rule, which insists on vows of poverty and other acts of asceticism. Her order was said to represent a kind of "active mysticism" in which service and involvement in the world was not excluded. Birgitta herself often traveled, seeking audiences with popes and kings. She also frequently took pilgrimages and would find herself overwhelmed by the amount of wickedness she found. She is often described as an Old Testament prophet because of her insistence of calling clerical and political figures to repentance.[87] She died in 1373, and she had significant influence on many subsequent women, including Margery Kempe and Julian of Norwich.

Birgitta wrote several books of visions, dictated to various scribes. These books, called the *Revelations*, were originally written in Latin, but they were quickly translated into a Middle English and several other languages. In them Birgitta writes as the bride of Christ and directs her visions to popes and kings alike. Like Hildegard, she presents her interpretations through her charismatic experiences. Her use of biblical imagery is found throughout her writings, and she often uses allegory to apply the biblical text directly to a contemporary issue. She discusses the story of Mary and Martha at great length in book six of the *Revelations*. Chapter 65 begins: "The Son of God says: 'Bride, there are two lives which are compared to

---

85. Early accounts of her life record that her mother, Ingeborg, while pregnant with Birgitta, survived a shipwreck and that afterward she had a vision that said she was saved "because of the goodness that is in your womb." Quoted in Julia Bolton Holloway, "Introduction," in *Saint Bride and Her Book: Birgitta of Sweden's Revelations*, trans. Holloway, LMW 6 (Newburyport, MA: Focus Texts, 1992), 3.

86. Mari Jørstad, "Birgitta of Sweden," in Taylor and Choi, *Handbook of Women Biblical Interpreters*, 74. It should also be noted that she named one of her daughters Martha after Martha of Bethany.

87. Jørstad, "Birgitta of Sweden," 74.

Mary and Martha; which lives if a man and a woman would follow he must first make clean confession of all his sins being himself truly sorry for them, having the desire never to sin again. The first life, as the Lord bears witness, Mary chose; and it leads to the contemplation of heavenly things and this is the best part and day's journey to everlasting health."[88] She then continues with an extended analysis of how the person who seeks to be Mary should live his life. This person must live scarcely with only enough food, drink, and clothing to survive. He must not take any joy in the praise of the world or be affected by anything that occurs in the world (other than people repenting and becoming lovers of God). Birgitta then argues, "Mary ought not to be idle any more than is Martha; but after he takes his necessary sleep, he ought to rise and with inward attentiveness of heart thank God" (6.65).[89] She argues that Marys must be diligent in prayer and in their labors. If someone is not able to work, however, he should not be too embarrassed, pointing to Christ as an example of someone who made himself poor that others should become rich.

She continues with a second parallel to Martha: "Fourth, Mary ought not to be covetous, no more than was Martha. But he ought to be truly generous; for Martha gives temporal goods for God, so ought Mary to give spiritual goods." Like the author of the Liber Graduum, Birgitta argues that Mary is also in service to others, only her service is spiritual, compared to Martha's physical service. Mary is to work hard so that others do not fall into sin. Those who choose the part of Mary are clearly expected to preach, and thus they should have proper discretion to know what to speak when, so that "Mary must with words, examples and prayers try the hearts of many" (*Rev.* 6.65). Birgitta's depiction of Mary shows her own commitment to a life of active mysticism. One should live an ascetic lifestyle, with a focus on growing in the love of God, but this should in turn lead the ascetic to loving the neighbor through preaching, hospitality, and other acts of service.

Birgitta then turns to the life of Martha, which she also praises, stating: "Yet the part of Martha is not evil, but praiseworthy and very pleasing to

---

88. Translations of Birgitta's *Revelations* come from *Saint Bride and Her Book*, trans. Holloway.

89. Birgitta often uses male pronouns when she speaking about Mary and Martha and those who strive to live like them, sometimes even switching between feminine and masculine identifiers. This can be confusing for the reader, but I believe this further supports the argument that these two characters were not limited to their gender.

God. Therefore I shall tell you how Martha ought to be governed. For he ought to have good things as well as Mary" (*Rev.* 6.65). These five things are (1) having right faith, (2) keeping the commandments of God, (3) keeping one's tongue from evil speech and one's hand from evil deeds, (4) fulfilling acts of mercy, and finally (5) loving God above all things. Birgitta argues (still speaking from the perspective of Christ) that this is how Martha lived:

> So did Martha, for he gave joyfully of himself, following my words and she gave all her goods for my love. And therefore she loathed temporal things, and sought heavenly things.... And therefore, she thought always on my charity and Passion and she was glad in tribulation and loved all as a mother. The same Martha followed me every day desiring nothing but to hear words of life. She had compassion on those who were grieving; she comforted the sick; she neither cursed nor said evil to any. But did not imitate the pushiness of her neighbor and prayed for all. Therefore every man who desires charity actively ought to follow Martha in loving his neighbor, to bring him to heaven. (6.65)

In this depiction of Martha, she appears to engage both physical acts of service such as caring for her neighbors, but also spiritual acts in that she constantly sought the words of life and sought heavenly things. Birgitta is clear, however, that the acts of Martha are only the first step. One should begin by seeking the life of Martha, but then should move into the life of Mary, because "in spiritual life, he who perfectly desires to be Mary must be Martha, laboring physically to my praise" (6.65). One must ascend from the life of Martha to the life of Mary.

That said, she concludes with a discussion of the relationship between Mary and Martha, using Lazarus and John 12 to make her argument: "But mark well that Martha, praying for her brother Lazarus when he was dead came first to me. But her brother was not yet raised until Mary came after, when she was called. And then for both sisters their brother was raised to life" (*Rev.* 6.65). She states that Lazarus represents an unperfect work. This is a work, that is good, but done for the wrong reasons and thus done poorly. For a work to be brought to life, she argues, one needs both Mary and Martha, "that is, when the neighbor is clearly loved for God and to God, and God alone is desired above all things" (6.65). Right motivation is loving one's neighbor (the part of Martha) for the sake of love of God (the part of Mary), which makes an action truly good in the eyes of God. She concludes:

> Therefore I said in the Gospel that Mary chose the better part, for then the part of Martha is also good, when he grieves for the sins of his fellow Christians; and then is the part of Martha better when he labors that men may continue in the good life wisely and honestly, and that only for the love of God. But the part of Martha is best when he beholds only heavenly things and the profit of souls. And the Lord enters into the house of Martha and Mary when the heart is fulfilled with good affections ... and thinking of God as always present and not only contemplating and mediation on his love, but laboring in that day and night. (6.65)

From this, it appears that Birgitta too was caught in the tension between the parts of action and contemplation. While she repeatedly emphasizes the part of Mary is the better choice, she is clear that the active life is still a necessary part of the Christian life. Even those who have ascended to the better part of Mary are still required to act out of their love of God and neighbor.

In this way Birgitta encapsulates a standard medieval reading of this passage in that she interprets the passage as central for understanding how to live the Christian life. It is creative and highly allegorical, and it reveals the inherent tension between action and contemplation. She places Mary above Martha but still holds on to Martha's part as good also. Her interpretation draws on Lazarus's resurrection to discuss the nature of a truly perfect action. Furthermore, even though she is a woman and throughout her ministry was concerned about women in the church, Birgitta does not interpret Mary and Martha as speaking only to women but rather as instructive to men and women. In fact, she uses oddly male pronouns most of the time when talking about how someone should live as Mary and Martha. Her work differs from her male counterparts in that, due to her gender, she speaks not in her own voice but rather as one receiving a message directly from Christ.

Teresa of Ávila

Teresa was born in 1515 in Ávila, Spain. She was given a rudimentary education in Spanish (but not Latin) by her mother at home before being sent to the Convent of the Incarnation, a Carmelite convent in Ávila, when she was in her late teens. Shortly thereafter, she experienced a three-year-long illness, during which she was unable to speak or walk. Later she attributed this illness to the laxity of her Carmelite convent and committed herself to a more strenuous form of asceticism.[90] She eventually began her own religious order, known as the Discalced Carmelites, based on this stricter form of asceticism.

Up until the mid-1550s, Teresa recounts suffering significant periods of spiritual trials and difficulties, but in 1554, she had two experiences/visions, which she describes as conversions. She subsequently had many more mystical experiences after these conversions. It is after this point that Teresa began writing. She wrote a number of books, including *The Book of Her Life*, *The Road to Perfection*, *The Interior Castle*, and others. She also wrote a small and controversial book called *Meditations on the Song of Songs*, an exegetical work on that biblical text. One of her confessors ordered her to destroy it, arguing two things.[91] First, he said, it might link her to the growing Protestant movement, with its focus on Scripture, and second, he said she should destroy it because she was a woman and her interpretations violated Paul's command that women not lead in church. Teresa supposedly burned her manuscript, but not before several copies were made. She defended her interpretation, arguing that even though she was a woman, she did not believe God would be offended by her study of Scripture: "I hold it as certain that we do not offend Him when we find delight and consolation in His words and works. A king would be happy and pleased if he saw a little shepherd he loved looking spellbound at the royal brocade and wondering what it is and how it was made. Nor must we make women stand so far away from enjoyment of the Lord's riches.... I am just like this shepherd boy" (*Med.* 1.8).[92] She made clear that she was not instructing men but rather exploring the goodness of God's word. Throughout all of her works, her knowledge of Scripture comes from her immersion in the prayers, readings, and liturgy of the text rather than her own study, but such immersion provided her with a foundation from which she was able to offer many of her own interpretations.

---

90. Carole Slade, "Teresa of Ávila," in Taylor and Choi, *Handbook of Women Biblical Interpreters*, 494. See also Kiernan Kavanaugh and Otilio Rodriquez, "Introduction," in *The Collected Works of St. Teresa of Ávila*, trans. Kavanaugh and Rodriguez (Washington, DC: Institute of Carmelite Studies, 1976), 1–31.

91. Slade, "Teresa of Ávila," 494.

92. Translations from Teresa's works come from *Collected Works of St. Teresa of Ávila*, trans. Kavanaugh and Rodriguez.

She discusses Mary and Martha in Luke 10:38–42 throughout many of her writings, and she highlights several common ways the two sisters are discussed. For instance, she writes in the *Book of Her Life* about how one must ascend to the contemplative life of Mary after being Martha. She records her struggles in attaining a contemplative state, arguing that what she needed was humility and therefore to wait for God to raise up her soul to the state of Mary. She writes: "I already began to say that there is a small lack of humility in wanting to raise the soul up before the Lord raises it, in not being content to meditate on something so valuable and in wanting to be Mary before having worked with Martha" (*Vita* 22.9). What is particularly interesting here is the emphasis that Teresa places on God raising up the soul. One ascends not by one's own effort, but one has to work alongside Martha, waiting and preparing for God to raise one. She repeats this idea throughout her work. Only God can raise one to the true contemplative life of Mary.

In *The Way of Perfection*, directed to the nuns in her convent, she writes about the absolute necessity of humility when it comes to the life of contemplation. She begins with an argument for practicing humility and preparation: "Prepare yourself so that God may lead you along this path [of contemplation] if He so desires. When he doesn't, you can practice humility which is to consider yourself lucky to serve the servants of the Lord and praise his Majesty because He brought you among them" (*Perf.* 17.1). God does not lead everyone down the same path, and even ones raised to the contemplative path should remain humble. It is impossible for everyone to be contemplative, and those who do not attain it should not feel as though they have failed. In order to emphasize this, she uses the example of Martha: "St. Martha was a saint, even though they do not say she was a contemplative. Well now, what more do you want than to be able to resemble this blessed woman who merited so often to have Christ our Lord in her home and give Him food and serve Him and eat at table with Him? If she had been enraptured like the Magdalene, there wouldn't have been anyone to give food to this divine Guest" (17.5).[93] She then compares Martha to those who are not raised to the contemplative life:

> Well, think of this congregation as the home of St. Martha and that there must be people for every task.... Let them recall that it is necessary for

---

93. Note here how Teresa conflates the two Marys. This is another example of how the conflation sometimes does not actually affect an interpretation.

someone to prepare His meal and let them consider themselves lucky to serve with Martha. Let them consider how true humility consists very much in great readiness to be content with whatever the Lord may want to do with them and in always finding oneself unworthy to be called His servant. If contemplating, practicing mental and vocal prayer, taking care of the sick, helping with household chores and working even at the lowliest tasks are all ways of serving the Guest who comes to be with us and eat, what difference does it make whether we serve in one way or the other. (17.5–6)

Thus, Teresa reiterates that even though the contemplative life might be better, one can still glorify and serve God in the active life. Therefore, the sisters should not worry.

In other places she writes about the beauty of the soul when the examples of Mary and Martha are joined together. She writes, "This is great favor for those to whom the Lord grants it; the active and the contemplative lives are joined. The faculties all serve God together: the will is occupied in its work and contemplation without knowing how; the other two faculties serve in the work of Martha. Thus Mary and Martha walk together" (*Perf.* 31.5). She continues with a story about someone she knows who was able to experience this sort of linking, and thus she knew it was possible. In *Meditations*, she presents a similar argument when she is reflecting on the phrase "sustain me with flowers" from Song 2:5: "I understand by these words that the soul is asking to perform great works in the service of our Lord and of its neighbor. For this purpose it is happy to lose that delight and satisfaction. Although a person will become more active than contemplative ... Martha and Mary never fail to work always together when the soul is in the state.... For these [acts of service] proceed from the tree of God's love and are done for Him alone" (*Med.* 7.3). She further develops this argument in the *Interior Castle*, when she states: "My sisters, let us desire and be occupied with prayer, not for the sake of our enjoyment, but so as to have the strength to serve.... Believe me, Martha and Mary must join together in order to show hospitality to our Lord" (*Int. Castl.* 7.4.12). She then addresses the argument that some might raise that Mary did not work when the Lord came to visit. She responds that she had already "performed the task of Martha" by washing and drying Jesus's feet with her hair (7.4.12). This proves to Teresa that Mary, whom she calls Magdalene, did not only sit in contemplation but also worked. Similarly, the sisters in her convent should strive to live in what she calls both exterior and interior sacrifice to God, and that both types of actions, those of Mary and Martha, should be rooted solely in their love of God.

Teresa discusses Luke 10:38–42 a final time in her short work *The Soliloquies*, a collection of meditations directed to God written throughout 1569. According to Kiernan Kavanaugh and Otilio Rodriguez, the style appears to be constructed to intentionally resemble the pseudo-Augustinian work *The Soliloquies*, which was a popular text in Spain, having been translated into Spanish and widely circulated. Teresa's version contains deeply personal and fervent prayers to God. In one such prayer, she reflects on Martha and her complaint to Jesus in Luke 10:40. She begins by wondering how she could possibly ask God to do anything else for her, only to remember Ps 4:2, for "you tell us to ask you and that you will not fail to give" (*Solil.* 5.1). This causes her to remember "the complaint of that holy woman Martha." From there, Teresa begins to explore the nature of Martha's complaint and Jesus's response to her:

> She did not complain only about her sister, rather I hold it is certain that her greatest sorrow was the thought that You, Lord did not feel sad about the trial she was undergoing and didn't care whether she was with you or not. Perhaps she thought you didn't have as much love for her as for her sister. This must have caused her greater sorrow than did serving the one for whom she had such great love; for love turns work into rest. It seems that in saying nothing to her sister, but in directing her whole complaint to you, Lord, love made her dare to ask why you weren't concerned. Your reply seems to refer to her complaint as I have interpreted it, for love alone is what gives value to all things; a kind of love so great that nothing hinders, it is the one thing necessary. (*Solil.* 5.1)

In Teresa's interpretation, Martha was not upset about her sister's lack of work, but rather at Jesus's seeming lack of concern for Martha's situation. Martha was worried that perhaps Christ did not love her or did not care whether she got to be near him too. According to Teresa, what Martha is looking for is confirmation of Jesus's love, which in turn is what she receives from him. Love is the one thing necessary. She concludes: "Shall I complain with this holy woman? Oh, I have no reason at all for I have always seen in my God much greater and more extraordinary signs of love than I have known how to ask for or desire" (5.1). She then returns to what her request actually is, not confirmation of God's love, like Martha, but rather that God would give her something so that she could give it back to him.[94]

In this short interpretation, Teresa discusses Martha's complaint in way that we have not previously seen. She argues that Martha is not angry or concerned at all about her sister but is completely focused on Jesus and his seeming lack of concern and love for her. Martha has not chosen to do too much; in fact, it is not about the work at all but entirely about God's love for her. This is what drives Martha to address Jesus, and in turn Jesus responds to her complaint, knowing her true concern, with love. This reading is not rooted in the familiar (even to Teresa) arguments about Mary and Martha as action and contemplation. This interpretation is rooted entirely in Teresa's reflection on the biblical story itself. Teresa wants to understand how the holy woman Martha could actually complain to Jesus, since that seems like an outrageous thing for a holy woman to do. This drives her interpretation, and from it, she concludes that she cannot ask God the same thing as Martha because she has been reassured repeatedly of God's love for her.

Like Hildegard and Birgitta before her, Teresa often casts her interpretations in terms of visions and prayers, but they reflect the same interpretive tendencies of the men around them. By studying these three women, one can see the various ways in which the story of Mary and Martha was actually being discussed and interpreted in communities of faith that primarily included women.[95] Furthermore, our study of these interpreters shows once again how Mary and Martha were not limited to their gender, but rather their story was used to develop theories of discipleship that were relevant to monks and laity, men and women, throughout the medieval period.

---

94. Teresa actually quotes Augustine here, referencing *Conf.* 10.29 to make her point.

95. It has been pointed out that even with these additional voices from women interpreters, we are still limited in the evidence available to us. We only have access to women's voices who were among a small subset of literate, highly educated women. These women had resources many women (and men) did not have access to, meaning their opinions and interpretations are lost to us. That said, these three women do provide important insight into how other set of communities of faith were reading this passages beyond the primarily male settings we have studied so far.

Concluding the Medieval Period

Medieval writers, drawing on the ideas of patristic thinkers, expanded on the distinction between the active and contemplative life, adapting it to fit their specific understanding of Christian discipleship. Thus, while one can see the same threads of interpretations weaving throughout this period, there are distinctive elements added. Repeatedly one sees the tension between the claim that a contemplative life is the better part and the reality of needing to be busy with many things. Finally, the conflation of Mary Magdalene and Mary of Bethany, alongside a rise in popularity of Martha, led to the two sisters receiving new characteristics, which in turn shifted interpretations.

Mary and Martha became fixtures of the culture as these two biblical figures were used to highlight current concerns. The better part became shorthand for monastic living. The sisters' images were depicted in illustrated manuscripts, churches, statues, and paintings throughout the medieval world, giving more people access to the story. The two sisters were two of the most well-known biblical women, and yet, while at times their story was tinged with sexist imagery (particularly applied to Mary), one sees that they were still being upheld as examples for Christians of both genders. Their visage was invoked when people were constructing their own images of Christian discipleship in order to understand how a Christian should actually live.

6
The Reformation and a Shift

> It is, therefore, a foolish attempt of the monks to take hold of this passage, as if Christ were drawing a comparison between a contemplative and an active life, while Christ simply informs us for what end, and in what manner, he wishes to be received.... It is true that this error is not of today, but is very old.
> — John Calvin, *Commentary on a Harmony of the Evangelists, Matthew, Mark and Luke*

> I'm already grinning and we haven't even started. I love women. I have great appreciation for men too, but I don't share their psyche. I get a huge kick out of women. We are just so women-y.... We've got a healthy population of Marys and Marthas in our group.
> — Beth Moore, "A True Tale of Two Sisters"

Introduction

The Reformation marks a significant shift in interpretations of Luke 10:38–42. During the patristic and medieval periods, the two sisters were primarily cast as representative of different Christian behaviors. While there was diversity and disagreement among these interpreters, the overall discussion followed the same internal logic, namely, that the story intended to teach its readers about the nature of Christian discipleship. During the Reformation, this approach to the text was deemed allegorical and as such was dismissed in favor of a more literal reading. Alongside this commitment to so-called literal readings of Luke 10, there was a renewed focus on women's roles as being primarily in the household. Women who chose to take religious vows were viewed with great skepticism, as the proper place for a woman to live out her faith was not a convent but in her own home as a wife and mother.

This focus on the household and the role of the housewife led to what Merry Wiesner labels "the death of two Marys" (meaning the Virgin Mary and Mary of Bethany) in favor of Martha, the diligent housewife.[1] That said, Martha was also often negatively depicted because she is not properly oriented in her work, and so she is scolded by Jesus. Thus, there is a call for women to live as a Martha in the household, while still remaining spiritual like Mary. This gendered interpretation grew in popularity throughout the Reformation and early modern period, replacing the threads of interpretation we saw in previous chapters.

In this chapter, I seek to accomplish three things. First, I present the readings of John Calvin and Martin Luther to show how they attempted to break with allegorical readings of the text while still retaining some elements of patristic readings. Second, I show how Luther and the other Reformers shifted the roles available to women by locating their place solely in the household. This led later generations to interpret Mary and Martha "literally" in the household as examples for women in their household. Finally, I show how modern readings, exemplified by Beth Moore and Elisabeth Schüssler Fiorenza, work within this framework when they interpret Luke 10:38–42. By doing so, I hope to show how the patristic and medieval readings offer the opportunity to remove this text from its current niche of women's texts, placing it back into the broader conversation on what these women and their interaction with Jesus can teach us about Luke's understanding of discipleship.

Reformers: John Calvin and Martin Luther

John Calvin and Martin Luther are the two most influential voices from the Reformation. As preachers, authors, and biblical exegetes, they introduced biblical interpretations that became the standard readings for the next several hundred years. Calvin's full-throated rejection of the active/contemplative interpretation and Luther's depiction of Martha as one seeking salvation through works led to significant shifts in future readings of Luke 10:38–42.

While both men rejected what they label as incorrect readings of the text, however, they continued to follow old patterns. Calvin's reading

---

1. Merry Wiesner, "Luther and Women: The Death of Two Marys," in *Disciplines of Faith: Studies in Religion, Politics and Patriarchy*, ed. Jim Obelkelvich, Lyndal Roper, and Raphael Samuel (London: Routledge, 2013), 297.

appears similar to that of John Chrysostom, and Luther, despite all his complaints to the contrary, still reads like a medieval thinker, finding in the two sisters two different types of Christians. In this way, Luther and Calvin stand at the crossroads between two different exegetical cultures. They are both indebted to the patristic and medieval interpreters and at the same time set the stage for new interpretive approaches.

John Calvin

John Calvin was born in 1509 in Noyon, a small city in northern France.[2] When he was fourteen years old, he was sent by his father to study at the College de la Marche in Paris, with the intent to enter the priesthood. After several years of liberal-arts education (with a particular focus on Latin and rhetoric) and the death of his father in 1531, Calvin returned to Paris, not to become a priest but to more fully immerse himself in humanistic studies. It was during this period (probably 1533) that Calvin converted to the Reformed faith.[3] After his conversion, Calvin was forced to leave Paris upon threat of arrest and spent the next several years traveling and writing, mostly in solitude, before landing in Geneva. He writes that he only intended on staying in Geneva for a single night but was convinced to stay and help lead the reform there.[4] After Geneva rejected his attempts at reform, he went to Strasbourg, where he continued to write and preach,

---

2. For more in-depth analysis of Calvin's life and influence, see the following works: David C. Steinmetz, *Calvin in Context* (New York: Oxford University Press, 2010); Alexandre Ganoczy, "Calvin's Life," trans. David L. Foxgrover and James Schmitt, in *The Cambridge Companion to John Calvin*, ed. Donald K. McKim (Cambridge: Cambridge University Press, 2004), 3–24; Bruce Gordon, *Calvin* (New Haven: Yale University Press, 2009); Emile Doumergue, *Jean Calvin: Les hommes et les choses de son temps*, 7 vols. (Lausanne: Bridel, 1899–1927); François Wendel, *Calvin: Origins and Development of His Religious Thought* (Durham, NC: Labyrinth, 1987); Alister E. McGrath, *A Life of John Calvin: A Study in the Shaping of Western Culture* (Oxford: Basil Blackwell, 1990).

3. Steinmetz, *Calvin in Context*, 8.

4. Calvin writes in his preface to his *Commentary on the Psalms:* "William Farel forced me to stay in Geneva not so much by advice or by urging as by command, which had the power of God's hand laid violently upon me from heaven.… When [Farel] realized that I was determined to study in privacy in some obscure place, and saw that he could gain nothing by entreaty, he descended to cursing and said that God would surely curse my peace if I held back from giving at a time of such great need. Terrified by his words … I gave up my journey and attempted to apply whatever gift

publishing his second edition of the *Institutes of the Christian Religion* in 1539 as well as several biblical commentaries. He also married Idellete de Bure, who had two children from a previous marriage. In 1539 he was invited back to Geneva, and in 1541 he returned, introducing substantial ecclesial and civic reforms. He died in Geneva in 1564 after a long illness. Calvin is the unquestioned shaper of the Reformed theological tradition.

As a biblical interpreter, Calvin describes his exegetical approach in his preface to his *Commentary on Romans*, written as a letter to his friend Simon Grynaeus.[5] In it he seeks to differentiate himself from the commentaries of other Reformers, notably Philipp Melanchthon and Martin Bucer. While he stresses that he has found their commentaries to be useful, he rejects the length at which Bucer discusses theological problems in each text and the brevity of Melanchthon, who focused only on major themes, which he says leads to many unfortunate omissions. His approach sought to find middle ground by writing on each verse of a chapter but by making his comments as brief as possible: "Both of us felt that lucid brevity constituted the particular virtue of an interpreter. And truly, since almost his only responsibility is to lay open the mind of the writer whom he has undertaken to explain, to the degree that he leads his readers away from it, he goes astray from his own purpose."[6] He argued that he had theological works, such as the *Institutes*, where he could work out theological and dogmatic concerns and that too much theological discourse in a commentary would hinder the average reader from getting much value out of it.

Furthermore, Calvin believed that being straightforward, while keeping to the literal and historical context of the passage, was key to good biblical interpretation.[7] He paid careful attention to the Greek and Hebrew, often addressing linguistic and cultural concerns. He was interested in what the biblical texts meant for their original audience, and this is often what he sought to convey in his commentaries. Because of this focus on

---

I had in defense of my faith." See *Calvin: Commentaries*, trans. Joseph Haroutunian, LCC 23 (Philadelphia: Westminster, 1958), 53.

5. For a fuller discussion of Calvin as biblical interpreter, see John R. Walchenbach, *John Calvin as Biblical Commentator: An Investigation in Calvin's Use of John Chrysostom as an Exegetical Tutor* (Eugene, OR: Wipf & Stock, 2010); John L. Thompson, "Calvin as Biblical Interpreter," in McKim, *Cambridge Companion to John Calvin*, 58–73.

6. Calvinus Grynaeo, *Ep.* 191 (CO 10:402 [Walchenbach]).

7. Thompson, "Calvin as Biblical Interpreter," 61.

the literal meaning of the text, Calvin had a complicated relationship with patristic and medieval biblical commentators. He rejected most allegorical or figurative readings and had many negative things to say about patristic writers, particularly Origen. Origen and other allegorists had distorted the text and should be ignored.

However, Calvin did appreciate a few key patristic thinkers, notably John Chrysostom, whose biblical interpretations had significant impact on him. In fact, Calvin intended to translate some of Chrysostom's homilies into French but died before he was able to complete the project. However, in the drafted preface to that work, he writes that there is value in reading many of the church fathers because they are resources provided by God to help understand the biblical text.[8] In particular, Chrysostom, with his focus on the plain meaning of the text, could help the layperson have a deeper understanding of the Bible. As we will see, all these factors come into play in his interpretation of Luke 10:38–42. Calvin strongly and repeatedly rejects the active/contemplative reading introduced by Origen. He engages with the literal level of the text in a straightforward and easily accessible way, and he draws on the work of Chrysostom in his final interpretation.

Calvin's primary discussion of Mary and Martha can be found in his *Commentary on the Harmony of the Gospels, Matthew, Mark and Luke*. In this commentary he attacks previous interpretations as deeply flawed, while also offering a nuanced reading of his own. He begins after a translation of the passage with this claim: "As this passage has been basely distorted into the commendation of what is called a Contemplative life, we must inquire into its true meaning, from which it will appear, that nothing was farther from the design of Christ, than to encourage his disciples to indulge in indolence, or in useless speculations. It is, no doubt, an old error that those who withdraw from business, and devote themselves entirely to a contemplative, lead an Angelical life."[9] Calvin believes the claim that this passage supports a contemplative life is a distorting of the actual meaning of the passage. He acknowledges that it is an old idea (though he does not explicitly mention Origen or any other patristic thinkers), but he still argues that it is an obvious error. He continues by claiming that the idea that the contemplative live is the best life was taken from Aristotle and not

---

8. Thompson, "Calvin as Biblical Interpreter," 63–64.
9. John Calvin, *Commentary on a Harmony of the Evangelists, Matthew, Mark and Luke*, trans. William Pringle, 3 vols. (Grand Rapids: Eerdmans, 1949), 2:142.

the Bible. He argues, "When peevish men gave themselves up to solitude and indolence, the resolution to adopt that course was followed by such pride, that they imagined themselves to be like the angels, because they did nothing."[10] In a clear rejection of the monastic life, he condemns the laziness of such people. He argues that the biblical witness is clear that God desires people to live an active life and to follow the call that God has placed on their lives.

He then turns to mock their reading of Mary as representing the contemplative life. He argues that she did not sit at Christ's feet her entire life:

> How absurdly they have perverted the words of Christ to support their own contrivance, will appear manifest when we have ascertained the natural meaning. Luke says that "Mary sat at the feet of Jesus," does he mean that she did nothing else throughout her whole life? On the contrary, the Lord enjoins his followers to make such a distribution of their time, that he who desires to make proficiency in the school of Christ shall not always be an idle hearer but shall put in practice what he has learned; for there is a time to hear, and a time to act.[11]

Calvin's own interpretation is one that we have already seen in the sermons of Chrysostom and others. Like Chrysostom, he says that the passage suggests the need for proper discernment. Once one has learned from Christ, one needs to practice the things learned, because Jesus is not advocating idleness. He concludes: "It is, therefore, a foolish attempt of the monks to take hold of this passage, as if Christ were drawing a comparison between a contemplative and an active life, while Christ simply informs us for what end, and in what manner, he wishes to be received."[12]

Having dismissed the allegorical reading, Calvin then presents what he calls the "natural meaning" of the text. Calvin argues that while Martha should be praised for hospitality in this text, she failed in two key ways. First, Martha was too extravagant in her practice of hospitality. She worked too hard and prepared more than Christ needed or asked for, leading to her distress. He argues, "Martha carried her activity beyond proper bounds; for Christ would rather have chosen to be entertained in a frugal manner, and at moderate expense, than that the holy woman should have submit-

---

10. Calvin, *Commentary on a Harmony*, 2:142.
11. Calvin, *Commentary on a Harmony*, 2:143.
12. Calvin, *Commentary on a Harmony*, 2:143.

ted to so much toil."[13] Here Calvin echoes Basil and Cyril of Alexandria: Martha's problem is that she prepared too many dishes for Jesus. Calvin is quick to note, however, that when Jesus says "one thing is necessary" he is not actually referring to one dish, like those who "give a very meager interpretation of these words."[14] Martha's first problem, nonetheless, is her extravagance. This leads to her stress, because if she had prepared less, she could have sat with her sister and listened. She should have known that Jesus would be satisfied with only a little.

Martha's second error, according to Calvin, is more grievous and directly results from her overly abundant hospitality:

> The second fault was, that Martha, by distracting her attention, and undertaking more labor than was necessary, deprived herself of the advantage of Christ's visit. The excess is pointed out by Luke, when he speaks of much serving; for Christ was satisfied with little. It was just as if one were to give a magnificent reception to a prophet, and yet not to care about hearing him, but, on the contrary, to make so great and unnecessary preparations as to bury all the instruction. But the true way of receiving prophets is, to accept the advantage which God presents and offers to us through their agency.[15]

She is so busy with serving that she is not able to take advantage of Christ's presence in her home. This leads her to another evil, namely, to her despising her sister's pious behavior. Even though Calvin grants that hospitality is a good thing, her incorrect orientation toward hospitality leads her to sin. He offers this as a warning to all Christians that "in doing what is right, we must take care not to think more highly of ourselves than of others."[16]

Calvin then begins his exegesis of Jesus's response to Martha with a particular focus on the phrases "one thing is necessary" and "Mary has chosen the best part." He first outlines several alternate interpretations that he has heard: the one thing as a dish (as previously discussed) and the one thing being unity. The one thing being unity is a reading we have seen

---

13. Calvin, *Commentary on a Harmony*, 2:143.
14. Calvin, *Commentary on a Harmony*, 2:144. It is unclear whether Calvin knows about the textual variant in this verse, as he does not mention it here, but it is clear that he knows interpretations that hold the "one or few things" as being a reference to hospitality and the number of dishes rather than the one thing being a spiritual need.
15. Calvin, *Commentary on a Harmony*, 2:144.
16. Calvin, *Commentary on a Harmony*, 2:144.

previously in Augustine, and Calvin labels this reading "ingenious" but still wrong. Calvin argues that when Jesus says one thing is necessary, he is referring to Martha's misplaced attention. She is not focused on the ultimate thing in this instance, which is learning from Jesus: "And yet Christ does not mean that everything else, with the exception of this one thing, is of no importance, but that we must pay a proper attention to order, lest what is accessory—as the phrase is—become our chief concern."[17] Martha has disordered priorities. In this way, Calvin again echoes Chrysostom, but places an even stronger emphasis on the dangers of this disordering.

Calvin then turns to Jesus's statement that Mary has chosen the good part. He begins by stressing that Jesus is not drawing a comparison between Mary and Martha, and he rejects any interpretation that seeks to place the two sisters at odds, labeling those interpreters "unskillful and mistaken."[18] Calvin argues that Jesus's statement is a simple claim that Mary is doing something good and should not be interrupted. He then writes his own understanding of Jesus's statement: "'You would have a good right,' [Jesus] says, 'to blame your sister, if she indulged in ease, or gave herself up to trifling occupations, or aimed at something unsuitable to her station, and left to you the whole charge of the household affairs. But now, when she is properly and usefully employed in hearing, it would be an act of injustice to withdraw her from it; for an opportunity so favorable is not always in her power.'"[19] Calvin's retelling of the story highlights his view that Mary is not being placed higher than Martha. Rather, Mary is simply doing what she should be doing, and Jesus is trying to encourage Martha to do likewise. He then concludes with a short discussion of what it means that this good part will not be taken away from Mary. This is the only phrase where he does not land on a firm interpretation. He notes that some interpret the phrase eschatologically, and surprisingly he does not have a problem with this interpretation. Another option (and the one he prefers) is that Jesus is referring to the fact that Martha should not take away Mary's current position at Jesus's feet, but he concludes that either is fine.

Calvin is detailed but does not digress into long theological discussions. His reading is highly accessible. What is particularly notable for our

---

17. Calvin, *Commentary on a Harmony*, 2:144.

18. Calvin, *Commentary on a Harmony*, 2:144. Also, see the similarities between this argument and Loveday Alexander's, who also argues that the primary problem with modern interpretations is the tendency to place Mary and Martha in tension.

19. Calvin, *Commentary on a Harmony*, 2:144.

purposes is his complete rejection of the action/contemplation dichotomy and his overall insistence that this reading is unbelievably foolish. That said, he does not fully reject all earlier readings, as his interpretation of the passage is highly similar to both Chrysostom's and Cyril's interpretation: the main message of the passage is one of discernment. Martha is not correctly oriented in her hospitality. She overdoes it, and that extravagance leads to her problems. Mary does not always sit and listen. She works too, but she recognizes when she should work and when she should listen.

Calvin's rejection of medieval readings continues in his other mention of Mary and Martha. In a treatise, *An Admonition Showing the Advantages Which Christendom Might Derive from an Inventory of Relics*, Calvin discusses the various relics scattered around Europe and how they lead to idolatry. He discusses the relics he knows in order to mock any claims that there might be a historical basis for them. He briefly discusses Mary (whom he calls Magdalene), Martha, and Lazarus and the tradition that they went to France to preach. We have already studied the legends that arose around Mary and Martha in the previous chapter, including the popular story of Martha slaying a dragon. Calvin seems to have knowledge of these stories and concludes: "For if ancient history be read and examined with judgment, it will be seen that this is the most stupid of all fables, and has not the least shadow of plausibility."[20] He is convinced that the extracanonical stories surrounding the two sisters should be rejected whole cloth.

Like his rejection of the active/contemplative dichotomy, this rejection also contributes to shifting interpretations about the two sisters. One should focus only on the words of the biblical text and attempt to get a literal understanding of the story. Reformation exegesis more broadly followed Calvin's lead in rejecting the active/contemplative interpretation, despite the fact that he followed a patristic author in his interpretation, which opened the door to new, more gendered interpretations. As Jaroslav Pelikan writes of the first Reformers, Calvin and Luther rejected some church traditions in the name of Scripture, but in many ways they still found those traditions important and even necessary. Their followers, however, rejected many of these traditional interpretations in their entirety.[21]

---

20. Calvin, *An Admonition Showing the Advantages Which Christendom Might Derive from An Inventory of Relics*, in *Tracts and Treatises*, trans. Henry Beveridge, 3 vols. (Grand Rapids: Eerdmans, 1958), 1:330.

21. Jaroslav Pelikan, *Luther the Expositor: Introduction to the Reformer's Exegetical Writings* (St. Louis: Concordia, 1959), 71–72. It should be noted that chronologically

Martin Luther

Martin Luther was the most influential figure of the Reformation.[22] He was born in 1483 in Eiselben, Saxony. Though not particularly wealthy, his father, Hans, spent a great deal on Luther's education, sending him to several schools before Luther enrolled in the University of Erfurt in 1501. After finishing his degree in 1505, Luther had a near-death experience in a thunderstorm, which prompted him to join the Erfurt Augustinian monastery. He studied theology in Wittenberg, receiving a doctorate in theology in 1512. He began teaching Bible and theology and continuing his own research. Over these years, he grew more and more disillusioned with some of the practices of the church, leading to the infamous *Ninety-Five Theses*, which he may or may not have physically posted to the door of Castle Church in Wittenberg.[23] After the publishing of the theses, Martin Luther began a series of books and treatises on the authority of the church and the authority of Scripture that eventually led to his excommunication in 1521. Pope Leo X argued that Luther's beliefs were heretical and that all of his writings should be banned. After refusing to recant at the Diet of Worms, Luther was forced to go into hiding, ending up at the Wartburg Fortress, hidden by his allies after an arrest warrant was issued for him. During this time he translated the Bible into German, a huge feat that he accomplished in three months. He was soon called back to Wittenberg, where he remained for the rest of his life. From here, he continued to debate his views of the authority of Scripture as well as weigh in on a number of sociopolitical issues. He also wrote a large number of biblical commentaries and sermons, producing a number of his own interpretations during this period. He married Katherina von Bora, a former nun, in 1525, and they had six children together. He died in 1546.

Luther preceded Calvin. However, his interpretation became more influential in later generations. This is why structurally he is placed here, in order to ensure a smoother transition into later interpretations.

22. For a more in-depth analysis of Martin Luther's life and influence, see the following works: Martin Brecht, *Martin Luther*, trans. James L. Schaaf, 3 vols. (Philadelphia: Fortress, 1985–1993); David M. Whitford, *Luther: A Guide for the Perplexed* (New York: T&T Clark, 2011); Heiko A. Oberman, *Luther: Man between God and the Devil*, trans. Eileen Walliser-Schwarzbart (New Haven: Yale University Press, 1989); James M. Kittelson, *Martin Luther: The Story of the Man and His Career* (Minneapolis: Fortress, 1986).

23. Whitford, *Luther*, 31.

6. The Reformation and a Shift

Unsurprisingly perhaps for someone whose catchphrase was *sola scriptura*, Luther dedicated much of his time to translating and interpreting Scripture. He viewed himself first and foremost as a biblical exegete, and his writings on the Bible make up over half of his published works.[24] He lectured on the book of Genesis for a decade and spent over two years preaching the first chapter of John's Gospel. Luther believed that the meaning of Scripture should always be clear, and he encouraged his readers to view his comments more as a scaffolding for their own study of Scripture. As he wrote in his conclusion to the *Kirchenpostille*: "And so my dear Christians, get to it, get to it, and let my exposition and that of all the doctors be no more than scaffold, an aid for the construction of the true building, so that we may ourselves grasp and taste the pure and simple Word of God and abide by it."[25] From this, one sees that Luther does not completely dismiss the work of previous biblical interpreters but cautions that readers should only view them as guides and not as an authorities.

Luther clearly prefers the literal sense of the text and equally rejects medieval readings that he views as twisting the real meaning of the text. But, as Mark Thompson notes, Luther often engages explicitly with Augustine and Jerome, as well as Origen, Ambrose, Gregory the Great, and others.[26] He uses their interpretations in his theological arguments on the sacraments, church doctrine, and other issues. He is, however, equally as comfortable rejecting them if he views them as being in error. As he writes in response to some critics: "This is my answer to all those who accuse me of rejecting all the holy teachers of the Church. I do not reject them. But everyone knows that at times they have erred as men will. Therefore I am ready to trust them only when they give me evidence for their opinions of Scripture which have never erred."[27] In reality, Luther's interpretative style often resembles many patristic writers. In fact, he more frequently

---

24. Pelikan, *Luther the Expositor*, 48. For another resource on Luther as biblical interpreter, see Mark D. Thompson, *A Sure Ground on Which I Stand: The Relation of Authority and Interpretive Method in Luther's Approach to Scripture*, SCHT (Milton Keynes: Paternoster, 2004).

25. Martin Luther, *Kirchenpostille* (trans. Thompson).

26. Thompson, *Sure Ground*, 252.

27. Martin Luther, *Grund und Ursach aller Artikel D. Martin Luther, so durch römische Bulle unrechtlich verdammt sind* (*LW* 32:11). Unless otherwise noted, all translations from Luther's works come from Jaroslav Pelikan's English translation of *Luther's Works*.

resembles the patristic medieval interpreters who preceded him than the Reformers who followed him.

We see this tension in Luther's interpretation of Mary and Martha in Luke 10:38–42. He discusses the two sisters in a number of places throughout his writings, because they represent for him not the dichotomy between action and contemplation but the difference between works and faith. That said, he wants to resist a so-called allegorical reading of the two women, and yet he still holds that these two real, historical women can emphasize the importance of faith. As Susan Karant-Nunn and Merry Wiesner-Hanks argue, "Mary and Martha are real women, not metaphors, but the primary purpose of their story is to emphasize the importance of faith (Mary) as opposed to works (Martha). Luther explicitly rejects the most common medieval allegorical interpretation, in which Mary had stood for the contemplative life and Martha for the active life in the world."[28]

This rejection is most clearly seen in Luther's homily on Mary's ascension. He begins this sermon with the following claim: "We can dismiss what has been said until now about the active and the contemplative life. Even if it comes from Augustine or others, I would cover up their words and let them be unknown."[29] Unsurprisingly, he also rejects the connection between the Virgin Mary and the two sisters of Bethany. As Beth Kreitzer notes, Luther was skeptical of the entire story of Mary's ascension and even more skeptical of a connection between Luke 10:38–42 and Mary's characteristics.[30] Mary the mother of Jesus does not appear in this Lukan account, and thus she should not be mentioned. He eventually concludes that this holiday should not be celebrated, but if one is going to preach on this day, one should stick to the text at hand and not attempt to integrate the Virgin into the story.[31]

Despite rejecting the action/contemplation dichotomy as well as the idea that the Virgin Mary represents the perfect balance of both, Luther has his own beliefs about the symbolic meaning of this passage, which

---

28. Susan C. Karant-Nunn and Merry E. Wiesner-Hanks, eds., *Luther on Women: A Sourcebook* (New York: Cambridge University Press, 2003), 60.

29. Luther, *Sermon on the Day of Mary's Ascension*; unless otherwise indicated, all translations of this work are by Karant-Nunn and Wiesner-Hanks.

30. Beth Kreitzer, *Reforming Mary: Changing Images of the Virgin Mary in Lutheran Sermons of the Sixteenth Century* (Oxford: Oxford University Press, 2004), 128.

31. Kreitzer, *Reforming Mary*, 128.

he precedes to lay out in this sermon. Luther argues that the story can be summarized in the following way: "Mary hears the word, Martha wants Mary to stop listening to the word, and Christ makes a judgment. I make a distinction between faith and works…. Faith is higher than life, and all people's works are transitory things; there is nothing except the word of God and faith."[32] For Luther, Mary does not need to do anything to receive the word of God; she only needs to have faith. This is why Jesus does not tell her to get up and help her sister. Luther acknowledges that Martha's works are not bad, but that they are not necessary for salvation. After all, Martha is a good cook who is trying to fill people's bellies, and these sorts of works "do not make you godly, but they make you useful."[33] They are not what is needed for salvation.

This leads Luther to transition into an even more abstract discussion, which focuses on Mary as the one who receives the gospel and Martha as the one who receives the law.[34] Martha does not realize her freedom because she has received the law, and this has made her feel trapped and leads to her unhappy demeanor. Mary has received the freedom that comes from the gospel, and thus whenever she works, she does so by choice, not necessity. We have not seen Martha being discussed in relation to the Law since Origen in *Fr. Luc.* 171, and yet here Luther returns to it, although with different conclusions.

He then reverses the entire contemplative/active reading by saying that if a person wants to be in a convent or a monastery, they should do it, but not because they feel obligated to do so. This is not the freedom that Mary had:

> If it is possible to be in convents or monasteries, good, be there. Anything that we do, we should do freely. Those who do not want to do it willingly, leave. If today one does not have the desire, return [from there] tomorrow. A Christian will not be bound; if he is willing, he will do it freely without force. Christ rules in the world in this way, and does not make Christians as we commonly do, putting them all in positions that are not free, in monasteries or convents. Just as he says "Martha, you are being forced, and you suffer from this." Mary stays quiet and yet she does work, with a willing heart, by choice.[35]

---

32. Luther, *Sermon on the Day of Mary's Ascension.*
33. Luther, *Sermon on the Day of Mary's Ascension.*
34. Luther, *Sermon on the Day of Mary's Ascension.*
35. Luther, *Sermon on the Day of Mary's Ascension.*

Thus, the one who feels compelled to enter a monastery or to remain there is not actually Mary, but rather a Martha, because she feels forced to do so, as if she must earn her salvation, which comes freely to her.

One finds a similar interpretation in one of his *Sermons on John's Gospel*. In it he returns to the example of Martha as one who strives to earn her salvation. He frames this sermon by stating that he is about to discuss the chief doctrine of the Christian faith as he understands it. He says that it can be fully understood by reading Christ's response to Martha in Luke 10:42: "Thus we hear Christ the Lord telling Martha in the Gospel: 'One thing is needful. Mary has chosen the good portion. You, Martha, are anxious about many things; you are busy. It is fine to work, to manage house and home, to be a burgomaster, to be a servant, to be a pastor. But this will not attain the goal. Mary has chosen and found the right thing to do. She is sitting at My feet and listening to what I am saying. This is proper; this is the right thing. This is the secret, just to hear Me. This alone does it.' "[36] He continues by noting that Mary too will eventually do work, but that her works are done out of the "righteousness of faith," not the righteousness of works. The core message of the gospel is that a person only needs to hear the word of God and believe it. Mary knows this, and thus she is the one praised in the story. Luther uses this as a warning to his hearers that they too should strive to be like Mary and not Martha: "Therefore wherever conscience, sin, life, death, or even God or the devil are concerned, bear in mind that you must disregard everything in the world. Let Martha go into the kitchen and wash dishes; let Martha put the house in order and you become a Mary Magdalene."[37] Luther concludes that this is Christ's gift to all Christians, that one only needs to hear his words and what Christ

---

36. Luther, *Sermons on St. John* (*LW* 2:247–48). See also Luther's *Lectures on Galatians*, where he uses Luke 10:42 to make almost the exact same point: "Or listen to Christ Himself, who gives the following answer to Martha when she is deeply concerned and finds it almost unbearable that her sister Mary is sitting at Jesus' feet, listening to His words, and leaving her to serve alone. 'Martha,' He says, 'you are anxious and troubled about many things; one thing is needful. Mary has chosen the good portion, which shall not be taken away from her.' Therefore a man becomes a Christian, not by working but by listening. And so anyone who wants to exert himself toward righteousness must first exert himself in listening to the Gospel" (*Lectures on Galatians* [*LW* 1:214]).

37. Luther, *Sermons on St. John* (*LW* 2:247–48). Note that Luther here conflates Mary of Bethany and Mary Magdalene.

meant when he said that he will give rest to all those who are heavy laden (Matt 11:28).[38]

Luther believes strongly that Mary is the sister who should be emulated because she understands that all one needs to do is listen to the Word. Let Martha go and do her housework, but it will not lead to her salvation.

One final interpretation is worth briefly discussing. The relationship between listening to the word and faith is found throughout Luther's works, but in his treatise *Concerning the Order of Public Worship*, he uses the story to justify the primacy of the word in a worship service. He writes in his conclusion:

> And this is the sum of the matter: Let everything be done so that the Word may have free course instead of the prattling and rattling that has been the rule up to now. We can spare everything except the Word. Again, we profit by nothing as much as by the Word. For the whole Scripture shows that the Word should have free course among Christians. And in Luke 10, Christ himself says, "One thing is needful," i.e., that Mary sit at the feet of Christ and hear his word daily. This is the best part to choose and it shall not be taken away forever. It is an eternal Word. Everything else must pass away, no matter how much care and trouble it may give Martha.

The one thing needful in this instance is the word of God. Thus, all worship services should privilege it over the "prattling and tattling" that he believes is currently at the forefront. Everything else is not eternal, as the word is, and thus of lesser importance, even though there are those who would prefer to spend their time on those lesser things. This highlights Luther's overall belief that listening to the Word, as Mary does in Luke 10:38–42, is the only thing necessary for salvation.

From Luther's interpretation of Luke 10:38–42, one should take away two key points. First, he rejects the active and contemplative reading in its entirety, suggesting it would be best that it be entirely forgotten. As a part of this rejection, he dismisses any parallels between the Virgin Mary and Martha and Mary, arguing instead that since the Virgin does not appear in the Lukan story, one should not try to force her into it. Second, he replaces the active and contemplative tension with faith and works. Instead of representing the active life, Martha now represents those who try to work for

---

38. Luther, *Sermons on St. John* (*LW* 2:247–48).

their salvation. Mary now represents the one who knows that listening and believing the gospel is the only thing needed. Like many interpreters before him, Luther does not dismiss the necessity of works but frames them around Christian freedom. One should not work because one has to do so but only out of joyful obedience as result of grace. In this way, Luther elevates Mary and places her as the paradigm that all Christians should follow. Martha, the cook and housekeeper, is not correctly oriented and is distracted by unnecessary things, as she is burdened by the self-righteousness that comes from trying to keep the law.

Thus, Luther and Calvin both reject the active and contemplative readings. After them, no Protestant interpreters embraced this interpretation, as it was seen as ignoring the actual details of the text. This was a marked shift in the Protestant era. Calvin and Luther's own interpretations, however, are markedly different from each other, suggesting that there was not one simple reading of the story even in the Reformation. Calvin chooses to focus on what he labels a more literal reading, emphasizing there is not competition between the two sisters and that the primary message is discernment. Luther, on the other hand, sees a tension between Mary and Martha and reads the story in light of his own concerns of the relationship between works and faith. Other Reformed thinkers followed these two interpretative threads. For instance, John Mayer argues in favor of discernment, one should listen when the Word is proclaimed, but this does not mean one should only sit and listen.[39] Richard Baxter, on other hand, follows a more Lutheran view, arguing that the one thing necessary is listening to Christ and having faith. Martha's work is misplaced.[40] Thus, the most common threads of the patristic and medieval period disappeared during the Reformation, though they were not replaced by one literal reading, despite an emphasis on reading literally.

It should also be noted that while there are more gendered overtones in the interpretations particularly in Luther (see, for instance, his repeated references to Martha as cook), these interpretations are not explicitly gendered. That said, another shift occurred in the Reformation that contributed to the rise of such gendered readings of Luke 10:38–42 in the coming centuries. This shift revolved around the rising emphasis of

---

39. John Mayer, *Commentary on the New Testament*, Luke 7:39, 373.
40. Richard Baxter, *The One Thing Necessary or Mary's Choice Justified* 2–3.

Christian women as primarily mothers and wives and the rising distrust of religious women. It is to this shift that we must now turn our attention.

Christian Women as Housewives and Mothers

Luther himself was one of the primary champions of this shift, in which women who entered convents were viewed skeptically. Luther believed that the proper place for a woman to live out her faith was not in the "abnormal" state of singleness but rather under either her husband or her father. There is an ongoing debate over Luther's overall opinions of women and whether we should view him as a champion of women's freedom or as a perpetrator of the patriarchy. Frustratingly, in many ways, he appears to be both.[41] For our purposes, what is important is Luther's elevation of marriage and his dismissal of religious celibacy. Luther replaced chastity and virginity with the virtues of marriage and motherhood. Luther was highly skeptical that anyone could remain celibate. As Wiesner argues, "Women choosing to remain celibate, however, were not only fighting their natural sex drive, which Luther and everyone else in the 16th century felt to be much stronger than men's but also the divinely imposed order which made woman subject to man."[42] As Luther himself writes in one of his treatises on marriage:

> Therefore, priests, monks, and nuns are duty bound to forsake their vows whenever they find that God's ordinance to produce seed and to multiply is powerful and strong within them. They have no power by any authority, law, command, or vow to hinder this which God has created within them. If they do hinder it, however, you may be sure that they will not remain pure but inevitably besmirch themselves with secret sins or fornication. For they are simply incapable of resisting the word and ordinance of God within them.[43]

It was unnatural to be a monk or nun because this choice contradicted God's natural order. As we have already seen, Luther rejects a reading of Luke 10:38–42 that suggests a monastic life is to be preferred, and here

---

41. For a fuller discussion of the secondary scholarship and the ongoing debate on Luther's view of women, see Karant-Nunn and Wiesner-Hanks, *Luther on Women*, 1–14.
42. Wiesner, "Luther and Women," 298.
43. Martin Luther, *The Estate of Marriage* (*LW* 45:19).

we find another example of his overall skepticism concerning celibacy and monastic vows. Luther believed that women in particular needed a husband to ensure that they did not stray from their faith. In fact, Luther argued that all women should remain in the household since that is the embodiment of their high calling: "What better and more useful thing can be taught in the church than the example of a godly mother of the household who prays, sighs, cries out, gives thanks, rules the house, performs the functions of sex and desires offspring with the greatest chastity, grace and godliness: What more should she do?"[44]

Luther knew of biblical women who did more than stay at home, women who taught, preached, and prophesied, but he believed that those women were unique to biblical times. Women should be silent, be obedient to their husbands, and find joy in staying at home, running the day-to-day tasks and raising their children: "The woman is like a nail driven into the wall.... She sits at home... For just as the snail carries its house with it, so the wife should stay home and look after the affairs of the household. She enjoys staying home, enjoys being in the kitchen ... does not enjoy going out ... does not enjoy speaking to others."[45] By doing this, women were able to fully live out their salvation as it was God's mercy to them after the sin of Eve.[46]

Thus, Luther's ideal woman began to resemble Martha of Bethany, the dedicated housekeeper, in many ways, even as he dismissed those women who previously had been identified as Marys because of their desire to sit at the feet of the Lord. As Wiesner concludes: "Thus Luther established Martha, the obedient wife serving God through daily household tasks, as the ideal women, belittling Mary her sister who chose to devote herself to learning Christ's teaching.... Luther added his voice, then, to widely accepted notions of the proper role of women, but the strength of that voice

---

44. Martin Luther, *Lectures on Genesis 26–30* (*LW* 5:331).
45. Martin Luther, *Lectures on Genesis 1–5* (*LW* 1:202–3).
46. Kirsi Stjerna (*Women in the Reformation* [Malden, MA: Blackwell, 2009], 33) argues, "The domestication of women led to the honorable callings of motherhood and marriage, advocated through theological argument, knitted with the Protestants' valorization of family and marriage as the cornerstones of society, on the one hand, but led to their reiteration of the Pauline rejection of women teachers and ministers, on the other. Just as the exclusion of women from public teaching roles and official forms of ministry continued, so too a status quo in gender relations was promoted both at home and in society, backed by biblical arguments about the created order of human life and the effects of the first sin."

and the power of his language gave contemporaries and followers new ammunition. His metaphors and imagery were repeated for centuries."[47] Wiesner's argument that Luther effectively eliminated a reading of Mary that would support women entering convents is accurate. In Luther's ideology, it is clear that women should be housewives. Their behavior should mimic that of Martha when she served the Lord. This is their holy calling. But this position introduced a new tension, because as we have seen in Luther's own interpretations of Luke 10:38–42, it is clear that Mary is the better sister. Elisabeth Moltmann-Wendel argues that it was during the Protestant Reformation that the image of Martha grew very complicated. Martha is practical and the ideal example of female behavior, yet also she is an example of works righteousness.[48] She is useful and yet ultimately misguided, because Christ takes no account of any good works. This led to women being told to be Martha and yet somehow maintain the ability to have faith alone in the midst of that work. Moltmann-Wendel holds that this tension is at root of modern interpretations: "Consequently, many women in the church, who even now tend to be identified with Martha, feel as though they are less valuable, even worthless."[49]

Thus, the Protestant Reformation, with its emphasis on Martha as an embodiment of works righteousness, combined with the idea that women should actually try to act like Martha in their everyday lives (and that the convent should be rejected entirely), led to a shift in reading Luke's story in later generations. After all, Luke 10:38–42 is about two women, and thus it led to a message in which the Protestant woman should be a Martha but maintain a Mary-like spirit of faith. The new holy woman was the one who could be both at the same time. Unlike in previous generations, when great religious men and women were said to combine both Mary and Martha in their lifetimes, now we see that it was solely applied to women, who were to be wives and mothers. This new generation of women were Mary and Martha because they could balance their spiritual life and their physical household tasks. This led to the popular British rhyme "Mary and Martha in one life, Make the perfect vicar's wife."[50]

To illustrate this, let us briefly turn to some examples of women being elevated as embodying both Mary and Martha due primarily to their

---

47. Weisner, "Luther and Women," 305.
48. Moltmann-Wendel, *Women around Jesus*, 21.
49. Moltmann-Wendel, *Women around Jesus*, 21.
50. Moltmann-Wendel, *Women around Jesus*, 21.

identities as wives/mothers. The first is an epitaph for Dorothy Selby, an English woman who died in 1641. She was married to William Selby and a lady-in-waiting to Queen Elizabeth I.[51] On her grave, after her biographical information and the fact that she was good at needlework, one finds the following inscription:

> She was in heart, a Lydia, and in tongue, a Hannah
> In zeale, a Ruth, and in wedlock, a Susanna
> Prudently simple, providently wary
> To the World, a Martha, and to Heaven, a Mary.[52]

Selby is described here as representing a number of biblical women, to illustrate her faith, her commitment to her marriage, and so on. For our purposes, the ending of the epitaph is particularly notable. It seems to present Selby as being externally a Martha, a dedicated and committed wife and daughter (both her husband and father are named on her grave), but internally and now in heaven she is Mary, faithfully listening to God. Selby is essentially being praised here for having a Mary heart in a Martha world.

This desire for wives to be both Martha and Mary can also be seen in the detailed eulogy *The Holy Life of Mrs. Elizabeth Walker*, written by her husband, Anthony Walker, after her death in 1690. In this work Anthony Walker explores the details of her life and her character as a wife and mother. He places his wife as the exemplar that all women should strive to follow. Near the beginning of this almost three-hundred-page work, he places his wife in the following frame: "She was Mary and Martha both unto perfection, and acted Martha's part with Mary's Spirit."[53]

---

51. Interestingly, Dorothy Selby is also credited with foiling the gunpowder treason by Guy Fawkes by writing an anonymous letter to her cousin warning him not to come to Parliament on November 5.

52. Thomas F. Ravenshaw, ed., *Antiente Epitaphes (from A.D. 1250 to A.D. 1800)* (London: Masters, 1878), 92. This epitaph is also cited in Christine Peters, *Patterns of Piety: Women, Gender and Religion in Late Medieval and Reformation England* (Cambridge: Cambridge University Press, 2003), but she identifies the Mary named here as referring to the Virgin Mary (227). I think it is more likely this is a reference to Mary of Bethany.

53. Anthony Walker, *The Virtuous Wife: Or, the Holy Life of Mrs. Elizabeth Walker, Late Wife of A. Walker, Sometimes Rector of Fyfield of Essex* (London: Robinson & Churchill, 1694), 51.

He returns to this comparison again when describing how she organized the household, treating even the drudgery of everyday life as a great joy, which is worth quoting in full:

> She was, as I touch'd before, Martha and Mary both unto Perfection, yet always acted Martha's Part with Mary's Spirit, (though Martha also was a good Woman;) she spiritualized her Worldly Businesses, behaved herself in her Family, as became one who was of the Family of the first-Born; made all her Imployments a Sacrifice, by performing them in obedience to God, whose Providence imposed them on her, in setting her in a Station, in which they were required of her; not only submitted to them as Mortifications … but with a willing Mind cheerfully engaged in them, accounting all as done to God, which his Appointment made her Duty: For if the Maid-Servant may sweep the House to God, by considering it as a Duty.[54]

Here Walker fully fleshes out what it meant that his wife was both fully Martha and Mary. She was able to do her worldly, everyday chores, but she made them spiritual. She did them all with a focus on God, not complaining but rejoicing in being able to do them. It was not only the duty she owed her husband and children but also the one she owed God. Thus, while she was doing the part of Martha, she maintained her Mary spirit. Walker does not condemn Martha, presenting her as a good woman, but it is clear that his wife succeeds in being holy because she is able to be Mary.

It is particularly important to remember that Walker is lifting up his wife as the example that all women should strive to follow in their daily life, which is why he goes into such great detail. He tells his readers how she organized her chores, how she educated her children, how she acted as wife, how she memorized Scripture, in order that they might do likewise. By the early modern period, this gendered reading had taken root. Women were no longer Mary and Martha if they were leading convents in the manner of Hildegard. Abbots were not embodying both by their service to the church and their desire to focus solely on God. Women were Marthas and Marys through their household tasks.

This call for women to be like Mary and Martha also leads to a tension, as caring for a household makes it difficult to focus one's attention on God. This tension is acknowledged in the treatise *The Ladies' Calling*, written by

---

54. Walker, *Virtuous Wife*, 88.

an English Protestant preacher, Richard Allestree, in the mid-1600s. In his section on widows and the correct structure of lives after their husbands' deaths, he argues:

> There are many things which are but the due compliances of a wife, which yet are great avocations, & interrupters of a strict devotion; when she is manumitted, from that subjection, when she has less of Martha's care of serving, she is then at liberty to choose Mary's part. She has her time and her fortune at her own command, and consequently may much more abound in the works both of piety and charity.... But the widow might devote herself to what degree she pleas'd, her piety has no restraint from any other inconsistent obligation, but may swell as high as it can.[55]

Allestree recognizes that being a godly and faithful wife will inherently mean that a woman cannot also dedicate much time to focus on the things of God. These tasks are "interrupters of a strict devotion." The benefit of being a widow, he argues, is that one is now set free from all those tasks, meaning one can choose the better part, like Mary. In this way, becoming a godly widow is a blessing because now one can focus on developing more piety.

Beyond eulogies and instruction manuals for women, gender also became an important interpretive detail in visual depictions of this passage. Images of Martha fighting a dragon disappeared; Martha as housekeeper and cook rose to the forefront. This is perhaps unsurprising given Calvin's rejection of Martha's time in France as the silliest of all fables. But even without the influence of Calvin, Martha as a cook was growing in popularity in the fifteenth–sixteenth centuries. For instance, on the *Magdalene Altar* at Tiefenbronn, painted by Lucas Moser in 1432, one finds an image of Martha, clearing away a table unnoticed, while her sister washes Jesus's feet. Similarly, in 1637, Pieter de Bloot depicted Martha's immense preparation of food as the main focus of his painting *Christ in the House of Mary and Martha*. The table is overflowing with a meal, while Martha stands unhappily in the background, addressing Jesus.

De Bloot's scene is representative of a trend to use a scene in order to create devotional paintings in which the story is placed in the background

---

55. Richard Allestree, *The Ladies' Calling, in Two Parts* (Oxford: Oxford University Press, 1673), 217, https://tinyurl.com/SBLPress4824a.

of the painting, while the moral of the story is placed in the foreground.[56] This can also be seen in the sixteenth-century painter Vincenzo Campi, whose work *Christ in the House of Mary and Martha* (undated) is entirely focused on Martha surrounded by food. In this painting, one can hardly see Mary and Jesus in the background, as the emphasis rests entirely on Martha and her preparations. The fish in the painting likely represent Martha's own place as a disciple, as fish were often used to depict an association with Christ.[57] Nonetheless, Martha is primarily being depicted a cook.

One of the most famous and debated depictions of Mary and Martha is also depicted in this style. In Diego Velázquez's *Christ in the House of Martha and Mary* (1618), one sees a young girl preparing food in a kitchen while an older woman looks on, appearing to point her to an image of Jesus, Mary, and Martha on the wall.[58] The girl is not looking at the painting but rather looks out of the painting toward the viewer, wearing a resigned and somewhat unhappy expression.

Velázquez, a Spanish painter who was highly influenced by Dutch painter Pieter Aertsen, used compositional inversion to highlight what he believed to be the primary message of the biblical story scene in the background. This piece has drawn great debate as art scholars continue to argue over the intended message of this painting and the intended relationship between the kitchen scene and the biblical scene behind it.[59]

---

56. Heller, "Sibling Rivalry," 258. See Pieter Aertsen, *Christ in the House of Martha and Mary* (1553), for another example of Flemish devotional painting of Mary and Martha. Jesus and the two sisters are almost completely hidden behind a large table covered in food. Heller suggests that perhaps this was to draw a sharp dichotomy between material things and spiritual things ("Sibling Rivalry," 256).

57. Tanya J. Tiffany, "Visualizing Devotion in Early Modern Seville: Velázquez's 'Christ in the House of Martha and Mary,'" *SCJ* 36 (2005): 438.

58. The modern title of this painting is *Kitchen Scene with Christ's Visit to Mary and Martha*, to emphasize the main scene in the painting. At the British Museum, however, where the painting is located, one still finds the original title.

59. There is an ongoing debate whether the biblical scene in the background should be considered a painting, a mirror, or a window into the next room. As Heller notes, "The spatial relationship between the two scenes is far more complicated [than most Flemish compositions] and as such remains a matter of art historical debate" ("Sibling Rivalry," 258). For an argument that the scene is a painting, see Jane Boyd and Philip F. Esler, *Visuality and Biblical Text: Interpreting Velazquez' Christ with Martha and Mary as a Test Case*, AASD 26 (Florence: Olchiski, 2004). For an argument that the scene is actually a glimpse into the next room, see Jonathan Brown, *Velazquez, Painter and Courtier* (New Haven: Yale University Press, 1986).

Fig. 6.1. Vincenzo Campi, *Christ in the House of Mary and Martha*. Sixteenth century. Source: Wikimedia.

Fig. 6.2. Diego Velázquez, *Christ in the House of Mary and Martha*. 1618. Source: Wikimedia.

Scholarship is also divided on how to properly interpret the meaning of the painting. It is only in the last two decades that the biblical context of the painting has been taken more seriously, as previously one could only find brief mentions that Martha represented action and Mary represented contemplation in this passage. Two recent interpreters, Tanya Tiffany and Ena Heller, have attempted to do this in recent years. Tiffany argues that Velázquez's Sevillan context mattered, and thus the painting should be studied for a deeper meaning than simply a parallel between work and contemplation.[60] She argues that Velázquez is presenting the life of Martha positively but as a step behind the contemplative life of Mary, depicted in the scene behind the kitchen. She argues that the kitchen scene shows good labor, focusing on the fish and the other details of the table.[61] Tiffany does not discuss the role of gender explicitly in her interpretation. For her, Velázquez is intentionally visualizing the ascent from the active life of Martha to the contemplative life of Mary.

On the other hand, Heller argues that this scene should be interpreted in light of the young girl's expression: "The young woman, like Martha, is unhappy with her chores; the older woman reminds her of the important things in life by pointing to the biblical scene. This shows that in 17th century Spain, just like in 16th century Holland or 14th century Italy, the story from Luke 10 continued to be used as a moral lesson for the young."[62] Heller's argument is compelling, though she also does not explicitly discuss whether this painting should be read in light of gender.

I take the position that the action/contemplation dichotomy should not be the primary exegetical lens for this painting and that the fact that the two main figures in the scene are two women should not be overlooked. This is not two men in a field or a mixed group engaged in some sort of task; rather, this is two women in a kitchen doing household chores. This clearly identifies the young girl preparing food as a Martha type, as Martha too was predominantly identified as a cook in this period. Her unhappiness appears as a mirror to the unhappiness of Martha in her complaint to Jesus. The older woman appears as a spiritual guide to remind her that she should consider the story of Luke 10:38–42 and Jesus's response to Martha. The young girl should not complain about her own household chores but embody Mary's better choice to focus on things of God. That said, there

---

60. Tiffany, "Visualizing Devotion," 433–53.
61. Tiffany, "Visualizing Devotion," 452.
62. Heller, "Sibling Rivalry," 258.

is no indication within the painting that the girl is being to encouraged to stop her cooking to pray, suggesting that an attitude adjustment is what is required: have a Mary spirit while you must be a Martha. It is as if the older woman points to the scene to remind the girl of Jesus's words to Martha to not complain and choose the better part. This painting is another example of a new reading that highlights Mary's devotion, while still calling women to be Marthas.

Thus, one can see that after the Reformation, the gender of Mary and Martha became important to interpretations of Luke 10:38–42 in ways previously unseen in the history of interpretation. As more literal translations called more attention to their gender and as the duty of Christian women was placed more and more firmly within the household, Mary and Martha began to become representative of Christian women. Luther and those who followed his exegetical tradition clearly depict women as needing to live as Marthas, but from a position of faith and devotion to the Word like Mary. The rejection of the action/contemplation paradigm, alongside many of the interpretations of the fathers, also adds to the strength of this reading. The virtues of Mary and Martha are placed before women as an example that they should follow, while the failures of Martha are offered as a warning.

That said, this is not the only reading that existed during this period. Many writers of the Counter-Reformation (see, for instance, Teresa of Ávila) continued to offer the action and contemplation dichotomy as a legitimate reading. Furthermore, Calvin follows Chrysostom in his own interpretation, arguing that this story teaches its hearers about the need for proper discernment. Luther's reading about faith and works also became a popular reading in the fifteenth century and beyond. Thus, like in the patristic and medieval periods, Luke 10:38–42 continued to be interpreted and reinterpreted in a variety of ways. What I am trying to show in this section, however, is that unlike in those previous periods, there was now a strong interpretive thread that focused on gender, leading the story to be read in light of women's roles in the home. At times this thread was even interwoven among other interpretative claims about Mary and Martha.

This trend can be seen in Thomas Adams, a seventeenth-century Protestant theologian, who wrote in his *Commentary on II Peter* (1633) on the virtues a woman should put on in order to be considered a godly women: "So she that gathers obedience from Sara, wisdom from Rebecca, chaste love from Rachel, faith from Mary, hospitality from Martha, humility from Anna, charity from Dorcas; she shall make her selfe a most excellent woman."[63] Women are supposed to be faithful like Mary and hospitable like Martha. Elsewhere in the same commentary, however, he debates the "papists'" view that contemplation is better than action and concludes, similar to Chrysostom, that the meaning of the passage is actually one of discernment because works sometimes are necessary.[64] Adams's interpretation reveals how the different interpretive threads of discernment, gendered values and the action/contemplation reading, exist together.[65]

Over time, however, this interpretative tendency to focus on the gendered values of the passage became more and more popular, leading to a fundamental shift in how this text was interpreted in the modern era. Gender, more often than not, became the starting point of interpretations of Luke 10:38–42. The story is about two women and Jesus, as concerns about the proper way to engage in Christian discipleship faded out of the discussion.

Evangelicals and Feminists: Placing the Modern Conversation in Context

Having analyzed the interpretative tendencies of the patristic, medieval, and Reformation eras, we can once again rejoin the modern conversation on Luke 10:38–42. Many evangelical writers and feminist scholars, despite disagreeing in most areas, have both focused on the gender of Mary and Martha as the primary exegetical focus of the passage. The plurality of interpretations, which we saw coexisting in previous eras, became secondary, and discussions that highlight gender and gender issues moved to the center. This is the case across the ideological spectrum. In the following section, I return to two examples of modern readings: Beth Moore, as a

---

63. Thomas Adams, *A Commentary or, Exposition upon the Divine Second Epistle General* (1633), 422. Interestingly, he follows with the virtues that the excellent man is supposed to embody: "These be good patterns to follow, as we pray for our Soveraigne, that not only he may be like some former Prince, but have the virtues of them all: the courage of Joshua, the heart of David, the head of Solomon, the zeale of Josiah, the integrity of Hezekiah, etc."

64. Adams, *Commentary or, Exposition*, 1334.

65. Another example of this mingling of different interpretive threads by the same author can be found in the lectures of William Allen, who at one point discusses the virtues of Mary and Martha and what their namesakes can learn from them while also discussing in another place how to remain focused on what is ultimate. See William Allen, *Certain Select Discourses on Those Most Important Subjects* (London, 1699), 29, 149.

representative of the evangelical view, and Elisabeth Schüssler Fiorenza, as representative of feminist biblical scholarship. Clearly, both evangelicalism and feminism are broader than these two perspectives, but Moore and Schüssler Fiorenza are both prominent and influential voices in their fields. Their specific interpretations of Luke 10:38–42 offer us insight into wider exegetical trends.

Beth Moore

Beth Moore (b. 1957) is one of the most influential and prolific female writers in American evangelicalism. After marrying and raising two children, Moore began to speak at women's groups about the Bible. In 1994, she founded Living Proof Ministries, an organization dedicated to introducing women to the study of Scripture. Moore views her calling to be "teaching women how to love and live on God's Word."[66] This has led her to write dozens of Bible studies and devotionals directed toward a female audience. It is not an exaggeration to state that millions of women have read her work, and many groups exclusively use her Bible studies. Despite having had no formal biblical training, Moore is a careful and often insightful exegete who is able to distill complex exegetical issues into an easily accessible form.[67] Though Moore has recently expanded parts of her platform to address men as well, she consistently emphasizes that she is not trying to have any authority over them. She does not describe herself as a preacher or a pastor but rather calls herself a speaker and a teacher for women.

Thus, it is not surprising that Moore begins her exegesis of Luke 10:38–42 with the following statement: "I'm already grinning and we haven't even started. I love women. I have great appreciation for men too, but I don't share their psyche. I get a huge kick out of women. We are just so women-y."[68] She goes on to discuss the vast differences among women and how within her friend group, "We've got a healthy population of Marys and Marthas."[69] She begins to describe these Marys and Marthas. Marthas,

---

66. "About Us," Living Proof Ministries, https://tinyurl.com/SBL4824b.

67. Moore has a degree in political science from Southwest Texas State University. She writes that she got her start in teaching the Bible after taking Bible doctrine courses that were offered at her church, Houston First Baptist.

68. Beth Moore, "A True Tale of Two Sisters," in *Jesus, the One and Only*, 199.

69. Moore, "True Tale of Two Sisters," 199.

for instance, rarely volunteer to pray, and when they do, it is usually very short. Marys, on the other hand, never plan luncheons.

Moore wants to celebrate this diversity and stresses that this passage should not be read as Mary is good and Martha is bad, but rather that the contrast is between good and better.[70] She stresses that Jesus loved Martha (citing John 11:5) "apron and all." She then turns to describe Martha's positives and negatives before discussing how women can learn from her behavior. Moore divides her exegesis into six points. First, she finds a contrast between the fact that "Martha opened her home, but Mary opened her heart."[71] She discusses the fact that Martha shows extravagant hospitality, and it is because of her actions that Mary is able to sit at Christ's feet in the first place. This is an example to all women to show hospitality to our neighbors. Martha's problem, however, is that she does not realize that what Jesus wants is her heart and attention more than he wants her hospitality. This is essentially an argument for women to have proper discernment, though Moore does not use this specific language.

Second, Moore argues that Martha's distraction teaches us that even noble people can forget to listen to God's word. She draws on the example of getting distracted during a sermon to show how easy it is to lose focus. She cites the Greek to show how distracted really means being pulled in different directions at the same time. In this way she sympathizes with Martha, arguing that "our culture may be entirely different, but women have had the same challenges from the beginning of time."[72] Connected to this danger of distraction, Moore then turns to her third point: ministry can be the biggest distraction when one is seeking intimacy with God. In this section, Moore writes: "You may faint when you see the Greek word for 'preparations.' The word is *diakonia*. It means 'service, attendance, ministry.' We are more familiar with the word *diakonos* meaning 'servant.' God's word is saying that if we are not careful, even our need-meeting, well-meaning ministries can distract us from what is most important."[73] Being busy, Moore argues, even if it is godly busy, often separates us from God. She believes that both the parable of the good Samaritan and this story show this point. The priest and Levite are so focused on doing God's

---

70. Moore, "True Tale of Two Sisters," 199.
71. Moore, "True Tale of Two Sisters," 200.
72. Moore, "True Tale of Two Sisters," 201.
73. Moore, "True Tale of Two Sisters," 201.

work that they are unable to serve the dying man. In same way, Martha is too busy serving God to hear from God.

This could potentially have been avoided if Martha had not forgotten "to keep the 'pre' in preparation."[74] This is Moore's fourth point. She emphasizes that in her experience in speaking at different conferences, she sees many Marthas, who are usually too wrapped up in the conference actually to participate in it. She then refers to several examples of women who intentionally made sure all the planning and details were taken care of before the conference started. These women were able to actually enjoy their work, because they had been good stewards of their time. In this way, they doubly honored God in their preparations. They were able to be Marys, having already been Marthas.

The fifth and sixth points focus on how Martha is not able to see what is ultimate because of her distraction. She misses how much Jesus loves her because she is too focused on her sister and on her work. She also misses the one thing that is necessary: "Christ's message is not that we should neglect family and responsibilities to pray and to study the Bible. His message is that many things are important but that one thing is essential: Him.... Shall we allow good to become the enemy of our best? The choice is ours."[75] Mary chooses Jesus; she does not let herself be swept up by other responsibilities. It is an intentional choice by Mary to focus on God. Moore concludes her interpretation by arguing that the purpose of this passage is to encourage us to make that choice daily. Women have a lot of distractions and have had them since the beginning of time, but we need to be intentional about choosing to focus on Jesus.

Overall, Moore offers an interpretation of Luke 10:38–42 that is meant to offer a challenge, specifically to women. She builds her exegetical argument by paying careful attention to the text itself. She emphasizes the positive ways in which Martha's character is described and the overall necessity of showing hospitality. She also rejects a dichotomy that suggests Martha should be viewed negatively. Like many interpreters before her, she stresses that this is a comparison between what is good and what is better. She also draws on the text's surrounding context and the original language to argue that improperly oriented service distracts from what is ultimate, by incorporating the parable of the good Samaritan in Luke

---

74. Moore, "True Tale of Two Sisters," 202.
75. Moore, "True Tale of Two Sisters," 203.

10:25–37 and a discussion of διαχονία. In these points, Moore's interpretation does not differ greatly from many patristic and medieval interpreters.

What separates her reading from those we have previously studied, however, is her repeated insistence that this story is about women and for women. She begins with the anecdotes that divide all women into the Mary camp or Martha camp, and she frequently returns to claims that all women in particular should relate to the themes in this story. Moore, without explicitly acknowledging it, recognizes the tension this sort of reading places on women. The work women are called to do is good and necessary, but also it is not ultimate. Thus, she offers strategies for how to do both. In particular, she suggests making sure one is diligent in preparing things ahead of time, so as to not be distracted when one is supposed to be focused on Jesus. In this way, Moore believes one can be both Mary and Martha.

Even though many of her exegetical points would apply to men as well, her focus is entirely on what this story says to women. She assumes that her audience will find themselves as either a Mary or a Martha, and she pastorally tries to reassure the Marthas that they are loved and that they have the choice to be a Mary.[76] Moore's interpretation reveals how this story operates as a guide for women's discipleship within evangelical circles. In Moore's case, this does not only appear to be limited to housework (though she frequently mentions it) but extends to other ministry settings. For her, this means women's conferences, however, and not in any settings that would place women in any sort of role other than support and hospitality. The story of Mary and Martha teaches women how to have proper discernment and time management so that they can focus on the most important thing: Jesus.

Elisabeth Schüssler Fiorenza

This sort of interpretation of Luke 10:38–42 is precisely what Schüssler Fiorenza and other feminist biblical scholars reject as patriarchal, setting up impossible goals for women rooted in unfair gender roles. In fact, Moore's interpretation in many ways stands as the implicit opponent against which Schüssler Fiorenza was fighting when she wrote her interpretation of Mary

---

76. It seems as though Moore considers herself a Mary more than a Martha, as she states that she has to struggle to show Martha's hospitality.

and Martha. Except, instead of arguing against it as a type of interpretation, Schüssler Fiorenza views it as the intended meaning of the original author. As she writes in *But She Said*: "This text is patriarchal because it reinforces the societal and ecclesiastical polarization of women. Its proclamation denigrates women's work while insisting at the same time that housework and hospitality are women's proper roles. It blames women for too much business and simultaneously advocates women's 'double roles' as super women. Women ought not to only be good disciples but also good hostesses, not only good ministers but also good housewives."[77] Schüssler Fiorenza rejects any reading that creates this tension between the two roles, as it places unrealistic expectations on women, and she believes that the text itself is the cause of this tension. She consequently seeks to reject the text as it stands in order to replace it with a more holistic, life-giving model for women.

In many ways, her interaction with Luke 10:38–42 is a prime example of her overall approach to the study of the New Testament. Schüssler Fiorenza (b. 1938) is the best-known feminist biblical scholar. Born in Germany and raised a Roman Catholic, she studied feminist theology and received a ThD from the University of Münster in 1964. Her book *In Memory of Her*, originally published in 1983, introduced a feminist-critical method for interpreting the biblical text. Her primary goal is to uncover previously ignored or forgotten contributions that women made to the development of Christianity. She emphasizes that the patriarchal systems that produced the New Testament ensured that influential women were not given their proper place in the history of Christianity. Women, in particular, need to reclaim these original leaders in the church, and thus her exegetical program is centered on a fourfold hermeneutic for achieving this.

First is a hermeneutic of suspicion, which questions the patriarchal structures and motives that produced the biblical texts. This stage involves a significant deconstruction of traditional readings. Second is a hermeneutic of remembrance, which seeks to reconstruct the women behind the text in order to reclaim their stories. This stage involves significant historical-critical research in an attempt to piece together lives of women during the first century. Third is a hermeneutic of evaluation and proclamation, which recognizes that the biblical words are actually only the

---

77. Schüssler Fiorenza, *But She Said*, 69.

words of flawed men and not of God. This allows the exegete to strip away those things that are harmful and allows new, liberative readings to be seen. Fourth is a hermeneutic of imagination. This requires an imaginative retelling of the biblical account that highlights instead of hides the importance of the women involved in the story. This exegetical program, particularly the hermeneutic of suspicion, set the standard for feminist study of the Bible.

She applies these four hermeneutics to the story of Mary and Martha in *But She Said: Feminist Practices of Biblical Interpretation*, published in 1992. She dedicates an entire chapter to uncovering the real contributions of Mary and Martha to the early church. First, she argues that Luke himself is clearly intending to create a dualistic structure in which the two women are pitted against each other.[78] This form of "dualistic antagonism," according to Schüssler Fiorenza, has guided most interpretations throughout Christian history and serves to effectively erase Mary and Martha and any contributions they might have made to the early church. Martha is depicted positively when she serves but negatively when she tries to stand up for herself. Mary is good only because she does not speak. Schüssler Fiorenza argues, "Mary, who receives positive approval, is the *silent* woman, whereas Martha, who argues in her own interest, is *silenced*.... Rather the narrative is prescriptive, pitting sister against sister in order to make a point."[79] This good women/bad women dichotomy as well as the limiting of a woman's speech leads Schüssler Fiorenza to reject the predominant reading as "kyrio-centric" and one that intentionally minimizes both Martha and Mary.

Schüssler Fiorenza then turns to her hermeneutic of remembrance. As we discussed in the second chapter, she argues that the fact that Martha is described repeatedly using διακονία language suggests that she participated in a diaconal ministry, one that was similar to the ministry of the Seven in Acts 6. She argues that Luke knew this and is seeking intentionally to diminish her ministry: "Luke 10:38–42 stresses that the *diakonein* of Martha is not the one thing needful and hence must be subordinated to 'listening to the word.' However, it must not be overlooked that the good portion chosen by Mary is not the diakonia of the word: it is not the preaching of the word, but rather listening to the word. The

---

78. Schüssler Fiorenza, *But She Said*, 60.
79. Schüssler Fiorenza, *But She Said*, 62.

characterization of Mary as a listening disciple corresponds to the narrative interests in playing down the leadership role of women."[80] Thus, she believes that Luke is able to diminish both Martha's and Mary's ministries because Mary participates in listening to the Word, but she does not actually preach it herself. While Luke knew of women and their ministries, Schüssler Fiorenza argues that he intentionally constructed his narratives about women to minimize depictions of female leadership in the early church. Mary and Martha were likely known to Luke's original audience, and thus he cannot fully ignore their importance.[81] She argues that the rhetorical structure of the entire travel narrative is intended to acknowledge women as Christian disciples but downplay their role as apostolic leaders in the early church. This is why Luke includes a story about Mary and Martha but constructs it in such a way that they are not recognizable as early Christian leaders.

The goal, then, of a feminist interpreter, according to Schüssler Fiorenza, is to reclaim Mary and Martha as early Christian female leaders of the church. A true feminist reading has to fully reject the patriarchal prejudice that is inherent in the narrative.[82] Allegorical readings like the ones we have seen throughout the history of interpretation cannot be viewed as feminist because they strip Mary and Martha of their "woman-ness," leaving them only as symbols, not real women who led the early church through the ministries of word and service. All of these readings, according to Schüssler Fiorenza, continue the antagonistic dualism that Luke embedded into his text and as such are also flawed. One must reject Luke's text in full and instead seek to rebuild it by looking behind his words.[83]

She then offers several possibilities for proclaiming this story. First, she suggests that a homily that emphasizes Mary's right to study and read as a liberating act could be a transformative message, particularly in lower and working-class communities since taking time for oneself could be considered luxurious and lazy. She argues this homily "could be liberative in a community where women's activity is restricted to caring and working for others in her family, on the job or in the church."[84] This sermon would be about women's freedom from tasks dedicated to the well-being

---

80. Schüssler Fiorenza, *But She Said*, 65.
81. Schüssler Fiorenza, *But She Said*, 66.
82. Schüssler Fiorenza, *But She Said*, 69.
83. Schüssler Fiorenza, *But She Said*, 70.
84. Schüssler Fiorenza, *But She Said*, 70.

of others, though she warns that the passage should not be used only to encourage reading the Bible, so as to become another burden.

Next she suggests that a feminist proclamation of Luke 10:38–42 would entirely reject a model that presented the women of the New Testament as carrying a double burden of both following Jesus and cooking and cleaning. Feminists should be careful not to present a reading that limits women both to teach like the male disciples and to clean, following traditional female roles. A good interpretation would emphasize how unfair such a claim is, as it still limits women to traditional roles even while taking on a host of new ones. Connected to this second possibility, she argues in her third point that feminist interpreters should find a way to reclaim what she labels servanthood ecclesiology.[85] She argues that this type of service is based in the freedom of choice: "The powerlessness of servanthood can be redemptive only when it results from free and conscious choice. Such freely chosen servanthood is not be understood as self-denial.... Rather it is said to be the capacity to look beyond ourselves to see the need of others." This sort of servanthood is mirrored in the life and death of Jesus, and when servanthood is freed from its patriarchal roots, in which servanthood is forced on women, it can critically challenge cultural norms.[86]

Another possibility for proclaiming this passage involves using it to create a feminist theology of ministry. In this theology, servanthood is not based in institutionalized structures of authority or power *over* but rather power *for*. This sort of women's ministry is not based in being subservient but rather in exercising their own power for the service of others. She argues this new vision for women's ministry and service would be understood as a "democratic practice of solidarity with all those who struggle for survival, self-love, and justice."[87] It is a discipleship of equals that moves beyond patriarchal structures that Luke's telling of Luke 10:38–42 supports.

Finally, Schüssler Fiorenza suggests that one can articulate this new, liberative vision for this story by imaginatively retelling it. A retelling would not leave Martha in the kitchen and would not leave Mary without her own voice. Schüssler Fiorenza acknowledges that there are a number of ways to participate in this dance of interpretation, but she also offers her own creative retelling to conclude her chapter. In her reconstruction,

---

85. Schüssler Fiorenza, *But She Said*, 71.
86. Schüssler Fiorenza, *But She Said*, 72.
87. Schüssler Fiorenza, *But She Said*, 73.

the discipleship of equality and service is at the forefront, told from the perspective of Martha, who claims that she is telling her story because "all kinds of men are writing down the stories about Jesus but they don't get it right. Some use even our very own name to argue against women's leadership in the moment. Our great-great granddaughters need to know our true stories if the discipleship of equals is to continue."[88]

In her account, the evening that Jesus spends at Martha's house in Bethany is one rooted in Jesus's teaching and the male disciples' discomfort on the topic of women's equality. At dinnertime, Jesus starts to go with Martha to help her prepare dinner, but the men want him to stay, leading to another women, Susanna, claiming that God's word is for all people and that Jesus's message is for both men and women. Jesus affirms Susanna's statement and then invites Martha to preside over the breaking of the bread and invites Susanna to teach the Torah lesson. She concludes: "There was grumbling among the men, but we women were excited by the new possibilities that God had opened up to us."[89]

This story, which is obviously dramatically different from the account in Luke, is what Schüssler Fiorenza believes is a more liberative narrative. Women are not accused of complaining; they are not silent. It is the men who are actually rebuked by Jesus for not fully accepting the ministry of women, rather than Martha rebuked for insisting her sister help. There is no dichotomy between the two sisters, and they are both seen as full disciples of teaching and service. This account embodies the discipleship of equals. She concludes her analysis by arguing that this story presents feminist scholars with the perfect opportunity to "not only reconceptualize historical and theological hermeneutics in rhetorical terms, but also to challenge biblical scholarship in general and feminist interpretation in particular to become sophisticated ... in the struggle for a more just church and world."[90]

Schüssler Fiorenza presents an interpretive model that most interpreters of Luke 10:38–42 would find perplexing. While she engages with the text as it currently stands from a historical-critical perspective, she completely rejects it. She finds the very construction of the text irredeemably patriarchal. She finds Luke's version intentionally to restrict women. She does not see this as interpretation of the passage but rather the original

---

88. Schüssler Fiorenza, *But She Said*, 74.
89. Schüssler Fiorenza, *But She Said*, 75.
90. Schüssler Fiorenza, *But She Said*, 76.

intent. She also rejects the entire history of interpretation of the passage, arguing that since the interpreters use the same patriarchal base text, they too are poisoned. In many ways, however, she creates a straw man when arguing against the history of interpretation, ignoring the men and women who interpreted this story as other than dichotomous. As we have seen in this book, there is a plurality of interpretations surrounding Luke 10:38–42, not just the action/contemplation divide. In particular, Schüssler Fiorenza rejects these abstract readings because she argues that they ignore the gender of Mary and Martha, turning them into symbols, saying that this also is a reflection of a patriarchal culture. Anyone who adopts these more allegorical readings is unable to consider their own readings feminist, since a truly feminist reading, in her mind, interprets this passage in light of Mary and Martha's gender. The only lens for the passage is that of liberating or limiting women.

Two Gendered Readings and a Way Forward

Thus, even though Beth Moore and Schüssler Fiorenza have radically different interpretations, they appear to agree on one thing: the story of Mary and Martha is a story about and for women. Moore's interpretation aligns with the tradition that began in the Reformation, one that reads the text literally and thus focuses solely on how the text speaks to women. Her entire exegetical framework is rooted in the basic concept that this story is about women's roles. Moore clearly wrestles with the tensions in this sort of reading, one that asks women to be all things at once. She acknowledges the difficulties and is very sympathetic to Martha, even as she reiterates that Mary made the better decision. Moore attempts to exegete the passage for women so that they can be encouraged to serve God as either a Martha or a Mary, and she ultimately concludes that this story is intended to teach women to focus on Jesus above all else. Moore would say that this is a liberative story for women.

Schüssler Fiorenza rejects this sort of reading. She clearly sees it as toxic, but more importantly she does not see exegetical models such as Moore's as an interpretative decision but rather the original intent of Luke. Thus, her interpretation is designed for reconstructing a narrative that does not have this sort of dichotomy. All four of her possibilities for proclaiming this text, as well as her creative retelling, focus on how to make this story one that elevates women to their proper place within both the history of Christianity and the church today. Her ultimate goal is for the story of Mary and Martha to be one that acknowledges the role women had in the early church, a church that had followed Jesus's own teachings about the equality of women as disciples in the kingdom of God. Reclaiming this history allows for women in the present also to claim equality. Women today can rebuild this earlier model of the church, one in which they share full equality with men.

I agree with Schüssler Fiorenza's claim that readings that place an impossible burden on women are toxic. That said, if we follow her model of fully rejecting the current text of Luke 10:38–42, there is very little for us to work with as biblical scholars. Moreover, I am concerned that Schüssler Fiorenza's complete insistence that interpretation be rooted in concerns about women in the church has inadvertently led to this text becoming pigeonholed into a small group of texts about women, allowing most of the church and biblical scholarship to overlook it. In this way, Mary and Martha are once again silenced, but in a different way than Schüssler Fiorenza fears.

In her book *Women and Power*, Mary Beard addresses this type of silencing when discussing the limits of women's speech throughout history.[91] She argues that traditionally, beginning as far back as Homer and moving through to the twenty-first century, women's speech has been rejected and ignored. If it is not ignored, it is usually mocked. History has wanted its women to be silent. She finds, however, that there is one exception. Women are allowed to speak if they are speaking on women's issues. This is the only form of permissible female speech. For instance, Beard observes that in most collections of the one hundred greatest speeches in history, one only finds women included if their speeches are about women's issues.[92] She points to the examples of Hillary Clinton and her famous speech at the United Nations (1995) and Sojourner Truth's famous speech "And Ain't I Woman?" (1851). Both of these speeches revolve around women's rights. Beard is quick to clarify she is not trying to claim that "women's voices raised in support of women's causes were not, or are not, important (someone has to speak up for women); but it remains the case that women's public speech has for centuries been 'niched' into that area."[93]

---

91. Mary Beard, *Women in Power* (London: Profile Books, 2017).
92. Beard, *Women in Power*, 24.
93. Beard, *Women in Power*, 25. Beard sees a similar trend in demands for more women in governing bodies. She argues that often people claim they want more women in Parliament so that "women's issues" can be discussed more often. Again, she

She argues that true equality of speech in the modern world would allow for women to speak not just about these issues but about all issues that affect our shared humanity.

Thus, we must ask ourselves in what ways modern interpretations of the story of Mary and Martha have been relegated to that niche of women's issues. Luke 10:38–42 is not women's speech in the same way that Beard is referring to literal women speaking on issues, but it is a story that predominantly features two women. In recent history, this feature of the story and the women's issues that it raises have completely dominated how the story is interpreted. Both Schüssler Fiorenza and Moore, for all their differences, view the story through this gendered lens. Similarly, this has led many men in the modern world to be comfortable overlooking the story and its potential contribution both to Lukan scholarship and Christian discipleship more broadly, simply because it is a woman's story that deals with women's issues. It has led to this passage losing its traditional place as a central passage in a larger discussion about the nature of Christian discipleship. Instead, this passage is now discussed most frequently in women's devotional guides and Bible and Gender sections at Annual Meetings of the Society of Biblical Literature. In this way, I believe that even feminist biblical interpreters find themselves in this trap when interpreting Luke 10:38–42.[94]

This raises the fundamental question of this study: Is there a way to interpret Mary and Martha's story that acknowledges and honors them as women without limiting them to only speak about issues of women in the church or women in Luke? Can this story about women instruct its readers about the complex nature of discipleship in Luke, a type of discipleship that includes both men and women? I reject readings that suggest that since this story features women it can only affect our understanding of women. If this story had featured two brothers, this story would be treated as a normative discussion of the tensions within Luke's conception of following Jesus.[95] This reinforces old patterns that male equals normative,

---

is clear that women's issues (childcare, domestic violence, equal pay, etc.) are important issues but rejects both their label and the claim that more women are need solely to address women's issues and not societal issues more broadly (86).

94. And perhaps inadvertently find themselves writing volumes on gender and the Bible.

95. See, for instance, Luke 15 and the parable of the prodigal son. This story about two brothers and their father is not discussed in light of what it teaches us about men.

while female equals idiosyncratic. There has to be a way out of this new kind of dichotomy when we interpret Luke 10:38–42.

I hold, contra Schüssler Fiorenza's argument that the history of interpretation is irredeemably flawed, that the reception history of this passage does offer modern readers a way forward. By engaging with the varied and nuanced interpretations of previous exegetical cultures, we are able to discover more interpretative options beyond a focus on gendered issues. The goal is not to suggest that we should attempt to somehow return to premodern readings of Luke 10:38–42 or to even suggest that the precritical readers were superior to modern readers. Rather, the goal is to rejoin a much older conversation so that we can uncover concepts in the text that our own exegetical cultures have overlooked. As Luke Timothy Johnson and William Kurz argue in *The Future of Catholic Biblical Scholarship*: "Rejoining a conversation that has long been abandoned requires hard historical labor and theological imagination. It is not easy or automatic. The point is not an easy nostalgia about the good old days (there is much in ancient interpretation that is unattractive) nor a simple imitation of perfect models (there is much in ancient interpretation that is inadequate). The point, rather, is a critical engagement that can enrich the present and enable a future."[96] The goal of studying these past interpreters is not to mimic them but rather to make us better interpreters in the present. Patristic and medieval interpreters were, no doubt, deeply embedded in a patriarchal system that devalued women. Very rarely do they offer modern readers a liberating message for women. Despite their creativity and piety, much of what they wrote explicitly about women is rightly condemned.

Yet, somewhat remarkably, the patristic and medieval interpreters of Luke 10:38–42 read this story about two women and focused on questions of discipleship and not on questions of women in the church. As we have seen, their contributions are diverse and vary in exegetical skill, but within this history, we find that Luke 10:38–42 is a central passage for an ongoing discussion about the construction of Christian discipleship, not a marginal text about a niche issue. Throughout this book, we have repeatedly seen that this text was a core passage for understanding the proper way for engaging in Christian behavior at large. Since the ancient interpreters do not speak with one voice, we also discover voices that do not simply focus on Mary and Martha as a good/bad dichotomy, but rather as

---

96. Johnson and Kurz, *Future of Catholic Biblical Scholarship*, 38.

illustrative of the need for proper discernment before acting. We discover voices that highlight the story as informing practices of hospitality. We find still others that find this story as the second prong of how to love God and love the neighbor. The history of interpretation reveals that we have many interpretative options, based in close readings of the text. Within these interpretative options, one finds a shared commitment to the idea that Luke offers his readers insight into how to practice the Christian faith properly. Mary and Martha appear not as examples for women but examples for all disciples who seek to follow Christ.

That said, I think Schüssler Fiorenza's argument that abstract readings turn Mary and Martha into mere symbols and not people should be addressed here more explicitly. To a certain extent, she is correct, but she ignores the ways in which allegory functioned in premodern interpretations. The Bible existed not only as a collection of past events but also as a living text for the present. This allowed men and women to represent not only their historical context but also the problems facing interpreters in their present settings. Biblical characters existed as both symbols of God's truth in the present and as historical figures. To suggest that, because an interpreter offered a so-called allegorical meaning, this interpreter did not view Mary and Martha as real sisters who followed Jesus, is seriously to misread patristic and medieval interpreters. Furthermore, as previously noted, Schüssler Fiorenza ignores all the interpreters, such as Chrysostom, Cyril, and Basil, who do not engage in allegorical readings at all. This book has shown how careful engagement with each writer on his or her own terms leads to a fuller understanding of how Luke 10:38–42 operated in the patristic and medieval periods.

Ultimately, through such critical engagement with these previous interpreters, we can remove this story from the niche market that has been designated for so-called women's speech. Furthermore, we place it in line with the broader tradition of the Christian faith. As this chapter has shown, it is only in relatively recent history that this story has become predominantly about women. By reclaiming a broader reading, we allow Martha and Mary to lead a conversation about Luke's understanding of discipleship specifically and conversations about best practices within the Christian faith more broadly.

Epilogue

> Let us consider, then, our busy involvement with many things.
> — Augustine, *Sermo* 104.3

This study has covered centuries of interpretation from early monks to modern feminists. Mary and Martha stood at the center of a number of debates about the nature of Christian discipleship, and they have proven to be lively characters. Martha left the kitchen to preach the gospel and slay dragons, only to return again to the kitchen, while Mary remarkably has encompassed all of the other Marys in the New Testament. The sisters have been the subject of sermons, commentaries, biographies, eulogies, and artwork. Their encounter with Jesus in Luke 10:38–42 did not remain within the pages of the biblical text. I conclude by asking (1) What has this project shown? (2) What questions have been raised by this research? and (3) What areas of research remain to be studied in the future?

What Has This Project Shown?

The analysis of patristic and medieval interpretations has disclosed several important insights, previously unseen or undervalued in scholarship.

(1) Precritical exegesis of Luke 10:38–42 is richer and more diverse than most scholars grant. Claims that all the readings were "allegorical," and based in Origen's interpretation of the action/contemplative paradigm, have been repeatedly shown to be false. Even Origen himself offers a more varied interpretation than is usually ascribed to him. While one of his interpretations is the popular claim that Martha represents action and Mary represents contemplation, he actually offers five different interpretative options for the passage. The ways in which Origen's interpretations were adopted by later interpreters, moreover, varied dramatically. Within the monastic tradition, for instance, different authors, while often aligning with the basic paradigm of action and contemplation, frequently diverged

from Origen concerning their conclusions on the relationship between contemplation and action in the present world. There was significant disagreement about the relationship between Mary and Martha, as some viewed the two sisters as representing different kinds of Christians, while others viewed them as representing different kinds of Christian behaviors. Some even rejected Origen's paradigm altogether, focusing instead on other aspects of the passage, such as the nature of godly hospitality and the question of proper discernment. Thus, while Origen should certainly be viewed as one of the most important interpreters of Luke 10:38–42, it is clear that modern readers should not assume that his interpretations were simply accepted whole cloth by the generations of interpreters who followed him. Rather, Origen and those later interpreters show that the reception history of Luke 10:38–42 is more complicated than a single allegorical reading.

(2) Even within interpretations that read Martha as representative of the active life and Mary as representative of the contemplative life, we find a constant emphasis on the biblical text itself. The specifics of Luke 10:38–42 are important for ancient interpretation. This means, for instance, that both Mary and Martha are depicted positively, following the positive language of the text itself. Throughout patristic and medieval writings, Martha is explicitly named as a positive figure alongside her sister, Mary. She is the one who had the privilege to serve Jesus himself, a role many interpreters envy. She is a faithful disciple of Christ. There is, to be sure, disagreement concerning her mistake in this story: some focus on her distraction and her misplaced concerns, while others latch onto the fact that her work is inherently temporal, whereas Mary's is eternal. Interpreters wrestled with Jesus's response to Martha. What is the nature of the better part? What is the one thing that is needed? Such recurring questions demonstrate the importance of the text. Thus, while interpretative traditions do shape later readings, I have shown that the majority of patristic readers continued to read closely the details of the biblical text itself. This is true not only in the immediate Lukan context of the story but also in the ways they place this text in conversation with the larger biblical witness. Theirs are not flat readings; they do not simply lift Mary and Martha out of their Lukan context in order to make allegorical claims.

(3) I have shown that the textual variants of Luke 10:41–42 gave rise to different interpretations. The unstable nature of the text itself had a significant effect on the history of interpretation. Basil, for instance, clearly uses a text that says "a few things are necessary," and in light of

this he interprets this story in terms of the few dishes that Martha should have prepared for Jesus. Augustine, on the other hand, uses a text that says "one thing is necessary," and he, in turn, interprets this one thing as unity with Christ. While text critics have acknowledged the importance of studying the reception history of textual variants for the sake of uncovering more reliable readings, I have presented in this study many concrete examples of how textual variants actually influenced interpretations throughout history.

(4) I have shown decisively that precritical exegesis does *not* focus on the gender of Mary and Martha as the starting point for their interpretation. In fact, I have shown that gender as a primary exegetical concern was a relatively late development in the history of interpretation, not appearing until after the Reformation. Such gender-focused readings that place a double burden on women to be both Mary and Martha appeared alongside the rise of the wife and mother as the ideal form of Christian woman. This interpretive thread requires women to be able both to clean and run their household and to maintain space for personal piety. While a dominant interpretation today, it is not in continuity with the rest of the history of interpretation. For most of Christian history, the defining characteristic of Mary and Martha was that their discipleship, and thus their story, is central to constructions of Christian discipleship. As we have seen, some interpreters focus on the relationship between acts of service and acts of prayer and study and ask how Luke 10:38–42 informs which one should be privileged. Some interpreters focus on the story as an example of practicing discernment: one should know when to serve like Martha and when to be still like Mary. The patristic and medieval interpreters are continually attempting to resolve the seemingly inherent tension within this story as they recognize that both sisters' behaviors are praiseworthy. Questions of how to actually put the message of this story into practice are central to most precritical exegesis. It is not a text that is meant simply to describe the role of two *women* in the church. In various ways, I have shown that earlier interpreters believed this story places a challenge on readers of all genders that should shape how they practice their faith.

(5) Finally, I have shown that there is intrinsic value in studying the reception history of a given passage when engaging in modern exegetical work. By expanding one's analysis of the text beyond what people have said in the last century, one is exposed to new questions and different answers being raised by the text. Oftentimes the exegete's own interpretative culture limits what she is able to see in the text. By taking the exegetical

questions of other cultures seriously, new ways of reading are opened up. This research can inform multiple avenues of exegesis, from text-critical questions to literary analysis. As biblical scholars, we have inherited a vast tradition of interpretation, with thousands of readers attempting to understand the text before us. This can be used to our benefit. This is not to say that simply because they read it first they read it better, but to argue that reading, particularly of sacred texts, should not be done in isolation. Biblical scholars have the opportunity to use this history to our advantage.

What Questions Have Been Raised by This Research?

1. How Should We Evaluate Various Interpretations of Luke 10?

There needs to be a way to evaluate the claims that are being made about the text, even across a wide range of exegetical cultures. They are not all equally good. There are better and worse ways of reading the story. I believe I have shown that better interpretations of Luke 10 are those that take into account its biblical context. Interpreters who illuminated the text, opening it up to new ways of reading, were the ones who placed the text in conversation with the larger biblical narrative.

These interpretations took at least three different forms. First, there are interpreters who pay explicit attention to the passage's narrative framework in Luke 10. We have seen readings draw on Luke's context explicitly, despite coming from so-called precritical eras. Take, for instance, Bede and Hugh of Saint Cher, both writing in the medieval period. They both find a connection between Luke 10:38–42 and the Lukan story of the good Samaritan in 10:24–37, and they argue that these stories illustrate the dual love of God and neighbor. More recently, John Donahue has made a similar move (as we saw in ch. 2).

Second, other interpreters use the narrative context more implicitly, moving within the larger context of Luke. One of the most important examples of this is Origen himself, who, despite the charges modern scholars make against his interpretations, pays careful attention to all the details of the text. In his second interpretation in *Fr. Luc.* 171, he frames his interpretation around the details of Martha welcoming Jesus "into her house" and Mary "sitting at his feet." These details, which Origen sees in other places throughout Luke's Gospel, influence his reading. He examines throughout his Lukan commentary what it means to welcome Jesus into his house to order to figure out what the house represents. Now, Origen is clearly not doing a modern word study, and his exegetical framework is clearly different from those of the modern era, but within his interpretations, one sees careful attention to untangling the difficult portions of the story by turning to other relevant pieces of Scripture. This adds an important depth to his interpretations, as they are rooted within the biblical narrative itself. Origen does not make loose claims about the text; his reading is based entirely within the narrative world of the story. We could make similar claims about Augustine's, Cassian's, and Cyril's reading. The text shapes their arguments.

Third, we can see those interpreters who move beyond the bounds of Luke to place Luke 10 in direct conversation with other biblical passages on the same themes. We can see this exegetical tendency in the work of John Chrysostom. He resists readings that would force the sisters into absolute positions, that is, Martha as the one who always works and Mary as the one who always sits and prays. Chrysostom is arguing against a form of interpretation that lifts this story out the larger biblical narrative to insist that Christians should never work (*Hom. Jo.* 44.1). He insists that the key to a better reading is to recount how this story interacts with other stories on the same topic.[1] He points to the example of Paul as a tentmaker and Matt 25 to show that the overarching biblical message is not one that condemns work. He also points to John 11 to show how much Martha is loved by Jesus. He further notes that since the gospels actually affirm the work that Martha does, a reading that condemns her behavior is flawed. Thus, this pushes Chrysostom to examine the text in light of this tension, leading him to argue that the problem within the text is not work but rather Martha's lack of discernment. Chrysostom focuses on placing the text in conversation with the large biblical world and not treating the

---

1. It is worth noting that many who read this from a monastic perspective also pay careful attention to the text within its biblical context. For instance, the author of the Liber Graduum draws strongly on the idea that Martha represents the Upright (the active) and Mary represents the Perfect (contemplative), and yet this entire framework is built on his analysis of the Bible as a whole. He is attempting to reconcile potentially conflicting commands, such as to sell all you have but to also take care of the poor, and the command to pray without ceasing alongside other commands to serve and love the neighbor. He also finds different biblical examples who appear to follow God in markedly different ways, and he reads the story of Mary and Martha in light of this larger conversation. He is not proof-texting, and his analysis that both sisters represent disciples reflects both a concern for the specific text of Luke 10:38–42 and a larger concern for how to interpret the entire Bible.

story as if it exists outside the specifics of the narrative itself and its larger biblical framework.

On the other hand, there are some interpreters who separate Luke 10:38–42 from its biblical narrative, presenting an acontextual reading. Chrysostom's opponents, for instance, appeared to lift the story out of the biblical narrative and treat it as a text that stood alone.[2] Similarly, during the medieval period, Mary and Martha at times became so synonymous with action and contemplation that they began to exist as these forms apart from their specific story. Within the modern era, particularly within the type of feminist-critical analysis that Schüssler Fiorenza recommends, the story of Mary and Martha is not just lifted out of its original Lukan context but out of the narrative framework of the story itself. Schüssler Fiorenza views the text as inherently corrupt and oppressive to women, and she eliminates the framework altogether and then turns to rebuild it. She argues that the story of Mary and Martha needs to be retold in order to be liberative. Yet her reading is not rooted in the actual details of the text but rather is a reconstruction based entirely on her own notions of gender equality in the early church with a thin veneer of historical criticism smoothed over the top.

What is particularly interesting is that Schüssler Fiorenza's creative retelling is not the first imaginative construction of the story of the two sisters. In fact, during the medieval period, as we have seen, biographies about Mary and Martha were popular. Both Schüssler Fiorenza and the medieval biographies move beyond the details of the biblical narrative in Luke 10:38–42, and thus it is worth briefly placing these medieval biographies and Schüssler Fiorenza's retelling in conversation with each other. On one hand, the medieval biographers create a fantastical world beyond the edges of the biblical narrative. After following Jesus during his earthly ministry and witnessing the resurrection, Mary and Martha travel far from Bethany, preaching the gospel and converting whole towns to Christianity. They perform miracles, slay dragons, and have mystical encounters with the risen Lord. They are apostolic figures who are quite literally forming the church through their actions, as people travel from all over to be discipled by the two sisters. In these narratives, Mary and Martha's narrative identity is not based in the fact that they are women. They are not con-

---

2. Though it should be noted that this assessment is due to Chrysostom's designation of their interpretation, since we do not have access to their reading except through him.

fined to the kitchen or expected to be wives and mothers. Rather, they are cast as powerful, Spirit-filled apostles who proclaim the gospel message. Throughout their narratives, both Mary and Martha are described in biblical imagery to achieve this goal.

On the other hand, Schüssler Fiorenza also participates in an imaginative telling of the story of Mary and Martha. Through her four-stage hermeneutic, she deconstructs the text as it is originally stands, and thus instead of casting her telling using biblical imagery, she mostly dismisses the text in its entirety, keeping only the smallest details from Luke, namely that Mary, Martha, and Jesus are there. Then she creates a story in which Jesus defends Mary and Martha from the sexist male disciples who wish to put Martha in the kitchen and not let women learn from him. This story does create a world in which Mary and Martha are given more explicit authority from Jesus himself and are cast in the narrative as important founders of the church who are telling their story. In the end, however, Schüssler Fiorenza's account is completely rooted in her attempt to liberate Mary and Martha from the text, and this ends up creating a narrative in which Mary and Martha's story is limited to their fight for equality in the early church.

When compared to the medieval biographies and their radical depiction of the two sisters, Schüssler Fiorenza's story falls flat. The medieval biographers were able to use the narrative framework and imagery of the biblical text to creatively retell it in such a way that Mary and Martha become powerful, Spirit-filled leaders of the church. This is the exact thing that Schüssler Fiorenza says she is attempting to do. This shows that one can use the biblical framework to tell the story of Mary and Martha in a creative way that empowers women, by simply and consistently presenting them as important founders of the church. Thus, I believe the medieval biographers end up with a more liberative interpretation for women than what Schüssler Fiorenza was attempting to do with her deconstruction and removal of all biblical context.

2. Is Gender the Current Starting Point for Interpretation?

Most modern interpretations turn on questions of gender and liberation for women. There is a repeated fixation on answering different questions about women and Christianity. From a historical-critical perspective, the question is: Does this story show that Luke was positively oriented toward women, or was he oppressive? Within ecclesial communities, the question is: What does this story teach Christian women about being Christian women? Thus the women issues become an interpretative framework, within both modern biblical studies and women's devotional material. As we have seen, the history of interpretation shows that this is not the only framework for approaching this text. The more traditional framework focuses on the question of discipleship: What does this text require of us? Not just require of women, but what does it require of us as disciples?

It is useful on this point to compare the works of Beth Moore and Teresa of Ávila. Both of these women are interpreting this story primarily for women, and yet, since they have a different starting point, their interpretations diverge substantially. Teresa interprets this passage repeatedly for the women within her community, but she does not interpret this passage as though it speaks only about women's issues. Rather, women's issues do not appear at all; the issues at the center of interpretation are issues of discipleship. She is concerned with exegeting this passage so that those in her community can understand the relationship between physical service and contemplative practices. She offers words of comfort as they strive to find a balance, but it is clear that if one removed her address of "sisters" in many of her interpretations then they would speak to men as well. She ultimately sees that this passage is calling all Christians to embody both the listening Mary did and the hospitality of Martha in order to fully love God and neighbor (*Med.* 7.3). Furthermore, she meditates on the passage in the *Soliloquies*, wrestling with the text itself to see what prompts Martha to make her complaint. Her answers are not rooted in a double burden that Martha must carry, but rather in the fact that Martha is concerned that Christ does not love her (*Solil.* 5.1). This excursus on why Martha would be upset reveals Teresa's focus on the nuances of the text itself, beyond the question of what the text might teach her as a woman.

This stands in contrast to Moore's interpretation, even though both women share a commitment to close readings of the biblical text. In many ways, Teresa is Moore's predecessor in the faith as she also focused on training women in the faith as she studied the Bible. Like Teresa, Moore mystically sees this story as Christ actually reaching out to teach about how to best know him. That said, Moore's interpretation begins with the concept that this story reveals truth about Christian women. Since everyone is either a Mary or a Martha, Luke's account is intended to speak about how Christian women should live. Moore also focuses on offering comfort as women try to live this out, but this is because she is aware of the double burden this story appears to place on women. Her interpretations repeatedly return to the unique message this story has for the Marys and Marthas of the present world. She notes that even though this story is thousands of years old, women are united in that we continue to share the same struggles. There is always too much to do, and like Martha, we need to be able to learn how to balance it so we can fully focus on Christ. Most Christian men reading this story would not find in Moore's interpretations much that they would think applies to them.

Thus, we can see how these two female interpreters are shaped by their exegetical starting point. Even though Moore and Teresa of Ávila have many things in common, their interpretations of Luke 10:38–42 differ in what the primary takeaways of this passage are. For Teresa, this story is about discipleship and how to properly practice the faith while balancing the demands of serving one's neighbor and the desire to sit always with the Lord. For Moore, this is a story for women to figure out how to balance the demands of womanhood while still making time for the Lord. These differences are subtle, and in one way, Moore's gender-focused interpretation still speaks to the tension of trying to serve the neighbor and find time for contemplative practices. Yet, by limiting the type of service to gendered service and by limiting the audience to only women, one can see how this text, despite its ability to speak to all, becomes only applicable to women. From this comparison, one can see how the starting point matters. If the first question is "How does this text speak to women?" this limits how the text can speak. Teresa of Ávila, a female interpreter, does not assume gender to be the starting point, and her interpretations are varied and creative, with careful attention to the details of the story, placing her among the most insightful interpreters of Luke 10:38–42.

3. Most Importantly, If We Dismiss an Exegetical Framework That Focuses on Gender, What Framework Should Replace It?

We are not precritical readers and thus cannot and should not adopt whole cloth medieval readings of Luke 10:38–42. But as I have shown, the modern focus on women's liberation often limits the voices of the women to speak to the church beyond questions of gender. How can modern readers of the text reclaim a reading of Luke 10:38–42 that rejects a framework that insists this text must only speak about gender and open it up to allow Mary and Martha to speak to larger questions?

First, I think we need to step away from questions of whether Luke was a misogynist when studying this passage. These questions are anachronistic and ultimately unhelpful, because the answer will always be both yes and no. Luke is not attempting to be liberative or oppressive in this depiction. By removing primary focus on this question, we can focus on Luke's actual concerns as they present themselves in the text and its context. At the end of this analysis, there is room, perhaps, for asking whether Luke's decision to use two women to tell this story should affect our conclusions, but it should be a secondary and not a primary concern.

Second, I think this study of the reception history has revealed that modern interpretations should take the narrative context of the story seriously. The development of critical exegesis supplies the exegete with a number of tools to use when interpreting Luke 10:38–42, but because of the gendered focus of most interpretations, the primary hermeneutic has been an attempt to uncover the historical Mary and Martha. This has led to the story being frequently out of its context and treated as a standalone unit. This intense focus on the historical-critical issues of the passage, particularly surrounding the question of the historical roles Mary and Martha played in the early church, has led to the text being even more pigeonholed into a women's text. As Loveday Alexander argues, a literary-critical approach opens up the story to new and potentially liberative readings, ones that push beyond the narrow construct of gender and allow the text to speak to all readers.[3] This sort of literary reading is not a rejection of feminist readings, but rather is deeply feminist as well, as it attempts to push a powerful passage about two women disciples into the mainstream discussions of discipleship in Luke.

What Areas of Research Remain to Be Studied in the Future?

I have touched on a number of other issues that deserve further study outside the bounds of the particular work.

1. While we have discussed the ways in which the Reformers introduced a new thread of interpretation, more research needs to be done with how those threads interacted with one another. There are still several unanswered questions about Reformation readings that need to be answered in

---

3. Alexander, "Sisters in Adversity," 213.

order to fully understand the ways the Reformation both broke with and continued previous interpretative models.

2. How to place Luke 10:38–42 into the larger context of Luke-Acts, not just the travel narrative and its immediate literary context, is another question that remains to be studied. My exegetical chapter focused primarily on the travel narrative, but I believe a larger analysis that places Luke 10:38–42 next to other passages on discipleship throughout Luke-Acts. For instance, how does Mary's listening to Jesus's words in Luke 10:39 compare to Luke 24, where Jesus opens up the Scriptures to the disciples on the walk to Emmaus and then to the Twelve in Jerusalem? A fuller analysis of the nature of discipleship in Luke-Acts that includes Luke 10:38–42 is an important next step to build off the work of this book.

3. The relationship between Luke 10:38–42 and John 11 in the history of interpretation is another question. Considerable scholarship has discussed the relationship between the two accounts from a source-critical perspective, but the ways in which the two stories influence each other in the reception history is also worth discussing. Due to space constraints, this book focused almost exclusively on the Lukan account, as it was the more popular narrative. That said, the story of Mary and Martha in John 11 is also an important account of the two sisters, often appearing tangentially within discussions of Luke's version. For example, one piece of evidence that Martha is also a beloved disciple of Christ comes from John 11, where it states that Jesus loves Martha and Mary. Furthermore, while scholarship has noted the active/contemplative dichotomy in the history of interpretation, little study has been given to the importance of Mary and Martha and their resurrection proclamations in John 11. This relationship is certainly an area that needs more research.

Conclusion

This project has shown that by engaging seriously with these precritical exegetical cultures, we can gain new insight into the text. It has shown the complexity of the story, with its presentation of two good characters with a question of what is most important. It has forced us to reconsider whether it is a few things or indeed only one thing that is necessary. It has allowed us to move beyond gendered readings and see more clearly its role in constructing a Lukan understanding of Christian discipleship, one that places service and listening to the word beside each other and asks the reader to consider alongside Martha how to decide what is ultimate.

These questions of discernment in the construction of Christian discipleship have mostly dropped out of modern discussions of Luke 10:38–42. By taking the precritical perspectives seriously, however, we can chart out a new way of reading, one that both liberates Mary and Martha by removing them from the niche of women's ministries and books on women in Luke and allows their story to speak about how all disciples should live.

Bibliography

Primary Sources

Adams, Thomas. *A Commentary or, Exposition upon the Divine Second Epistle General*. London, 1633.

Allen, William. *Certain Select Discourses on Those Most Important Subjects*. London 1699.

Allestree, Richard. *The Ladies' Calling, in Two Parts*. Oxford: Oxford University Press, 1673. https://tinyurl.com/SBLPress4824a.

Augustine. *The Works of Saint Augustine*. Edited by Boniface Ramsey. 50 vols. Hyde Park, NY: New City Press, 1990–2013.

Basil of Caesarea. *Ascetical Works*. Translated by M. Monica Wagner. FC 9. Washington, DC: Catholic University of America Press, 1962.

———. *Letters and Select Works*. NPNF 2/8.

The Book of the Elders: Sayings of the Desert Fathers; The Systematic Collection. Translated by John Wortley. CSS 240. Collegeville, MN: Liturgical Press, 2012.

The Book of Steps, The Syriac Liber Graduum. Translated by Robert Kitchen and Martien Parmentier. CSS 196. Kalamazoo, MI: Cistercian, 2004.

Birgitta of Sweden. *Saint Bride and Her Book: Birgitta of Sweden's Revelations*. Translated by Julia Bolton Holloway. LMW 6. Newburyport, MA: Focus Texts, 1992.

Bede. *Homilies on the Gospels*. Translated by Lawrence T. Martin and David Hurst. Kalamazoo, MI: Cistercian, 1993.

Bernard of Clairvaux. *Selected Works*. Translated by G. R. Evans. New York: Harper Collins, 2005.

Calvin, John. *Commentary on a Harmony of the Evangelists, Matthew, Mark and Luke*. Translated by William Pringle. 3 vols. Grand Rapids: Eerdmans, 1949.

———. *Calvin Commentaries*. Translated by Joseph Haroutunian. LCC 23. Philadelphia: Westminster, 1958.

———. *Tracts and Treatises on the Reformation of the Church*. Translated by Henry Beveridge. 3 vols. Grand Rapids: Eerdmans, 1958.
Cassian, John. *Conferences*. Translated by Colm Luibheid. New York: Paulist, 1985.
———. *The Conferences of John Cassian*. NPNF 2/11.
Clement of Alexandria. *The Exhortation to the Greeks; The Rich Man's Salvation; To the Newly Baptized*. Translated by G. W. Butterworth. LCL. Cambridge: Harvard University Press, 1919.
———. "Stromateis." *ANF* 2.
Chrysostom, John. *Baptismal Instructions*. Translated by Paul William Harkins. ACW. New York: Paulist, 1988.
———. *The Homilies of S. John Chrysostom on the Gospel of St. John*. Translated by G. T. Stupart. 2 vols. Oxford: Parker, 1848–1852.
———. *Homilies on Paul's Letter to the Philippians*. Translated by Pauline Allen. Atlanta: Society of Biblical Literature, 2013.
———. *Homilies on the Gospel of John*. NPNF 1/14.
———. *On Virginity; Against Remarriage*. Translated by Sally Rieger Shore. SWR 9. Lewiston, NY: Mellen, 1983.
———. *The Preaching of Chrysostom: Homilies on the Sermon on the Mount*. Edited and translated by Jaroslav Pelikan. Philadelphia: Fortress, 1967.
———. *Six Books on the Priesthood*. Translated by Graham Neville. Crestwood, NY: Saint Vladimir's Seminary Press, 1964.
Cyril of Alexandria. *A Commentary upon the Gospel according to Saint Luke*. Translated by Robert Payne Smith. Piscataway, NJ: Georgias, 2009.
Eckhart, Meister. *The Complete Mystical Works*. Translated by Maurice O'C Walshe. New York: Crossroads, 2009.
———. *Sermons*. Translated by Claud Field. New York: Cosimo, 1909.
Epictetus. *The Discourses, as Reported by Arrian, the Manual, and Fragments*. Translated by W. A. Oldfather. 2 vols. LCL. Cambridge: Harvard University Press, 1926–1928.
Ephrem. *Saint Ephrem's Commentary on Tatian's Diatessaron*. Translated by Carmel McCarthy. JSS 2. Oxford: Oxford University Press, 1993.
Eusebius. *History of the Church*. Translated by Philip R. Amidon. FC 133. Washington, DC: Catholic University of America Press: 2016.
Evagrius. *Evagrius of Pontus, the Greek Ascetic Corpus*. Translated by Robert E. Sinkewicz. OECS 13. Oxford: Oxford University Press, 2006.
Grimlaicus, *Rule of Solitaries*. Translated by Andrew Thorton. CSS 200. Collegeville, MN: Liturgical Press, 2011.

Gregory the Great. *Forty Gospel Homilies.* Translated by David Hurst. CSS 123. Kalamazoo, MI: Cistercian, 1990.

Harkin, Franklin, and Frans van Liere, trans. *Interpretation of Scripture: Theory; A Selection of Works of Hugh, Andrew, Godfrey and Richard of St Victor, and Robert of Melun.* VTT 3. Turnhout: Brepols, 2012.

Hildegard of Bingen. *The Letters of Hildegard.* 3 volumes. Translated by Joseph E. Baird and Radd. K. Ehrman. New York: Oxford University Press, 1994.

Ignatius of Antioch. *Letter to the Smyrnaeans.* Pages 99–105 in *Early Christian Writings: Apostolic Fathers.* Edited by Andrew Louth. Translated by Maxwell Staniforth. London: Penguin, 1987.

Ignatius of Loyola. *Spiritual Exercises and Selected Work.* Translated by George E. Ganss. CWS. New York: Paulist Press, 1991.

Josephus. Translated by H. St. J. Thackeray et al. 10 vols. LCL. Cambridge: Harvard University Press, 1926–1965.

Leclercq, Jean, ed. *Bibliotheque national: Catalogue generale des manuscrits Latin.* Paris, 1966.

The Life of St. Mary Magdalene and Her Sister Saint Martha: A Medieval Biography. CSS 108. Translated by David Mycof. Kalamazoo, MI: Cistercian, 1989.

Luther, Martin. *Luther on Women: A Sourcebook.* Edited by Merry Wiesner-Hanks and Susan Karant-Nunn. Cambridge: Cambridge University Press, 2003.

———. *Luther's Works.* Edited by Jaroslav Pelikan. 75 vols. St. Louis: Concordia, 1956–2011.

Musonius Rufus. *Fragment 3 (That Women Too Should Study Philosophy)* in *Moral Exhortation: A Greco-Roman Sourcebook.* Edited by Abraham Malherbe. Philadelphia: Westminster, 1986.

Origen. *Commentary on the Epistle to the Romans: Books 1–5.* Translated by Thomas P. Scheck. FC 103. Washington, DC: Catholic University of America Press, 2001.

———. *Commentary on the Gospel according to John: Books 1–10.* Translated by Ronald E. Heine. FC 80. Washington, DC: Catholic University of America Press, 1989.

———. *Homélies sur S. Luc: Texte latin et fragments grecs.* Edited by Henri Crouzel, François Fournier, and Pierre Périchon. SC 87. Paris: Cerf, 1962.

———. *Die Homilien zu Lukas in der Übersetzung des Hieronymus und die griechischen Reste der Homilies und des Lukas Kommentars.* Translated by Max Rauer. GCS. Origenes Werke 9. Berlin: Akademie Verlag, 1959.

———. *Homilies 1–14 on Ezekiel.* Translated by Thomas P. Scheck. ACW 62. New York: Newman, 2010.

———. *Homilies on Genesis and Exodus.* Translated by Ronald E. Heine. FC 71. Washington, DC: Catholic University of America Press, 1982.

———. *Homilies on Luke.* Translated by Joseph T. Lienhard. FC 94. Washington, DC: Catholic University Press, 1996.

———. *On First Principles.* Translated by G. W. Butterworth. Gloucester, MA: Smith, 1973.

———. *The Philocalia of Origen: A Compilation of Selected Passages from Origen's Works Made by St. Gregory of Nazianzus and St. Basil of Caesarea.* Translated by George Lewis. Edinburgh: T&T Clark, 1911.

———. *The Song of Songs: Commentary and Homilies.* Translated by R. P. Lawson. ACW 26. Westminster, MD: Newman, 1957.

Possidius. "Life of St. Augustine." Pages 69–124 in *Early Christian Biographies.* Translated by Roy J. Deferrari. FC 15. Washington, DC: Catholic University of America Press, 1952.

Pseudo-Macarius. *The Spiritual Homilies and the Great Letter.* Translated by George A. Maloney. New York: Paulist, 1992.

The Sayings of the Desert Fathers. Translated by Benedicta Ward. Kalamazoo, MI: Cistercian, 1975.

Teresa of Avila. *The Collected Works of St. Teresa.* 2 vols. Translated by Kiernan Kavanaugh and Otilio Rodriquez. Washington, DC: Institute of Carmelite Studies, 1976.

Theodore of Mopsuestia. *Commentary on the Gospel of John.* Translated by Marco Conti. Edited by Joel C. Elowsky. Downers Grove, IL: IVP Academic, 2010.

Thomas F. Ravenshaw, ed. *Antiente Epitaphes (from A.D. 1250 to A.D. 1800).* London: Masters, 1878.

Walker, Anthony. *The Virtuous Wife: Or, the Holy Life of Mrs. Elizabeth Walker, Late Wife of A. Walker, Sometimes Rector of Fyfield of Essex.* London: Robinson & Churchill, 1694.

Secondary Sources

Alexander, Loveday C. "Sisters in Adversity: Retelling Martha's Story." Pages 197–213 in *A Feminist Companion to Luke*. Edited by Amy-Jill Levine. Cleveland: Pilgrim, 2004.
Amar, Joseph P. "Christianity at the Crossroads," *RelLit* 43.2 (2011): 1–21.
Augsten, Monika. "Lukanische Miszelle." *NTS* 14 (1968): 581–83.
Baker, Aelred. "One Thing Necessary." *CBQ* 27 (1965): 127–37.
Baum, Armin Daniel. *Lukas als Historiker der letzten Jesusreise*. Zurich: Braukhas, 1993.
Baur, Chryosotomus. *John Chrysostom and His Time*. Translated by M. Gonzaga. 2 vols. Westminster, MD: Newman, 1959.
Beard, Mary. *Women in Power*. London: Profile Books, 2017.
Bendemann, Reinhard von. *Zwischen ΔΟΞΑ and ΣΤΑΥΡΟΣ: Eine exegetische Untersuchung der Texte des sogenannten Reiseberichts im Lukasevangelium*. BNZW 101. Berlin: de Gruyter, 2001.
Bonnardiere, Anne-Marie La. "Les deux vies: Marthe et Marie (Luc 10:38–42)." Pages 400–411 in *St. Augustin et la Bible*. Bible de tous les Temps 3. Paris: Beauchesne, 1986.
Bovon, Francois. *Luke 2: A Commentary on the Gospel of Luke 9:51–19:27*. Hermeneia. Minneapolis: Fortress, 2013.
Boyd, Jane, and Philip F. Esler. *Visuality and Biblical Text: Interpreting Velazquez' 'Christ with Martha and Mary' as a Test Case*. Arte e Archeologia. Studi e documenti 26. Florence: Olschki, 2004.
Brecht, Martin. *Martin Luther*. Translated by James L. Schaaf. 3 vols. Philadelphia: Fortress, 1985–1993.
Brennan, Irene. "Women in the Gospels." *NBf* 52 (1971): 291–99.
Brooten, Bernadette J. *Women Leaders in the Ancient Synagogue*. BJS 36. Chico, CA: Scholars Press, 1982.
Brown, Jonathan. *Velazquez, Painter and Courtier*. New Haven: Yale University Press, 1986.
Brown, Peter. *The Body and Society: Men, Women and Sexual Renunciation in Early Christianity*. New York: Columbia University Press, 2008.
Brutscheck, Jutta. *Die Marta-Maria Erzählung: Eine redaktionskritische Untersuchung zu Lk 10:38–42*. BBB 64. Frankfurt am Main: Hanstein, 1986.
Bultmann, Rudolf. *The History of the Synoptic Tradition*. Translated by John Marsh. Peabody, MA: Hendrickson, 1994.

Busse, Ulrich. *Die Wunder des Propheten Jesus: Die Rezeption, Komposition und Interpretation der Wundertradition im Evangelium des Lukas*. FzB 24. Stuttgart: Verlag Katholisches Bibelwerk, 1997.
Caird, G. B. *The Gospel of Luke*. PNTC 3. New York: Penguin, 1963.
Cameron, Michael. "Augustine and Scripture." Pages 200–214 in *The Cambridge Companion to Augustine*. Edited by David Vincent Meconi. Cambridge: Cambridge University Press, 2014.
Caner, Daniel. *Wandering, Begging Monks: Spiritual Authority and the Promotion of Monasticism in Late Antiquity*. Berkley: University of California Press, 2002.
Carter, Warren. "Getting Martha out of the Kitchen." Pages 214–31 in *A Feminist Companion to Luke*. Edited by Amy-Jill Levine. Cleveland: Pilgrim, 2004.
Carroll, Thomas K. *Preaching the Word*. MFC 11. Wilmington, DE: Glazier, 1984.
Cassidy, Richard J. *Jesus, Politics and Society: A Study of Luke's Gospel*. MaryKnoll, NY: Orbis Books, 1978.
Chadwick, Owen. *John Cassian*. 2nd ed. Cambridge: Cambridge University Press, 2008.
Collins, Billy. "Introduction to Poetry." Page 58 in *The Apple That Astonished Paris*. Little Rock: University of Arkansas Press, 2006.
Collins, John N. *Diakonia: Re-interpreting the Ancient Resources*. New York: Oxford University Press, 1990.
———. "Did Luke Intend a Disservice to Women in the Martha and Mary Story?" *BTB* 28 (1998): 104–11.
Colwell, Ernest C. "Method in Evaluating Scribal Habits: A Study of $\mathfrak{P}^{45}$, $\mathfrak{P}^{66}$, and $\mathfrak{P}^{75}$." Pages 106–24 in *Studies in Methodology in Textual Criticism of the New Testament*. NTTS 9. Leiden: Brill, 1969.
Constable, Giles. *Three Studies in Medieval Religious and Social Thought*. Cambridge: Cambridge University Press, 1995.
Contreni, John J., Richard Marsden, and E. Ann Matter. "The Patristic Legacy to c. 1000." Pages 505–35 in *From 600 to 1450*. Vol. 2 of *The New Cambridge History of the Bible*. Edited by Richard Marsden and E. Ann Matter. Cambridge: Cambridge University Press, 2012.
Conzelmann, Hans. *The Theology of St. Luke*. Translated by Geoffrey Buswell. Minneapolis: Fortress, 1961.
Crawford, Matthew. *Cyril of Alexandria's Trinitarian Theology of Scripture*. Oxford: Oxford University Press, 2014.
Creed, J. M. *The Gospel according to Luke*. London: Macmillan, 1930.

Crouzel, Henri. *Origene et la "Connaissance Mystique."* MLST 53. Paris: de Brouwer, 1961.

Csanyi, Daniel. "Optima Pars: Die Auslegungsgeschichte von Lukas 10,38–42 bei den Kirchenvatern der ersten vier Jahrunderte." *StudMon* 2 (1960): 5–78.

D'Angelo, Mary Rose. "Women Partners in the New Testament." *JSFR* 6 (1990): 65–86.

Danielou, Jean. *Origen*. Translated by Walter Mitchell. New York: Sheed & Ward, 1955.

Danker, Frederick W. *Jesus and the New Age: A Commentary on St. Luke's Gospel*. Philadelphia, Fortress, 1988.

Dargan, Edwin Charles, *History of Preaching*. 2 vols. New York: Hodder & Stoughton, 1905.

Davies, Stevan. "Women in the Third Gospel and the New Testament Apocrypha." Pages 185–97 in *"Women Like This": New Perspective on Jewish Women in the Greco-Roman World*. Edited by Amy-Jill Levine. EJL 1. Atlanta: Scholars Press, 1991.

Dawsey, James M. "Jesus's Pilgrimage to Jerusalem." *PerpRelSt* 14 (1987): 217–32.

Dayton, Hellen. "On the Use of Luke 10:38–42—Jesus in the House of Mary and Martha—for Instruction in Contemplative Prayer in the Patristic Tradition." Pages 205–12 in *Archaeologica, Arts, Iconographica, Tools, Historica, Biblica, Theologica, Philosophica, Ethica*. Edited by J. Baun, A. Cameron, M. Edwards, and M. Vinzent. StPatr 44. Leuven: Peeters, 2010.

Donahue, John R. *The Gospel in Parable: Metaphor, Narrative and Theology in the Synoptic Gospels*. Philadelphia: Fortress, 1988.

Dörries, Hermann. *Symeon von Mesopotamien: Die Überlieferung der messalianischen 'Makarios' Schriften*. TUGAL 55. Leipzig: Hinrichs, 1941.

Doumergue, Emile. *Jean Calvin: Les hommes et les choses de son temps*. 7 vols. Lausanne: Bridel, 1899–1927.

Edwards, Otis Carl. *A History of Preaching*. Nashville: Abingdon, 2004.

Ernst, Allie M. *Martha from the Margins: The Authority of Martha in Early Christian Tradition*. VCSup 98. Leiden: Brill, 2009.

Evans, Craig F. "The Central Section of St. Luke's Gospel." Pages 37–53 in *Studies in the Gospels: Essays in Memory of R. H. Lightfoot*. Edited by D. N. Nineham. Oxford: Basil Blackwell, 1957.

Evans, G. R. *Bernard of Clairvaux*. New York: Oxford University Press, 2000.

Farag, Lois. *St. Cyril of Alexandria: A New Testament Exegete*. Piscataway, NJ: Gorgias, 2007.

Fee, Gordon D. *To What End Exegesis*. Grand Rapids: Eerdmans, 2001.

Fitschen, Klaus. *Messalianismus und Antimessalianismus: Ein Beispiel ostkirchlicher Ketzergeschichte*. Göttingen: Vandenhoeck & Ruprecht, 1998.

Fitzgerald, Allen, ed. *Augustine through the Ages: An Encyclopedia*. Grand Rapids: Eerdmans, 1999.

Fitzmyer, Joseph. *The Gospel according to Luke*. 2 vols. AB 28–28A. Garden City, NY: Doubleday, 1981–1985.

Ganoczy, Alexandre. "Calvin's Life." Translated by David L. Foxgrover and James Schmitt. Pages 3–24 in *The Cambridge Companion to John Calvin*. Edited by Donald K. McKim. Cambridge: Cambridge University Press, 2004.

Gordon, Bruce. *Calvin*. London: Yale University Press, 2009.

Goulder, Michael. "The Chiastic Structure of the Lucan Journey." Pages 195–202 in *Studia Evangelica 2*. Edited by F. L. Cross. Berlin: Akademie, 1964.

Grant, Robert M. "The Citation of Patristic Evidence in an Apparatus Criticus." Pages 117–24 in *New Testament Manuscript Studies*. Edited by M. M Parvis and A. Wikgren. Chicago: University of Chicago, 1977.

Grant, Robert M., and David Tracy. *A Short History of the Interpretation of the Bible*. Minneapolis: Fortress, 1988.

Green, Joel B. *The Gospel of Luke*. NICNT. Grand Rapids: Eerdmans, 1997.

Grillmeier, Aloys. *Christ in Christian Tradition*. Translated by John Bowden. New York: John Knox: 1965.

Grundmann, Walter. *Das Evangelium nach Lukas*. THNT 3. Berlin: Evangelische Verlaganstalt, 1971.

Guillamont, Antoine. 'Les "arrhes de L'Esprit" dans le Livre des degres.'" Pages 107–13 in *Memorial Mgr Gabriel Khouri-Sarkis*. Leuven: Secrétariat du Corpus, 1969.

Guy, Jean-Claude. *Jean Cassian: Vie et doctrine spirituelle*. Paris: Lethielleux, 1961.

Hanson, Richard P. *Allegory and Event: A Study of the Sources and Significance of Origen's Interpretation of Scripture*. London: SCM, 1959.

Harmless, William. *Augustine in His Own Words*. Washington DC: Catholic University Press of America, 2010.

Hausherr, Irenee. "L'erreur fondamentale et la logique de Messalianisme." *OCP* 1 (1935): 328–60.

Heffner, Blake. "Meister Eckhart and a Millennium with Mary and Martha." *LQ* 5 (1991): 171–85.
Heintz, Michael. "Pedagogy of the Soul: Origen's Homilies on the Psalms." PhD diss., University of Notre Dame, 2008.
Heller, Ena Giurescu. "Sibling Rivalry: Martha and Mary of Bethany." Pages 244–61 in vol. 2 of *Women from the Margins: Women of the New Testament and their Afterlives*. Edited by Christine E. Joynes and Christopher C. Rowland. BMW 27. Sheffield: Sheffield Phoenix, 2009.
Hunt, Hannah. *Clothed in the Body: Asceticism, the Body and the Spiritual in the Late Antique Era*. Abingdon: Ashgate, 2012.
Hylen, Susan. *The Modest Apostle: Thecla and the History of Women in the Early Church*. Oxford: Oxford University Press, 2015.
Jipp, Joshua W. *Divine Visitations and Hospitality to Strangers, An Interpretation of the Malta Episode in Acts 28:1–10*. NovTSup 53. Leiden: Brill, 2013.
Johnson, Luke Timothy. *The Gospel of Luke*. SP 3. Collegeville, MN: Liturgical Press: 1991.
———. *The Literary Function of Possessions in Luke-Acts*. SBLDS 39. Missoula, MT: Scholars Press, 1977.
Johnson, Luke Timothy, and William S. Kurz. *The Future of Catholic Biblical Scholarship: A Constructive Conversation*. Grand Rapids: Eerdmans, 2002.
Kelly, J. N. D. *Golden Mouth: The Story of John Chrysostom, Ascetic, Preacher and Bishop*. Ithaca, NY: Cornell University Press, 1995.
Kerrigan, Alexander. *S. Cyril of Alexandria: Interpreter of the Old Testament*. Rome: Pontifical Biblical Institute, 1952.
Kittelson, James M. *Martin Luther: The Story of the Man and His Career*. Minneapolis: Fortress, 1986.
Klostermann, Erich. *Das Lukasevangelium*. HNT 5. Tübingen: Mohn, 1919.
Kopallik, Joseph. *Cyrillus con Alexandrien, eine Biographie nach den Quellen*. Mainz: Kircheim, 1881.
Koperski, Veronica. "Women and Discipleship in Luke 10:38–42 and Acts 6:1–7: The Literary Context of Luke-Acts." Pages 161–96 in *A Feminist Companion to Luke*. Edited by Amy-Jill Levine. Cleveland: Pilgrim, 2004.
Kreitzer, Beth. *Reforming Mary: Changing Images of the Virgin Mary in Lutheran Sermons of the Sixteenth Century*. Oxford: Oxford University Press, 2004.

Laland, Erling. "Die Marta-Maria Perikope Lukas 10:38–42." *StTh* 13 (1959): 70–85.

Lane, D. J. "Book of Grades, or Steps." *The Harp* 14 (2001): 81–88.

Levine, Amy-Jill, ed. *A Feminist Companion to Luke*. FCNTECW 3. Cleveland: Pilgrim, 2004.

Liere, Frans van. *Introduction to the Medieval Bible*. Cambridge: Cambridge University Press, 2014.

Lobkowicz, Nicholaus. *Theory and Practice: History of a Concept from Aristotle to Marx*. Notre Dame: University of Notre Dame Press, 1967.

Louth, Andrew. *The Origins of the Christian Mystical Tradition from Plato to Denys*. Oxford: Oxford University Press, 1981.

Lubac, Henri de. *History and Spirit: The Understanding of Scripture according to Origen*. Translated by Anne Englund Nash. San Francisco: Ignatius, 2007.

———. *Medieval Exegesis*. Translated by Mark Sebanc. 4 vols. Grand Rapids: Eerdmans, 1998.

Malherbe, Abraham. ed. *Moral Exhortation: A Greco-Roman Sourcebook*. Philadelphia: Westminster, 1986.

Marshall, I. Howard. *The Gospel of Luke*. NIGNT 3. Grand Rapids: Eerdmans, 1978.

Martens, Peter. "Metaphors for Narrating the History of Biblical Interpretation." Paper presented at the Annual Meeting of the Society of Biblical Literature. San Antonio, Texas. November 20, 2016.

———. *Origen and Scripture: The Contours of an Exegetical Life*. Oxford: Oxford University Press, 2015.

Matter, E. Ann. Review of *L'Exégèse chrétienne de la Bible en Occident médiéval*, by Gilbert Dahan, *Speculum* 77 (2002): 1272–74.

Mayer, Wendy, and Pauline Allen. *John Chrysostom*. London: Routledge, 2000.

McGuckin, John Anthony. *St. Cyril of Alexandria: The Christological Controversy, Its History, Theology and Texts*. Crestwood, NY: Saint Vladimir's Seminary Press, 2004.

———. "Cyril of Alexandria: Bishop and Pastor." Pages 205–36 in *The Theology of Cyril of Alexandria*. Edited by Thomas G. Weinandy and Daniel Keating. London: T&T Clark, 2003.

McGrath, Alister E. *A Life of John Calvin: A Study in the Shaping of Western Culture*. Oxford: Basil Blackwell, 1990.

Meer, Frederick van der. *Augustine the Bishop: The Life and Work of a Father of the Church*. Translated by Brian Battershaw and G. R. Lamb. London: Sheed & Ward, 1961.

Menot, Michel. *Sermon choisis*. Edited by Joseph Nève. Paris: Librairie spéciale pour l'histoire de France, 1924.

Metzger, Bruce. *A Textual Commentary on the New Testament*. Stuttgart: United Bible Societies, 1975.

Meyvaert, Paul. "A New Perspective on the Ruthwell Cross: Ecclesia and Vita Monastica." Pages 130–42 in *The Ruthwell Cross*. Edited by Brendan Cassidy. Princeton: Princeton University Press, 1992.

Moessner, David Paul. *Lord of the Banquet: The Literary and Theological Significance of the Lucan Travel Narrative*. Minneapolis: Fortress, 1989.

Moltmann-Wendel, Elisabeth. *The Women around Jesus*. London: SCM, 1982.

Moore, Beth. *Jesus, the One and Only*. Nashville: Broadman & Holman, 2013.

Muller, Hildegund. "Preacher: Augustine and His Congregation." Pages 297–309 in *A Companion to Augustine*. Edited by Mark Vassey. Chichester: Wiley-Blackwell, 2012.

Noël, Filip. *The Travel Narrative in the Gospel of Luke: Interpretation of Luke 9:51–10:28*. Collectanae Biblica et Religiosa Antiqua 5. Brussels: Voor Wetenschappen en Kunsten, 2004.

Oberman, Heiko A. *Luther: Man between God and the Devil*. Translated by Eileen Walliser-Schwarzbart. New Haven: Yale University Press, 1989.

Ocker, Christopher, and Kevin Madigan. "After Beryl Smalley: Thirty Years of Medieval Exegesis, 1984–2013." *JBRec* 2 (2015): 87–130.

O'Keefe, John J. "'A Letter That Killeth': Toward a Reassessment of Antiochene Exegesis, or Diodore, Theodore, and Theodoret on the Psalms." *JECS* 8 (2000): 83–103.

Olsen, Derek. *Reading Matthew with Monks: Liturgical Interpretation in Anglo-Saxon England*. Collegeville, MN: Liturgical Press, 2015.

Pelikan, Jaroslav. *Luther the Expositor: Introduction to the Reformer's Exegetical Writings*. St. Louis: Concordia, 1959.

Peters, Christine. *Patterns of Piety: Women, Gender and Religion in Late Medieval and Reformation England*. Cambridge: Cambridge University Press, 2003.

Peters, Diane E. "The Early Latin Sources of the Legend of St. Martha: A Study and Translation with Critical Notes." MA diss., Wilfrid Laurier University, 1990.

———. "The Legends of St. Martha of Bethany and Their Dissemination in the Later Middle Ages." *ATLASP* 48 (1994): 149–64.

———. "The Life of Martha of Bethany by Pseudo-Marcilia." *TS* 58 (1997): 441–60.

Plested, Marcus. "The Christology of Macarius-Symeon." Pages 593–96 in *Cappadocian Writers, Other Greek Writers*. Edited by M. F. Wiles and E. J. Yarnold. StPatr 37. Leuven: Peeters, 2001.

Posse, Otto, ed. *Urkunden der Markgrafen von Meissen und Landgrafen von Thuringen 1100–1195*. Leipzig: Gieseke & Devrient, 1889.

Power, Kim. *Veiled Desire: Augustine on Women*. New York: Continuum, 1996.

Price, Robert M. *The Widow Traditions in Luke-Acts: A Feminist Critical Survey*. SBLDS 155. Atlanta: Scholars Press, 1997.

Quasten, Johannes. *Patrology*. 4 vols. Westminster, MD: Newman, 1960.

Radler, Charlotte. "Actio et Contemplatio/Action and Contemplation." Pages 211–22 in *The Cambridge Companion to Mysticism*. Edited by Amy Hollywood and Patricia Beckman. Cambridge: Cambridge University Press, 2012.

Ramsey, Boniface. "John Cassian: Student of Augustine." *CS* 28 (1993): 5–15.

Ravaisson-Mollien, Félix. *Rapports ou Ministre de l'Instruction Publique sur les Bibliothèques des Départements de l'Ouest: Suivis de pièces inedites*. Paris: Schneider & Langrand, 1841.

Réau, Louis. *Iconographie de l'Art Chrétien*. 3 vols. Paris: Presses Universitaires de France, 1955–1959.

Reicke, Bo. "Instruction and Discussion in the Travel Narrative." *Studia Evangelica* 73 (1959): 206–16.

Reid, Barbara E. *Choosing the Better Part? Women in the Gospel of Luke*. Collegeville, MN: Liturgical Press, 1996.

Reinhartz, Adele. "From Narrative to History: The Resurrection of Mary and Martha." Pages 161–84 in *"Women Like This": New Perspective on Jewish Women in the Greco-Roman World*. Edited by Amy-Jill Levine. EJL 1. Atlanta: Scholars Press, 1991.

Rengstorf, Karl H., ed. *The Complete Concordance of Flavius Josephus*. 4 vols. Leiden: Brill, 1973–1983.

Robbins, Vernon K. "New Testament Texts, Visual Material Culture, and Earliest Christian Art." Pages 13–54 in *The Art of Visual Exegesis: Rhetoric, Texts, Images*. Edited by Vernon K. Robbins, Walter S. Melion, and Roy R Jeal. ESEC 19. Atlanta: SBL Press, 2017.

Roux, Renato. "The Doctrine of the Imitation of Christ in the Liber Graduum." Pages 259–64 in *Biblica et Apocrypha, Ascetica, Liturgica*. Edited by Elizabeth A. Livingstone. StPatr 30 Leuven: Peeters, 1997.

Royse, James. *Scribal Habits in Early Greek New Testament Papyri*. NTTSD 36. Leiden: Brill, 2007.

Rücker, Adolf. *Die Lukas Homilien des HL. Cyrill von Alexandrien: Ein Beitrag zur Geschichte der Exegese*. Breslau: Drugulin, 1911.

Russell, Norman. *Cyril of Alexandria*. London: Routledge, 2000.

Schaberg, Jane. "Luke." Pages 275–92 in *The Women's Bible Commentary*. Edited by Carol A. Newsom and Sharon H. Ringe. Louisville: Westminster John Knox, 1992.

Schneider, Gerhard. *Evangelium nach Lukas*. ÖTK 3. Gütersloh: Gütersloher Verlagshaus, 1977.

Schneider, Jürgen. "Zur Analyse des lukanischen Reiseberichtes." Pages 207–29 in *Synoptische Studien*. Edited by Josef Schmid and A. Vögtle. Munich: Zink, 1953.

Schottroff, Luise. *Lydia's Impatient Sisters: A Feminist Social History of Early Christianity*. Translated by B. M. Rumscheidt. Louisville: Westminster John Knox, 1995.

Schüssler Fiorenza, Elisabeth. *But She Said: Feminist Practices of Biblical Interpretation*. Boston: Beacon, 1992.

———. "A Feminist Critical Interpretation for Liberation: Martha and Mary: Lk 10:38–42." *RIL Life* 3 (1986): 21–36.

———. *In Memory of Her: A Feminist Theological Construction of Christian Origins*. New York: Crossroads, 1984.

———. "The Practice of Biblical Interpretation: Luke 10:38–42." Pages 172–97 in *The Bible and Liberation: Political and Social Hermeneutics*. Edited by Norman K. Gottwald and Richard A. Horsley. Maryknoll, NY: Orbis Books, 1992.

Seim, Turrid Karlsen. *The Double Message: Patterns of Gender in Luke and Acts*. Nashville: Abingdon, 1994.

Smalley, Beryl. "The Gospels in the Paris Schools in the Late Twelfth and Early Thirteenth Centuries: Peter the Chanter, Hugh of St. Cher, Alexander of Hales, John of La Rochelle." *FS* 39 (1979): 230–54.

———. *The Study of the Bible in the Middle Ages*. Notre Dame: University of Notre Dame Press, 1952.

Steinmetz, David C. *Calvin in Context*. New York: Oxford University Press, 2010.

Stjerna, Kirsti. *Women in the Reformation*. Malden, MA: Blackwell, 2009.

Stewart, Columba. *"Working the Earth of the Heart": The Messalian Controversy in History, Texts and Language in AD 431*. Oxford: Clarendon, 1991.

———. *Cassian the Monk*. New York: Oxford University Press, 1998.

Stoffels, Joseph. *Die mystische Theologie Makarius des Aegypters: Und die Ältesten Ansätze Christlicher Mystik*. Bonn: Hanstein, 1908.

Swartley, William. *Israel's Scripture Traditions and the Synoptic Gospels: Story Shaping Story*. Grand Rapids: Baker Academic, 1994.

Taylor, Marion Ann, and Agnes Choi, eds. *Handbook of Women Biblical Interpreters: A Historical and Biographical Guide*. Grand Rapids: Baker Academic. 2012.

Thompson, John L. "Calvin as Biblical Interpreter." Pages 58–73 in *The Cambridge Companion to John Calvin*. Edited by Donald K. McKim. Cambridge: Cambridge University Press, 2004.

Thompson, Mark D. *A Sure Ground on Which I Stand: The Relation of Authority and Interpretive Method in Luther's Approach to Scripture*. Studies in Christian History and Thought. Milton Keynes: Paternoster, 2004.

Tiffany, Tanya J. "Visualizing Devotion in Early Modern Seville: Velázquez's 'Christ in the House of Martha and Mary.'" *SCJ* 36 (2005): 433–53.

Torjesen, Karen Jo. *Hermeneutical Procedure and Theological Method*. PTS 28. Berlin: de Gruyter, 1986.

Volker, Walter. *Das Vollkommentheitsideal des Origenes: Eine Untersuchung zur Geschichte der Frömmigkeit und su den Anfängen christlicher Mystik*. Tübingen: Mohr, 1931.

Vööbus, Arthur. *History of the Asceticism in the Syrian Orient*. CSCO 184. Leuven: Secrétariat du Corpus, 1958.

———. "Liber Graduum: Some Aspects of Its Significance for the History of Early Syrian Asceticism." *PETSE* 7 (1954): 108–28.

Walchenbach, John R. *John Calvin as Biblical Commentator: An Investigation in Calvin's Use of John Chrysostom as an Exegetical Tutor*. Eugene, OR: Wipf & Stock, 2010.

Wasserman, Tommy. "Bringing Sisters Back Together: Another Look at Luke 10:41–42." *JBL* 137 (2018): 439–61.

Weaver, Joanna. *Having a Mary Heart in a Martha World: Finding Intimacy with God in the Busyness of Life*. Colorado Springs: Waterbrook, 2000.

Wellhausen, Julius. *Das Evangelium Lucae*. Berlin: Reimer, 1904.

Wendel, François. *Calvin: Origins and Development of his Religious Thought*. Durham, NC: Labyrinth, 1987.

Whitford, David M. *Luther: A Guide for the Perplexed*. New York: T&T Clark, 2011.

Wiesner, Merry. "Luther and Women: The Death of Two Marys." Pages 295–308 in *Disciplines of Faith: Studies in Religion, Politics and Patriarchy*. Edited by Jim Obelkelvich, Lyndal Roper, and Raphael Samuel. London: Routledge, 2013.

Witherington, Ben, III. *Women in the Ministry of Jesus: A Study of Jesus' Attitudes in Women and their Roles Reflected in this Earthly Life*. SNTSMS 51. New York: Cambridge University Press, 1984.

Wyant, Jennifer S. "Giving Martha Back Her House: Analyzing the Textual Variant in Luke 10:38b." *TC* 24.

Zuffi, Stephano. *Gospel Figures in Art*. Translated by Thomas Michael Hartmann. Los Angeles: Getty Publications, 2002.

Ancient Sources Index

Hebrew Bible/Septuagint

Genesis
1	87
1–3	133
22:11	60
43:34	65

Exodus
3:4	60
18:22	58

1 Samuel
3:10	60

3 Kingdoms (LXX)
10:8	145–46

Psalms
4:2	220
5:3	146
15:5	65
27:4	138
36	80
66:9	146
72:26	66
73:28	137
86:11	146
88:22	58
118:57	66
121:3	146

Ecclesiastes (or Qoheleth)
1:13	49
3:10	49
5:19	49

Song of Songs (or Canticles)
2:5	219

Ezekiel
1:8	179

Ancient Jewish Writers

Josephus, *Ag. Ap.*
1.247	41

New Testament

Matthew
6:34	153, 155
9:20	200
11:28	237
13:1	79
25	154, 269
26:6–13	200

Mark
4:38	57
13:3–9	200

Luke
1:1–4	76
1:2	77
1:38	54
2:9	57
2:38	57
4:39	46
5:1	54

Luke (cont.)
6:47	54
7	52, 158, 160
7:29	54
7:36–50	41, 52, 69, 116, 158, 200
7:37	80
7:38	116
7:39	238
8:1–3	45–46, 48, 51
8:2	200
8:4	79
8:4–15	54
8:14	54, 60
8:16	79
8:18	66
8:21	54
8:24	58
8:35	53
8:39	80
9:43–45	37
9:51	34–35
9:51–56	39
9:51–10:24	41
9:51–10:28	34
9:51–19:27	2, 34
9:52	35
9:52–53	42
9:53	35
9:56	35
9:57	35
9:57–62	39
10	17, 26, 28, 30, 32, 42, 48, 51, 168, 223, 237, 247, 268–69
10–11	29
10:1	35
10:1–12	39, 42
10:5–7	44
10:6	42
10:6–9	67
10:9	42
10:10	42
10:12–15	42
10:13–15	39
10:16	54
10:16–23	39
10:24–37	39, 268
10:25–37	11, 19, 42, 67–68, 253
10:38	1, 35, 39–42, 44, 67, 198
10:38–42	1–2, 4, 5–15, 17, 19–20, 22, 24–31, 33–35, 39–41, 45, 67, 69, 72, 74, 81, 88, 91, 93, 106, 112, 114–15, 117–23, 125–26, 134, 143–44, 152, 155, 157, 159, 167, 169–70, 174, 178–79, 186, 189, 191, 195–200, 204, 206, 208, 210, 218, 220, 223–24, 227, 234, 237–39, 241, 247–50, 252–55, 257–63, 265–70, 273–76
10:39	53, 59, 145, 275
10:39–40	1
10:40	46–48, 56, 59, 61
10:40–42	1, 56
10:41	22, 59–60, 155
10:41–42	11, 22–23, 29, 34, 59, 62, 67, 69, 83–84, 117, 153, 158, 169–70, 194, 266
10:42	22–23, 148, 191, 196, 198, 236
11:1–13	39, 67–68
11:1–14	68
11:10	67
11:14–36	39
11:28	54, 68
11:37–52	69
11:37–53	39
12:1–12	39
12:13	58
12:13–21	39
12:22	60
12:22–53	39
12:37	46
12:46	66
12:54–13:30	39
13:22	35
13:31	35
13:31–14:24	39
13:33	35, 37
14:1–6	69
14:7–11	69
14:12–14	69
14:15–24	69

14:25	35	24:13–35	41
14:25–35	39		
14:35	54	John	
15	261	6:8–11	117
15:1–32	39	6:26–27	153–55, 157
15:11–32	58	6:27	113
16:1–13	39	6:27–29	155
16:14–31	39	9	166
17:1–9	51	11	26, 28, 269, 275
17:1–10	39	11–12	82, 158
17:7–10	47	11:1–44	1
17:11	35	11:2	23
17:11–19	39, 52	11:5	251
17:20–21	39	11:17–44	28
17:22–18:8	39	11:20	116
18	88	12	148, 158, 171
18:9–14	39	12:1	44
18:15	39	12:1–8	200
18:15–17	39	12:3	200
18:18–25	39	13:8	66
18:19	84	20	161
18:21	86	21	142
18:26–34	39		
18:30	34	Acts	
18:31	35	1:17	47, 65
18:34	34	1:25	47
18:35–43	39	2:22	54
19:1	35	4:4	54
19:1–10	41	4:32–37	52
19:1–27	39	6	29, 48
19:6	43	6:1–4	47–48
19:10	34	6:1–7	5, 14
19:11	35	6:12	57
19:28	35	9:4	60
19:29–46	35	10:1–48	41
19:44	34	10:22	54
19:46	34	10:25	52
19:48	34	11:1–18	41
20:1	57	13:7	54
21:38	34	13:44	54
22:24–27	48	15:7	54
22:26–27	46	16	53
22:31	60	16:15	44
24	275	17:6–7	43
24:4	57	17:7	41, 43

Acts (cont.)

19:10	54
20:7–12	202
22:3	53
28:1–10	41

Romans

2:28–29	85
2:29	85, 120
8:26	58

1 Corinthians

3:2	95
7:32–35	61
9:24	146
13:9	66
13:11	80

2 Corinthians

1:22	96
3:18	83

Ephesians

1:14	96
1:18	66

Philippians

3	137
3:16	146

Colossians

1:12	66
3:1–2	87

1 Timothy

2:15	55
5:6	161

Hebrews

13:1	167

James

2:25	43

Christian Writers

Apostolic Constitutions

2.63.1–6	156

APalph

5	182

Augustine, *Confessionum libri XIII*

3.4.9	133
10.29	221

Augustine, *De catechizandis rudibus*

7	131

Augustine, *De doctrina christiana*

1.35.39	134
4.5	132
4.29	132
4.46	132
10.14	133–34

Augustine, *De virginitate*

20	161

Augustine, *Enarrationes in Psalmos*

50.1	130–31
103.4.1	133
138.1	131

Augustine, *Contra Faustum Manichaeum*

4.2–9	133
7.2–48	133

Augustine, *In Evangelium Johannis tractatus*

15.18	134
124.5	142

Augustine, *Quaestionum evangelicarum*

2.20	141

Augustine, *Sermones*

103.2	135–36
103	137

Ancient Sources Index 297

103.3	141
103.4	130, 137
103.5	135, 138
104–4	134
104	143
104.2	139, 141
104.3	13–37, 140
104.4	138
104.5	146
104.6	140, 144
169	134
169.17	136, 138
179	134
179.3	146
198.1	130
255	134, 138, 140
255.2	135–36
265.9	131
339.4	140
352	134
355.2	128
339.4	132, 140

Aquinas, *Contra impugnantes Dei cultum et religionem*
1	185
4	185

Aquinas, *Summa Theologica*
2.2 q. 182	185

Bede, *In Evangelium Lucae libros VI*
3.10	181

Bernard, *Sermones*
2	186
2.2.5–6	183
2.7	184
3.4	184
51.2.2	184
57	184

Bonaventura, *In Evangelium Lucae*
71–75	196

Brigitta of Sweden, *Revelations*
6.65	214–16

Bruno of Segni, *Commentaria in Lucam*
1.10.22	182–83

Calvin, John, *An Admonition*
1:330	231

Calvin, John, *Commentary on a Harmony*
2:142	227–28
2:143	228–29
2:144	229–30

Calvin, John, *Commentary on the Psalms*
	225–26

Calvinus Grynaeo, *Epistula*
191	226

Cassian, *Conferences*
1.7	107
1.8	106, 107
23	106
23.3	109–10
23.5	110

Clement of Alexandria, *Quis dives salvetur*
10	88

Distinctiones monastiche 196

Ephrem, *Commentary on the Diatessaron*
8.15	115–16

Eusebius, *Historia ecclesiastica*
6.2.15	73
6.3.19–11	73

Evagrius, *Rerum monachalium rationes*
3	108

Gregory the Great, *Homiliae in Ezechielem*
  1.3   179
  2.2.7   181

Gregory the Great, *Moralia*
  6.37   179

Grimlaicus, *Rule of Solitaries*
  42–45   182

Herbord of Michelsberg, *Dialogue de Ottone ep Bamberbensi*
  1.41–42   212

Hildegard of Bingen, *Answers to Thirty-Eight Questions*   210

Hildegard of Bingen, *Letters*   186
  1:54, 83, 130   212
  2:12   212
  2:139   212
  77r   210
  84r   212
  94r   211
  113r (2.58)   211
  194   211
  194r   211
  329   211, 212

Hildegard of Bingen, *Scivias*   209

Hugh of Fouilloy, *De claustro animae*
  2.10   188

Hugh of Saint Cher, *Commentaria in Lucam*
  10   185

Idungus of Regensburg, *Dialogs duorum monachorum*
  1.5   189

Ignatius, *To the Smyrnaeans*
  10.1   41

Ignatius of Loyola   24

Innocent III, *On Renunciation*   191–92

Isodore of Seville, *Liber de variis quaestionibus*   49

Isodore of Seville, *Sententiae*
  3.15   180

Jerome, *Epistula*
  84.8   73

Joachim of Fiore, *Concordia novi ac veteris testamenti*
  5.16   186
  5.71   186

John Chrysostom, *De Anna*
  5.1   151

John Chrysostom, *Catech. ult.*
  3.17   152

John Chrysostom, *Homiliae in epistulam i ad Thessalonicenses*
  6.1   156

John Chrysostom, *Homiliae in Matthaeum*
  19.5   151

John Chrysostom, *Homiliae in Joannem*
  44   151
  86.1   161

John Chrysostom, *Homiliae in epistulam ad Philippenses*
  4   163
  9   161
  11   163

John Chrysostom, *De sacerdotio*
  4.8   150
  5.2   149, 150

Ancient Sources Index

5.8	150	Luther, Martin, *Lectures on Genesis 1–5*	
John Chrysostom, *Ad populum Antiochenum de statuis*		1:202–3	240
2.4	150	Luther, Martin, *Lectures on Genesis 26–30*	
		5:331	240
John Chrysostom, *De terrae motu*		Luther, Martin, *Sermon on the Day of Mary's Ascension*	235
15	149, 151		
John Chrysostom, *De virginitate*		Luther, Martin, *Sermon on St. John*	
46.1	162	2:247–48	236, 237
46.2	162		
62.1	163	Origen, *Commentarius in Canticum*	
		prol.	81, 82
Liber Graduum		2.1	145
1	95	10.1	86
2	95		
2.1	95	Origen, *Commentarii in evangelium Joannis*	
3.11	94		
3.12	96, 97	1.91	77
3.13	96, 97	9.6–17	166
3.13–14	97		
3.14	98	Origen, *Commentarii in Romanos*	
3.15	95	2.5.4	84
3.11	94	2.7.2	85
9	95	2.11.4	85
14.2	94	2.13.24–36	85
19	95	2.13.36	85
19.40	98	2.14.4	85, 85
20	95	3.2.8	85
		4.1.4	85
Luther, Martin, *Concerning the Order of Public Worship*	237	4.2.6	85
		4.9.4	84
Luther, Martin, *Estate of Marriage*		Origen, *Fragmenta in librum primum Regnorum*	
45:19	239		
		2	76
Luther, Martin, *Grund und Ursach*	233		
		Origen, *Fragmenta in evangelium Joannis*	
Luther, Martin, *Kirchenpostille*	233	80	76, 82
Luther, Martin, *Lectures on Galatians*		Origen, *Fragmenta in Lucam*	
1:214	236	113	80
		114	79
		120	79

Origen, Fragmenta in Lucam (cont.)
121	79
122	79, 83
124	80
171	9, 74–78, 82–83, 85–87, 107, 116, 119, 145, 183, 235, 268
174	79
226	86

Origen, Fragmenta ex commentariis in evangelium Matthaei
10	83

Origen, Homiliae in Exodum
8.1	76
12.2	87

Origen, Homiliae in Genesim
1.7	88

Origen, Homiliae in Judices
1.4	76

Origen, Homiliae in Numeros
27	81

Origen, Homiliae in Psalmos XXXVI
4.1	81
5.1	81

Origen, Philocalia
1.10	71

Origen, De principiis
preface 1	87
1.1.6	87
4.1.7	87
4.2.4	74, 83
4.4.10	81

Odo of Canterbury, *De assumptione* 196

Possidius, *Life*
1	128
4	128

5	130
31	129
31.4	129

Pseudo-Macarius, *Homiliae*
9.12	103
10	102
10.1–2	102
12.16	101, 102
12.17	102
17.4	101
17.7–8	104
18.10	103
24.4	103
24.6	103, 104
46.3	103

Reiner of St. Laurence, *Vita Wolbodonis*
3	212

Richard of St. Victor, *Explicatio in Cantica Canticorum*
8	198

Richard of St. Victor, *Sermones*
33	184–85

Rudolf, *Vita Lietberti ep Camaeracensis*
7	212

Robert Pullen, *Sententiae*
7.23–25	185

Siegfried of Mainz, *Mainzer Urkundenbuch*
1	188–89

Simon of Tournae, *Disputationes*
4.1	191
4.2	191

Stephen of Murot, *Regula*
35	187

Stephen of Murot, *Sententiae*
10.4	187

Stephen of Tournai, *Epistulae*
   1   187–88
   8.15   192

Teresa of Ávila, *The Interior Castle*
   7.4.12   219

Teresa of Ávila, *Meditations*
   1.8   217
   7.3   219, 272

Teresa of Ávila, *Way of Perfection*
   17.1   218
   17.5   218
   17.5–6   218–19
   31.5   219

Teresa of Ávila, *Soliloquies*   220
   5.1   220, 272

Teresa of Ávila, *Vita*
   22.9   218

Thomas a Kempis, *Imitatio Christi*
   2.8, 11   185

William of Thierry, *Meditative orationes*
   11.19   190

        Greco-Roman Literature

Epictetus, *Diatribi*
   3.9.19   49
   3.19.1   50

Modern Authors Index

Adams, Thomas 248–49
Alexander, Loveday C. 1, 18–19, 29, 40, 51, 55–56, 58, 69, 230, 274
Allen, Pauline 147–49
Allen, William 249
Allestree, Richard 244
Amar, Joseph P. 115
Augsten, Monika 63
Baird, Joseph E. 209–10, 212
Baker, Aelred 23
Baum, Armin Daniel 36
Baur, Chryosotomus 147, 149
Beard, Mary 31, 260–61
Bendemann, Reinhard von 35–36
Beveridge, Henry 231
Bonnardiere, Anne-Marie La 24–25, 140–142
Bovon, Francois 1–2, 18, 21, 23, 33, 40–41, 44, 50–51, 56, 60–61, 63, 65–66, 75, 118
Boyd, Jane 245
Brecht, Martin 232
Brennan, Irene 7, 16
Brooten, Bernadette J. 54
Brown, Jonathan 245
Brown, Peter 162
Brutscheck, Jutta 20–21, 35, 44, 53, 56
Bultmann, Rudolf 21
Busse, Ulrich 36
Butterworth, G. W. 74, 81, 83
Caird, G. B. 63–64
Cameron, Michael 133
Caner, Daniel 156–57
Carroll, Thomas K. 126–27, 147, 150–151, 153
Carter, Warren 8, 13, 21, 42
Cassidy, Richard J. 16
Chadwick, Owen 106, 108
Choi, Agnes 209, 213, 217
Collins, Billy 11
Collins, John N. 14, 45–46
Colwell, Ernest C. 44
Constable, Giles 1, 27, 173, 179–80, 184–86, 190–92, 194–95, 197, 199, 205–7, 212
Contreni, John J. 177
Conzelmann, Hans 36–37
Crawford, Matthew 164, 166
Creed, J. M. 64
Crouzel, Henri 76–78
Csanyi, Daniel 25, 71, 75–76, 89, 155
D'Angelo, Mary Rose 21
Danielou, Jean 74
Danker, Frederick W. 16, 20
Dargan, Edwin Charles 127, 164
Davies, Stevan 16
Dawsey, James M. 36
Dayton, Hellen 112, 118
Deferrari, Roy J. 129
Donahue, John R. 16–17, 19–20, 29, 55, 67–70, 185, 268
Dörries, Hermann 99
Doumergue, Emile 225
Edwards, Otis Carl 127
Ehrman, Radd K. 209–10, 212
Ernst, Allie M. 25–26
Esler, Philip F. 245
Evans, Craig F. 36
Evans, G. R. 183
Farag, Lois 164, 166

Fee, Gordon D.	22–24, 62–64	Lawson, R. P.	81
Fitschen, Klaus	155–56	Leclercq, Jean	190
Fitzgerald, Allen	ix	Levine, Amy-Jill	5, 8, 16, 18, 21
Fitzmyer, Joseph	16, 19, 21, 34, 64–65, 71	Lewis, George	71
		Lienhard, Joseph T.	9, 75–76
Ganoczy, Alexandre	225	Liere, Frans van	174–78
Gordon, Bruce	225	Lobkowicz, Nicholaus	76
Goulder, Michael	37	Louth, Andrew	100
Grant, Robert M.	23, 151	Lubac, Henri de	74, 90, 176–77
Green, Joel B.	16, 19	Luibheid, Colm	105, 107
Grillmeier, Aloys	103	Madigan, Kevin	175
Grundmann, Walter	60	Maloney, George A.	99–101
Guillamont, Antoine	96	Malherbe, Abraham	53
Guy, Jean-Claude	106, 242	Marshall, I. Howard	47, 61–62
Hanson, Richard P.	74	Martens, Peter	11–12, 72–74, 76, 83, 86–87
Harkin, Franklin	175–76		
Harkins, Paul William	152	Martin, Lawrence T.	181
Harmless, William	128, 132	Matter, E. Ann	175, 177
Haroutunian, Joseph	226	Mayer, Wendy	147–49
Hausherr, Irenee	92	McCarthy, Carmel	115–16
Heffner, Blake	24, 197	McGrath, Alister E.	225
Heine, Ronald E.	77, 87	McGuckin, John Anthony	164
Heintz, Michael	85	Meer, Frederick van der	128–30
Heller, Ena Giurescu	26–27, 71, 245, 247	Menot, Michel	199
		Metzger, Bruce	1, 42, 44, 62–63
Holloway, Julia Bolton	213–14	Meyvaert, Paul	205
Hunt, Hannah	100	Moessner, David Paul	36
Hurst, David	158, 181	Moltmann-Wendel, Elisabeth	6, 55, 197, 208, 241
Hylen, Susan	54		
Jipp, Joshua W.	41–42	Moore, Beth	4–5, 31, 223–24, 249–53, 259, 261, 272–73
Johnson, Luke Timothy	19, 20, 35, 38–40, 54, 134, 262		
		Müller, Hildegund	129
Karant-Nunn, Susan	234, 239	Mycoff, David	173, 201–2
Kavanaugh, Kiernan	217, 220	Neville, Graham	150
Kelly, J. N. D.	147–48, 152	Noël, Filip	34–37
Kerrigan, Alexander. S.	164	O'Keefe, John J.	152
Kitchen, Robert	92–95	Oberman, Heiko A.	232
Kittelson, James M.	232	Ocker, Christopher	175
Klostermann, Erich	64	Olsen, Derek	178
Kopallik, Joseph	164	Parmentier, Martien	92–95
Koperski, Veronica	5, 8, 16, 21, 48	Pelikan, Jaroslav	151, 231, 233
Kreitzer, Beth	234	Peters, Christine	242
Kurz, William S.	134, 262	Peters, Diane E.	195, 200, 203–4
Laland, Erling	17	Plested, Marcus	92
Lane, D. J.	93	Posse, Otto	187

Power, Kim	161	Tracy, David	151
Price, Robert M.	5, 8, 17–18	Volker, Walter	78
Pringle, William	227	Vööbus, Arthur	92–93
Quasten, Johannes	148–49, 152, 164–65	Wagner, M. Monica	117
Radler, Charlotte	24	Walchenbach, John R.	226
Ramsey, Boniface	139, 143	Walker, Anthony	242–43
Ravaisson-Mollien, Félix	194	Walsh, Maurice O'C.	10, 193
Ravenshaw, Thomas F.	242	Ward, Benedicta	113
Rauer, Max	75	Wasserman, Tommy	23, 64
Réau, Louis	203–4	Weaver, Joanna	4
Reicke, Bo	37	Wellhausen, Julius	64
Reid, Barbara E.	8, 14–15, 45, 53	Wendel, François	225
Reinhartz, Adele	21	Whitford, David M.	232
Rengstorf, Karl H.	41	Wiesner, Merry	224, 234, 239–41
Robbins, Vernon K.	204	Witherington, Ben, III	21
Rodriquez, Otilio	217	Wortley, John	113–14
Roux, Renato	98	Wyant, Jennifer S.	45
Rücker, Adolf	165	Zuffi, Stephano	207
Russell, Norman	164–65		
Schaberg, Jane	7		
Scheck, Thomas P	84		
Schneider, Gerhard	19		
Schneider, Jürgen	37, 39		
Schottroff, Luise	21		
Schüssler Fiorenza, Elisabeth	5–7, 11, 14, 16–18, 31, 45, 55, 71, 122, 224, 250, 253–63, 270–71		
Seim, Turrid Karlsen	8, 14–17, 41, 45, 55		
Shore, Sally Rieger	162		
Sinkewicz, Robert E.	108		
Smalley, Beryl	175, 177, 185		
Smith, Robert Payne	165, 167		
Steinmetz, David C.	225		
Stewart, Columba	92, 96, 99–100, 102–3, 106, 108–9, 111		
Stjerna, Kirsti	240		
Stupart, G. T.	153–54		
Swartley, William	36		
Taylor, Marion Ann	209, 213, 217		
Thompson, Mark D.	233		
Thompson, John L.	226–27		
Thorton, Andrew	182		
Tiffany, Tanya J.	245, 247		
Torjesen, Karen Jo	74		

Subject Index

action, 9, 54–56, 75–76, 89, 111–12, 119, 180–85, 195–98, 216, 247–49, 255–56. *See also* active life
active life, 9, 26, 76, 78, 142, 179, 181–85, 194, 201–4, 228, 234, 266
Alexandria, 72–73, 84, 88, 120, 164–66
    Alexandrian School, 151–52, 166
allegory, 74, 176, 176, 213, 263
Antioch, 148–52, 155, 156
    Antioch school, 151–52
anxious, 2, 17, 60, 110, 117, 153, 236. *See also* worry
Augustine, 22–25, 28, 30, 128–47, 149, 154, 159–60, 170–71, 178–79, 181, 184, 230, 233–34, 265, 267
asceticism, 17, 73, 91, 93, 97–98, 100–102, 113, 115, 147, 213, 217
Basil, 22, 115–19, 121, 170, 194, 229, 263, 226
Bede, 180–82, 185, 206
"the better part," 1–2, 62–68, 70, 83, 86–88, 90, 97, 105–13, 120, 137–43, 155–57, 160, 171, 183–90, 206, 210–12, 216, 222, 244, 266
Birgitta of Sweden, 208, 213–16, 221
bishops, 126, 130, 147, 156, 165, 192, 212
Calvin, John, 31, 223–31, 238, 244, 248
Cassian, John, 22, 29, 72, 105–12, 118, 120–22, 139, 143, 181–82, 195
celibacy, 94, 161, 239–40
church
    early, 6–8, 13–15, 20–21, 25, 37, 45, 53, 59, 126, 255–56, 260, 270–71, 274
    evangelical, 4–5, 8, 12, 13, 28, 249–50, 253

church (*cont.*)
    gentile, 82–85, 120
    medieval, 30, 158, 173–78, 188–95, 204–8, 222
    present and future, 126, 134, 143–44, 180
Chrysostom, John, 22, 28, 30, 126, 147–64, 170–71, 183, 197, 200, 225, 227–28, 230, 248–49, 263, 269
Clement of Alexandria, 22, 25, 88–89
clergy, 157, 170, 186
conflation of Marys, 158, 171, 195–204, 207, 218, 222
contemplation, 9, 75–78, 87–89, 107–11, 119–22, 140, 142, 178–79, 183–87, 191, 196–99, 205–6, 216–19, 234, 247–49, 265–66. *See also* contemplative life
contemplative life, 76–78, 88, 114, 118, 179, 180–84, 194, 198–201, 203–7, 218–20, 227–28, 247, 266
criticism
    feminist, 5–8, 10–12, 17, 26–27, 55, 122, 249–50, 253–59, 274
    form, 8, 17–18, 23
    historical, 8, 11, 13–18, 33, 35–36, 226, 234, 254, 258, 262–63, 271, 274
    literary, 11, 19–22, 33–70, 274–75
    textual, 1–2, 22–24, 29, 39–45, 59, 62–65, 69, 107, 169–70, 194, 229, 266–67
Cyril of Alexandria, 22–24, 30, 164–71, 194, 229, 263
desert fathers, 29, 105–6, 112–15, 117, 157

development, spiritual, 73–75, 78–82, 90, 120
diakonia, 14, 45–46, 251. *See also* service
discernment, 114, 126, 154–57, 160, 170–71, 181, 183, 228, 231, 238, 248–49, 267
distraction, 4, 48–51, 56–59, 61, 87–90, 107–8, 251–52, 266
dragon-slaying, 202–4, 207–8, 231, 244
Epictetus, 49–51, 88, 127
Ephrem, 115–16, 121
Evagrius, 22, 105–6, 108, 117
gaze, 107–8, 112, 121, 146, 210
Good Samaritan, 1, 11, 19–20, 25, 29, 40, 67, 185, 251–52, 268
Gregory the Great, 22, 158, 179, 233
heaven, 49, 98, 102, 109–10, 138, 181, 193, 195, 203, 210, 212, 215, 225, 242
Hildegard of Bingen, 208–12, 221, 243
hierarchy, 99, 105, 118–19, 147, 207
hospitality, 10, 17, 20–21, 40, 45, 51, 56, 59, 61, 64, 67–70, 98, 107–11, 117–19, 121, 135–36, 143–44, 154–55, 167–71
host, hostess, 4, 18–19, 24, 34, 40, 42–43, 52, 58, 169–70, 202–3
Isidore, 180–83
Jerome, 2, 22, 73, 195, 233
laity, 160, 179, 186, 211–12, 221
Lazarus, 1, 42, 44, 96, 116, 158–59, 184, 200, 215, 231
Liber Graduum, 29, 91–99, 104–5, 111–12, 120–22, 157, 188–89, 214, 269
listening to the word, 33–34, 52–54, 63, 68, 117, 138–40, 144–47, 157, 160, 235, 237, 255–56, 275
Luther, Martin, 31, 224, 232–40
Lydia, 44, 53, 242
Messalianism, 25, 92, 100, 155–56
mixing, co-mixing, 96, 102–3, 20
monasticism
  early, 29, 77, 91–93, 100, 105–6, 113, 117, 118, 125, 140, 143, 156–57, 165, 170–71
  medieval, 30, 178–79, 182–83, 186–90, 194–96, 205–6, 210–11, 213, 216–17, 222

Mary, Mother of Jesus, 164, 174, 195–97, 234 *See also* conflation of Marys
Mary Magdalene, 158, 197–201, 204–5, 207–8, 212, 218–19, 222, 231, 236, 244. *See also* conflation of Marys
meal, meals, 7, 47, 61, 63, 65, 113, 117, 154–55, 207, 219, 244. *See also* hospitality
Meister Eckhart, 9, 24, 190, 192–94
Origen, 2, 9–11, 22–25, 29, 71–91, 97–98, 105, 108, 111, 115, 116, 118–23, 145–47, 178–79, 227, 233, 235, 265–69
Perfect, the, 93–98, 105, 120–22, 157, 269
perfection, Christian, 75, 78–81, 86, 88, 90–91, 93, 98–101, 104–5, 109, 111, 118, 120, 142–43, 162, 182, 193, 196, 242
prayer, 3, 37, 47, 67–68, 81, 92–94, 114, 144, 154, 184, 190, 194, 201, 212, 214, 219–20, 267
Pseudo-Macarius, 22, 29, 96, 99–105, 112, 120–21, 139, 181
Pseudo-Marcillia, 203–4
purity, 81, 104, 107–9, 193, 233, 239
repentance, 37, 80–81, 149, 198, 211–13
reward, eschatological, 46, 65–66, 94, 98, 101, 116, 122, 138, 140–44, 169, 180
salvation, 9–10, 78, 88, 94, 139, 154, 224, 235–40
Septuagint, 48–49, 58, 60, 65
sermon, development of, 126–28
service, 6, 9, 14, 15–16, 33, 41–50, 58–59, 61–68, 72, 75, 77, 104–2, 122, 134–36, 139–44, 157, 173, 178–80, 190, 194, 214–15, 219, 251–52, 256–58, 267, 272–73
Silvanus, 112–15, 121, 157, 182
sitting at the feet, 48, 52–56, 80–82, 86, 116, 145–47, 154, 192
soul, 9, 18, 51, 64, 74, 78–83, 101–4, 108, 114, 120–21, 163, 196, 201, 211, 218–19
Stoicism, 49, 102–3, 126–27
synagogue, 79, 82–85, 120, 126–27
Teresa of Avila, 208, 216–21, 248, 272–73

travel narrative, 11, 20–21, 34–40, 42, 54, 68, 256
unity, 95 n 45, 133, 137, 206, 229, 267
Upright, the, 93–99, 105, 120–22, 157, 269
visual exegesis, 174, 204–8, 244–48
Vulgate, 22, 194–95
Walker, Elizabeth, 242–43
wealth, 94, 148–49, 157, 162–63, 170–71
worry, 3, 60–61, 107, 219. *See also* anxious